EVIL MINDS

Understanding and Responding to Violent Predators

Robert J. Meadows
California Lutheran University

Julie M. Kuehnel
California Lutheran University

Upper Saddle River, New Jersey 07458

Library of Congress Cataloging-in-Publication Data
Meadows, Robert J.
Evil minds : understanding and responding to violent predators / Robert J. Meadows and Julie M. Kuehnel.
p. cm.
Includes bibliographical references and index.
ISBN 0-13-048613-2
1. Violent offenders. 2. Violent crimes. 3. Victims of violent crimes. I. Kuehnel, Julie M. II. Title.
HV6133.M43 2004
364.3—dc22

2003026359

Publisher: Stephen Helba
Executive Editor: Frank Mortimer Jr.
Assistant Editor: Sarah Holle
Production Editor: Linda Duarte, Pine Tree Composition
Production Liaison: Barbara Marttine Cappuccio
Director of Manufacturing and Production: Bruce Johnson
Managing Editor: Mary Carnis
Manufacturing Buyer: Cathleen Petersen
Creative Director: Cheryl Asherman
Cover Design Cooridinator: Miguel Ortiz
Cover Designer: Carey Davies
Cover Image: Getty Images/Digital Vision
Editorial Assistant: Barbara Rosenburg
Marketing Manager: Tim Peyton
Formatting and Interior Design: Pine Tree Composition
Printing and Binding: Phoenix Book Tech Park

Pearson Education Ltd.
Pearson Education Singapore, Pte. Ltd.
Pearson Education Canada, Ltd.
Pearson Education—Japan
Pearson Education Austrailia PTY, Limited
Pearson Education North Asia Ltd
Pearson Educación de Mexicao, S.A. de C.V.
Pearson Education Malaysia, Pte. Ltd.
Pearson Education, Upper Saddle River, New Jersey

10 9 8 7 6 5 4 3 2 1
ISBN 0-13-048613-2

CONTENTS

PREFACE

Most of us are curious about those individuals who are capable of engaging in predatory violence: serial killers, mass murders, child molesters, and rapists. Who are they? Why do they do what they do? How did they get that way? What can be done about them? Those of us who teach and study in the social sciences are also fascinated by these questions, and we approach them through the theories, concepts, and research of our own disciplines: psychology, sociology, criminology, and criminal justice. This text is an effort to understand these "evil minds" by using a multidisciplinary perspective.

The idea for this book grew out of our experiences teaching a course on the topic of evil minds. We discovered that our students' natural curiosity about the "monsters" among us provided a vehicle for also teaching them about the theories, constructs, and methods that various disciplines in the social sciences employ to understand and respond to these evil minds. Unfortunately, we also discovered that there were no texts that really incorporated this multidisciplinary approach into a study of this topic. This book is an effort to close that gap.

We also wanted to write a text that you would find engaging. To accomplish this goal, we have employed a case study approach to illustrate the content, as well as pedagogical features to engage you in applying and evaluating what you are learning. At the end of each chapter are Discussion Questions and Activities that invite you to be active rather than passive learners. Most chapters include self-check boxes so that you can check your understanding as you read. Highlight boxes include related material and interviews with professionals involved in the field.

The text is divided into three sections. The first section, which addresses theories of victimology, includes chapters that describe the motives, methods, and backgrounds of the various types of sexual predators and murderers. That is, who are these people, and why do they victimize? What you will find is that broad categories such as rapists and serial killers contain subtypes of individuals who commit their crimes for different reasons that are reflected in how they select victims and carry out their offenses.

In the second section we try to respond to the question, How did these evil minds get that way? Predatory violence does not spring from a single seed but rather is rooted in maladaptive psychological development, neurological dysfunction, and mental disorder, and is nourished by maladaptive social influences. Theory and research into biological, psychological, and social factors that interact to produce a John Wayne Gacy or a Bobby Joe Long continue to be developed. Therefore, we have included a chapter on the research methods employed by social scientists to find answers and to assist you in becoming informed consumers of such information.

The last section addresses how we respond to predatory offenders. The natural and behavioral sciences contribute in different ways to investigate such crimes. The justice system creates laws and delivers punishment to these offenders. Chapters Nine and Ten introduce you to the way that this process happens. For sex offenders, who are likely to be released into the community at some point, is treatment a viable option? Does time in prison stop them from committing further offenses? These questions and an overview of treatment approaches are the subject of the final chapter. After you have completed this text, we think you will see that as a society, we should focus more intensely on prevention and early intervention to reduce predatory violence.

For instructors, there is an instructor's guide to accompany the text. This guide includes objective, short-answer, and essay questions for each chapter; suggestions for in-class demonstrations; supplemental lecture material; and ideas for structuring an interactive course.

ACKNOWLEDGMENTS

This book would not have been possible without the assistance of many people. We would like particularly to acknowledge those who shared their time and experience in interviews: Dr. Jeffrey Teuber, Senior Psychologist at Atascadero State Hospital; Dr. Mark Weideranders, Research Program Specialist; and Frank Salerno, Retired Los Angeles County Sheriffs Detective. Graduate student Chandler Marrs scoured databases and libraries to find relevant articles, and because of her interest in the topic, helped draft the chapter on neurological contributions to violence. Our undergraduate students in our spring 2002 and 2003 Criminal Psychology course were also very helpful in finding interesting case studies to use in the book, as well as reviewing and making many helpful suggestions for improving the early manuscript. Claire Gordon, a graduate student at California Lutheran University, provided valuable research assistance. Our faculty secretary, Pat Egle, not only provided emotional support but also patiently incorporated multiple additions, subtractions, and reorganizations into the multiple drafts of each chapter; and somehow she kept it all straight!

We would also like to thank the following people who reviewed our manuscript: Anne Lanning, Rockingham Community College, Wentworth, North Carolina; Diane Learny, Southwest Missouri State University, Springfield, Missouri; John Mason, Upper Iowa University, Fayette, Iowa; Judith Sgarzi, Mount Ida College, Newton Center, Massachusetts; and Prabha Unnithan, Colorado State University, Fort Collins, Colorado.

Finally, we wish to thank California Lutheran University for granting us sabbaticals to give us our running start on the manuscript.

About the Authors

Dr. Julie M. Kuehnel earned her doctorate in Educational Psychology at the University of Texas and is a licensed clinical psychologist in California. She is currently Professor/Chair of Psychology at California Lutheran University, where she teaches undergraduate and graduate courses. She came to CLU with experience as an Assistant Research Psychologist at UCLA specializing in behavior therapy; as a private practice clinician; and as a trainer/consultant to Camarillo State Hospital, Atascadero State Hospital, and the Center for the Improvement of Child Caring. Dr. Kuehnel coauthored the *Handbook of Marital Therapy* and articles and book chapters on the treatment of mental disorders.

Dr. Robert J. Meadows is an Associate Professor of Criminal Justice and is Director of the Graduate Program in Public Policy and Administration at California Lutheran University. Dr. Meadow's research and teaching interests include legal issues in criminal justice, private security, violence and victimization, and delinquency. He authored a book on Saudi Arabian justice and a parent's guide for coping with difficult teenagers. He also authored *Understanding Violence and Victimization* for Prentice-Hall Publishing, now in its third edition. Dr. Meadows is a member of the Academy of Criminal Justice Sciences and the American Society of Industrial Security.

Part One

Violent Predators: Types and Patterns

There are a number of types of criminal predators who stalk vulnerable and available victims. Becoming a victim of a violent predator can occur anywhere, without warning, when the opportunity presents itself. Violent predators broadly characterized as serial killers or sex offenders are not all alike. Some are more organized in their criminal behaviors than others. Most are sociopathic outcasts who were raised in deplorable family conditions and who suffer from a variety of mental disorders. However, some of these offenders are socially adept and thus are able to move about society victimizing others for years. Their choice of victims varies according to opportunity, age, gender, or some physical or behavioral attribute of the intended victim. Typologies based on modus operandi (method of procedure) and motives assist in better understanding these predators. Chapter One considers victimology, specifically addressing how or why certain people are victimized. By exploring the dynamics of violence, it becomes painfully clear that scores of evil predators learned or acquired their violence at an early age. Victimization can occur through situations and routine activities. In other words, simply being in a particular place at the wrong time or associating with deviant types can result in harm. Growing up in a violent family can also increase the risk of victimization, both within and outside the family. In addition, victimology addresses the issue of active and passive victim precipitation.

Chapter Two focuses on sexual predators, including rapists and child molesters. Like murderers, sexual predators are of several types. Some may victimize children, others prefer adults. A sexual predator may be a stranger or someone close to the victim, such as a teacher, parent, or member of the clergy. Also, there are sexual predators who torture and kill their victims. In other words, there is some obvious overlap between killers and sexual offenders. Case studies representing the various types of sex offenders and their motives are offered.

Chapter Three addresses mass, spree, and serial killers. In this chapter we explore the motives and methods of each type, along with the various subcategories of each. Although these killers may have different motives and tactics, they are similar in terms of their mental instabilities or social deficiencies. Some see murder as a challenge, other as a right. Many murder for thrill, excitement, or revenge on some individual or group. And of course, a number of these killers may commit suicide rather than face capture. Case studies are presented to assist in differentiating the various types.

CHAPTER 1

MONSTERS AND THEIR VICTIMS: THE DANCE

LEARNING OBJECTIVES

After studying this chapter, you will

- Learn how crime rates are measured
- Learn about violent crime rates and trends
- Learn about four major theories of victimization
- Understand why some persons are targeted for victimization by violent offenders
- Be able to identify situations conducive to victimization

INTRODUCTION

A man in his thirties posing as a talent agent approaches two young teen girls in a shopping mall, promising both of them a modeling contract if they agree to accompany him to his studio. He is attractive, well dressed, and convincing, and he even has a camera and business cards. He flatters the girls, telling them that they are perfect for a new teen magazine he purports to represent. The unwitting victims, swayed by his adoring attention, agree to accompany him to his studio. Several days later, the girls' sexually abused and mutilated bodies are found in a wooded ravine.

Distraught over his unhappy relations with his parents, a sixteen-year-old boy decides to run away from home. While hitchhiking, he accepts a ride with two men.

The men strike up a conversation with the young boy, empathizing with his plight and offering both food and shelter for a few days. They take the boy to their home, where they sodomize and torture the young victim. His headless torso is later found in a dumpster.

These cases represent examples of the creative and cruel tactics employed by violent perpetrators to obtain victims. **Victimology** explores the dynamics of victim-offender relationships and studies how and why some people are victimized by crime. Whereas criminology and criminal psychology focus on criminal behavior and motives, victimology seeks understanding as to the relationship between the victim and the offender. A killer or sadistic rapist is driven by many motives, usually abnormal sexual appetites or the need for power and control over an unsuspecting weaker person. The methods used to secure the victims are left to the twisted imagination of the offender. Child molesters, for example, know how to gain access to their victims by employing methods to coax their unwitting victims into dangerous situations without using force.

Victim selection varies according to the perverted needs of the offender. Some victims are targeted for crime by their appearance, age, type of social standing, race, or sex. Others are chosen because of their associations, lifestyle, or vulnerability. And a number of victims are simply in the wrong place at the wrong time, as in the case of an innocent person shot during a rival gang war.

Victims of violent predators such as serial killers and rapists are often selected for their vulnerability and sex, such as a lone female or a child walking alone in an isolated area. These predators will go to great effort to avoid detection. For that reason, many of them carefully plan their crimes and escapes; also, many unknowing victims may be stalked for months before they are attacked. This chapter will examine victimization theory and the dynamics of victim-offender relationships. But first, a word about how crime victim statistics are gathered and what trends they reveal about violent victimization.

MEASURING CRIME AND VICTIMIZATION

Reporting crime is often characterized as an action on the part of a victim of the crime. However, violent crimes can come to the attention of police through persons other than the victim, such as witnesses, relatives, or neighbors. Yet, many crimes go unreported. An abused spouse may never report his or her victimization out of fear of losing his or her spouse or of embarrassment. What we know about crime in the United States comes from official reports of crime gathered from law enforcement agencies nationwide and from surveys or self-report data about crimes that may not have been reported to law enforcement agencies.

There are three major sources reporting criminal victimization in the United States. The first source are reported offenses, tabulated by the Federal Bureau of Investigation, which include both serious and nonserious offenses. When a crime occurs and the police are notified, an official report is made and becomes part of the **Uniform Crime Report (UCR)** system. It is from the Uniform Crime Reports that crime rate and trends are calculated. Data included in the FBI's UCR program are provided by approximately 17,000 law enforcement agencies representing 94 percent of the nation's population as established by the U.S. Bureau of the Census. The Violent Crime Index a subject of data from the UCR: as measured by the Federal Bureau of Investigation includes murder, forcible rape, aggravated assault, and robbery.

The chance of a crime's being officially reported increases with severity. Crimes resulting in injuries are likely to be reported to police. Fifty-six percent of victimizations in which the victim was injured, compared with 40 percent of violence in which the victim emerged uninjured, were reported to the police. Seventy-five percent of all violent victimizations in which the victim was *seriously* injured and 90 percent of violence in which the victim sustained a gunshot wound were reported to the police (*Reporting Crime to the Police, 1992–2001, 2003*). However, it should be noted that health-care workers in most states are required to report to the police anyone injured by a firearm, as well as suspected cases of child abuse. These mandated reporting laws assist in the reporting process.

The second major source for tabulational victimization is the National Crime Victimization Survey (NCVS). Despite laws and the seriousness of the crime, not all crime is officially reported. Victims of violent crimes may refuse to report a crime because of embarrassment, fear, and the like. The victim may also be part of a criminal act and therefore unwilling to report the offense. A common example is the situation in which a person seeks a prostitute but is later robbed and beaten by the seller of pleasure. Chances are that the aggrieved customer will not report the offense to authorities, because once reported, it becomes a matter of public record. The topic of underreporting leads us to considering other ways of determining victimization, the National Crime Victimization Survey and self-reports.

The **National Crime Victim Survey (NCVS)** is conducted by the U.S. Bureau of Justice Statistics. The data are gathered from household surveys and by U.S. census interviewers and therefore include unreported victimizations. The NCVS chronicles crime information, including the following:

- Crime records
- Profiles of crime victims
- Relationships of the victims and the offenders
- Weapon usage

Figures released by the National Crime Victimization Survey (Rennison, 2001) reveal that violent crime rates fell 15 percent between 1999 and 2000, resulting in the greatest annual percentage decline and the lowest rates of violent crime recorded since the inception of the NCVS in 1973. Almost every demographic group considered between 1999 and 2000 experienced this decline in violent victimization rates. The rate at which males, females, whites, blacks, and non-Hispanic persons were violently victimized decreased significantly between 1999 and 2000. Why did this change occur? Crime education programs may be responsible, as well possible trends and strict sentencing laws. However, we must recognize that nearly half of all violent crime is neither discovered nor reported. The NCVS information indicates that only 48 percent of violent victimizations were reported to the police in 2000.

The third major source of reporting crime is referred to as unofficial self-reports. **Self-report studies** are used to demonstrate the prevalence, as well as the incidence, of offending, by supplying comprehensive information about offenders. However, this information is generally limited to juvenile offenders and victims. The problem with relying on self-reports is that victims either may not always be honest in their reporting or may not accurately report the event.

There are inherent problems in all methods of crime reporting. Yet, for the best estimates of the actual number of crimes, NCVS data are clearly preferable to UCR data. For the best estimates of offender characteristics such as race and gender, self-report data and victimization data are preferable to UCR arrest data. However, UCR data is superior in providing the geographic distribution of street crime.

Victim Characteristics

For the consideration of victimization rates for all violent crimes combined, the data consistently demonstrate that the most likely victims are males under the age of 25 who are victimized by someone of their own race (FBI, 1999). However, when rape, murder, and serial killings are considered separately, the picture shifts.

Rape. Females are more likely than males to be victims of sexual abuse as children and of sexual assault as adults. Although fewer than 5 percent of completed and attempted rapes were reported to law enforcement officials, in about two-thirds of rape incidents, the victim did tell another person, such as a friend or family member.

Females identified friends or acquaintances as the offender(s) in a substantial portion of the violence that they experienced. Thirty-seven percent of overall violent crime and 42 percent of rapes and sexual assaults occurred at the hands of a person whom the female victim considered a friend or an acquaintance (these figures are also supported by the FBI).

In studies of rape incidents among college women, data from the National Institute of Justice reveal that the following four main factors consistently increased the risk of sexual victimization: (1) frequently drinking enough to get drunk; (2) being unmarried; (3) having been a victim of a sexual assault before the start of the current school year; and (4) living on campus (for on-campus victimization only).

Murder. Seventy-five percent of murder victims are male. The large majority are over 18 years of age, and most (approximately 51 percent) knew their assailant.

In regard to murder, arguments are the predominant circumstance leading to this crime. According to supplemental data, 29 percent of the murders resulted from an argument. Felonious activities, such as forcible rape, robbery, and arson, precipitated almost 17 percent of the murders. Although almost half of murder victims are blacks (in disproportion to their representation in the U.S. population), other murder victimization data revealed by the Federal Bureau of Investigation indicate that murder is most often intraracial. In 2000, 94 percent of black murder victims were slain by black offenders, and 86 percent of white murder victims were slain by white offenders. The weapon of choice in most murders is a firearm, which was used in 66 percent of the murders. By firearm type, handguns accounted for over fifty percent of the murder total.

Serial Killer Victims. In an examination of 337 cases of serial killings, Hickey (2002) found that the number of victims of serial killings has risen substantially since 1950. However, keep this finding in perspective. Although the number of victims of murder in general averages between 9 and 10 per 100,000 population, the number of victims of serial killers is a tiny fraction of this population. Distributed over 20 years, the rate for serial killing is only .02 per 100,000 population. In other words, despite media hype, you are more likely to be hit by lightning than to be the victim of a serial killer! However, there are some interesting similarities and differences in the victimology for serial killers and for murder in general (FBI, 1999; Hickey, 2002).

Victims of both murders in general and of serial killers are more likely to be

- young adults;
- members of the same race as that of the killer;
- residents of urban areas; and
- persons of lower socioeconomic classes.

However, victims of serial killers, unlike victims of murder in general, more likely

- are females;
- are persons unknown to the killers; and
- will be killed by hands-on methods such as strangulation, stabbing, or beating (victims of female serial killers are most likely to be poisoned).

These comparisons represent only general probabilities based on data gathered from a variety of sources. That is, serial killers also kill children, the elderly, males, and family members, and they sometimes use guns to kill. As we will also see in later chapters, violent predators often are more selective in their victims than these data would indicate.

General crime statistics provide information that reveal trends in violent crime, but this is only part of the picture. Victimologists are also interested in better understanding why certain individuals become victims of crime. Subsequently, they have used additional information to develop theories of victimization that take into account the actions and lifestyles of victims that may facilitate victimization.

VICTIMIZATION THEORY

Crime and victimization data lead us to probe into the theory of victimization or the reasons why some are violently victimized. Through examining the situation in which the victimization occurred, along with victim characteristics, including lifestyle, behavior, and so on, a researcher may draw conclusions about causal factors related to crime and victimization.

It is nearly impossible to predict who will be victimized by violence at any given time. The terrorist attacks on September 11, 2001, remind us of our vulnerabilities to the evil intentions of dedicated monsters. How could anyone have predicted the horrible deaths that occurred on that dreadful day? Another tragic example was the sniper shootings in the Washington, D.C., area in 2002. Innocent persons, while conducting daily routine activities, were shot by two depraved gunmen whose only motive was pleasure. For the discussion of the dynamics of victimization theory, we divided the subject into routine activities, family risks, deviant lifestyle, and active and victim precipitated behavior (Figure 1–1). It is not our intent to maintain that these are totally discrete categories—clearly there is some overlap and congruence among them. However, we feel that there are some distinctions in explaining violent victimization.

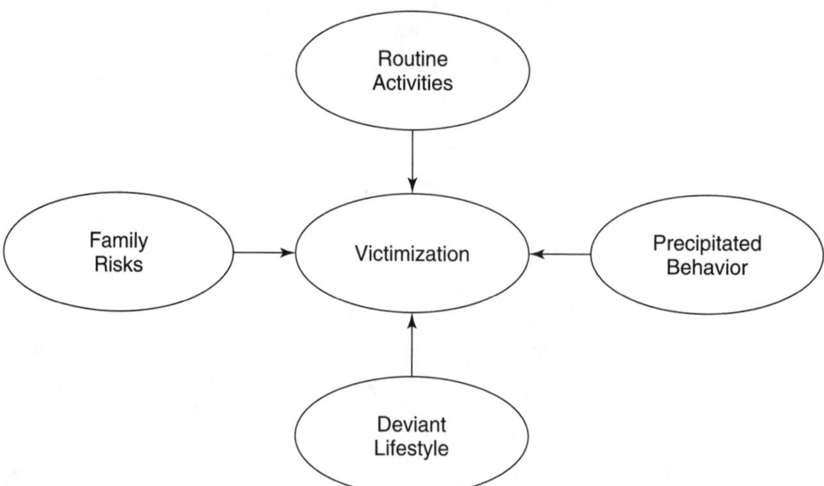

Figure 1–1 Victimization by Routine Activities, Family Risks, Deviant Lifestyle, and Victim-Precipitated Behavior

Routine Activities Theory

Victimization is explained by examining the **routine activities theory** (see Figure 1-2). The theory focuses on everyday activities of people, such as driving to work and running errands. Also, the theory addresses how particular situations influence

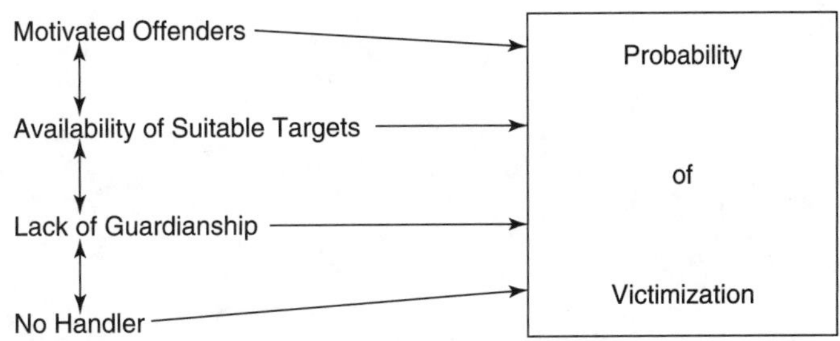

Figure 1–2 Routine Activities Paradigm. *(Cohen and Felson, 1979)*

interactions between victims and offenders. The routine activity approach assumes that most criminal acts require the following:

- Motivated offenders,
- Suitable targets,
- The absence of capable guardians, and
- No person to control the actions of the offender. (Cohen and Felson, 1979: 589).

A motivated offender is one who is provoked, idle, or bored. He or she may be driven by sexual desire, thrill, money, or control. The motivated offender may have a mental disorder, forming a basis for impulsive violent behavior (e.g., sociopathy). In choosing a suitable target, the offender considers opportunities such as the location of the victim-target, an escape route, and rewards for committing the crime. The opportunity to complete the crime and get away with it is another factor considered. Guardianship refers to the protection measures available to the potential victim. The presence of family, neighbors, bystanders, friends, and authorities helps to establish guardianship, which can serve to displace or discourage an offender. Cohen and Felson add that the convergence of suitable targets and the absence of capable guardians "may even lead to large increases in crime rates without necessarily requiring any increase in structural conditions that motivate individuals to engage in crime." Furthermore, they write, "if the proportion of motivated offenders or even suitable targets were to remain stable in a community, changes in routine activities could nonetheless alter the likelihood of their convergence in space and time, thereby creating more opportunities for crimes to occur" (Cohen and Felson, 1979: 589).

The final element of the theory—and one recently added by Felson—is the influence of a "handler." In other words, if the previous three conditions exist, the victimization will not occur if the offender is with a law-abiding person who discourages

Case Example: Routine Activities

Sexual child predator Wesley Allen Dodd was executed in the state of Washington in 1993 for the murder and sexual torture of three boys. Dodd boasted that a "sexual predator/child molester is always alert and ready for situation or possibility that may arise" (a motivated offender). If he saw a victim he liked (suitable target), he wrote down the address, with plans to return hoping to catch the child alone (absence of guardians). He would make note of any isolated areas near the victim's home and marked them on a map. Dodd would also attend children's movies and would frequent playgrounds (target-rich environments) hoping to find and lure an unsuspecting child. The activities of the children were routine, but to a dedicated predator, were an opportunity.

criminal behavior (e.g., a parent). This handler is a type of unofficial controller who serves to prevent the offender from committing an offense.

The theory comes to life in poverty-stricken neighborhoods where the presence of disenfranchised young people without work or school or solid family attachments creates greater opportunity for interpersonal conflict. In other words, geography, space, and the activities of persons within these settings generate opportunities for crime. In a study by Crutchfield (1989: 494), high rates of both unemployment and underemployment are associated with higher criminal violence at the neighborhood level, because the conditions create a "critical gathering of young angry males" in a potentially explosive situation. Potential victims and the violators are forced to coexist or compete for existing resources. Also, high rates of unemployment or underemployment may increase the opportunity for spousal and intimate violence for the same reasons.

As the number of opportunities or interactions between offenders and targets multiplies, the need for guardianship likewise becomes more important. Imagine living in a decaying community where prostitution, gang activity, and street corner drug-dealing are commonplace. Many unfortunate families, such as the poor and recently arrived immigrants, are forced to live in such communities without suitable guardianship. Places with abandoned buildings or rundown housing with absentee owners (slumlords) are attractive to criminals such as drug dealers who are seeking areas to do business without the fear of detection or property owner complaints.

Research has indicated (Skogan and Maxfield, 1981; Wilson and Kelling, 1982) that environmental conditions such as the activities of rowdy youths, broken windows, prostitution, loitering, litter, noise, and obscene behavior contribute to community disorder. Such visible conditions, moreover, actually signal social decay that prompts an invitation to criminality and victimization.

Studies conducted by the U.S. Department of Housing and Urban Development found that how a building is built or how a public space is designed has a major impact on the amount of crime that occurs in that space (Cisneros, 1995). In other words, victimization may be caused by the physical layout of the property or community. Poorly designed property provides an offender with hiding places or easy access for escape, which are factors in seeking a suitable target.

Income is also a factor in victimization. Data reported by the NCVS indicated that families earning less than $8,000 per annum were victimized at a rate of 60 per 1,000 persons, as opposed to persons with incomes of $75,000 or more in which the violent victimization rate was only 22 per 1,000 persons.

Low income translates into living conditions and situations conducive to victimization, suggesting a lack of guardianship. In these communities, women, children, the homeless, and the elderly are often targeted for crime because of the perceived ease by predators to commit assaults without detection, along with the knowledge that these victims are unlikely to report their assaults for fear of retaliation.

Neighborhood crime rate is linked with individual risk of victimization and is a significant predictor of assault and violent victimization (Sampson and Lauritsen, 1990). In these settings, males were more likely than females to be victimized by strangers, with 54 percent of the male victims of violence stating that the offender was a stranger (Rennison, 2001).

Another study found that respondents who view their neighborhoods as unsafe at night are significantly more likely to be victimized than respondents who feel safe (Miethe and Meier, 1990). In contrast, research has indicated that well-integrated localities, such as gated communities, actually lower the risk of violent victimization because in such communities the residents tend to know who belongs or to have rapid law-enforcement responses (Lee, 2000).

One of the earliest theoretical approaches in studying victim-offender relationships was presented by a Romanian lawyer (Mendelshon, 1963). His basic premise was that criminal victimization resulted from **situational factors** in which the person finds oneself. The location, not the victim's personal behavior or lifestyle, often defines the probability of becoming a crime victim. In other words, the victim may be totally innocent or unaware of impending harm.

The victim may be either in the wrong place at the right time or in the right place at the wrong time. The victim may be taking part in legitimate activities, walking to his or her car, sitting at home, or jogging through a park. An acquaintance, a stranger, or a family member may commit the victimization. However, in most cases it is a stranger who commits violent crimes under these conditions. The key to understanding situational victimization is the relative unpredictability of the circumstances. In murders committed by strangers, over 25 percent are unsolved. Moreover, these offenders have a better than 80 percent chance of going unpunished.

On January 16, 1997, Ennis Cosby, son of entertainer Bill Cosby, was murdered on a Los Angeles freeway. His only mistake that evening was getting a flat tire. A motivated offender happened to be nearby and saw the opportunity (suitable target, lack of guardians) to victimize. In the well-known O. J. Simpson murder case, Ronald Goldman was slain along with Nicole Brown Simpson. The primary target appeared to be Simpson's ex-wife, but Goldman was killed because he just happened to be at the scene returning a pair of glasses.

We can apply the routine activities theory to the workplace. About 900 work-related homicides occurred annually. As to **occupation-related victimization**, studies indicate that a person's work may increase the likelihood of victimization. Between 1993 and 1999 in the United States, an average of 1.7 million violent victimizations per year were committed against persons age 12 or older who were at work or on duty, according to the National Crime Victimization Survey (NCVS). It is not surprising that police officers experienced workplace violent crime at rates higher than all other occupations (261 per 1,000 police officers). After police officers, persons working in the mental health field (e.g., social workers and counselors) were ranked second, followed by retail sales workers, who were victimized in the workplace at a rate of 20 per 1,000. Transportation workers (cab drivers) and teachers also reported victimizations. Although most workplace victimizations did not involve a weapon, transportation workers, sales clerks (e.g., in convenience stores), and law-enforcement officers reported more weapon assaults (guns, knives, clubs, etc.) than did those in other occupations (see Table 1-1).

The data in Table 1-1 suggest that workplace victimization is associated with occupations in which contact with undesirables and determined offenders are part of an employee's routine activities. In response to that threat, many businesses have increased their guardianship through enhanced security measures.

Although some occupations are linked by routine activities to the potential for victimization, other connections are more difficult to explain and may occur at unexpected times and locations. The U.S. Postal Service reported that 38 employees died violently and unexpectedly between 1986 and 1994. A more recent example occurred when a number of employees of an Internet consulting firm in Massachusetts were

Highlight 1-1

In some cases, the presence of a guardian in an apparently safe situation does not stop a motivated offender.

A tragic example of a totally innocent victim's being raped and murdered is that of 12-year-old Polly Klaas. During a slumber party in October 1993, Polly Klaas was abducted at knifepoint from her Petaluma, California, home. She was later found murdered. The monster Richard Allen Davis, a paroled sex offender, was convicted and executed for the murder.

The unsolved murder of JonBenet Ramsey, a child of 6, who was brutally murdered in her own home between December 25 and 26, 1996, is yet another gruesome example. In addition, the abduction of Elizabeth Smart from her home in Utah in 2002 is further evidence that the sanctity of the home did not protect these children from murder or abduction.

TABLE 1-1

Victim's Occupational Field	Percent of Workplace Victims Victimized by an Offender with a Weapon
Transportation	31.7
Retail sales	23.3
Law enforcement	23.2
Other field	22.0
Mental health	14.9
Teaching	10.9
Medical	10.5

Source: U.S. Department of Justice, Office of Justice Programs.

murdered by Michael McDermott, a software technician at the firm. One day he appeared at work bearing a semiautomatic rifle, a 12-gauge shotgun, and a pistol. He methodically and callously waded through the company's accounting offices, fatally shooting seven coworkers, some of them at close range.

America learned a painful lesson on September 11, 2001, about the extent of criminal motivation. The guardianship or security measures that day were inadequate to deter these murderous offenders. However, since September 11, travelers have been confronted with stricter controls or, shall we say, improved guardianship. Thus, although increased guardianship measures may cause inconvenience for many, given the constant threat of violent crime, such vigilance may be the best response.

Family Risks

Circumstances, activities, and the acts of strangers are not the only source of victimization. Unscrupulous family members also increase the risk of future victimization.

The risks of victimization from family relationships are categorized into three areas. First, a child living in a household in which there is a parent or guardian who batters a spouse is also at risk of assault by the batterer. Data from the 1985 National Family Violence Survey, for example, revealed that the greater the amount of violence against a spouse, the higher the chance of physical abuse against a child living in the same home (Ross, 1996). Accordingly, O'Keefe (1994) found a relationship between the amount of husband-to-wife violence witnessed and father-child physical abuse. The abuser of one victim seems to find other targets in proximity to the first act of violence.

A second risk factor for violent victimization occurs when the quality of parental supervision and/or supervisory control is lacking. Research on the children of battered women shows that these children indeed suffer from poor parenting because battered parents are consumed with their own safety and because the stress they are under prevents them from providing guidance and protection for their children (Bingham and

Harmon, 1996; Holden and Ritchie, 1991). Other characteristics consistent with violent households include inconsistent child-rearing and more negative disciplinary practices (Holden and Ritchie, 1991). In these settings, a child may turn to a criminal lifestyle or, as in many cases, may join deviant subcultures that increase their risk of later victimization.

A third risk factor is the psychological consequences or trauma in witnessing or being exposed to violence. Such experiences may have a variety of effects on a child, which may make them vulnerable to victimization as they grow older (Campbell and Lewandowski, 1997; Edlenson, 1999). Children in families who witness or experience violence at home may display long-term developmental problems such as mental instability and other cognitive disorders (Edlenson, 1999).

One consequence of witnessing domestic violence may be traumatic stress and anxiety in the children themselves. And individuals suffering from post-traumatic stress disorder (PTSD) and traumatic anxiety have been shown to be at higher risk for revictimization (Arata, 1999; Kilpatrick et al., 2003). In addition to traumatic anxiety, another effect of exposure to domestic violence, based on learning theory, is that children may be socialized into the acceptance of violence and the inevitability of victimization (Jaffe, Wilson, and Wolfe, 1986). They may see violence as an appropriate solution to interpersonal conflict and as a means to an end between intimate partner or others. Some research suggests that children who live in violent homes do not necessarily have to witness the abuse to be affected by it (Jaffe et al., 1990). Children can be exposed to the violence by hearing the assault or seeing its consequences in the form of injury to family members or damage to the home.

In an ironic twist, children who are victims of family violence or who witness violence in the home are at greater risk of later using violence against others. As we will see in later chapters, often the violent victimizer was once a victim himself or herself.

Deviant Lifestyle

The third theory of victimization is referred to as victimization through one's chosen lifestyle. In this theory, a victim may be acquainted with the offender or may undertake a lifestyle in which contact with undesirable types is common (excluding certain occupations as previously discussed). In other words, either the environment in which the victim lives or frequents, or the quality of his or her associations raises the probability of victimization. Lifestyle factors contributing to victimization may be normal, such as frequenting bars or areas known as trouble spots.

A person's lifestyle may reflect his or her personal behavior or pleasures conducive to victimization. Thus, if a person uses drugs or is a heavy drinker and frequents areas known for high crime, the risk of being a victim increases (Gottfredson, 1981; Sacco and Johnson, 1990).

More recent evidence on background factors suggests that childhood abuse, mental illness, and physical health limitations predispose a person to adult physical and sexual victimization in general population studies (Gidycz, Hanson, and Layman,

1995; Kilpatrick et al., 2003). Why is this the case, and what does it have to do with lifestyle? It is argued that a lower self-esteem due to prior victimizations may actually lower one's ability to perceive harm, and therefore the victim engages in risky lifestyles or occupations such as prostitution or associating with deviant types.

The development of the **deviant lifestyle theory** of victimization is credited to Hindelang et al. (1978). The theory posits that patterns of victimization reflect variations in lifestyles and activities. Those engaged in the criminal subculture are undertaking a deviant lifestyle, which can either get them arrested or victimized. Prostitutes are frequently placed in vulnerable situations with unknown persons (customers), and many violent predators choose prostitutes as victims. The famed English serial killer Jack the Ripper confined his attacks on impoverished women of the streets of London who were forced to rely on prostitution for their income. As such, it was easy to acquire victims in desperate need of funds. Street prostitutes are frequently the target of serial killers and other sexual predators.

Many troubled teenagers run away from home and engage in risky lifestyles and activities such as selling drugs and hitchhiking. They may not consciously choose to become a crime victim, but because of their associations and behaviors or their need for companionship, they become victimized. In one reported case, a troubled teenage runaway was subjected to weeks of physical and sexual abuse and forced into prostitution. The victim met the offender at a party, and later they became friends. After hours of binge drinking, the girl passed out and then woke up to find herself naked, wearing handcuffs and shackles. The victim was beaten and forced to perform oral sex. She was later reportedly hog-tied and sexually assaulted with candlesticks and a baseball bat, and later was forced to prostitute herself. She was fearful of leaving her tormentor.

Case Example: Deviant Lifestyle

Arthur Shawcross, a serial killer from Rochester, New York, sought out street prostitutes. He would prowl the low-income areas of Rochester late at night, seeking a prostitute victim. After engaging in sex, he strangled his victims and dumped their bodies in rural areas.

Famed serial killer Jeffrey Dahmer prowled low-end gay bars for victims. After selecting his victims, he would lure them back to his apartment for sex and then kill them. To avoid detection, he would cut up their bodies, cannibalize some body parts, and place the remaining body parts in containers for decomposition and disposal.

These offenders targeted easy victims whose deviant lifestyles (prostitution) or activities (frequenting bars) made them more likely to come into contact with predators.

(Branswell, 1997). The victim suffered horribly, but her chosen lifestyle contributed to her unfortunate victimization.

Homelessness is a lifestyle that correlates with being both a criminal and a victim. Homelessness creates interaction with violent others, making one more vulnerable to victimization. It also provides an environment in which violent attitudes are learned and supported as a means of survival. Homeless or placeless persons adopt violent values to avoid victimization (Baron, 1997). Studies indicate that those who reported the least victimization on the street also reported more supportive attitudes toward violence (Baron et al., 2001). In other words, kill or be killed or the proverbial "survival of the fittest" is the cultural message in some communities. And of course, the chances of serious injury improve each time violence is used against another.

Active and Passive Victim-Precipitated Behavior

The final perspective on the theory of victimization is the role of the victim leading up to the crime. Known as the theory of victim-precipitated behavior, the theory seeks to understand how a victim may contribute to his or her injury. The theory is closely aligned with deviant lifestyle, with the exception that victim-precipitated events can result from legitimate lifestyles or interactions with others that evolve into victimization.

One of the first criminologists to focus on the victim-offender relationship (as opposed to situations or locations) was Von Hentig (1967: 384). He believed that personal characteristics of the victims, which prompted certain behaviors, were important in explaining victimization. Personal vulnerability to crime was associated with low intelligence, depression, susceptibility to anger, or the need for stimulation. Because of their behavior, people with these characteristics may find themselves in situations leading to personal harm, albeit unintended.

Self-Check 1-1

Which theory best describes the victimology for each of the following examples? RA — Routine Activities; FR — Family Risk; DL — Deviant Lifestyle.

___ 1. Susan ran away from her abusive step father when she was 16. She is living with Mark, who is very controlling and jealous and who periodically "knocks her around."

___ 2. Alex worked as a street prostitute and was beaten to death by one of his "johns."

___ 3. Jason works as a counselor in a free clinic in a rough part of town. On his way to his car after work, he was robbed and shot.

___ 4. Alison, who is 9, was molested by a male teacher at her school.

Key: 1—FR; 2—DL; 3—RA; 4—RA.

Victim-precipitated behavior occurs through active or passive participation in crime. **Active participation** occurs when a victim is directly responsible for his or her injury by creating the situation for injury. A bully who picks a fight with another but then becomes the beaten party is an active participant.

A well-publicized example of a victim-precipitated incident resulting in a murder occurred in July 2000. A 44-year-old father, Thomas Junta, upset over the way his son's hockey practice was being conducted, fought with the son's coach. Junta beat the coach, Michael Costin, to death. Witnesses testified that Costin and Junta both were "belligerent the day of the fight, exchanging profanities and brawling in front of children." Some witnesses said that Costin "threw the first punch" (Associated Press, 2002). Although Junta deserved conviction, an argument could be made that Costin precipitated the event.

The emphasis on the behavior of the victim in murder was researched by Wolfgang (1957), who found higher proportions of such victim characteristics as alcohol in the blood and previous arrest, particularly for assault, in victim-precipitated homicides than were found in non-victim-precipitated homicides. He argues that "in many cases the homicide victim has most of the major characteristics of an offender." In other words, they both may be using drugs and engaging in some illegal activity.

These characteristics tend to expose some individuals to greater risk of being victimized. The higher rates of victimization for young black males, for example, can be explained by their accessibility to offenders (many of whom are armed), resulting from deviant behaviors. The greater the degree of social interaction among individuals who share these characteristics, the more likely violent victimization will occur (Hindelang et al., 1978).

Associates of drug dealers and other criminals, who become victimized, are active participants. An extreme form of active precipitation occurs when two offenders engage in a criminal enterprise, such as drug dealing. After the deal has been completed, one offender assaults the other and steals the profits. However, this type of victim-precipitated behavior is rarely reported, even though a crime was technically committed.

Engaging in violent conduct increased the likelihood of also being the recipient of violence. It is overwhelmingly evident that there is a very small likelihood for nonviolent actors to be the targets of violence, and therefore it is safe to conclude that nonviolent adolescents by no means constitute the pool of victims of violence.

Passive participation occurs when, as a result of naïveté or ignorance, a passive participant becomes a victim. Picking up hitchhikers or hitchhiking itself may lead to victimization. Noncriminal women who associate with deviant males may not be involved in criminal activity, but their associations create the opportunity for assault and robbery. Such women, because of sheer gullibility, put themselves into situations in which victimization is likely and escape is impossible.

Internet technology has prompted many innocent and lonely persons to seek companionship only to become victimized. Pedophiles, for example, look for loners or children with low self-esteem; and since many children use computers, they become easy prey. It is less likely that they will talk about the overtures to friends, and they are susceptible to someone's trying to befriend them. The pedophile feeds on these opportunities, posing as the much-needed friend or companion.

Routine alcohol usage is associated with sexual assaults, in that the victim's passive participation may result in victimization. A recent comprehensive review by Kantor and Asdigian (1997) examined four types of association between women's alcohol use and their victimization by males: (1) women's intoxication provokes male violence; (2) women's intoxication is a reaction to/coping mechanism for being abused; (3) women's intoxication is related to victimization through men's drinking behavior; and (4) women's intoxication is related to victimization because of childhood abuse experiences. Their review suggests that there is an association, but no direct causal mechanism, between women's drinking and abuse by male partners.

Passive participation was found by Synovitz and Byrne (1998) in a study of 241 college women victimized by rape. The researchers found three predictors of becoming a rape victim. The first was the number of sexual partners that the women had. The more men a woman dates and engages in sex with, the greater the likelihood of rape. The high number of sexual partners might not allow time to set parameters for a caring relationship.

The second predictor, dressing provocatively, also was significant in predicating sexual assault. Dressing provocatively may be viewed as "sexy and seductive and may cause miscommunication between men and women."

A third predictor is alcohol usage. Women who drink alcohol in the dating situation may exhibit behavior such as excessive friendliness that may be misinterpreted by men as seductive. Of course, this finding is not to suggest that the victim is responsible or that the offender isn't culpable; however, victim behavior, whether active or passive, may encourage victimization.

Self-Check 1-2

For each of the following examples, identify whether there was Active (A) or Passive (P) participation by the victim.

1. In domestic violence murders, researchers found that long-term abuse suffered by women is a precursor to killing their abusive mate (Brown, 1986: 57–79); an abusive husband's efforts to control and restrict his wife's lifestyle can result in his murder (Daly and Wilson, 1988: 294–295).
2. Women who are victims of domestic violence are at risk for being killed by their abusive partner, especially when they try to leave.

Key: 1—A; 2—P.

Conclusion

Theories of victimization such as crime theory seek to understand the interaction between the victim, offender, and location or situation surrounding the attack. By examining lifestyle, family influences, routine activities, and victim behavior, we find that there is a degree of interrelatedness. Some people are victimized through their choice of associations or lifestyles, and others through random or unpredictable events; and in some situations, people may invite their own victimization. Simply stated, dangerous times, dangerous places, and associating with dangerous people increase victimization. High-risk activities, including certain types of employment, are possible invitations to victimization. The geographical setting and socioeconomic level of community influence the probability of victimization. This finding is not to suggest that place predicts crime, but we know that many criminals consider environmental conditions conducive to crime commission and escape.

Discussion Questions and Activities

1. How can the reporting of violent crimes be increased?
2. Provide an actual or a hypothetical example for each of the four major theories of victimization. Discuss how each theory applies to each example.
3. Visit a community in transition or decay, and then indentify the number of possible sources of violence that could lead to victimization.
4. Scan various news sources for articles pertaining to crime and violence. Are you able to determine what role the victim played in the offense?
5. Conduct a confidential survey of students or other groups, and then determine how many were victimized by crime (assault, theft, etc.). How many reported the crime to the police?
6. Identify two websites that provide information for suvivors of rape and two websites for survivors of child molestation. For each of the four sites, write the URL and provide the following:
   a. Source (i.e., organization, profession) and date posted
   b. Summary of the type of information that is provided
   c. Evaluation of the source—is it credible/authoritative? Why, or why not?
   d. Evaluation of the information. Would it be useful/helpful to victims of sexual crimes? Why, or why not?
7. Women are most often victims of rape. However, males are also victims of rape, but they often do not report it. Why do you think this is the case? Do you think that there are any gender-tied reactions to being sexually victimized? Explain.

8. According to Hickey (2002), the most common stranger-victims of serial killers are college females and prostitutes. Using two of the theories of victimization, explain why this is the case. What do these two groups of women have in common that makes them more likely victims?

Key Terms

Active participation
Deviant lifestyle theory
National Crime Victim Survey (NCVS)
Occupation-related victimization
Passive participation
Routine activities theory
Self-report studies
Situational factors
Uniform Crime Report (UCR)
Victimology

References

Arata, C. M. 1999. Sexual re-victimization and PTSD: An exploratory study. *Journal of Child Sexual Abuse, 8*(1): 49–65.

Baron, S. W. 1997. "Risky lifestyles and the link between offending and victimization." *Studies on Crime and Crime Prevention 6:* 53–72.

Baron, S. W., L. W. Kennedy, and D. R. Forde. 2001. "Male street youths' conflict: The role of background, subcultural, and situational factors." *Justice Quarterly* Vol I.

Bingham, R. D. and R. J. Harmon. 1996. Traumatic stress in infancy and early childhood: Expression of distress and developmental issues. In C. R. Pfeffer (Ed.), *Severe stress and mental disturbance in children* (pp. 499–532). Washington, D.C.: American Psychological Association.

Branswell, B. 1997. "Teenage horror." *Maclean's*, v. 110, p. 88.

Brown, A. 1986. "Assaults and homicides at home." *Advances in Applied Psychology 3.*

Campbell, J. C. and Lewandowski, L. A. 1997. Mental and physical health effects of intimate partner violence on women and children. *The Psychiatric Clinics of North America, 20*(2): 353–374.

Cisneros, H. (1995). "Defensible space: Deterring crime and building community." U.S. Department of Housing and Urban Development.

Cohen, L. and M. Felson. 1979. "Social change and crime rate trends: A routine activity approach." *American Sociological Review 44:* 588–608.

Crutchfield, R. D. 1989. "Labor stratification and violent crime." *Social Forces 68:* 489–512.

"Dad convicted in hockey death." 2002. Associated Press, Monday, Jan. 14.

Daly, M. and M. Wilson. 1988. *Homicide.* New York: Aldine-DeGruter.

Edlenson, J. L. 1999. Children's witnessing of adult domestic violence. *Journal of Interpersonal Violence, 14*(8): 839–870.

Federal Bureau of Investigation. 1999. *Uniform Crime Reports.* Department of Justice, Washington, D. C.

Fishman, G., G. S. Mesch, and Z. Eisikovits. 2002. "Variables affecting adolescent victimization: Findings from a national youth survey." *Western Criminology Review 3*(2). [Online.] Available: *http://wcr.sonoma.edu/v3n2/fishman.html.*

Gidycz, C. A., K. Hanson, and M. J. Layman. 1995 "A prospective analysis of the relationships among sexual assault experiences." *Psychology of Women Quarterly 19:* 5–29.

Gottfredson, M. R. 1981. "On the etiology of criminal victimization." *The Journal of Criminal Law and Criminology* 72(2): 714–726.

Hickey, E. 2002. Serial murderers and their victims (3rd ed.). Wadsworth.

Hindelang, M. J., M. R. Gottfredson, and J. Garofalo. 1978. *Victims of Personal Crime: An Empirical Foundation for a Theory of Personal Victimization.* Cambridge, Mass.: Ballinger.

Holden, G. W., and K. L. Ritchie. 1991. "Linking extreme marital discord, child rearing, and child behavior problems: Evidence from battered women." *Child Development 62*(2): 311–327.

Jaffe, P., S. Wilson, and D. A. Wolfe. 1986. Promoting changes in attitudes and understanding of conflict resolution among child witnesses of family violence. *Canadian Journal of Behavioral Science 18*(4): 356–366.

Jaffe, P., D. Wolfe, and S. K. Wilson. 1990. *Children of Battered Women.* Newbury Park, Calif.: Sage.

Kantor, G. K. and N. Asdigian, 1997. "When women are under the influence: Does drinking or drug use by women provoke beatings by men?" In M. Galanter (Ed.), *Recent Developments in Alcoholism, Volume 13; Alcohol and Violence.* New York: Plenum.

Keane, C. and R. Arnold. 1996. "Examining the relationship between criminal victimization and accidents: A routine activities approach". *The Canadian Review of Sociology and Anthropology 33:* 457–479.

Kilpatrick, D., B. E. Saunders, and D. W. Smith. 2003, April. *Youth Victimization: Prevalence and Implications.* National Institute of Justice. Washington, D. C.

Lee, M. R. 2000. "Community cohesion and violent predatory victimization: A theoretical extension and cross-national test of opportunity theory." *Social Forces* 79(2): 683–706.

Mann, C. 1988. "Getting even? Women who kill in domestic encounters." *Justice Quarterly 5.*

Mendelshon, B. 1963. "The origin of the doctrines of victimology." *Excerpta Criminologica*

Miethe, T. D., and R. F. Meier. 1990. "Opportunity, choice, and criminal victimization: A test of a theoretical model." *Journal of Research in Crime and Delinquency* 27: 243–266.

Mooney, D. R. and M. Rodriguez. 1996, Winter. "California healthcare workers and mandatory reporting of intimate violence." *Hastings Women's Law Journal* 7, *(1):* 85–111.

O'Keefe, M. 1994. Linking marital violence, mother-child/father-child aggression, and child behavior problems. *Journal of Family Violence 9*(1): 63–78.

Rennison, C. M. 2001. "Criminal Victimization 2000 Changes 1999–2000 with Trends 1993–2000." Washington, D. C.: U. S. Department of Justice, Bureau of Justice Statistics.

Reporting Crime to the Police, 1992–2001. 2003. U.S. Department of Justice, Office of Justice Programs, Bureau of Justice Statistics.

Ross, S. M. 1996. Risk of physical abuse to children of spouse abusing parents. *Child Abuse & Neglect 20*(7): 589–598.

Sacco, V. F. and H. Johnson. 1990. *Patterns of Criminal Victimization in Canada.* Ottawa: Statistics Canada.

Sampson, R. J. and J. L. Lauritsen. 1990. "Deviant lifestyles, proximity to crime, and the offender-victim link in personal violence." *Journal of Research in Crime and Delinquency 27:* 110–139.

Skogan, W. G. and M. G. Maxfield. 1981. *Coping with Crime: Individual and Neighborhood Reactions.* Beverly Hills, Calif.: Sage Publications.

Synovitz, L. B. and T. J. Byrne. 1998. "Antecedents of sexual victimization: Factors discriminating victims from nonvictims." *Journal of American College Health 46:* 151–158.

Von Hentig, H. 1967. *The Criminal and His Victim.* Hamden, Conn.: Archon.

Wilson, J. Q. and G. L. Kelling. 1982. Broken windows: The police and neighborhood safety. *Atlantic Monthly 329:* 29–38.

Wolfgang, M. E. 1957. "Victim-precipitated criminal homicide." *Journal of Criminal Law, Criminology and Police Science 48:* 1–11.

CHAPTER 2

SEXUAL PREDATORS

LEARNING OBJECTIVES

After studying this chapter, you will

- Become familiar with data on sexual offenders
- Become familiar with the research explaining sex offenders
- Learn about the types of rapists and child molesters
- Through cases studies, learn about the motives and methods of sexual predators
- Understand key legislation aimed at punishing sexual offenders

INTRODUCTION

Sex crimes are often regarded as the most evil and offensive to society, especially when children are targeted. Victims of sexual predators may be acquainted with the offender, who may be a neighbor, parent, mentor, coach, teacher, or member of the clergy. Also, both the offender and the victim represent all social levels of society as evidenced by recent reports of sexual abuse by teachers and members of the clergy. Sex offenders are often described as self-serving egotists, dedicated to satisfying their twisted passions at the expense of an unwilling or naive victim. For many, the hedonistic need for control and dominance are classic motives of the predator. Moreover, some offenders achieve an even greater satisfaction through torture and murder. The dynamics of the encounter may be opportunistic, planned, or associated with another crime, such as burglary. Most reported sex offenses are classified as rape, assault with intent to commit rape, contributing to the delinquency of a child involving sexual misconduct, sodomy, indecent exposure, and indecent liberties with children (molesting).

The dimensions of sex crimes and offender behavior are complex, incorporating a variety of motives and preferences. Sex crimes may be physically violent or accomplished through trickery or deceit. There are sexual offenders who prefer children, some who prefer the elderly, others who prefer victims in the same age range, and still others for which age or sex or physical condition is no boundary.

As we will discover, some offenders practice paraphilic behavior for their psychosexual pleasure. It is surprising that there are offenders who experience remorse and guilt; however, others, such as sadistic offenders, have no feelings for their victims. There are ritualistic offenders who develop complex fantasies and act them out, and there are offenders who act out impulsively with little or no thought beyond immediate sexual gratification (Hazelwood and Warren, 2000).

This chapter addresses the motives and methods of violent and serious sex offenders, focusing primarily on serial rapists, pedophiles, and child molesters. A discussion of women sex offenders is also presented.

Sex Crime Data

Most violent sex offenders are males who assault female victims, with females accounting for a small percentage of known offenders; likewise, adult males account for a small percentage of victims, at least those who choose to report the victimization. In some cases, the victim and the offender are of the same sex, and it is quite common for both the victim and the offender to have had a prior relationship as family members, intimates, coworkers, or casual acquaintances.

Statistics published by the United States Department of Justice, Bureau of Justice Statistics, report that on a given day, there are over 200,000 offenders convicted of rape or sexual assault under the care, custody, or control of corrections agencies, and that nearly 60 percent of these offenders are under conditional supervision in the community. It is interesting that nearly one-fourth of those serving time for rape in state prisons had been on probation or parole at the time of the offense for which they had been in prison. In cases of rape, victims report that in nearly 3 out of 4 incidents, the offender was not a stranger. In a high percentage of sex crimes, the victims are usually children.

In addition to the many unfortunate emotional consequences of sexual assault, data indicate that more than half of spousal rapes, rapes by ex-spouses, and stranger rapes resulted in victim injury, whereas about a quarter of parent-child rapes resulted in major injury. Many rape victims are physically harmed, with nearly 6 in 10 rapes involving a knife, resulting in victim injury (National Criminal Justice Reference

Service, 1997). In addition to committing sex crimes, sexual offenders may display a number of behavioral disorders influencing their behavior.

Paraphilias

Many sex offenders exhibit a variety of sexual disorders, which are referred to as paraphilias. A sexual **paraphilia** is characterized by recurrent intense sexual urge and sexual arousal involving either (1) nonhuman objects, (2) the suffering or humiliation of oneself or one's partner (not merely simulated), or (3) children or other nonconsenting persons. Paraphilic behavior, sexual urges, or fantasies often cause significant distress in social, occupational, or other important areas of functioning (American Psychiatric Association, 1994).

Consensual sexual behaviors, such as sadomasochism, do not impair life functioning or are not considered a paraphilia because they do not meet all the diagnostic criteria. Some of the most common paraphilias include sexual arousal to children (pedophilia), objects (fetishism), watching unaware others undress or engage in sexual activity (voyeurism), and inflicting pain on self (masochism) or others (sadism).

In addition, there are a number of less common but bizarre paraphilias such as necrophilia (sexual relations with a dead person); zoophilia (sex with animals); obscene phone calls; and fascination with feces, urine, or enemas. There are no limits as to one's sexual appetite or behavior, and although some paraphilias are extreme and appalling, they nevertheless are practiced by a number of sex offenders. Paraphilias are discussed in more detail in Chapter Eight.

The importance of knowing about paraphilia is that many sex offenders also suffer from one or more of these paraphilic conditions, which may provide insight into what motivates offender behavior (Abel et al., 1988). Some rapists, for example, demonstrate paraphilic behavior by collecting items from their victims, such as jewelry or undergarments. And sexual sadism, bondage, and voyeurism (photographs of the victim) may also be part of the offender's repertoire. Paraphilias are not crimes as long as they remain fantasies (i.e., to fuel masturbation or arousal with a consenting adult) but are crimes when acted out with a nonconsenting person. They do, however, fuel the fantasies and actions of many sex offenders.

SERIAL RAPISTS

> "I am plagued by repetitive thoughts, urges, and fantasies of the degradation, rape, and murder of women. I cannot get those thoughts out of my mind." (Quote by serial rapist and murderer Michael Ross, who was sentenced to death for raping and killing 8 women.)

One of the most evil and despicable types of predatory offenders are serial rapists. Such people commit two or more rapes over a particular time period, not stopping with one victim but continuing over a period of months or years until apprehended. Serial rapists may attack several victims in a relatively short time frame, halt their assaults for several weeks or so, and then begin again whenever the urge arises. Sex offenders employ various methods in committing their crimes, such as kidnapping, stalking, or breaking and entering into a dwelling.

As with many criminal types, there are certain common behavioral characteristics of serial rapists. Burgess (1986) and her colleagues found that over 80 percent of the violent sex offenders they studied engaged in compulsive and chronic masturbation and constant daydreaming; were socially isolated; were more likely to force fellatio and anal intercourse upon their victims; and had an average to superior intelligence. The first three behaviors were reported to be consistent from childhood to adulthood, and they were also found in serial killers as well.

In a study of juvenile rapists and sex offenders, it was found that the offenders had high rates of learning disabilities and academic dysfunction; behavioral and health problems, including substance abuse; and disorders of conduct resulting from inconsistent or abusive parents. They also had observed difficulties with impulse control and judgment (Hunter, 2000). The psychological state and resulting behaviors of the rapist often define the type of sexual predator that he or she becomes. In examining the criminal motives and behaviors of rapists, the following two basic types are offered: the acquaintance-contact rapist and the power-anger rapist.

Acquaintance-Contact Rapists

Acquaintance-contact rapists are the most common type, but their crimes are rarely reported. The reason is that the victims know their offenders from casual dating or through a social or business relationship. Also, the embarrassment or fear associated with reporting the offenses outweighs the need to prosecute. Acquaintance-contact rapists believe that men are independent, aggressive, competitive, and strong, whereas women are viewed as passive, dependent, and accepting play-toys. In dating relationships, this perception leads the acquaintance-contact rapist to believe that women want sex (and that he is God's gift), that women owe him sex, but that they play games and act uninterested only to turn him on.

This rapist feels that even though a woman appears to be reluctant, she actually wants him to overcome her objections and take the initiative. He may disregard a woman's signals of unwillingness, misinterpret her resistance as teasing, or decide that she has no right to refuse him. The classic rationalization of an acquaintance-contact rapist is "She came on to me" or "She dressed like she wanted it."

Acquaintance-contact rapists are not conspicuously deviant in either personality or sexuality, and most may have responsible jobs or high social standing in the community, with no previous record of sexual assaults. In fact, they often use their status or charisma to seduce victims. The motivation is sexual conquest, or the completion of initiated sexual contact. So-called date rapists fall under this typology. To accomplish their objectives, they often use alcohol or other drugs to lower the defenses of the

Case Example: Acquantance-Contact Rapists

Andrew Luster

> "This is what I dream about. A beautiful strawberry-blonde, passed out on my bed, waiting for me to do with her what I will." (Quote by Andrew Luster, convicted rapist.)

The great-grandson and heir to cosmetics tycoon Max Factor was convicted of rape in Ventura, California. He cruised college bars and beach areas for victims. During his 2002 trial and in anticipation of a conviction, the playboy surfer and stock trader fled the jurisdiction. He was convicted and sentenced to prison for 124 years. He was on trial for rape and sodomy of several unconscious victims, drug possession, poisoning, and sexual battery. Prosecutors charged Luster with using the date-rape drug gamma hydroxybutyrate (GHB) and liquid ecstasy, to incapacitate his victims. A search of Luster's home revealed sex tapes involving over a dozen young female victims. Cocaine and assorted illegal firearms were also found. Luster maintained that he was innocent, saying that the alleged victims were willing participants in the sex movies and that they pretended to be asleep.

victim. This technique allows rapists to assign equal responsibility for what happens to the victim. In other words, the rationale of the rapist is that if the victim voluntarily went with the offender and had a few drinks, then the victim is a willing participant regardless of other factors.

College students are particularly prone to this type of sexual victimization. Studies on college campuses have indicated that over half of a representative sample of more than 1,000 female students at a large urban university had experienced some form of unwanted sex. The study revealed that in casual dating 43 percent of steady dating partners perpetrated 12 percent of these acts (Abbey et al., 1996).

In both of these cases, the offenders used deceit and drugs to secure their victims. Although physical violence may have not been used and there was an acquaintance relationship, both offenders are considered to be predators and guilty of rape. The lack of voluntary consent on the part of the victim is at issue, not the act.

Power-Anger Rapists

The most feared rapists are referred to as the **power-anger rapists.** In this grouping, the literature generally identifies four types of rapists (Hazelwood and Burgess, 1987; Swanson, Chamelin, and Territo, 2000):

- Power-assertive
- Power-reassurance

- Anger-retaliatory
- Anger-excitation

In a **power-assertive rape,** forceful aggression and intimidation of the victim are employed to meet the predator's strong need to control and dominate the victim. A direct and overpowering initial assault is employed, which often results in multiple rapes of the victim. Since power-assertive rapists like to make their victims totally submissive from the start, they may begin with an anal assault, with their preference being oral sex. Also, the rapist will use a great deal of profanity, demeaning language, and humiliation toward the victim. To overcome a victim's resistance, the rapist will say, "If you don't want to get hurt, give up" or "You want it as bad as I, so enjoy it."

Power-assertive rapists usually select victims close to their own age group and will often take their victims to isolated location where they will humiliate their victims by tearing off their clothes. These rapists will typically operate in a comfort zone, such

Case Example

Allen

Allen was an only child raised in an affluent two-parent family. Both of his parents were working professionals, who were often absent because of business trips. During the parents' frequent absences, a nanny cared for Allen. There was no evidence of abuse or family discord. His parents frequently favored Allen with gifts and a generous allowance. Allen, who is handsome and well educated, is regarded as a womanizer. He enjoys cruising nightclubs, seeking female companionship. He is also known to seduce many of his female coworkers and clients, married and single alike. Allen is proud of his sexual conquests, often bragging about his relations to male friends. Although many women find Allen charming and irresistible, he has been known to intoxicate his dates, leaving them defenseless. He believes that if they return home with him and engage in festive drinking, they are consenting to having sexual relations with him.

On several occasions, Allen has become frustrated with the reluctance of his dates to accommodate his sexual tastes, which include anal intercourse and filming the sexual encounters. Rather than using force to gain compliance, Allen employed the drug rohypnol to incapacitate his dates. Rohypnol intoxication causes impaired judgment and impaired motor skills, and can make a victim unable to resist a sexual attack. The combination of alcohol and rohypnol is also particularly hazardous because together, their effects on memory and judgment are greater than the effects resulting from either taken alone. The drug reduces the victims to unconsciousness, allowing the rapist total freedom and control.

In Allen's case, he would videotape his victims to prove his conquests. Allen shared many of his photos with friends and even placed them on the Internet. A number of victims discovered the photos and filed complaints. The evidence was later used to convict the 35-year-old optometrist of several date rapes.

as a particular neighborhood that is familiar. Also, these rapists are geographically mobile, preferring to pick up hitchhikers or stranded motorists. As with many offenders, alcohol and/or drugs are usually taken prior to the act. The sex act often involves sexual bondage or the use of duct tape to further incapacitate the victim. These rapists don't rape as frequently as other predator rapists—this type is known to select victims every 2 to 3 weeks.

Power-assertive rapists are selfish and egotistic; and although there is usually no fondling, kissing, or foreplay, their **motive** is not to harm their victims but rather to overpower and possess them sexually. Power over their victims is their means of psychologically affirming their "macho" identity to themselves. Victim accounts tend to confirm that these rapists exhibit extremely inflated "egos" or self-conception. After the act, these rapists are known to leave their victims emotionally traumatized, often naked by the side of the road or in an isolated area. But unlike other rapists, they prefer to keep things "foolproof," not taking any trophies or souvenirs.

As to specific methods employed by the power-assertive rapist, the following are reported methods that they use (Flynn, 1993):

- The victim can be either preselected or opportunistic (too good to pass up, such as a hitchhiker).
- The age range tends to be the same but can vary with opportunity.
- The victim is chosen by availability, accessibility, and vulnerability.
- The location is victim-dependent.
- A weapon can be involved or can be substituted by higher levels of force.
- Physical aggression is used to initially overpower the victim.
- The victim may be held captive in some fashion while being raped.

Power-reassurance rapists use a more planned, single rape-attack strategy. They may exhibit voyeuristic behavior or may stalk their victims, as in the case of erotomanic offenders, who pursue celebrities before attacking their victims. Erotomanic offenders are unusually obsessed with a particular target and will take extreme measures to be with their intended victims.

The core fantasy motivating these rapists is that their victims will enjoy and eroticize the rape (or sexual encounter) and subsequently will fall in love with the rapists. It is not unusual for these rapists to revisit their victims' home after the rapes or even to make follow-up contacts by telephone, since from the rapists' point of view, the sexual encounter was more of a date than a rape. The motive is to compensate for their feelings of inadequacy. During the rape, they will often ask or demand that the victims reassure them about their sexual prowess. As with power-assertive offenders, power-reassurance rapists generally prefer victims in their own age range; however, they are fairly geographically stable.

If they have an unsuccessful rape attempt, there will be another attempt nearby in the same evening. Their cycle of rape is usually more frequent than that of the power-assertive rapists, usually occurring within two weeks. This short time period

Case Example: The Power-Assertive Rapist

Will is a 25-year-old single male employed as a construction worker. He has no steady girlfriends and has few male friends. Although he was an average student in high school, Will dropped out of school in the eleventh grade shortly after his parents divorced. During his teen years, Will was arrested a number of times for theft and underage drinking. As a teenager and into his adult years, Will resisted authority of any kind, thereby making it difficult for him to hold a job, do well in school, or establish meaningful relationships. Aside from partying, the only recreational activity he enjoyed was bodybuilding. While drinking at a local bar, he met a divorcee. After several drinks, he invited her to go to another bar to meet some friends. She accompanied him, but while en route, he detoured to a secluded area not far from the bar. He made sexual advances, which were rejected by the victim. She demanded that he take her back to the bar. Will became angry and threatened to beat her if she didn't undress and do what she was told. Despite pleas to let her go, Will stated, "You bitches are all alike . . . you want it as much as I do . . . so don't play fucking games with me." Will slapped her across the face, pushing her from the car down to the ground. He forced her to remove her clothes and lie facedown. He performed anal intercourse and then ordered her to orally copulate him. The victim later reported that he had a difficult time ejaculating. Will took the victim's driver's license and told her that if she called the police, he would "know where to find her." Will left the victim stranded along the side of a road.

may be explained by their feelings of social or sexual inadequacy; thus, as the effects of one rape dissipate, the offenders quickly seek another victim to reassure themselves.

These rapists are collectors (a fetish behavior) because they often take trophies or souvenirs from their victims and keep detailed records of their "conquests." Such collections include panties, bras, blouses, jewelry, and so forth. In addition to fetishism, they exhibit paraphilic behavior of voyeurism and may also be transvestites, thereby explaining their need to frequently reassure their feelings of sexual adequacy.

The following are methods used by power-reassurance rapists (Groth, 1979):

- Their victims are generally strangers or live in the same area as the rapists.
- They target several victims in advance.
- They engage in surveillance of victims.
- They engage in voyeurism.
- They make obscene phone calls.
- Their attacks occur in the late evening or early morning.
- Their victims will either be alone or be with small children.

- The attack will last a short period of time; the duration will increase with victim passivity.
- They may take personal items such as undergarments or photographs.
- Verbalizations are consistent with the need for reassurance.
- The locations of attacks will remain within the same general vicinity.
- They may keep a record of their attacks.
- They are most likely to terminate the rape if the victim resists.
- They may recontact the victim.

Anger-retaliatory rapists have deep anger toward women and use sex as a means to punish or get even. Because the motive is anger rather than sexual gratification, they will use more physical aggression than is necessary to accomplish the rape. The crime itself is usually not premeditated but is more likely opportunistic. The actual sexual assault will take little time; once the pent-up anger is vented, these rapists quickly leave. These rapists tend to attack women who are somewhat older or who symbolize another female figure such as a mother, a spouse, or an ex-girlfriend who has angered or betrayed them. Like power-assertive rapists, they like to tear the

Case Example: The Power-Reassurance Rapist

Robert is married with two children. He has no criminal history. However, Robert feels that he has not done particularly well in any part of his life (social, academic, employment). His marriage is one of convenience, not one of love or satisfaction. Lately, Robert has been having disturbing thoughts of homosexuality. These obsessive thoughts have forced him to question his own sexual identity and masculinity. To compensate for these feelings, Robert would visit nightclubs seeking a female companion for the evening. After several unsuccessful pickup attempts, Robert drove to shopping malls seeking female victims. He would fantasize about how he would abduct them and rape them. He believed that after the rape, the victim would fall in love with him. One afternoon he saw a woman walking in a mall parking lot. He followed the victim to her vehicle, positioning himself so that she wouldn't see him. He kidnapped the victim at knifepoint and drove her to an isolated wooded area. Robert tied her hands behind her back and raped her. He kept asking the victim whether he was "as good as her husband" and whether "he felt good inside her." The victim stated that he needed to be constantly reassured that he was sexually powerful and in control. And to avoid angering the rapist and suffering further injury, the victim played along, assuring him that he was a good sexual partner. After the rape, Robert wanted to meet the victim again. The victim arranged a meeting, resulting in Robert's arrest and conviction.

clothing off their victim and will often hit the victim in the breasts or stomach with their fists.

Because their anger is toward women in their life or women in general and is simply displaced on an available victim, the retaliation does not eliminate the direct source of hate, and the behavior will likely repeat when the anger escalates (approximately every 6 months to 1 year). In other words, a rape may be triggered by an unpleasant event resulting in a violent attack for the purposes of retaliation, getting even with and taking revenge on women (Keppel, 1997). The method employed by anger-retaliation rapists includes an unplanned sporadic attack. These rapists may use a weapon to force compliance (Turvey, 1996).

Anger-excitation rapists are often referred to as sadistic rapists. They enjoy and are sexually aroused by inflicting pain and punishment on the victim. One sadistic rapist stated the following: "She kept screaming for me to stop cutting her nipples, but I loved it. My power over her and her begging made me even more excited. I loved the pain as much as the sex."

The prolonged torture of their victims energizes these rapists' fantasies and arousal, temporarily satisfying their need for domination and control. The attack is vicious and prolonged: these rapists have methodically planned and executed this kind of behavior before. Victims of sadistic rapists are usually strangers who may or may not fit their idea of what a "nice" victim would be (prostitutes, etc.).

In sexual acts, there is never any attempt at foreplay, except for unusual licking and bites upon the buttocks or back. Such rapists typically use bondage, and while the

Case Example: The Anger-Retaliatory Rapist

Carl is a 40-year-old single man. When Carl was 6 years old, his mother abandoned him and his father. For years, Carl's father reminded him that his mother was a whore and never to trust any women. However, his father eventually remarried a younger woman. When Carl was 18, his father was hospitalized for several weeks. His stepmother began drinking heavily, and one evening she walked into his bedroom nude, attempting to seduce him. Carl, angered with the situation, left home. He later joined the U.S. Marine Corps and had an outstanding service record. After he left the service, Carl got a job as an electrician. He dated occasionally but spent most of his time with his male friends. One evening Carl got into an argument with a female at a local nightclub. The women humiliated him by calling him an insecure bastard. He left the club angry, thinking that women are just "plain bitches and whores." While driving home, he observed an older female jogging near a secluded park. Carl parked his car and hid near the jogging trail. As the woman passed, Carl grabbed her by the throat, hit her in the face, ripped her clothes off, and raped her in the brush. The victim later recounted how Carl kept referring to her as a whore and used profanity toward her.

Highlight 2-1

Victims of sadistic rapists may also be wives or girlfriends who have undergone extreme emotional, physical, and sexual abuse for many years. Intimate victims are often too fearful to report the offense, and a number of them may actually feel that they deserve the humiliations and the punishments delivered by their abusive partners. Victims who have survived these tragic experiences have reported extreme mood swings in the offender during their relationships, vacillating between extreme anger toward and compassion for the victim.

victims are bound, their clothes will be cut off or torn from the body. The rapists will take the victim to a preselected location, where they may torture the victim with various instruments for hours or days. They will often use recording devices to relive the experience, and murder may result after such offenders become bored. It is worth noting that this particular type of rapist may have a "public" life as a married, educated, white-collar worker. And some, of course, have criminal records with a prison background, who are seeking revenge on society as a whole. Drugs and/or alcohol are usually present in the situation.

There are a number of methods employed by the anger-excitation rapist (Turvey, 1996):

- These rapists often select an occupation that allows them to act as authority figures, thereby putting them in a position to identify and acquire victims (to impersonate law enforcement, security officer, etc.).
- Rapes are planned in exacting detail.
- Rapes are executed methodically.
- The rapist presents the image of a loving and sincere individual.
- The rapist assesses and chooses vulnerable victims for seduction.
- The rapist has a preference for adult victims.
- Victims will likely be nonaggressive and have low self-esteem.
- The rape kit brought with the offender to the scene contains weapons, bindings, and any sexual apparatus.
- The rape lasts for an extended period of time (the majority last more than 24 hours).
- The rapist is very prolific and has a high victim count.
- The victim is lured to an area over which the rapist has complete control (vehicle, basement, garage).
- This rapist is most likely to kill the victims.

Case Example: The Anger-Excitation Rapist

A women in her early thirties lived with her boyfriend Ken for over two years. At first, the victim reported that Ken was kind to her. They both used cocaine, which resulted in the victim's becoming addicted. After a while, Ken's sexual demands became more perverse. He often demanded that she perform unusual sex acts with him and participate in group sex acts with some of his friends. Ken would videotape the acts. Ken's demands and abuse became more violent, and he enjoyed inflicting pain. Ken would whip her, insert large objects into her rectum, and bind her hands behind her back. He would often hold a knife to her throat while performing anal intercourse and would demand that she beg for her life. The victim reported that as the pain and torture increased, Ken became more excited and controlling. Fearing for her life, the victim finally left the situation and reported him to the police. The police subsequently learned that Ken sadistically raped and murdered three women while living with the victim. Ken's background was full of abuse as a child. He was sexually abused by his father and was often forced to watch as his father raped Ken's sister. Ken's mother was a weak person who suffered from depression and various physical aliments. Ken never completed high school and was in and out of juvenile hall. Ken worked at various odd jobs, drifting from city to city. Ken had an arrest record for drug use, driving while intoxicated, and indecent exposure. Ken was obsessed with pornography, especially the type depicting bondage and sexual exploitation of women.

These rapists are very dangerous, and their aggressiveness is likely to increase with each new victim. Their arousal seems to escalate with each encounter, because of the excitement caused by the hunt (Hazelwood et al., 1989).

As presented by the preceding typologies, there are a variety of motives attributable to rape offenders. Sexual conquest, control, power, anger, and hatred of women are the dominant forces. Some offenders carefully select a certain type of victim, whereas others are more spontaneous, striking at the most available target. A rape can also result in the killing of the victim, which is most likely to occur with the sadistic rapist. As addressed in the next chapter, serial killers often rape and torture their victims before killing them.

In summarizing the crime characteristics and behavior of serial rapists, the research suggests the following (Hazelwood and Warren, 1989: 10–17):

- Rape offenders are often loners, harboring insecurity and low self-esteem.
- Fantasy is often a prelude to rape.
- Some offenders suffer from one or more sexual paraphilias.
- The majority of the rapes are premeditated.
- Trickery or deceit was used most often in initiating contact with the victim.

- A threatening presence and verbal threats were used to maintain control over the victim.
- Minimal or no force was used in the majority of instances.
- The victims physically, passively, or verbally resisted the rapists in slightly over 50 percent of the offenses.
- The most common offender reaction to resistance was to verbally threaten the victim.
- Slightly over one-third of the offenders experienced a sexual dysfunction, and the preferred sexual acts were vaginal rape and forced fellatio.
- Low levels of pleasure from the sexual acts were reported by the rapists.
- The rapists tended not to be concerned with precautionary measures to protect their identities.
- Approximately one-third of the rapists had consumed alcohol prior to the crime, and slightly fewer reported using some other substance.

PEDOPHILES AND CHILD MOLESTERS

The essential features of pedophilia are "recurrent, intense, sexual urges and sexually arousing fantasies, of at least six months duration, involving sexual activity with a prepubescent child." (Quote from *The Diagnostic and Statistical Manual of Mental Disorders* (DSM-IV-R), American Psychiatric Association).

Few criminal offenses are more despised than the molestation or sexual abuse of children; molesters are not just pot-bellied, middle-age men trolling for adolescent victims in public parks, playgrounds, or video arcades. As we will learn, these offenders represent all demographics and employ a variety of tactics to secure a victim.

General Characteristics

Little is understood in terms of the number of incidences or proportion of the population who commit sexual offenses against children. In a number of cases, such crimes are not reported because of embarrassment, public censure, and so forth. Victims of incest, for example, may not come to the attention of authorities unless a third party discovers the crime, such as a teacher or a neighbor. And, most pedophiles are relatives, friends, or neighbors of the child victims.

Some pedophiles expose themselves, but usually exhibitionists do not approach the child sexually, achieving their pleasure from the reaction of the victim. Some simply want to fondle the child. When sexual activity occurs, it often involves oral sex or touching the genitals of the child. In most cases (except incest), pedophiles do not attempt penetration. However, when pedophiles demand penetration, they may use threats or force to gain compliance. In these cases, the victims are usually older children. Whereas rapists commonly use force, pedophiles are less likely to use physical force or inflict pain upon the victim. Pedophiles are more likely than rapists to respond to their victim's pain and suffering by ceasing their activity (Bogaert et al., 1997). They will use "lures" to gain the victims trust, such as promising rewards or gifts if the victim participates in some act. Also, it is not unusual for the pedophile to groom the victim for weeks or months before committing a sexual act.

Victims. Pedophiles choose girls as their victims twice as often as they choose boys. If the victim is a girl, the perpetrator will most likely be someone in the family, and the sexual offense is more likely to take place in the home of the victim. If a boy is the victim of a pedophile or child molester, he is likely to be older and to be assaulted by a stranger, and the sexual offense is more likely to take place away from the victim's home. Levels of sexual self-esteem in adulthood are higher in those children who have experienced sexual offenses before they were 9 years old than in those who have experienced sexual abuse when they were older than 9 years of age (Murray, 2000).

Personality. As to personality, one study conducted in England employing the Eysenck Personality Questionnaire indicated that pedophiles scored high on introversion, depression, and sensitivity (Ames and Hovston, 1990). Subsequent studies confirmed these traits and added as additional factors emotional immaturity, fear of functioning in adult heterosexual relations, and social introversion (Levin and Stava, 1987).

How do pedophiles explain themselves? In a clinical interview, child molesters frequently offered some kind of explanation for their behavior. Pollock and Hashmall (1991) drew 250 justificatory statements from the interview records of 86 child molesters at the Clarke Institute of Psychiatry in Toronto. The researchers grouped the sample into six thematic categories. The justification given most often (by 29 percent of the sample) was that the victim had consented. Having been deprived of conventional sex was the rationalization of 24 percent of the pedophiles. Additional reasons given were intoxication (stated by 23 percent), with 22 percent claiming that the victim initiated the sexual activity. The case of John Geoghan, a Catholic priest from Boston who was defrocked in 1998, is one of the most egregious examples of pedophilia in the priesthood. Even after undergoing therapy, he continued to molest young boys, and it is estimated that he molested over 130 boys during his career. He was sentenced to a ten-year prison term, but was murdered in prison.

The most common characteristic in the psychological profile of pedophilia is that the perpetrator is male, who may be heterosexual, homosexual, or bisexual. He might prefer an adult or a child, a male or a female, as a sexual partner.

Explaining Pedophilia

Research indicates that sex offenders demonstrate different levels of physiological sexual arousal. The use of **plethysmographic** assessment, which is the measurement of penile volume changes in response to sexual stimuli (photos of nude children, etc.) has demonstrated an ability to discriminate between pedophiles and comparison groups of

Case Example: Father John Geoghan

Father John J. Geoghan was an incurable pedophile. He was ordained in 1962, retired from active ministry in 1994, and was defrocked by the Catholic Church in 1998. Geoghan served in 6 parishes across the Boston area during his years as a priest because he was moved each time a parishioner discovered or complained that he was molesting children. The church did ensure that Geoghan received therapy and psychological evaluations for his offenses but failed to completely remove Geoghan from the priesthood. Father Geoghan preyed on young boys from poorer families. He explained, "The children were just so affectionate, I got caught up in their acts of affection. Children from middle-class families never acted like that toward me, so I never got so confused." Geoghan's victims were usually young prepubescent boys. One victim said that Geoghan had him "close his eyes and repetitively recite 'Hail Mary's'" while the priest fondled him and performed oral sex on him. In addition to physical acts of abuse, Geoghan also made sexually explicit telephone calls to children in his parishes. By 1996, Geoghan had been taken out of 4 parishes in a row for child sex abuse. A psychological profile found Geoghan to be "a homosexual pedophile," having "a personality disorder with compulsive, dependent and schizoid traits."

nonmolesters, as well as among subgroups of child molesters defined by victim gender preference and by relationship to the victim (Freund and Blanchard, 1989). Incest offenders, for example, demonstrate far less sexual arousal in response to children than do extra familial child molesters.

There is evidence that child molestation may be related to an offender's recapitulation of his own sexual victimization. The pedophile is the type of offender who is typically abused before the age of 14, and this experience will often manifest itself in a deviant sexual arousal pattern in his adult years (Pendergast, 1991).

A significant number of the Roman Catholic priests accused of abusing children were molested themselves, many by other members of the clergy. Psychosocial histories of priest sex offenders from the past 12 years show that over 50 percent of the priests treated were abused as children. This estimate is much higher than that for the male abuser population at large, which is placed at about 30 percent. A noted example is Father Paul Shanley, who was charged in 2002 with raping a boy. He became a central figure in the nationwide abuse scandal, who admitted to a Boston Archdiocese administrator that a priest, a faculty member, and a pastor had abused him (Zoll, 2002).

Several studies on the backgrounds of pedophiles were conducted by Greenberg, Bradford, and Curry (1993) in the Department of Psychiatry at the University of Ottawa, Canada. They studied 135 pedophiles and 43 hebephiles who had admitted to their offenses. Hebephiles are sex offenders who prefer children between 13 and 16 years of age, whereas pedophiles chose children 12 years or younger as their victims. Among the perpetrators, 33 percent chose only boys, 44 percent chose only girls, and

23 percent had sexually abused both boys and girls. In response to questioning, 42 percent of the pedophiles and 44 percent of the hebephiles claimed to have been sexually abused in their own childhood. Members of both groups appeared to choose victims in accordance with their own ages at the time of their own experience as sexual victims.

Another factor leading to sexual molestation is the molester's apparent lack of social competence. A variety of studies have documented the inadequate social and interpersonal skills, underassertiveness, and poor self-esteem that characteristize individual offenders (Marshall, Barbaree, and Fernandez, 1995; Marshall and Mazzucco, 1995).

A history of early antisocial behavior is often a precursor of later sexual aggression. Pedophiles who committed their first sexual offense in adolescence had histories of being disruptive in school (verbally or physically assaulting peers and teachers); showed high levels of juvenile antisocial behavior; and, as adults, manifested a greater degree of nonsexual aggression. In other words, for this group, sexual offenses are part of a longer criminal history, reflecting an antisocial lifestyle and impulsive behavioral traits that probably had been present from childhood (Quinsey, Rice, and Harris, 1995).

A critical factor predictive of sexual offending is the lack of a consistent caregiver. Thus, "caregiver inconstancy" reflects frequent changes in primary caregivers and short time periods spent with any single caregiver; it also reflects the permanence and consistency of the child's interpersonal relationships with significant adults. Caregiver inconstancy is a powerful predictor of the degree of sexual violence expressed in adulthood (Prentky, Knight, and Lee, 1996). This experience interferes with the development of long-term supportive relationships, increasing the likelihood of an attachment disorder. Attachment disorders may be characterized by intense anxiety, distrust of others, insecurity, dysfunctional anger, and failure to develop normal age-appropriate social skills. Attachment disorder is often found in children raised in various foster homes. Thus, specifiable early childhood experiences may lead to interpersonal deficits and low self-esteem that severely undermine development of secure adult relationships. Individuals having interpersonal and social shortcomings are more likely than others to turn to children to meet their psychosexual needs.

Typologies

Not all sex offenders who prey on children are alike in their preferences, patterns, and backgrounds. Consequently, typologies have been developed to differentiate these offenders. The most common typologies are preferential molesters versus situational molesters, and fixated versus regressed offenders.

Preferential molesters are often referred to as classic **pedophiles** (Lanning, 1992). Preferential molesters are sexually attracted to children and frequently fantasize about having sex with them. They are often collectors of child pornography. These molesters use seduction tactics to engage in sexual relations with children. Such tactics include courting the child with attention and providing gifts. They are often persons in authority, such as teachers and members of the clergy who place themselves in jobs or activities that put them in regular contact with children.

Preferential molesters generally repeat their crimes, are very obsessed with their victims, and are often very secretive. They may never go public or share their fantasies with anyone, and it is not unusual for them to marry a single mother to gain or continue access to her children. Maintaining access to children at all costs is one of the defining trademarks of pedophilia/preferential molesters. It is not unusual for them to practice a number of paraphilic behaviors such as voyeurism, exhibitionism, and frotteurism in addition to their pedophilia. They practice oral sex, penetration of the rectum or vagina, and intercourse.

A number of pedophiles rationalize their behavior as normal. Also, some truly believe that sex with children is a healthy, normal practice. There are even organizations for pedophiles, such as **NAMBLA**, which stands for the North American Man Boy Love Association. The organization supports friendly and close relationships with a boy, supporting the perverse view that man-boy sexual relationships are healthy. The organization manifesto states that "they will not necessarily include any sexual intimacy, nor will it necessarily exclude it." A boy lover's fascination focuses primarily on the "boyish" and "childish" traits that are particular to any boy.

The recent sex scandals involving priests suggest that many are preferential molesters. Most preferential molesters prefer young boys. When a victim gets older, their sexual interest in the child decreases, causing them to pursue a younger victim. It is possible that some preferential molesters may become sadistic, inflicting pain upon their young victims.

There are some cultures allowing early sexual relations with adults. In the Netherlands, the law allows children ages 12 to 16 to make their own decision about sex, though if the parents feel the relationship is exploitative, they can ask the authorities to investigate.

Situational molesters, in contrast to preferential molesters, may or may not repeat their crimes and can have many different motivations for their crimes. And those motives, surprisingly, are often not of a sexual origin. In other words, the sexual abuse of a child may be a spontaneous act influenced by alcohol or drugs while the molester is experiencing some underlying stress.

In the situational type (Lanning, 1992), there is no true sexual preference for children (although an individual may escalate into a preferential type). These molesters usually act on an opportunity such as working at a day-care center or school. The situational molester seeks vulnerable victims, who may include their own children. Situational molesters suffer from low self-esteem and are usually under a great deal of stress that drives their need for relations with children. In incest cases, for example, a father with low self-esteem and poor relations with his spouse may seek relations with his daughter.

Groth (1979) offers the most frequently cited classification of child molestation. He divides offenders into the categories of fixated and regressed. The **fixated offenders** are characterized by having a compulsive attraction to children that begins when the offenders are adolescents. They have had virtually no age-appropriate relationships with someone of the opposite sex. In addition, most of the fixated offenders equalize their own behavior to the child's and believe themselves to be a pseudo-peer of the victim. The **regressed offenders'** child molesting emerges when they are adults and is usually precipitated by external stressors, which include such problems as alcohol and drug usage.

When combined, these two typologies demonstrate the variation in those who sexually abuse children (see Table 2-1). Keep in mind that these are general categories that may not reflect all possible variations and nuances.

Finkelhor (1984) suggests that there are four components that contribute to the making of a pedophile/child molester. The four components present complementary processes, which help explain the diversity of the behavior of sexual abusers.

The first component is sexual arousal. In order for an adult to be aroused by a child, there has to be early conditioning to sexual activity with children, which may have been reinforced by frequent masturbation. The second component is emotional congruence. There is comfort in relating to a child and the satisfaction of emotional need through the sexual abuse. This component is usually present when the abuser has intelligence, displays immaturity, or suffers from low self-esteem. The third component is referred to as **blockage.** Appropriate sexual opportunities may have been blocked by bad experiences with age-appropriate adults, or by evidence of sexual dysfunction, limited social skills, or marital disturbance. The final component is disinhibition, which is the loss of control through mental deficits, psychosis, alcohol, drugs, stress, or dysfunctional families.

Feeding the Lust: The Internet and Pornography

A popular medium used to seek out victims and disseminate child pornography is the Internet. Since preferential pedophiles are typically sexually obsessed with children, they constantly fantasize about having sex with children, and it is not uncommon for

TABLE 2-1

Child Molester Typologies

	Preferential	Situational
Regressed	Prefers children. Has had age-appropriate sexual attraction, but preference developed in adulthood.	Prefers adults. Under stress turns to children.
Fixated	Prefers children. Preference developed in adolescence—has always preferred children.	May prefer either adults or children. Has never been able to develop age-appropriate relationship—turns to children.

Self-Check 2-1

For the following case, (1) identify the typology from Table 2-1 that best fits John and why, and (2) determine how this case fits each of Finkelhor's four components that make a child-molester.

John is an only child raised by a deeply religious single mother. She demanded that he participate in church activities several times a week and that he read Bible verses to her every day. John was small in stature, and many kids at school and in his neighborhood teased him about his small size and inability to participate in sports. Consequently, John's mother became overprotective, often chasing away kids who bothered her son. As a result of peer disapproval, John became a loner, devoting his time to reading, watching TV, and playing with imaginary friends. John was an average student who posed no disciplinary problems in school. In elementary school, he was described by his teachers as shy and reclusive. As John entered adolescence, he seemed to become more withdrawn. His school grades dropped, and he became interested in adult sex magazines and would secretly masturbate to the pictures. He would routinely peek into the windows of his neighbors' house, hoping to see them undressing or engaging in sex. Once when John's mother was babysitting Ken, a 6-year-old boy, John began fondling the boy. He soon realized that the fondling and acceptance by the young boy gave him a feeling of control and satisfaction. The fondling grew into more overt acts, including oral copulation. John began to fantasize about other young children and would attend movies frequented by young children. He would follow them to the restroom and offer money if they would let him "touch them." In one case, a child ran from the theater, crying that "someone was trying to hurt him." John was arrested and ordered to attend court-imposed counseling. However, his fantasies toward young boys continued. He masturbated frequently and became obsessed with child pornography. John got a job as a janitor at a private elementary school. After a few months on the job, he became friendly with two second-grade boys. He would give them gifts and help them with their schoolwork. He would question them about sex, and after several visits, he asked if he could touch their private parts. He told them that as a janitor, he was also responsible for determining that all students were clean. He would orally copulate the boys, telling them that the act was part of the cleaning process, and that if they told anyone, a terrible disease would harm them and their families. John was later arrested and sentenced to prison for attempting anal intercourse on one of the boys.

(1) John is probably a situational-fixated offender. (2) Early conditioning—masturbation to child-sex fantasies; emotional congruence—encounter with Ken made him feel accepted; blockage—loner, rejected by peers; disinhibition—rigid mother, loneliness.

computer pedophiles to spend dozens of hours per week engaged in on-line child exploitation. The *Seattle Times* reported that by 1998, more than 1,500 suspected pedophiles in 32 states had been identified through various chat rooms on America's most popular Internet service (Malkin, 1999). Evidence of the extent of Internet pornography was revealed in 1998, when U.S. Customs officials smashed one of the largest organizations of child pornographers ever uncovered. More than 200 suspects were arrested across the world in a strike named Operation Cheshire Cat. The target was an Internet-based organization called The Wonderland Club, whose name was derived from Lewis Carroll's *Alice in Wonderland*, long a symbolic favorite of the pedophilic underworld.

The club trafficked in some of the most vile child pornography ever seen, including the rape of children. They also screened live sexual abuse of children to their members. The victims were often members' relatives.[1]

Collections of pornography are often considered the pedophile's most valued possession (Lanning, 1992). It represents years of work and symbolizes, in tangible form, his innermost sexual fantasies and thoughts. The collection will consist of slides, commercial photos, souvenirs, toys, Polaroids photos, and virtually any other type of material that relates to or displays any minute reference to child sex.

Police have found that the older the pedophile, the more extensive the collection. Pornographic collections serve crucial needs for pedophiles. First, child erotica and pornography are used in their crimes. Pedophiles will display this material to victims to lower their inhibitions and introduce them to the possibilities of sex with an adult. This is a very important step in the seduction process. Second, pedophiles will use the material for their own sexual gratification.

Pedophiles use photographs in the arousal phase prior to sexual activity with victims. Still others will use photographs of the abuse to blackmail their victims into further sexual activity. In other words, erotic pictures are used to induct the victims into the offender's sexual fantasies. Thus, law-enforcement officials are always on the alert to the onslaught of pornography on-line.

Clearly, pedophiles in general, and computer pedophiles in particular, are very good at identifying potential victims. Typically, they look for children who are loners or who appear to be neglected or alienated from normal activities. These vulnerable children can be found on-line in great numbers; such children may spend large amounts of time on-line looking for acceptance and understanding. Also, the computer pedophile will easily recognize these children and will fulfill the children's emotional needs.

By fulfilling these needs, the computer pedophile gains the child's trust, thereby allowing the pedophile to talk the victim into engaging in sexual acts.

SUMMARY

To sum up the general characteristics of a child molester, it can be stated that

- Most perpetrators are men.
- They may be heterosexual, homosexual, or bisexual.
- Some are married, and some have children.
- The age of the molester can range from the teens to middle age.

- Molesters are thought to begin their actions in the late teens.
- Molesters choose girls as their victims twice as often as they choose boys.
- If the victim is a girl, the perpetrator will most likely be someone in the family, and the sexual offense is more likely to take place in the home of the victim.
- If a boy is the victim, he is likely to be older and to be assaulted by a stranger, and the sexual offense is more likely to take place away from the victim's home.
- Many acts of child molestation are single acts that are not repeated.
- Pedophilia tends to be chronic, and recidivism may be more likely if the perpetrator is homosexual.
- Pedophiles tend to have a history of sexual abuse or neglect by a parent or an acquaintance.
- Pedophiles often collect child pornography to fuel their fantasies.

WOMEN CHILD-MOLESTERS

Although women rarely have been identified as perpetrators in studies of pedophilia, there is growing evidence that women sexually abuse children. In California for the year 2002, for example, only 103 of the 9,746 women incarcerated in prison were sex offenders. This finding compares with over 12,000 men serving time as sex offenders (Dolan, 2002). In a study of women who have sexually abused children (Faller, 1987), it has been found that many of the women had significant difficulties in psychological and social functioning. About half had mental problems, such as retardation and psychotic illness.

More than half of the women pedophiles had chemical dependency problems, and close to three-fourths had maltreated their victims in other ways in addition to the sexual abuse. As with their male counterparts, there were strong and consistent patterns of childhood social isolation, alienation, and lack of development of interpersonal skills and competence among perpetrators. Mathews et al. (1989) studied 16 female sexual offenders who were in a treatment project in Minnesota. As with male offenders, most women studied were themselves victims of childhood sexual abuse, and many were also victims of physical abuse.

The Mathews study offers three categories of female sex offenders:

- Teacher-Lover
- Predisposed
- Male-Coerced

The Teacher-Lover

"A female teacher was accused of having sex with a student. The teacher, a librarian at the school, was indicted on two counts of sexual abuse for reportedly molesting a 13-year-old girl who worked in the library at the school. The teacher has a small child and is married." (Quote from *The Arizona Republic,* February 12, 1999.)

The teacher-lover is generally involved with prepubescent and adolescent males with whom she relates as a peer. Her **motive** is to teach her young victims about sexuality, and she really does not see the acts as harmful. The teacher-lover is also referred to as the Mrs. Robinson type from the 1970s movie *The Graduate.* Many of these liaisons between women and teens are based on an emotional connection rather than on some physical need. Also, some offenders and even their victims defend their relations as true love, not some fleeting affair. The famous 1997 case of Mary Kay Le Tourneau serves as an example of this type. The 35-year-old grade schoolteacher, who was also married and the mother of four children, was convicted of having sexual relations with a 13-year-old student. The relationship resulted in her bearing two children with the adolescent. Le Tourneau continues to hold a romantic obsession for the boy. He has repeatedly insisted that he doesn't see himself as a victim. The teacher is presently serving a prison sentence in the state of Washington.

The Predisposed Offender

"A 27-year-old woman has avoided a prison term by admitting to a sexual relationship with her 14-year-old stepson. . . . She gave birth to a child fathered by the boy. . . ." (Quote from States News Service, August 19, 1998.)

The predisposed offender is usually a victim of severe sexual abuse that was initiated at a very young age and may have persisted at various stages over a long period of time. In this dysfunctional setting, the abuse is usually perpetrated by the father or stepfather, with the victim's mother ignoring the act or refusing to acknowledge it.

In later years, the victim may suffer from depression or the inability to maintain close relationships. She feels estranged from others, often as the result of insecurity. If the victim marries, she may become overly dependent on her spouse, and if the spouse is nonresponsive or abandons her, she may become desperate for comfort and turn to her children for support. For example, a mother may sleep with her adolescent son for comfort and security, a practice that may later develop into sexual relations with the child. The mother initiates the encounter to satisfy her **need for belonging and attachment.** Her motives are based on **emotional intimacy** rather than sexual pleasure.

This category also includes true women pedophiles who have an assortment of mental illnesses. It has been reported that over 50 percent of female pedophile sex offenders have molested their own children, particularly their daughters (Dolan,

2002). Some of these women may seek volunteer babysitting jobs to get the opportunity to molest. Also, these women are often sadistic, inflicting pain on young children in their care.

The Male-Coerced Offender

The male-coerced female offender acts initially in conjunction with a male who has previously abused children. She exhibits a pattern of extreme dependency and nonassertive behavior, and she may initiate the sexual abuse herself. Her victims are children both within and outside the family. This type will often do anything to please her partner, who is often very abusive and controlling. In a famous Canadian case, Paul Bernardo and his wife Karla were known as the perfect couple by their neighbors. However, they were accused of 43 sex attacks with young girls and a string of sadistic killings. The couple was convicted of sadistically slaughtering two teenage girls, including the brutal murder of Karla's 15-year-old sister, whom Karla assisted Paul in raping. Videotapes also showed Karla in a lesbian sex orgy with teenage victims. Evidence surfaced that Bernardo had a hot temper and often beat Karla; eventually she reported him to the police. They were both sentenced to prison.

RESPONDING TO SEXUAL PREDATORS

There are a number of treatments and punishments for sexual predators. The treatments available are addressed in Chapter Eleven. As for legal responses, states have not been idle in responding to the real or perceived threat of reoffending sexual predators. Most states have passed sexual predator statutes that require sexual offenders judged likely to reoffend to be civilly committed until they are judged to be no longer at risk.

The sexual predator laws are applied to those who are about to be released from prison following the completion of their sentences. To commit an individual, the state must prove that (1) the person has committed sexual offenses in the past, (2) the person currently suffers from a mental disorder, and (3) the person is likely to commit a sex offense in the future. The **civil commitment** follows a jury trial in which the jury finds that the person is likely to engage in predatory acts of sexual violence in the future.

The constitutionality of these statutes was challenged in ***Kansas vs. Hendricks***, and on June 23, 1997, the U.S. Supreme Court handed down a 5 to 4 decision confirming the constitutionality of the statute.

The difficulties in predicting dangerousness have not stopped courts from using such predictions in sexual offender commitment proceedings, and it is well-established that there is no constitutional barrier to using such predictions in legal proceedings, including those that result in loss of liberty (Janus and Meehl, 1997).

Conclusion

The motives and characteristics of sex offenders are varied and often unpredictable. A number of sex offenders exhibit paraphilias, others are impulsive, acting on instant anger or revenge; and still others plan their acts carefully. Rapists are generally more physically violent than pedophiles, but in either case, an innocent or unsuspecting victim is targeted. Some victims are seriously injured, and others may be killed. As with many other violent offenders, sex offenders have a history of abuse and neglect. This history, however, does not excuse their repulsive behavior, but it allows us to understand their deviance, in order to develop strategies to investigate and possibly treat their addictions. And yes, some offenders may be treated, but many will idle away in prison for life, possibly becoming sexual victims themselves. Clearly, society is intolerant of sex offenders, as evidenced by registration and notification laws. The trend will continue to view sex offenders as serious offenders in need of close supervision and punishment.

Discussion Questions and Activities

1. There are four types of power-anger rapists. Compare/contrast their methods of operation (how they attack their victim and what they say or do to the victim). Explain how their differences demonstrate the type of rapist that they are. Use elements of the cases provided in the chapter for examples.
2. What three characteristics/behaviors are constant from childhood to adulthood in serial rapists? Show how these characteristics might contribute to the careers of one subtype of the power-anger rapist.
3. Discuss the difference between a preferential pedophile and a situational child molester. What might be the implications of this difference for treatment or early intervention?
4. How might paraphilias lead to sex offending?
5. Make a graphic organizer (visual/pictorial representation) of how the three types of women child molesters differ from each other.
6. Compare and contrast the motives, victim characteristics, and perpetrator characteristics of female versus male pedophiles/child molesters. Compare two cases from the chapter (one male, one female). Why do you think that the perpetrators are overwhelmingly male?
7. On the basis of probabilities, identify as many characteristics as you can of suspects (i.e., male, female, family member, acquaintance, stranger, etc.) that you would look for in each of the following cases:

a. John (age 12) was molested at the community center.
b. Suzie (age 6) was molested in her home; the perpetrator inflicted unnecessary/gratuitous pain.
c. Joe (age 14) was molested but claims that he and the perpetrator are in love.

8. What ethical problems are associated with sexual predator civil commitment laws? Do you feel that the laws are too strict? Why, or why not?
9. Defend or refute the argument that "rape is about power and control and not sex."

Key Terms

Acquaintance-contact rapist
Anger-excitation rapist
Anger-retaliatory rapist
Civil commitment laws
Fixated molesters
Hebephilia
Kansas vs. Hendricks
NAMBLA
Paraphilia
Pedophiles
Plethysmographic
Power-anger rapists
Power-assertive rapist
Power-reassurance rapist
Preferential molesters
Regressed molesters
Situational child molesters

References

Abbey, A., L. T. Ross, D. Mcduffie, and P. Mcauslan. 1996. "Alcohol and dating risk factors for sexual assault among college women." *Psychology of Women Quarterly 20*(1): 147–169.

Abel, G. G., J. V. Becker, B. A. Cunningham-Rather, M. Mittleman, and J. L. Rouleau. 1988. "Multiple paraphilac diagnoses among sex offenders." *Bulletin of the American Academy of Psychiatry and the Law 15.*

American Psychiatric Association. (1994). Diagnostic and statistical manual of mental disorders (4th ed.).Washington, DC:

Ames, M. A. and D. A. Hovston 1990. "Legal, social, and biological definitions of pedophilia." *Archives of Sexual Behavior 19:* 333–342.

Bogaert, A. R, S. Bezeau, M. Kuban, and R. Blanchard. 1997. "Pedophilia, sexual orientation, and birth order." *Journal of Abnormal Psychology 106:* 331–335.

Burgess, A., J. Douglas, R. D'Agostino, C. Hartman, and R. Ressler, 1986, Sept. "Sexual killers and their victims: Identifying patterns through crime scene analysis." *Journal of Interpersonal Violence 1* (3): 288–308.

Dolan, M. 2002. "Not Only Men Are Molesters." *Los Angeles Times*, p. A-1.

Doren, D. M. 1998. "Recidivism base rates, predictions of sex offender recidivism, and the 'sexual predator' commitment laws. *Behavioral Sciences and the Law* 16: 97–114.

Faller, K. C. 1987. "Women who sexually abuse children." *Violence and Victims 2*(4): 263–276.

Finkelhor, D. 1984. *Child Sexual Abuse: New Theory and Research.* New York: Free Press.

Flynn, 1993. *The Unmasking: Married to a Rapist.* New York: Free Press.

Freund, K. and R. Blanchard. 1989. "Phallometric Diagnosis of Pedophilia." *Journal of Consulting and Clinical Psychology 57:* 100–105.

Gordon, D. 1998, March. "Keeping sex offenders off the streets." *State Legislatures*, pp. 32–33.

Greenberg, D. M., J. Bradford, and S. Curry, 1993. "A comparison of sexual victimizations in the childhoods of pedophiles and hebephiles." *Journal of Forensic Sciences* 38: 432–436.

Groth, A. N. Men Who Rape: The Psychology of the Offender, Plenum Press, 1979.

Hazelwood, R. R. and A. N. Burgess. 1987. *Practical Aspects of Rape Investigation. A Multidisciplinary Approach.* New York: Elsevier North–Holland.

Hazelwood, R. R. Reboussin, and J. Warren, 1989. "Serial rape: Correlates of increased aggression and the relationship of offender pleasure to victim resistance." *Journal of Interpersonal Violence 4 (1):* 65–78.

Hazelwood, R. R., and J. Warren. 1989. "The serial rapist: His characteristics and victims." *FBI Law Enforcement Bulletin* (58): 10–17 and 11–18.

Hazelwood, R. R. and J. I. Warren. 2000. "The sexually violent offender: Impulsive or ritualistic." *Aggression and Violent Behavior 5:* 3.

Hunter, J. A. 2000. "Understanding juvenile sex offenders: Research findings and guidelines for effective management and treatment." Juvenile Forensic Evaluation Resource Center (Virginia Department of Criminal Justice Services).

Janus, E. S. and P. E. Meehl. 1997. Assessing the legal standard for predictions of dangerousness in sex offender commitment proceedings. *Psychology, Public Policy, and Law 3:* 33–64.

Keppel, R. D. 1997. *Signature Killers.* New York: Pocket Books.

Keppel, R. D. and R. Walter. 1999. Profiling killers: A revised classification model for understanding sexual murder. *International Journal of Offender Therapy and Comparative Criminology* Vol. 10: 137–150.

Lanning, K. V. 1992. *Child Molesters: A Behavioral Analysis for Law Enforcement Officers Investigating Cases of Child Sexual Exploitation.* Arlington, Va.: National Center for Missing and Exploited Children.

Levin, S. M. and Stava, L. 1987. "Personality characteristics of sex offenders: A review." *Archives of Sexual Behavior 16:* 57–79.

Malkin, M. 1999. AOL's Online Cops AWOL on Pedophiles. *The Seattle Times*, Oct. 26.

Marshall, W. L., H. E. Barbaree, and M. Fernandez. 1995. "Some aspects of social competence in sexual offenders." *Sexual Abuse: A Journal of Research and Treatment* 7: 113–127.

Marshall, W. L. and A. Mazzucco. 1995. "Self-esteem and parental attachments in child molesters." *Journal of Research and Treatment* 7: 279–285.

Mathews, R., J. K. Matthews, and K. Speltz, 1989. *Female Sexual Offenders: An Exploratory Study.* Orwell, Vt.: Safer Society Press.

Murray, J. B. 2000. "Psychological profile of pedophiles and child molesters." *Journal of Psychology.* Vol 134: 2.

National Criminal Justice Reference Service. 1997. *Bureau of Justice Statistics.* Washington, D.C.

Pendergast, W. E. 1991. *Treating sex offenders in correctional institutions and outpatient clinics: A guide to clinical practice.* New York: Haworth.

Pollock, N. L. and J. M. Hashmall. 1991. "The excuses of child molesters." *Behavioral Sciences and the Law 9:* 53–59.

Prentky, R. A., R. A. Knight, and A. F. S. Lee. 1996. "Risk factors associated with recidivism among extrafamilial child molesters." *Journal of Consulting and Clinical Psychology* Vol. 16: 220–236.

Quinsey, V. L., M. E. Rice, and G. T. Harris. 1995. "Actuarial Prediction of Sexual Recidivism." *Journal of Interpersonal Violence 10:* 85–105.

Sex Offenses and Offenders: An Analysis of Data on Rape and Sexual Assault, *1997 U.S. Department of Justice Office of Justice Programs Bureau of Justice Statistics*

Swanson, C. R., N. C. Chamelin, and L. Territo. 2000. *Criminal Investigation.* Boston: McGraw Hill.

Turvey, B. E. 1996. *Behavior Evidence: Understanding Motives and Developing Suspects in Unsolved Serial Rapes through Behavioral Profiling Techniques.* San Leandro, Calif.: Knowledge Solutions.

West, D.J. 1987. *Sexual Crimes and Confrontations: A Study of Victims and Offenders.* Brookfield, Vt: Gower Publishing Co., Ltd., pp. 163–164.

Zoll, R. 2002. "Many Accused Priests Were Once Abuse Victims Themselves, Experts Say; Pedophilia: Clinicians estimate two-thirds of clergy suspected of sex offenses were molested as youths." *Los Angeles Times,* May 18.

NOTE:

1. *The Washington Post* reported this story September 3, 1998. *Time* magazine also reported on this case in their issue of September 14, 1998.

CHAPTER 3

MURDERING MINDS

LEARNING OBJECTIVES

After studying this chapter, you will

- Understand the difference between mass, spree, and serial killers
- Gain knowledge as to the typologies of mass killers and serial killers
- Understand the difference between organized and disorganized killers
- Examine and compare the motives and methods used by male and female serial killers
- Learn through case studies about the backgrounds of famous killers

INTRODUCTION

"Sex is one of my downfalls. I get sex any way I can get it. If I have to force somebody to do it, I do ... I rape them; I have killed them ... I've done that. I've killed animals to have sex with them, and I've had sex while they're alive." (Quote from serial killer Henry Lee Lucas.)

There are a variety of motives for murder. A murder may be for financial gain, as in the case of a plotting spouse who has his or her partner murdered in order to collect on a lucrative insurance policy. As experienced in the tragic events of September 11, 2001, murders are motivated by distorted and fanatical religious or political philosophy. History is replete with brutal murders committed for political, religious, or personal reasons. German dictator Adolph Hitler was responsible for ordering the mass murder of over 10 million Jews, as part of his regime's morbid philosophy of ethnic cleansing and his personal hatred of Jews. And, not to be outdone, Soviet leader Joseph Stalin is believed to have killed over 20 million Russian citizens through his forced policies of farm collectivization, denouncements, and personal vendettas.

In 2003, a coalition of women's groups from Mexico and the United States called for a joint task force to investigate the murders of hundreds of women in the Mexican border town of Ciudad Juarez. As of May 2003, over 270 people have been murdered in the town since 1993. In one month, the bodies of 8 women were discovered in a cotton field near the border with the United States. Many of the victims' bodies had been "hollowed out" with their organs removed, suggesting the work of a serial killer, satanic cult, or some other organized crime effort (Jordan and Sullivan, 2003).

On a more personal level, murder may be planned to eliminate witnesses, protect the identity of an offender, or to retaliate, as is often the case with street gangs. Yet, most murders result from uncontrolled passion, jealousy, or rage by an estranged spouse, family member, or acquaintance. Still, a number of killers seek victims for pleasure or sport as in the case of the random sniper killings in the Washington, D.C., area in 2002.

This chapter addresses murder committed by violent predatory killers, as opposed to murderers who kill out of financial gain, heat of passion, for the elimination of witnesses, political gain, or personal revenge. Violent predatory murderers are known as mass murderers, spree killers, and serial killers. We will delve into the mind and methods of each, with most attention focusing on serial killers.

Organized and Disorganized Murderers

Killers may be disorganized or organized in their crime patterns and behavior (Holmes, 1996). Once the crime scene is discovered, the offender type and criminal methods dictate whether the crime is disorganized or organized. As we will learn, most mass and spree killers usually display disorganized behavior, whereas serial killers are often organized because they usually have above average intelligence and are more methodical in their planning and commission.

Compared with disorganized offenders, **organized offenders** are described as more intelligent; more socially competent; more likely to be responding to some precipitating situational stressor; and more likely to show care, planning, and control in the criminal act. An organized killer plans the murder and brings along tools (rope, handcuffs, chloroform, etc.) to facilitate the crime. As to the crime scene the organized killer is very aware of evidence at the scene and will devote time to clean or destroy evidence. The killer may move the body to hide or bury it in an attempt to delay

Case Example: Ted Bundy—An Organized Killer

Ted Bundy would be known by many names, and he would kill and harm many women. Friends described him as handsome, charming, and smart. To his girlfriends, he was romantic and tender. Ted Bundy was illegitimately born in 1946. He attended law school. Ted started dating Leslie Holland in 1965, and he fell in love with her. But she broke the relationship off in 1967. After the painful breakup, Bundy went into politics and worked in many campaigns. He and Holland reunited and became engaged. However, he left her in 1974. Bundy began murdering women in that same year. Most of the women he murdered had a resemblance to his former fiancé, Leslie Holland. It is unclear as to how many women he killed. Some estimates claim between 30 and 40. Bundy's methods were unique, relying on women's caring: sometimes he wore a cast on his arm to get women to help him. He would stalk women and enter their homes at night. Bundy would carry an ice pick, a crowbar, a ski mask, a mask made of pantyhose, some rope, and a pair of handcuffs to many of his murders. Bundy was convicted in 1979 and electrocuted ten years later.

discovery, and also may take articles, jewelry, or clothing as trophies or souvenirs. Organized killers may be socially adept, hold a responsible job, and even have a family.

Disorganized killers, by contrast, are lonely and more socially awkward than the organized type. Their murders usually display their anger at their victims, with most disorganized offenders having low IQs or suffering from a mental disorder. The killing is not planned and is usually done on the spur of the moment as a result of opportunity or as the result of spontaneous actions and frenzied assaults. Disorganized killers usually do not bring any tools to the crime scene but bring a weapon. Also, there is usually no contact with the victim prior to the murder. After the killing, they do not care whether evidence is left at the crime scene and are generally unconcerned about the discovery of the crime. Unlike the organized killer, they will not move the body nor attempt to hide or bury it. That is the case because there is usually a high degree of violence and confusion taking place at the murder scene, where planning is either ignored or overlooked. Disorganized killers might be involved further with the dead victim (mutilation, necrophilia, cannibalism, etc.) and may also take a souvenir. It should be noted that some serial killers display the characteristics of both a disorganized and an organized killer.

Although there is a distinction between organized and disorganized killers in terms of characteristics and methods, some crime scenes may be mixed, and it is possible that organized killers may become reckless and disorganized as their crimes continue. Ted Bundy's murders became more brutal and reckless with each new victim. Bundy would leave bite marks on his victims, which were later used to convict him. It seems as if the excitement and rush associated with the killing supersedes the need to protect the crime scene. As the crimes increase, care and planning diminish because

Case Example: Disorganized Killers

Born in 1934 to a prostitute mother, Charles Manson was arrested many times for theft, stealing cars, and pimping. He spent half of his childhood in prison or juvenile halls. In 1967, Charles Manson started getting followers who saw him as a father figure and as God. Manson would initiate orgies with his "family," and everyone would comply. On August 9, 1969, he ordered his followers to drive into a wealthy area and kill. Manson's followers broke into director Roman Polanski's home, where the pregnant Sharon Tate, Abigail Folger, Jay Sebring, Voytek Frykowski, and Steven Parent were murdered. Sharon Tate was found on the floor, a rope tied around her neck, connecting her to Jay Sebring, who was beaten so badly that it was hard to identify him. Steven Parent was found dead in his car; Frykowski and Folger were found outside on the lawn. There was much evidence left at the scene, and the murderers scrawled the words "Pig" and "Helter Skelter" on the door and walls. The following evening they repeated their blitz attack in another home, that of Leno and Rosemary LaBianca. They were mutilated, tied up, and murdered. Leno had a fork and knife stuck in his chest. There were also words scrawled on the walls of the LaBianca residence. Charles Manson, Susan Atkins, Charles "Tex" Watson, Patricia Krenwinkel, and Leslie van Houten were eventually caught, and convicted of murder. All are currently still in prison.

the killer becomes too relaxed, overconfident, or less concerned about getting caught. The information in Table 3-1 describes the differences between the two types of killer in terms of behavior, background, and so forth.

MASS MURDERERS

> "The recent bunch of accused killers are "very self-centered, very self-absorbed ... angry who derive extraordinary pleasure from savage vengeance they wreak on one another." (Quote by Shawn Johnston, a psychologist in private practice in California.)

The first type of killer for discussion is the mass murderer. This type kills a number of victims, usually four or more, often in one location, over a short span of time, usually hours. If the killings are committed in more than one location, they are part of a "continuous" action, as in the case of a mentally disturbed employee who kills several coworkers and later murders his family. The victims may be selected at random and attacked, or the victims may be a target group chosen as "scapegoats." Mass murderers frequently conclude their killing by taking their own life or by behaving so recklessly that the police are forced to kill them. When this latter outcome occurs, it is often referred to as **suicide by cop**—death from a hail of police gunfire.

TABLE 3–1

Characteristics of Organized and Disorganized Killers

Disorganized Offenders	Organized Offenders
IQ is below average, 80–95 range	IQ is above average, 105–120 range
Is socially inadequate	Is socially adequate
Lives alone, usually does not date	Lives with partner or dates frequently
Had absent or unstable father	Had stable father figure
Had family emotional abuse, inconsistency	Had family physical abuse, harshness
Lives and/or works near crime scene	Is geographically/occupationally mobile
Has minimal interest in news media	Follows the news media
Usually is a high school dropout	May be college educated
Has poor hygiene/housekeeping skills	Has good hygiene/housekeeping skills
Keeps a secret hiding place in the home	Does not usually keep a hiding place in the home
Has nocturnal (nighttime) habits	Has diurnal (daytime) habits
Drives a clunky car or pickup truck	Drives a flashy car
Needs to return to crime scene to relive memories	Needs to return to crime scene to see what police have done
May contact victim's family to play games	Usually contacts police to play games
Has no interest in police work	Is a police groupie or wanabee
Experiments with self-help programs	Doesn't experiment with self-help
Kills at one site, considers mission over	Kills at one site, disposes at another
Usually leaves body intact	May dismember body
Attacks in a "blitz" pattern	Attacks using seduction into restraints
Depersonalizes victim to a thing or it	Keeps personal, holds a conversation
Leaves a chaotic crime scene	Leaves a controlled crime scene
Leaves physical evidence	Leaves little physical evidence
Responds best to counseling interview	Responds best to direct interview

Adapted from R. Holmes. 1996. *Profiling Violent Crimes*. Sage Publications. Thousand Oaks, California.

The demographics of mass killers are fairly consistent, in that most are middle-aged males who are white and reared in relatively stable, lower-middle-class backgrounds. Mass killers are usually people who aspire to more than they can achieve, and when they see their ambitions thwarted, they focus the blame on other people or society in general. They are often excluded from a group to which they wish to belong, and as a result, may develop an irrational, and eventually homicidal, hatred for that group (school, work groups, racial groups, etc.).

Many school shooters—students who kill teachers and/or other students—fall into this category.

The weapon of choice of the mass murderer is usually a semiautomatic weapon, rifle, or handgun. And the attacks usually take place at a public gathering spot such as a restaurant, school, or workplace.

Case Example: Mass Murderer Kip Kinkel

In 1998, a 15-year-old Oregon high school student, Kip Kinkel, was expelled from school for bringing a loaded gun to class. He returned to school and opened fire in the cafeteria, killing 2 students and wounding 22 others. Following the rampage, investigators found his parents dead in separate rooms of their suburban home. After Kinkel had murdered his parents, he spent the night with their bodies in the home, booby-trapped the house with bombs, stole the car, and drove twenty minutes to school the next morning with the intent to kill as many people as he could.

What drives these mass murderers to hunt and indiscriminately kill? It can be said that mass murderers suffer from a variety of disorders, prompted by social or familial factors, mental disease, social ostracism, and the like. There is no single theory to explain their motives. However, some common similarities in their precrime behavior are extreme anger and desire for revenge because of some real or perceived injustice or harm.

A mass killer may be triggered by a traumatic experience in his life, like a divorce or separation from a significant other, or loss of a job. Such killers may have a personal motive, or may be unhappy with various social political issues.

Mass Murderer Types

The motivational typologies of a mass murderer generally fall into five groups (Holmes and Holmes, 2001): disciple murderer, family annihilator, disgruntled employee, pseudo-commando, and set-and-run killer (Table 3-2).

The first type, the disciple murderer, follows the commands of a cult leader like Charles Manson, of terrorist leaders, and of other irrational political demagogues. Once these killers fall under the influence of a leader, they desire only to please their

TABLE 3-2

Typology of Mass Killers

Type	Motive
1. Disciple	Pleasing a charismatic, ideological religious or political leader
2. Family annihilator	Revenge, jealousy, suicide ("compassion")
3. Disgruntled employee	Anger against an employer or coworkers
4. Pseudo-commando	Hatred of a particular group
5. Set-and-run	Self-esteem, property destruction, enjoyment, fame

Case Example: Disciple Killer Jim Jones

Jim Jones, the son of a Ku Klux Klansman, considered himself the reincarnation of both Jesus and Lenin. As an ordained minister, Jones presided over a church in San Francisco, where he received numerous humanitarian awards and became the chairman of the city's Housing Authority. However, he was a controversial preacher who advocated revolutionary suicide to protest against racism and fascism. In 1977, facing community pressure, Jones moved his ministry to Jonestown, Guyana. Many of the congregation sold their belongings, giving all their assets to Jones, and followed him to Jonestown. In 1978, Congressman Leo Ryan from San Francisco went on a fact-finding mission to investigate alleged human rights abuses at Jonestown. After Ryan had spent only a day at the jungle compound, a congregation member tried to stab him. Ryan decided to leave with his party and 18 temple members who wanted to return to the United States. Other members of the cult followed the group to the airstrip and then opened fire, killing Ryan, 3 journalists, and one of the departing members. Eleven others were injured. Hours later, fearing other intrusions, Jones ordered his followers to drink from a tub of grape-flavored Kool-Aid laced with potassium cyanide and tranquilizers. Over 900 dedicated followers subsequently died. Children were killed by poison squirted into their mouths with a syringe. The adults died of poisoning, and some were shot by security guards as they attempted to escape. Jim Jones reportedly killed himself. Within a few months of the mass deaths, other People's Temple members who had survived also committed suicide, with one mother slitting the throats of her 3 children.

leader or the cause that the leader promotes. So-called **killer cults** fall into this category. Killer cults tend to be led by charismatic megalomaniacs who pit themselves and their beliefs against society, follow apocalyptic visions, and are absorbed with lust and power and the need for control over their followers. In most cases, their beliefs stem from twisted interpretations of established religious or political doctrines. Probably one of the most notorious examples of a disciple killing is the 1977 Jonestown massacre, led by the notorious reverend Jim Jones.

The second type of mass murderer is the family annihilator. Killers of this type exhibit the most mental problems, typically launching into a burst of violence against those with whom they live. Their killings are often based on jealousy or revenge against another family member such as an estranged spouse. This type will kill everyone in the family and will commit suicide rather than face capture. Annihilators may lie in wait for more family members, or they may travel some distance to kill relatives. Strangers are usually spared as victims of these attackers. In other words, they see their family as the cause of their own failures, often killing their own children to get even with an estranged spouse or killing family members out of so-called compassion. A father may kill his spouse and then kill his children before committing suicide. The

Case Example: Family Annihilator Mark Barton

Angry after losing a chunk of money trading on the Internet, Mark Barton beat his family to death and then headed to two brokerage offices, where he opened fire, killing 9 people and wounding 12. Barton escaped and shot himself to death after a five-hour manhunt that ended when police stopped his van at a gas station. The bodies of Barton's wife, his son, and his daughter were later found. The children's bodies were in their beds, with sheets pulled up to their necks and towels around their heads so that only their faces showed. A handwritten note left by Barton provided insight into his motives:

> To Whom It May Concern:
>
> Leigh Ann is in the master bedroom closet under a blanket. I killed her on Tuesday night. I killed Matthew and Mychelle Wednesday night. There may be similarities between these deaths and the death of my first wife, Debra Spivey. However, I deny killing her and her mother. There's no reason for me to lie now. It just seemed like a quiet way to kill and a relatively painless way to die. There was little pain. All of them were dead in less than five minutes. I hit them with a hammer in their sleep and then put them face down in a bathtub to make sure they did not wake up in pain. To make sure they were dead. I am so sorry. I wish I didn't. Words cannot tell the agony. Why did I? I have been dying since October. I wake up at night so afraid, so terrified that I couldn't be that afraid while awake. It has taken its toll. I have come to hate this life and this system of things. I have come to have no hope. I killed the children to exchange them for five minutes of pain for a lifetime of pain. I forced myself to do it to keep them from suffering so much later. No mother, no father, no relatives. The fears of the father are transferred to the son. It was from my father to me and from me to my son. He already had it and now to be left alone. I had to take him with me. I killed Leigh Ann because she was one of the main reasons for my demise as I planned to kill the others. I really wish I hadn't killed her now. She really couldn't help it and I love her so much anyway. I know that Jehovah will take care of all of them in the next life. I'm sure the details don't matter. There is no excuse, no good reason. I am sure no one would understand. If they could, I wouldn't want them to. I just write these things to say why. Please know that I love Leigh Ann, Matthew and Mychelle with all of my heart. If Jehovah is willing, I would like to see all of them again in the resurrection, to have a second chance. I don't plan to live very much longer, just long enough to kill as many of the people that greedily sought my destruction. You should kill me if you can.
>
> Mark O. Barton

Case Example: Susan Smith's Confession

When I left my home on Tuesday, Oct. 25, I was very emotionally distraught. I didn't want to live anymore! I felt like things could never get any worse. When I left home, I was going to ride around a little while and then go to my mom's. As I rode and rode and rode, I felt even more anxiety coming upon me about not wanting to live. I felt I couldn't be a good mom anymore, but I didn't want my children to grow up without a mom. I felt I had to end our lives to protect us from any grief or harm. I had never felt so lonely and so sad in my entire life. I was in love with someone very much, but he didn't love me and never would. I had a very difficult time accepting that. But I had hurt him very much, and I could see why he could never love me. When I was at John D. Long Lake, I had never felt so scared and unsure as I did then. I wanted to end my life so bad and was in my car ready to go down that ramp into the water, and I did go part way, but I stopped. I went again and stopped. I then got out of the car and stood by the car a nervous wreck. Why was I feeling this way? Why was everything so bad in my life? I had no answers to these questions. I dropped to the lowest point when I allowed my children to go down that ramp into the water without me. I took off running and screaming "Oh God! Oh God, no!" What have I done? Why did you let this happen? I wanted to turn around so bad and go back, but I knew it was too late. I was an absolute mental case! I couldn't believe what I had done. I love my children with all my (a picture of a heart). That will never change. I have prayed to them for forgiveness and hope that they will find it in their (a picture of a heart) to forgive me. I never meant to hurt them!! I am sorry for what has happened and I know that I need some help. I don't think I will ever be able to forgive myself for what I have done. My children, Michael and Alex, are with our Heavenly Father now, and I know that they will never be hurt again. As a mom, that means more than words could ever say. I knew from day one, the truth would prevail, but I was so scared I didn't know what to do. It was very tough emotionally to sit and watch my family hurt like they did. It was time to bring a peace of mind to everyone, including myself. My children deserve to have the best, and now they will. I broke down on Thursday, Nov. 3, and told Sheriff Howard Wells the truth. It wasn't easy, but after the truth was out, I felt like the world was lifted off my shoulders. I know now that it is going to be a tough and long road ahead of me. At this very moment, I don't feel I will be able to handle what's coming, but I have prayed to God that he give me the strength to survive each day and to face those times and situations in my life that will be extremely painful. I have put my total faith in God, and he will take care of me.

offender's logic is to save the children the pain and embarrassment of living without parents or of having a parent who is a killer.

The case of an Atlanta "day trader," Mark O. Barton, is an example of a family annihilator and of a disgruntled employee (the next type).

Another example of the family annihilator is Susan Smith, a housewife who murdered her two children in 1994. Smith, distraught over a love affair, released the safety brake on her car and let it roll down the boat ramp with her sons still strapped inside in the back seat. For nine days, she insisted that a black man had commandeered her car, and she begged tearfully on nationwide television for her sons' safe return. Unlike many other family annihilators, she did not take her own life, but she ultimately confessed to the murders and was sentenced in 1995 to life in prison. Her confession describes her feelings and motives for the murders (Herald-Journal, 1994.).

The third type of mass murderer is the disgruntled employee. Many acts of workplace violence involving firearms are the result of an employee's targeting coworkers or management. Usually this type is a former employee or someone about to lose his or her job. In other cases, these murderers are on medical or mental disability leave, or they have recently been disciplined by a supervisor. Often they have been a long-term employee who may have had previous conflicts with coworkers or a particular supervisor. It is believed that they are lashing out at some perceived unfairness, and usually having complained of strict management or unfair treatment. An example of this type is the former postal worker Patrick Henry Sherrill.

Case Example: Disgruntled Employee Patrick Sherrill

On August 20, 1986, postal employee Patrick Sherrill placed two .45 Colt government-issue semiautomatics, a .22 caliber pistol, and ammunition in his mailbag and then drove to work as usual. Sherrill was angry because his supervisors had admonished him for not working hard enough. He was denied a request for transfer and was facing possible termination from his long-time postal job. In high school football, the Marine Corps, and the U.S. Postal Service, he had always given his best. Now he was going to be fired. However, Sherrill decided to get even. When Sherrill arrived at work the following day, he systematically flushed out several employees who were hiding. Working fast and efficiently, he took less than five minutes to slaughter everyone in the large work area of the building. Having traveled in a circle through the building, Sherrill fired less than 50 bullets, killing 14 employees and wounding 7 in less than 15 minutes. Sherrill raised the pistol to his head and squeezed off one final round. When the body count was tallied, it became the third largest mass murder by a lone gunman in United States history. Psychiatrists who had never met Sherrill attributed his behavior to "factitious posttraumatic stress disorder," a term for self-induced battle fatigue from the Vietnam War. In addition, Sherrill was a lonely man who lived with his mother, without many social outlets.

Case Example: Pseudo-commando James Huberty

In 1984, unemployed security guard, gun enthusiast, and Vietnam veteran James Huberty donned his military camouflage pants and said to his wife, "Society had its chance. I'm going hunting. Hunting Humans." Armed with three powerful semiautomatic weapons, he drove to a McDonald's restaurant, parked his car, and casually walked into the restaurant in broad daylight. He began shooting at customers at random, stopping only to reload. He reloaded all his weapons twice as he circled the room, killing anyone he found still alive. In little over an hour, Huberty slaughtered 21 people, including many children, and wounded 20. A sniper's bullet ended his bloody rampage. Huberty, unable to hold a job, decided to move to California from his native Ohio. His wife worked, but Huberty believed that less qualified people were taking jobs from him, particularly minorities. Huberty suffered from depression and various mental disorders but refused to seek medical assistance. Huberty claimed that the only real friend he had in life was his dog.

The fourth type is the pseudo-commando. This type stockpiles guns, assault rifles, grenades, and other exotic weapons. They are similar to the disgruntled employee, with the exception that they target strangers. Their victims are often minorities or belong to some definable group.

Their attack is usually the result of careful planning and a desire to lash out against the world, which is "not right" in some way. These offenders may be quite

Case Example: Set-and-Run Killer John Leonard Orr

John Leonard Orr, a former fire department captain and admitted serial arsonist, was convicted for four arson murders in a 1984 hardware store fire. Also, in 1998, he was convicted for the arson-murders of 4 people who died in a fire at a retail center. Orr was considered an expert in fire investigation who wrote a manuscript "Points of Origin" (which was later made into a movie), about an arsonist who torches businesses across California. The book was discovered when he was arrested in 1991. Like the character in his book, Orr was in the habit of setting fires to develop material for the book. The novel was about a fireman-turned-arsonist who got sexual pleasure from his crimes. Orr was also convicted of starting several brush and house fires in the Los Angeles area in 1990 and 1991, one of which destroyed 67 hillside homes. Orr, who was a respected arson investigator in Southern California, was often called upon for training and consulting. He was a family man with no obvious mental disorders. However, his need for recognition and the excitement of starting fires overwhelmed him.

geographically mobile, and their killings usually end with a police officer's bullet—suicide by cop. Charles Whitman exemplified the pseudo-commando. In 1966, he barricaded himself for nearly two hours in the tower at the University of Texas, armed with several high-powered weapons, killing 14 people and wounding many more. His killing rampage ended when a police sniper shot and killed him. Whitman, who came from a wealthy family in Florida, was a gifted student, an accomplished pianist, an Eagle Scout, and a former marine. Whitman's anger, however, was prompted by several incidents. His abusive father brutally disciplined him and also beat his mother. While a marine, Whitman was disciplined for gambling, usury, and unauthorized possession of a nonmilitary pistol. He was demoted and eventually discharged. Whitman had a scholarship to the University of Texas, but it was withdrawn because of poor grades.

The set-and-run killer is the final type of mass killer. This type appears to be motivated by a desire to "go down in infamy" or to satisfy a desire for public recognition. These killers may plant an explosive device in a crowded location or set fire to a structure. Unlike most other mass killers, they are not suicidal. They set or plant somewhere a device on a timer and then flee the scene when the explosion goes off or a fire begins. Set-and-run killers take delight in watching the destruction and misery that follow, often masturbating and gloating over their gruesome accomplishment.

The typologies of mass killers are not mutually exclusive. A hate killer, for example, could be classified as either a pseudo-commando or disgruntled employee who may feel that minorities are taking his job or interfering with a promotion. The killer may seek revenge on coworkers at work or may attack innocent persons representing a particular racial or ethnic group. In any event, a mass killer normally strikes quickly, targeting many victims in one location.

SPREE KILLERS

We now visit the category of **spree killers,** a combination of mass killers and serial killers, who target people at different locations and times. Like the mass killer, a spree killer is usually a white male between 20 and 30 years of age, who kills many people by shooting. However, the killing occurs over a period of time, stretching from several days to weeks, or longer.

Spree killers generally are motivated by personal revenge against someone known to them or kill to prevent arrest or capture after committing another crime, such as robbery or rape. However, they may also kill for sport or the thrill. Spree killers usually select victims randomly, but will target those who meet their personal needs at the time. They may kill for money or sex, or simply because they are hungry or in need of a vehicle to escape from a crime scene.

Spree killers are usually highly disorganized because their killings aren't well planned but are the result of spontaneous need. They often leave a trail of evidence allowing the police to track their escape. Also, it is not uncommon for spree killers to operate with someone else, such as a girlfriend or crime partner.

Case Example: Spree Killer Andrew Cunanan

Andrew Phillip Cunanan was a conspicuous, even flashy figure on the San Francisco gay scene. He assumed a variety of guises, from a Hollywood hotshot with a Riviera mansion, a naval officer, and a graduate of Choate and Yale. He dressed impeccably and sipped only the finest champagne. He was by all accounts extremely good company, both vivacious and well informed. With a desperate need for attention, he was compelled to prove that he was someone of stature. Cunanan was a male mistress or gigolo, who kept company with a succession of older gay men who would lavish him with clothes, cars, money, and gifts. His relationships appeared to be purely superficial and sexually exploitive, and his primary source of income was the money his lovers were willing to provide in exchange for sex. After being jilted by lovers because he had AIDS and experiencing financial problems, Cunanan began a cross-country journey that turned into a killing spree on April 25, 1997. He purchased female clothing so he could disguise himself in drag. He was taking revenge on people he suspected of having given him AIDS, first traveling to Minnesota to seek his former lover. His first victim was Jeffery Trial, a companion of his former lover David Madson. Trial was bludgeoned to death with over two dozen savage hammer blows to the face and head. Afterward, Cunanan shot David Madson several times. Cunanan fled to Chicago, where he somehow gained entrance to the home of a 72-year-old real-estate mogul named Lee Miglin. There is no evidence that Cunanan had ever met the man before. What Cunanan needed from this millionaire developer was cash, a change of clothes, and a new getaway car. For reasons unknown, Cunanan reportedly subjected Miglin to a horrific form of torture, wrapping the victim's head in duct tape with breathing space at the nose, then stabbing him repeatedly with pruning shears before cutting open his throat with a gardening saw. Heading eastward in Miglin's green 1994 Lexus, Cunanan next killed a 45-year-old cemetery caretaker named William Reese in New Jersey, shooting the victim in the head with the same .40-caliber pistol he had used to slay Madson, then stealing Reese's red pickup truck. Andrew Cunanan not only killed gay acquaintances for revenge but also killed random bystanders to eliminate witnesses. His last victim was celebrated fashion designer Gianni Versace, who was gunned down outside his home in Miami. In the end, Cunanan killed 5 people, and eventually he killed himself in a Miami Beach houseboat as the police closed in.

MALE SERIAL KILLERS

"I'm the most cold blooded sonofabitch you'll ever meet." (Quote by serial killer Ted Bundy.)

Serial killers differ from mass murderers and spree killers in that the killings are separate ("serial"), usually with a cooling-off period between kills, but escalating over a period of time, sometimes years; and they will continue until the killer is apprehended or dies. The killing tends to be one on one, and there is usually no (or very little) previous connection between the perpetrator and the victim. The literature consistently describes the serial killer as a white male, 25 to 35 years of age.

Although there may be a "pattern," or "victim" trait, individual murders rarely display an obvious or a rational motive. Their main motives are sex (even though the act of sex may or may not take place), power, manipulation, domination, and control. The sex motive is usually rape for an organized killer and sadism for a disorganized killer (Douglas, 1997; Hickey, 2002).

There is usually a high degree of redundant violence, or overkill, where the victim is subjected to a disproportionate level of brutality, such as numerous stabbings. This excessiveness may be due to anger or pent-up frustrations resulting from early abusive childhood experiences of the killer, or due to displaced anger, seeing the victim as a person who resembles someone who rejected or humiliated the killer. Research has indicated that sadistic rapists who murder elderly women are motivated by the need for power or anger or a combination of both, rather than for sexual gratification (Pollock, 1988). They have a need to punish, dominate, and control the elderly female victim, who represents an authority figure or an actual woman over whom the assailant wants power.

Although rare, serial killers have been around for some time. The **Baron Gilles de Rais,** a fifteenth-century French aristocrat, military hero, and companion to Joan of Arc, was responsible for murdering hundreds of peasant children.

The baron declared that torturing the innocent was entirely for his own pleasure and physical delight. He was unbelievably bold in gathering victims, sending servants out to round up children and take them back to his castle. He enjoyed killing and sodomizing young boys before and after decapitating them. He sometimes masturbated over the entrails and enjoyed watching his servants butcher the boys. Because he was a baron, no one cared about the disappearing children around his castle. The baron's reign of terror came to an end when the Duke of Brittany dug up the mutilated remains of 50 boys in his castle. He confessed to 140 killings, but it is believed that the body count could have been as high as 300. On October 26, 1440, Gilles was simultaneously burned and hanged.

The first known serial killers in the United States were two cousins named Micajah and Wiley Harp, sons of Scottish immigrants who lived in North Carolina. The two cousins left home in 1775, with plans to become slave-owners in Virginia. They soon became sidetracked by the American Revolution and instead became outlaws,

Highlight 3-1

"The wish to inflict pain on others is not the essence of sadism. The central impulse to have complete mastery over another person, to make him/her a helpless object of our will, to become the absolute ruler over her, to become her god, to do with her as one pleases, to humiliate her, to enslave her are means to this end. And the most radical aim is to make her suffer. There is no greater power over another person than that of inflicting pain on her ... to force her to undergo suffering without her being able to defend herself. The pleasure is in the complete domination of another person." (Quote by serial killer Mike DeBardeleben)

roving the North Carolina countryside, stealing and kidnapping and raping farmers' daughters. During their tyranny, they reportedly kidnapped 3 women whom they allowed to live as their wives. After the women bore children, the Harps would execute the children. By 1797, the two had 5 credited kills and continued their killing spree into Tennessee and Kentucky. Their predominant method for disposing of bodies was to gut their victims and fill the body cavity with rocks so that they would easily sink when thrown into a body of water. After the governor of Kentucky issued a $300 reward, the two were finally captured and executed. The Harps were believed to have had as many as 40 victims, though the true number may never be known.

Although the United States is considered the leading serial killer nation, other nations have had their share of serial killers. One of the most prolific killers of all time is Pedro Alonso Lopez, who is believed to have killed over 300 children. A native of Colombia, his prostitute mother kicked him out of their home at age 8 for fondling his younger sister. By 1978, he claimed to have killed more than 100 girls in Peru. He moved to Colombia and Ecuador, where he averaged about 3 kills a week. Lopez targeted girls because they were "more gentle and trusting, more innocent." Across the globe in Russia, Andrei Chikatilo, known as the Russian Hannibal Lecter, also preyed on children. He stalked many of his victims in train and bus stations, and he had a penchant for disembowelment and mutilation. He was also a cannibal and a sadist. His macabre twelve-year killing spree was uncovered in 1982.

John Douglas, a senior FBI analyst, estimates that thirty to fifty serial killers are active in the United States at any one time. Any city large enough to have significant prostitution, a drug culture, "street people," and runaway kids is an ideal setting for such predators.

Methods

The victim profile for an individual serial killer is usually the same, such as prostitutes, hitchhikers, children, the elderly, or a lone female. The victims may also have the same or similar attributes in gender, age, race, general appearance, residence, and the like. Serial killers also usually stick very closely to a modus operandi, but they may change with experience or emotion, as in the case of Richard Ramirez (known as the Night Stalker), who terrorized Los Angeles in the 1980s. The following is from an interview with the investigator assigned to the Night Stalker investigation:

> Ramirez sort of broke the mold of how we used to look at serial killers because historically you looked at serial killers just based on M.O. . . . modus operandi . . . and that's how you linked cases . . . they killed the same way . . . they picked the same type of victim . . . same type of approach . . . whatever it was . . . same type of day . . . all that stuff. Richard was all over the board . . . he had victims that were as young as six years old that he didn't kill . . . he kidnapped . . . and sexually molested . . . and the oldest victim was eighty-three that he killed . . . male . . . female . . . he attacked on the street and he entered homes. His method of killing changed . . . he used guns to kill . . . he used knives . . . he strangled manually . . . he used a ligature . . . suffocated and stomped a woman to death with his foot . . . he did everything but poison so he really jumped around so that his M.O., for lack of a better term, was that as he got comfortable in entering a house . . . if he ever entered a house and there was a male and a female . . . he always executed the male . . . and then he would sexually attack the female . . . usually leave her alive . . . if there was any resistance . . . he would kill them both . . . it was like that. Once he got into that pattern, he changed guns for example, during that pattern . . . used guns that he had used once before and used them again and he hadn't used them in between. Even when he was in that pattern . . . he stomped one woman to death with his foot . . . so he kept changing and that was the difficult thing about him . . . is connecting all the cases. (Interview with retired Los Angeles Detective Frank Salerno.)

Most serial murderers prefer the methods of strangulation, suffocation, or stabbing, because they prefer to personalize their killing by using their hands rather than a weapon. Serial killers often act on a sexual fantasy, living in a dream world in their early years, until they act out for real in adulthood. Even in adulthood, the killers may first imagine the crime over and over in their minds, for months or even years. And before they begin killing, serial killers may fantasize about particular methods of killing or may have recurrent thoughts of inflicting pain on others (Ressler et al., 1988). Viewing pornographic material may fuel their fantasies; and for some, a need for excitement may first he expressed by killing small animals or setting fires. As the killers age, the fantasies become uncontrollable and consuming, resulting in the search for human victims.

As their hunt begins, the killers have a very clear image of the preferred victim: children, a lone female, or an elderly person. Also, the killers may prefer certain locations such as parking lots, woodlands, or streets. After they have found their victims, they may stalk or study them and may even plan where they will dispose of the body. The kill phase is the moment of climax for these killers. They may spend time with the victim, torturing and mutilating until they become bored. Many of these killers photograph or videotape their victims, to relive their experiences.

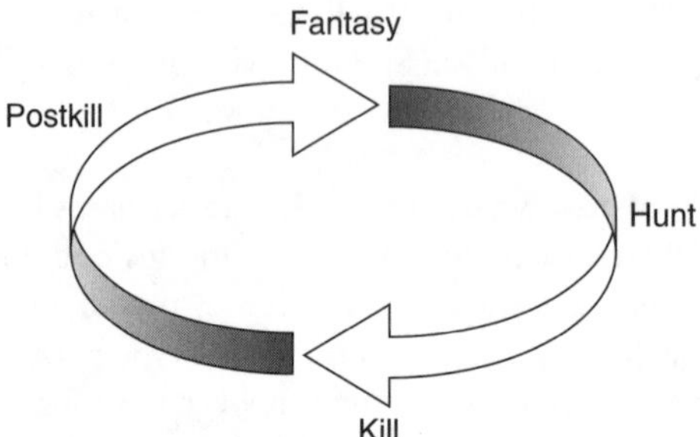

Figure 3-1 Fantasy Cycle of Serial Killers

After the kill, the serial killers may feel some temporary satisfaction; but soon depression will set in, and the necessity to feed their perverted needs will begin the **fantasy cycle** again (see Figure 3-1). In other words, as each murder occurs, the killers may be disappointed or unfulfilled, causing them to act out again to achieve a greater satisfaction or to improve upon their sadistic methods. Serial killers have been known to return to the scene of the murder and relive their fantasy by having sex with the corpse or by further desecrating the body.

Early Indicators

Many killers share common childhood characteristics. In a study of 36 incarcerated serial killers, it was revealed that many displayed similar behavior traits as children. The top ten traits in order of frequency were daydreaming, compulsive masturbation, isolation, chronic lying, enuresis (bed-wetting), rebelliousness, nightmares, destroying property, fire setting, and stealing (Ressler et al., 1988).

Another background characteristic frequently mentioned in the literature of serial killers is what is known as the **"MacDonald triad"** (MacDonald, 1963) (Figure 3–2). As youngsters they enjoyed torturing animals, liked setting fires, and suffered from enuresis (Bed-wetting). They enjoyed torturing animals and setting fires because it satisfied their need for power and control. The explanation of enuresis, or bedwetting, may be linked to a lack of control, to anxiety, or to hatred toward their parents.

Some serial killers had brain damage, learning disabilities, or an addiction to alcohol and/or drugs. (Williams and Seaman, 1997). Serial killers come from all different social classes, but many are reared in abusive environments, marked by family instability or poor parenting (Cleary and Luxemburg, 1993; Ressler et al., 1988). Stud-

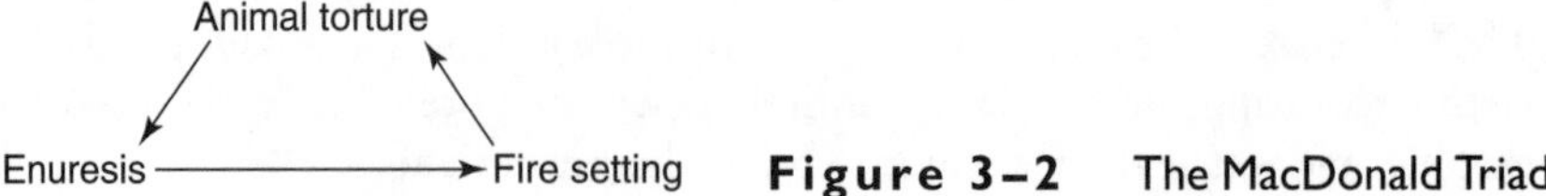

Figure 3-2 The MacDonald Triad

ies have indicated that violent offenders who were sexually abused as children are more brutal in their killing than those who were not.

In one study, Ressler, Burgess, Douglas, Hartman, and McCormack (1986) reviewed the case histories of 28 sexual murderers. The murderers were categorized into two groups on the basis of whether or not they were sexually abused as children. They found numerous differences between the two groups. As expected, all of the dependent variable differences (e.g., nightmares, cruelty to animals, assaultiveness) were higher in the abused subgroup. Furthermore, over 75 percent of the abused group mutilated their victims as compared with 40 percent of the nonabused group. Serial killers learn behaviors that encourage violence and that will one day lead to multiple murders (Holmes and De Burger, 1988).

The parents of serial killers often displayed psychological and behavioral problems, such as alcoholism and drug use; typically moved around a great deal; or frequently changed occupations, thereby creating feelings of detachment. Over 69 percent of the serial killers interviewed in one study had a family history of alcoholism, and over half of the serial killers reported psychiatric problems and sexual abuse in their families (Ressler et al., 1988). Norris (1988) asserts that patterns of parental abuse, violence, neglect, childhood cognitive disabilities, and familial alcoholism and substance abuse are typical factors in serial killers' backgrounds.

There is almost always "a clear history of abuse, usually by the mother." Norris maintains that many serial killers such as Ed Kemper, Henry Lee Lucas, and Charles Manson all suffered "extraordinary abuse by dominant females in a home that lacked the presence of a male." In other words, serial killers never truly bond to their family (Ressler et al., 1988). In addition, this inability to bond extends to peers, resulting in very few friendships and reflecting failures in the realm of interpersonal relationships. Along with negative experiences with the mother, a positive view of the father is rare among serial killers; 72% report a lack of attachment to, and no positive image of, their fathers (Ressler, 1988). A classic example on how to raise a serial killer is the family background of Henry Lucas, who claims to have murdered over 100 people.

Typologies

There are a number of serial killer typologies, which speak to the motives and modus operandi of many of these offenders. Ronald Holmes, a criminologist at the University of Louisville who specializes in the study of serial murder, has identified four **subtypes of serial killers** (Holmes and De Burger, 1988): visionary, mission-oriented, hedonistic, power-oriented. (Table 3–3).

The visionary killer types feel compelled to murder because they hear voices or see visions ordering them to kill certain kinds of people. Visionary killers are often psychotic, fixated on certain types of victims. There have been a number of visionary serial killers identified over the years, with David Berkowitz being one of the most famous.

The mission-oriented type seek to kill a specific group of people who they believe are unworthy to live and without whom the world would be a better place.

TABLE 3-3

Typology of Serial Killers

Type	Motive
Visionary	Responding to a higher order after hearing voices
Mission-oriented	Cleansing society of "undesirables"
Hedonistic-comfort	Obtaining thrills and excitement, sex, and money
Power-oriented	Exerting power and control

They are not psychotic; in fact, their everyday acquaintances frequently will describe them as fine citizens. These killers focus on prostitutes, the elderly, children, or any group that the killers feel don't deserve to live. Many hate killers—so-called "angels of death"—fall into this category as well. Arthur Shawcross fits the description of a mission-oriented serial killer. The famed Green River killer Gary Ridgway is another example. He is credited with murdering 48 women who were mostly prostitutes.

Case Example: Serial Killer Henry Lee Lucas

Henry Lee Lucas, suspected along with his partner Otis Toole of hundreds of sadistic murders, was told by his mother at an early age that he was evil and would probably die in prison. A part-time prostitute, his mother would often bring home customers (with his legless father shouting in the next room), and Lucas would observe their sexual encounters. He remembered an incident in which his mother finished with a customer and then shot the customer in the leg with a shotgun. Blood splattered over the boy. His mother chose to dress him as a girl, putting ribbons in his hair. Malnourished, dirty, and smelly, he was an outcast to his peers. Subjected by his mother to severe abuse, she once beat him unconscious with a two-by-four, forced him to drink urine, and burned him with cigarettes. She would not feed him, forcing him to eat out of the garbage. Destroying anything that he showed interest in, she made a point of shooting to death his pet mule and then beat him because it cost so much to dispose of the body. His favorite sexual fantasies as a child were torturing his mother to death (Dietz, 1986). He developed an inability to love. Once he had a severe injury to his eye. Having developed a nurturing relationship with his schoolteacher, she once tried to defend him in a fight with another boy. In the process, she accidentally struck Lucas, opening up the eye wound. Since then, he had to wear a glass eye. While an early teen, he had sex with his half-brother. After this event, he began to kill animals and copulate with their remains. He skinned animals alive. Lucas committed his first murder at the age of fifteen. It is not surprising that his second murder was that of his mother. When Lucas killed, he became sexually potent.

Case Example: Visionary Killer David Berkowitz

> "The demons never stopped. I couldn't sleep. I had no strength to fight. I could barely drive. Coming home from work one night, I almost killed myself in the car. I needed to sleep . . . The demons wouldn't give me any peace." (Quote by David Berkowitz.)

David Berkowitz was given up for adoption just after his birth. He was adopted by a childless couple. From all accounts, he had a normal childhood with no clear warning signs of violence. Perhaps the most significant factor in his life was that he was a loner. Because he was always big for his age, he always felt different from and less attractive than his peers. All through his youth, he was uncomfortable with other people. He was violent and was considered a bully who assaulted neighborhood kids for no apparent reason. After his mother's death from cancer, his grade average nose-dived. He began to imagine that her death was a part of some plan to destroy him. He became more and more introverted. His father remarried a woman who did not like Berkowitz. The couple moved to a Florida retirement community without him, leaving him to drift, absent of a purpose or a goal. Berkowitz continued to exist until his fantasy life had become stronger than his real life. He joined the U.S. Army in the summer of 1971 and served for three years. He was an excellent marksman, particularly proficient with the rifle. Anger and frustration with women, coupled with a bizarre fantasy life, occupied his mind when he got out of the Army in 1974. After returning from the service, Berkowitz held jobs as a security guard and taxi driver. His social life and sexual relationships with women, however, were nonexistent. The only consummated sexual experience he had with a woman was with a prostitute in Korea, resulting in his contracting a venereal disease. Berkowitz claimed that demons were driving his life. In his diseased mind, demons lived with the dogs of his neighbors, and their howling was the way they ordered David to go hunting for blood, particularly the blood of pretty young women. Since he felt rejected by women, he decided to get revenge. One evening he took a large hunting knife and drove around for hours looking for a young female victim. The demons would let him know when he found the right woman. He saw a young woman and attacked her from behind, stabbing her in the head. Her screaming scared David off, and she was able to escape. Stalking women had become a nightly adventure for him. Constantly on the hunt, he would choose young, attractive women victims. If he killed a man, he did so because the man was in the wrong place at the wrong time. If he didn't find a victim, he would go back to the scenes of his earlier murders and try to recall them, reportedly masturbating over the thoughts of his previous victims. For thirteen months Berkowitz terrorized New York City. In the end, he was responsible for six murders, with many more severely injured people. He confessed to the murders and received life imprisonment.

Case Example: Mission Killer Arthur Shawcross

Arthur John Shawcross was born on June 6, 1945. At an early age, Shawcross was beginning to show the first signs of abnormal behavior, especially after his little brother was born. He became a chronic bed-wetter and was still talking like a baby until he was 6 years old. The following year, he started running away from home, which family members dismissed as merely a ploy to gain attention. By the time he was 8, other behavioral problems began to surface. Arthur seemed to hate children younger than himself and teased them until they cried. He became obsessed with one of his sisters and ignored his other sister and younger brother. He invented imaginary friends and spoke with them in strange voices. His classmates constantly teased him, thus sending him into a rage. By and large, Arthur was a loner whose abnormal behavior made it hard for him to mix and communicate with others. Shawcross constantly ran away from home and often carried an iron bar on the bus to threaten other children. By the time he entered the third grade, his behavior deteriorated, as did his grades. He was given a series of psychological tests, which indicated that his behavior was due in large part to his feelings of inadequacy and rejection and to a growing hostility that he felt toward his parents, particularly his mother.

As the years passed, Arthur grew increasingly violent and would often beat up the neighborhood children. He became well-known for his explosive temper. Also, he began breaking into houses, stealing from local businesses, and setting fires. Shawcross claimed that by the age of 14, he was regularly having oral sex with his sister and cousin. Shawcross served in the U.S. Army in Vietnam, where he enjoyed the experience of killing and raping village women. Also, he claimed to have attacked several Asian prostitutes, some as young as 11. In 1972, Shawcross raped, tortured, and murdered an 8-year-old girl. Shawcross pleaded guilty to manslaughter and was sentenced to twenty-five years in prison. Because of an unjust correctional decision, he was released on good behavior. Upon his release, he moved to Rochester, New York, where he had a relationship with a woman. However, Shawcross prowled the streets of Rochester and killed his first prostitute there in 1988. By the time of his capture, he was responsible for killing 11 women, mostly prostitutes, whom he despised. Shawcross was convicted in 1990 and is serving life in prison with no possibility of parole.

The hedonistic type kills for the thrill of it. Such killers enjoy the act of killing and particularly take pleasure in the challenge of hunting victims. Sexual arousal fueled by extreme fantasy is common with this type of killer. Also, there are several subcategories of this type referred to as sadistic killers, lust killers, or those who kill for financial gain. There is no lack of serial killers of this type; for example, Bobby Joe Long and Ed Kemper are categorized as hedonistic predators who kill strangers or family members, often torturing and/or mutilating their victims (Ward, 1995). The

Case Example: Hedonistic Killer Ed Kemper

Ed Kemper was a sadistic necrophiliac. Kemper had death fantasies since early in his childhood. Ed liked decapitating his sisters' dolls and playing gas chamber. He also enjoyed killing, torturing, and mutilating animals. In 1963, at the age of 15, Kemper killed his grandparents, just to see how it would feel. Ed was committed to a maximum security mental hospital in 1963 but was released six years later. When he got out he had physically changed. He had grown to 6 feet, 9 inches tall and weighed 300 pounds. His appearance alone frightened people. Between the years 1971 and 1973, Kemper racked up six victims, all hitchhiking women students. He killed, decapitated, and dissected the victims, then proceeded to rape their corpses. In 1973, he hammered in his mother's skull, then proceeded to decapitate her, rape her corpse, and jam her severed larynx down the garbage disposal. He propped her head on the mantel for use as a dart board. Kemper phoned his mother's friend, inviting her to a surprise dinner. When she arrived, he clubbed her over the head, strangled her, and decapitated her. Kemper turned himself in to the police. He admitted to have kept the hair, teeth, and skin of some victims as trophies. He also admitted to having practiced cannibalism, saying that he had sliced some flesh off two victims' legs and had cooked it in a macaroni casserole. When he was asked what punishment would fit the crimes he had committed, he said, "death by torture." Instead, he was sentenced to life in prison and is currently serving his sentence in Vacaville Prison.

deadly sniper attacks in the Washington D.C. area in 2002 fall under hedonistic killings. Two men, John Allen Muhammad and his juvenile companion Lee Boyd Malvo, shot and killed individuals in Montgomery, Alabama, and Baton Rouge, Louisiana, then headed north where they randomly gunned down 10 victims and wounded four others in Maryland, Virginia, and Washington, D.C. Their motive for the killings appeared to be nothing more than sport.

A subcategory of hedonistic killers are referred to as comfort killers, who kill for financial gain. This group includes hit men who are paid to kill as a business deal; the "black widow," who marries and kills her spouses for inheritance or insurance money; and boarding-house owners, who kill their boarders and continue to collect their social security checks. These killers are usually very organized. Although they may enjoy killing, their primary motive is to make their own lives more comfortable.

The power-oriented types kill because they enjoy exerting ultimate control over their victims. These murderers are not psychotic, but they are obsessed with capturing and controlling their victims and forcing them to obey their every command. Serial killer John Wayne Gacy, responsible for killing 33 young boys, would lure his young victims into being handcuffed. Once the youths were securely manacled, he would kill them by pulling a rope or board against their throats as he raped them.

Case Example: Power-Oriented Killer Michael Swango

Michael Swango was one of the most prolific serial killers in history, victimizing nearly 60 persons, either fatally or nonfatally. However, he was charged with only 4 murders during his medical career, which spanned nearly 20 years. He traveled from hospital to hospital, state to state, and country to country to avoid further inquiries when questions were raised regarding his competency and rumors were rampant regarding his involvement in mysterious deaths and illnesses. Swango's career as "Dr. Death" began at Southern Illinois University (SIU) when he was accepted into their medical program in 1979. Immediately, the deaths of 5 patients, all by lethal injection, were attributed to Swango. Swango's medical licenses in both Illinois and Ohio were suspended, so he decided to move to Virginia. While in Virginia, he worked as a career counselor from 1987 to 1989, nonfatally poisoning 3 coworkers; and as a lab technician from 1989 to 1991, nonfatally poisoning 2 coworkers.

He was assigned to work at Northport Veteran's Hospital, Long Island, New York, beginning in June 1993. After four months, coworkers began to notice a pattern of deaths, all following "care" administered by Swango. By October 1993, he was fired not only for his involvement in the deaths but also for fraudulent admission, the staff having discovered the felony charge for battery and charges for nonfatal poisonings. Swango disappeared when the FBI issued a warrant for his arrest but later surfaced in Zimbabwe, Africa, more than a year later. In Africa, 5 deaths, including that of a coworker, as well as 2 nonfatal poisonings, were attributed to Swango. Swango also poisoned those he had a personal relationship with, which included his wife, a girlfriend and her four children, and a landlord in Africa. He expressed no sense of empathy for the deaths of his patients and enjoyed being the doctor to deliver the news of death to worried relatives. While working, he scrawled the word "DIED" in large red letters over the patients' names as though he were celebrating or bringing attention to their passing. When a 22-year-old girl suddenly died under his care, he kicked his feet up on a table when he delivered the news and said, "She's dead now, you can go look at her." Swango stated to one of his coworkers that "the best thing about being a doctor" was "to come out of the emergency room with a hard-on to tell some parents that their kid had just died from head trauma." It gratified him to see others in pain, especially when he was the party responsible for the pain. Excited by death and disaster, while working as a paramedic, he would oftentimes show up at the scene of violent tragedies while off duty. Even as a boy, he was thrilled by violent deaths and disaster, frequently seeking out such events or news of them and obsessing about them. Since his boyhood, he collected clippings from newspapers reporting violent deaths or disasters, and he pasted them into scrapbooks; his father also collected such clippings. One of Swango's most prominent traits was his narcissistic personality, which was evident in many aspects of his life. He expressed a need for control that was obvious in his obsession with physical fitness: control over his appearance, his girlfriends, and life and death.

FEMALE SERIAL KILLERS

"I was right behind her. I choked her with the phone cord ... She was holding on, trying to get the cord off. I pulled her down. She was on her back. I hit her in the head with a bottle. I lost it. I was so consumed ... I don't know the time span in there—must have been very quick. She must've stopped moving, and I left. As I walked out, she had a little wallet thing. I grabbed it. I left and proceeded to shop up a storm." (Quote by Dana Sue Gray, female serial killer.)

The "gentler sex" is not immune from violent behavior, as exemplified by the appalling actions of Susan Smith, **Aileen Wuornos,** Andrea Yates, and other well-known killers. Although females account for only a minor portion of all violent crime in the United States, there has been an increase in the number of violent crimes committed by women since 1970. Because female serial killers are few, they have always been something of an anomaly in criminology. As Eric Hickey (2002: 213) describes them, "Women can be just as lethal as males, but they use different methods to achieve their goals."

There is a history of women who have killed and tortured others for pleasure. The Hungarian Countess Elizabeth Báthory, born in 1560, was one such example. Elizabeth was the niece of the king of Poland. The countess had her own, very peculiar streak of cruelty toward servants—if they were female. Báthory punished them by placing a piece of paper between a woman's toes and setting it on fire. If a servant failed to press the countess's garments adequately, a hot iron would be held to the servant's face until she was scarred for life. These treatments often resulted in death, but that outcome was neither surprising nor disappointing to the callous countess. It is likely that as many as 650 women and girls, some as young as 12 years of age, lost their lives to her blood lust. One of the most striking and troubling things about this real-life horror story is its female-on-female character. All the murder victims were female, as were the procurers and torturers (Codrescu, 1995).

According to Deborah Schurman-Kauflin in her book *The New Predator* (2000), most women killers had a history of cruelty toward animals and levels of isolation that

Case Example: Black Widow Killer Belle Gunness

Belle Sorrenson Gunness, a Norwegian-American, insured her first husband and two of her children before killing them in the early 1900s and then collecting the money. She took her other two children to Indiana and bought a pig farm there, which she turned into a graveyard. Her second husband was next. He was found under a large meat grinder, his skull crushed. Belle soon put "lonely hearts" ads in a newspaper, and those men who answered her ads disappeared. It was also later revealed that she killed her children before fleeing. (Source: *http://www.crimelibrary.com*)

fed self-absorbed fantasies. Also, like their male counterparts, the sources of their violence include attachment disorders, abandonment, harsh discipline, and abuse. Studies on women who kill, for example, indicate that "motherless mothering," or the absence of positive mothering, shaped their early behavior. In other words, their mothers were neglectful, alcoholic, or mentally ill. Drug or alcohol abuse in their family of origin was common, including history of self-drug-usage. And as with men, many women experienced serious childhood harm and serious adult harm, including physical and sexual abuse by others (Crimmins, et al., 1997). Unfortunately, many violent women were exposed to multiple experiences of damage that influenced their lives and their ability to parent children or maintain normal relationships (see the case of Aileen Wuornos).

Methods and Motives

Kelleher and Kelleher (1998) argue that female serial killers are more successful, careful, precise, methodical, and quiet in committing their crimes than are men. Most had no prior criminal records. The authors examined 100 cases since 1900 and found an average duration of 8 years before the killers were caught—double the time for the male serial killer. Hickey's (2002) subsample of 62 female serial killers revealed the following information. More than nine out of ten were white, and two-thirds acted alone. Many are considered "black widows" (women who kill their spouses, remarry, and kill again) or health-care providers who kill their patients. Also, they tended to be older and to get away with their crimes for a longer period of time than did their male counterparts. For female serial killers, the most common weapon of choice is poison, followed by guns, and the most common motive is financial (hedonistic-comfort killers).

The methods and motives of female serial killers are presented in Table 3-4.

TABLE 3–4

Methods and Motives of Female Serial Killers

Method	Motives
1. Poison (80%)	1. Money (74%)
2. Shooting (20%)	2. Control (13%)
3. Bludgeoning (16%)	3. Enjoyment (11%)
4. Suffocation (16%)	4. Sex (10%)
5. Stabbing (11%)	5. Drugs, cult involvement, cover-up of feelings of inadequacy (24%)
6. Drowning (5%)	

From Serial Murderers and Their Victims (with CD-ROM) 3rd edition by HICKEY. © 2002. Reprinted with permission of Wadsworth, a division of Thomson Learning: www.thomsonrights.com. Fax 800-760-2215.

Case Example: Female Serial Killer Aileen Wuornos

Aileen Wuornos was born Aileen Pittman in Rochester, Michigan, in 1956. Her teenage parents separated months before she was born. Her father served time in Kansas and Michigan mental hospitals as a deranged child-molester. Also, her mother, who was unable to handle her responsibilities, left Aileen and her brother in her parents' care in early 1960. Their grandparents legally adopted Aileen and her brother Keith. At age six, Aileen suffered scarring facial burns while she and Keith were setting fires with lighter fluid. A rebellious child, she was constantly getting into trouble at school. At age 14, she became pregnant, delivering her son at a Detroit maternity home in 1971. Her brother allegedly fathered the child. After her grandmother died, her grandfather forced her and her brother out of his home. Aileen dropped out of school to work the streets full-time, traveling around and earning her way as a teenage hooker. In 1974, using the alias Sandra Kretsch, she was jailed in Jefferson County, Colorado, for disorderly conduct, drunk driving, and firing a .22-caliber pistol from a moving vehicle. She eventually hitched a ride to Florida, where she continued her prostitution. Aileen was subsequently arrested for armed robbery of a convenience store, resulting in a prison sentence. After release, she was later arrested for trying to pass forged checks at a bank and was named as a suspect in the theft of a pistol and ammunition. Aileen borrowed the alias Lori Grody from an aunt in Michigan. Eleven days later, the Florida Highway Patrol cited Aileen for driving without a valid license. Later, she was arrested in Miami under her own name, charged with auto theft, resisting arrest, and obstruction by false information; police found a .38-caliber revolver and a box of ammunition in the stolen car. She worked the bars and truck stops, thumbing rides to snag a trick when all else failed, to supplement her income as a prostitute. Wuornos began killing the men whom she solicited. In Florida, she killed 7 men, each of the encounters starting out as an ordinary proposition for sex. Then, at various points while engaging in sex, she would perceive the relationship as becoming abusive, pull out a .22-caliber handgun, and shoot her victims repeatedly in the chest or sometimes in the back of the head. She would then rob her victims and hide their bodies in the woods along the I-95 corridor. However, she defended her killings as self-defense, claiming that the men tried to rape her. Her lesbian lover of six years (who also assisted in her apprehension but never participated in the murders) provided testimony against her, destroying her self-defense claim. Sentenced to death, Wuornos was executed in 2002.

Like male serial killers, women may act either alone or with a partner. When acting alone, they are often mature, careful, deliberate, socially adept, and highly organized. As with the black widow killers, they tend to favor a specific weapon, like poison, lethal injection, or suffocations. Those acting in partnerships tend to be younger, aggressively vicious in their attack, sometimes disorganized, and usually unable to plan carefully.

As to victim selection, Newton (1993) compiled an exhaustive accounting of 183 female murderers, finding that 70 percent meet the definition of a serial killer. Regarding their victims, these female serial killers showed a different profile from that of males: 45 percent killed family members, 26 percent murdered friends or acquaintances, 10 percent took the lives of those left in their care (wards, charges, or patients), 19.5 percent were "mixed" predators, whereas only 11 percent murdered strangers. They usually attacked victims in diverse locations. (See the case of Aileen Wuornos presented on the previous page).

CONCLUSION

In comparing mass, spree, and serial killers, we find that most perpetrators are white males. In mass killings, the offender is motivated by revenge against coworkers, students, or society at large. Innocent parties unrelated to the offender may be targeted, as in the case of terrorist or hate killings. Also, the killings may take place at one location. In spree killings, the offender may be involved with other crimes such as robbery, in which murder is committed to conceal the identity of the perpetrator. Moreover, the killings may be geographically dispersed as the offender moves about to escape capture or to commit additional crimes. Serial killers target certain type of victims and usually plan their killings in advance. The motivations of male serial killers are usually based on sex, power, or hedonism. Their behavior may be organized or disorganized. Women serial killers are rarer, but revenge against a family member or acquaintance or financial incentive usually motivates their offenses. Also, they are more likely to use less violent methods such as poison to accomplish their crimes. Despite the methods or killer types, there are common characteristics in the backgrounds of these predators, such as abuse, family dysfunction, mental illness, and the like. This is not to suggest that abuse, mental disorder, and deplorable social economic factors are requirements; there may also be unexplained reasons for the actions of these killers.

DISCUSSION QUESTIONS AND ACTIVITIES

1. Create a graphic organizer (visual metaphor) to differentiate the perpetrator characteristics, motives, and modus operandi of the five types of mass killers.
2. Reread the Barton letter and the Smith confession from these family annihilators. What psychological themes are common to these cases?
3. Compare the motives and methods of serial killers and mass killers.
4. When you come upon the scene of a rape/murder, you notice that the female victim was raped and tortured pre mortem; that the perpetrator brought the knife that was used and took it away; left no prints (wore gloves); and brought duct tape to tie up the victim. Also, there is evidence that the victim invited the perpetrator

in. Would you be looking for an organized or a disorganized killer? Why? On the basis of your assessment, what characteristics would you look for in a suspect?

5. Discuss the typologies of serial killers. Are these typologies useful? Why, or why not?
6. What would cause an organized killer to become disorganized?
7. Make a chart comparing women serial killers and male serial killers in terms of family background, methods, motives, and victims. Why do you think that female serial killers have a "longer career" than their male counterparts? (Think of the types of victims, the modus operandi, etc.)
8. Critique the MacDonald triad in terms of predicting violent behavior. Why does it make sense?
9. What role does fantasy play in the creation of a serial killer? In terms of typical background characteristics, why do you think that fantasy is psychologically important to the future killer?
10. Show how the background of Aileen Wuornos (case example of a female serial killer) exemplifies the background characterstics of female murderers found in Schurman-Kauflin's study.

Key Terms

Aileen Wuornos
Baron Gilles de Rais
Disorganized killers
Fantasy cycle (of serial killers)
Killer cults
MacDonald triad
Organized killers
Spree killers
Subtypes of serial killers
Suicide by cop
Types of mass killers

References

Braidhill, K. 1998. "To Die For." *Los Angeles Magazine*, November.

Codrescu, A. 1995. *Blood Countess.* Simon & Schuster. New York, NY.

Cleary, S. and J. Luxemburg. 1993. Serial murderers: Common background characteristics and their contribution to causation. Paper presented to the annual meeting of the American Society of Criminology, Miami, Fl.

Crimmins, S., S. Langley, H. H. Brownstein, and B. J. Spunt. 1997. Convicted women who have killed children: A self-psychology perspective. *Journal of Interpersonal Violence:* Feb.

Dietz, P. E. 1986. Mass, Serial and Sensational Homicides. *Bulletin of the New York Academy of Medicine 62* (5): 477–491.

Douglas, J. 1997. *Journey into Darkness.* Pocket Books.

Geringer, J. 2000. *Michael Swango: Doctor of Death.* The Crime Library. Retrieved March 12, 2002, from the World Wide Web. *http://www.crimelibrary.com/serial6/swango.*

Herald-Journal, *Susan Smith Confesses,* Spartanburg, SC, November 3 1994.

Hickey, E. 2002. *Serial Murderers and Their Victims* (3rd ed). Belmont, Calif.: Wadsworth.

Hill, S. 1994. Nurture-born killers: The motivation and personality development of the serial killer. *http://www.wright.edu/~shill/killers.htm*

Holmes, R. 1996. *Profiling Violent Crimes.* Newbury Park, Calif: Sage.

Holmes, R. M. and J. De Burger. 1988. *Serial Murder.* Newbury Park, Calif.: Sage Publications.

Holmes, R. and S. T. Holmes. 2001. *Mass Murder in the United States.* Newbury Park, Calif.: Sage.

Jordan, M. and K. Sullivan. 2003. "Federal Officials in Mexico Join Murder Probe. Dozens of Women Killed in Border City May Have Been Slain for Their Organs." *Washington Post Foreign Service,* May 11. p. A16:

Kelleher, M. D. and C. L. Kelleher. 1998. *Murder Most Rare.* New York: Dell.

MacDonald, J. M. 1963. The threat to kill. *American Journal of Psychiatry 120*: 125–130.

Newton, M. 1993. *Bad Girls Do It: An Encyclopedia of Female Murderers.* Port Townsend, Wash: Loompanics Unlimited.

Norris, J. *Serial Killers: The Growing Menace.* New York: Bantam Doubleday.

Pollock, N. L. 1988. Sexual assault of older women. *Annals of Sex Research 1:* 523–532.

Pollak, O. 1950. *The Criminality of Women.* Philadelphia: University of Pennsylvania Press.

Ressler, R. K., A. W. Burgess, J. E. Douglas, C. R. Hartman, and R. B. D'Agostino. 1986. Sexual killers and their victims: Identifying patterns through crime scene analysis. *Journal of Interpersonal Violence (1)*: 288–308.

Ressler, Robert K et al. 1988. *Sexual Homicide.* Lexington, Mass.: D.C. Heath & Company.

Schurman-Kauflin, D. 2000. *The New Predator: Women Who Kill.* New York: Algora.

Stewart, J. B. 1999. *Blind Eye.* New York: Touchstone.

Ward, B. B. 1995. *In the Mind of a Monster.* Boca Raton, Fl.: Cool Hand Communications, pp. 69–95.

Williams, C. and D. Seaman. 1997. *The Serial Killers: A Study in the Psychology of Violence.* London: Virgin Publishing.

Part Two

Sources of Predatory Violence: Pieces of the Puzzle

In the previous section, we described the various faces of the "monsters" among us, but this question remains: how did they get that way? What psychological, family, social, and/or biological factors produce such antisocial behavior? Are they all mentally ill? Psychological and sociological theories can be applied to explain this phenomenon, as can the findings of research. Currently, social scientists cannot provide a unified and definitive answer to the question "How did they get that way?" either theoretically or on the basis of research findings. The reason for this condition is that such a complex human phenomenon as predatory violence is difficult to study retrospectively (after an individual has become a "monster"), and as with most complex human behavior, the cause-effect pathway is also complex. Therefore, as you study the following chapters, it is important to keep in mind the principles of multifinality and equifinality.

The *principle of multifinality* means that the *same experience or biological factor can result in different outcomes*. For example, a childhood marked by sexual abuse may lead to an adult who is depressed/suicidal *or* suffers from borderline personality disorder *or* is abusive toward his or her own children *or* is normal *or* is a child molester. Additional psychological, social, and/or biological elements interact with a sexually abusive childhood to produce different results. For that reason, even though most child molesters have a childhood history of sexual abuse, the converse is not true: most sexually abused children do not become child molesters. We can say only that the experience of childhood molestation, when combined with other biological and/or social factors, increases the likelihood of later sex offending.

The second principle to keep in mind is the *principle of equifinality*. That is, there are *multiple pathways to the same outcome*. For example, not all serial killers have horrendous childhood histories *or* demonstrate neurological deficits *or* suffer from a mental disorder. The pathways to becoming a serial killer or sexual predator vary. Although each of the preceding factors alone or in combination can increase the risk for predatory violence, they are not all necessary to produce this outcome. The pathways that lead to a life of predatory violence are heterogeneous, not homogenous.

This section is based on a bio-psycho-social model of the development of patterns of violent and predatory behavior.

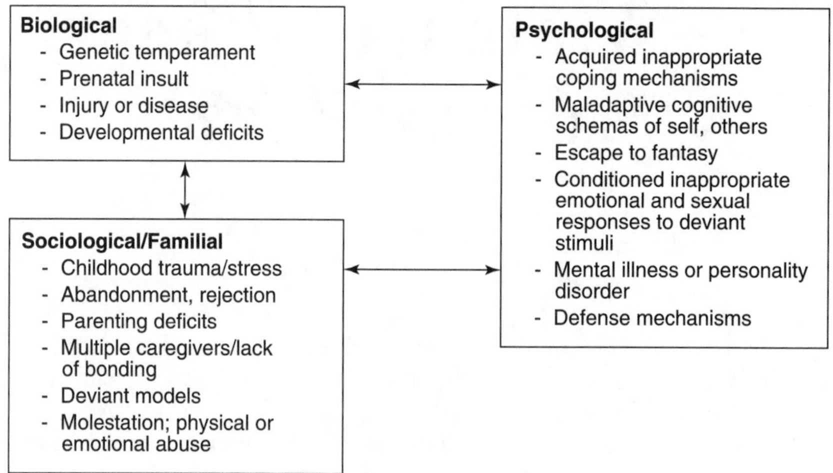

Notice that in this model, biological, psychological, and social/familial factors interact to produce a sexual or violent offender. However, within each category, there are multiple potential pathways to deviance (equifinality), and no individual factor alone can produce a deviant outcome (multifinality).

As you study the following chapters, keep in mind that as with all complex human behaviors, psychologists, sociologists, and neuroscientists can each contribute pieces of the puzzle, but the principles of multifinality and equifinality limit our ability to identify a single pathway to becoming a serial violent offender.

CHAPTER 4

HOW TO CREATE A MONSTER ACCORDING TO PSYCHOLOGICAL THEORIES OF DEVELOPMENT

LEARNING OBJECTIVES

After studying this chapter, you will

- Be able to synthesize three theoretical perspectives on how adaptive and destructive personalities develop
- Be able to identify the assumptions, structures, and dynamics of personality development described by Freud
- Be able to identify the assumptions and principles of learning that learning/cognitive theorists rely on to explain personality
- Understand the contribution of genetic trait/dispositional theory to conceptualizing personality development
- Learn how each of the three perspectives may be applied to analyze maladaptive/destructive behavior and attitudes
- See how these three perspectives may be integrated to provide insight into pathological personality development.

INTRODUCTION

Psychological theory is not alone in providing understandings of how deviant behavior, feelings, and attitudes develop. This has also been the domain of literary works. Conrad's *The Lord of the Flies* paints a picture of British schoolboys descending into savagery when left without the civilizing influence of authority. Mary Shelley's *Frankenstein* points to the effects of parental and social rejection in the development of a monster. However, psychological theory uses the lens of science to help us organize observations by identifying principles, constructs, and dynamics that tie together these observations into a coherent whole. Good theory also helps us generate hypotheses to be tested through systematic observations in the laboratories or through field research. The relationship between theory and research is dynamic; theories generate research but are also informed and modified by research.

Highlight 4-1

Before continuing, test your own assumptions about personality development. Write the letter of the response that most closely reflects your own opinion next to each item. A = mostly agree, D = mostly disagree.

___ 1. Most of our behavior is motivated by unconscious factors.

___ 2. Adult behavior problems have their roots in traumatic early childhood experiences.

___ 3. All humans are naturally aggressive and sexual; it is only the civilizing influence of parents and society that inhibits their expression.

___ 4. People *learn* to be good or *learn* to be bad, depending on what their environment rewards.

___ 5. Both prosocial and antisocial personality development are greatly influenced by what we observe people around us doing.

___ 6. How we learn to interpret situations strongly affects how we will react to the situation.

___ 7. Adult personality is largely the product of inherited predispositions.

___ 8. Our environment can only modify our basic ways of reacting within genetically programmed limits.

___ 9. Basic personality characteristics such as sociability, anxiousness, and excitability are biologically determined from birth.

Key: If you agreed with items 1–3, you are comfortable with the psychodynamic perspective. Items 4–6 reflect the learning/cognition perspective, and items 7–9 reflect trait/dispositional theories.

Case Example: Richard Ramirez, the Night Stalker

After his mother's tough pregnancy, baby Richard was born in Texas to Mercedes and Julian Ramirez in February 1960. He entered a family with three older brothers, Rubin, Joseph and Robert and an older sister, Ruth. Because his mother was busy working, Ruth (described as the perfect child) did much of the mothering. When he was two, a dresser fell on Richard's head, causing a severe concussion. Richard's brother Rubin got into trouble in school, fighting and bringing home bad report cards. Later, Rubin would begin sniffing glue and burglarizing homes. His father frequently responded to Rubin's bad behavior by beating him with a garden hose. Julian also reacted to minor frustrations with violent self-destructive rages. For example, when he had trouble repairing the car, he began cursing and beat his head on the side of the house until blood ran down his face. Julian's rages escalated, and he often beat his children until they were black and blue as well as directing his rage towards himself.

When Richard was in fifth grade, he had a seizure during class and was diagnosed with epilepsy. The seizures continued, and he was embarrassed to be put in a special class in school where the teacher began molesting him and even followed him home to engage him in sex. The final insult came when Richard was kicked off the football team because of his seizures.

About this time, Richard's cousin Mike returned from Vietnam, full of stories about killing, raping, and mutilating victims. He even shared with Richard pictures of his perverted sexual acts. Richard found them sexually arousing, and he would often masturbate to these pictures when he was alone. Richard hung out with Mike, smoking pot and listening adoringly to his stories until one day Mike became annoyed with his wife and shot her in front of Richard. Mike was found insane and committed to a mental hospital.

After Mike left, Richard spent most of his time alone, smoking pot and fantasizing about unusual violent and sexual scenarios. At 13, he joined his older brother Rubin in L. A., where they burglarized homes. Richard loved looking through people's things while he fantasized about bondage, feeling powerful.

Richard returned home and spent his days hunting small animals, gutting them and feeding their entrails to his dog (he had dropped out of school). Conflict with his father continued, and Richard's sister Ruth and her new husband took him in. Ruth's husband, however, was a voyeur and included Richard in his nightly activities. Richard progressed to actually entering the homes and enjoyed watching people sleep while fantasizing about bondage, often masturbating in their houses.

Meanwhile, cousin Mike was released from the mental hospital and reconnected with Richard. They spent almost all their time together, being each other's only friend; they believed that other people were hostile and unfair to them.

At 18, Richard returned to L. A., began burglarizing homes to support his drug habit (cocaine and PCP), and raped his first victim. He tied her up in vari-

(continued)

ous bondage positions while raping her. He felt powerful and began to follow the teachings of the Church of Satan; he felt that Satan, unlike the God of his Catholic upbringing, would love him no matter what. Richard spent the next 7 years doing drugs, burglarizing, raping, torturing, and finally murdering victims in their homes. He terrorized the Los Angeles area as the Night Stalker until he was caught in August 1985 (Carlo, 1996).

In our quest to put the pieces of the "monster" puzzle together, it would be useful if psychology had achieved consensus around only one theory of personality development. Unfortunately, this is not the case. There are a variety of theories that endeavor to explain both deviant and normal personality development. They differ because they were developed in different times and places that held particular worldviews of human nature and were often influenced by world events (i.e., world wars, social upheavals). Even the personal experiences of theorists themselves often informed their theories. Theories also differ because theorists made their observations on different groups: clinical patients, laboratory animals, or college students. However disparate their roots, the classical traditions in personality theory advance our understanding of how an individual may become the "monster" among us. As you review the following theoretical traditions, you may feel that these theories are the result of a "four blind men and the elephant" exercise, and you may be right. However, although each theorist may be describing only one part of the elephant, together they may provide a glimpse of the wiley pachyderm!

Consider the case of Richard Ramirez—how did baby Richard grow up to be the Night Stalker? Each theory of personality development would offer different interpretations.

The theories that we will explore represent three theoretical traditions: psychodynamic theory, learning/cognitive theory, and trait/dispositional theory.

Psychodynamic Theory

Freud's theory, first articulated in the late 1800s, has been extremely influential in shaping our views of why people behave and think as they do. The public, in general, have adopted Freudian thinking into their interpretations of behavior, especially Freud's idea of **psychic determinism.** That is, all behavior has a cause, and often the cause is unconscious. Freud's theories have been revered, modified, rejected, resurrected, and extended, and they have had heuristic impact across many disciplines (Martin, Mutchnick, and Austin, 1990). Although Freud himself did not treat violent criminals, his broad theory has often been applied to the study of violent human behavior.

Assumptions about Human Nature

Freud assumed that humans, like animals, are born with basic biological instincts that drive all personality development, both deviant and normal (Freud, 1949). These instincts are *Eros* (life instinct) and *Thanatos* (death instinct). Eros includes the sexual instincts and the drive to preserve the species and ourselves. The psychic energy of Eros is referred to as **libido.** Libido can be aimed at others (love) or self (narcissism), and includes sadism and masochism (pleasure in giving or receiving pain). Thanatos is the drive to return to an inanimate state and is associated with the desire for both self-destruction and, when externalized, aggression. Thus, as human beings, we come into this world in a state of conflict between the psychic forces of life (sex, preservation) and death (self-destruction and aggression).

Freud further assumed that although these instincts are the primary motivation for our thoughts and actions, we are unaware that they are the driving force behind our conscious needs and motives. In other words, we are all **unconsciously driven** to satisfy these basic animalistic instincts. How they are restrained, channeled, and acted out is established in early childhood and comes primarily from relationships with caregivers (mostly Mom) and to a lesser extent from family and the broader society. The lifelong patterns that emerge from this interaction may be prosocial, neurotic, and self-destructive, or may be antisocial and are expressed in a variety of ways. For example, the mass murderer who shoots up a McDonald's, the smoker, the anorexic, and the hang glider may all be unconsciously driven by Thanatos.

The Structure and Development of Personality

Freud (1960) postulates three parts, or agents, of the personality, the id, ego, and superego. From infancy to about 6 months, we are all **id.** That is, we are ruled purely by our inherent biological instincts, and we operate on the pleasure principle; we want what feels good, and we want it now. Therefore, if an infant is hungry, it wants to be fed immediately whether it is the middle of the night or whether Mom is in the middle of the mall. Delaying gratification is not an option. Further, the id operates with what is called **primary process** thinking—images rather than symbolic thought such as language. Therefore, infants imagine what they want and expect it to appear; they cannot plan or problem solve. The id does not disappear at 6 months; its instincts remain the unconscious driving force of our personality throughout life. The id with its instincts is the energy source or motor for the personality; without this part of the personality, we would not be motivated to do anything, and we would be unanimated lumps. On the other hand, it is easy to see that if personality development stopped with the id, we would all be sitting around wetting our pants when we needed to, expecting food to magically appear, and satisfying our sexual urges at will. The reason we are not doing these things is that the second structure of the personality, the ego, develops beginning at about 6 to 8 months.

The **ego** emerges as the infant becomes aware that she or he is separate from the people and objects around her or him (Freud 1960). The ego is the interface between the desires of the id and the real world and therefore operates on the reality principle. Ego functions are both internal, to gratify the needs of the id, and external, to provide awareness of external stimuli and their relationship to pleasure or pain, to remember through symbolic thinking how to meet these needs in the real world, to delay gratification, to plan and problem solve (Freud, 1949). In other words, if we are hungry we do not just sit around imagining a Big Mac (id); rather, we remember how to get in the car and go to McDonald's, and we delay gratification until we can get there (we don't just eat the nearest doorknob!). Or if we can't get to McDonald's, we problem solve and think of alternate ways to satisfy our hunger. All of this is the result of operating on the reality principle and using the **secondary process thinking** (symbolic thinking such as language) of the ego. The violent offender who has weak ego development is impulsive. For example, the perpetrator who breaks into a house to rob may impulsively rape a woman whom he finds at home. On the other hand, sexual predators who have strong ego development may carefully select victims and plan their attacks so that they will not be caught or interrupted.

Both the id and the ego are amoral. If personality development stopped with the development of the ego, we would all be psychopaths—meeting our sexual and aggressive instincts through careful planning. The reason that we are not is because of the development of the superego.

The **superego** develops between the ages of 3 and 5 years through the resolution of the Oedipus complex (Freud, 1960). The superego operates on the morality principle and is developed mostly through parental influences as they socialize us to the values and morals of society. These internalized values and morals serve as our conscience and restrain the unacceptable desires of the id by making our egos feel guilty and anxious when these desires press for expression (Freud, 1964). The superego morality is not realistic; it is perfectionistic. The conscience part of the superego has perfectionistic standards for what we should not do—thoughts, feelings, and actions that are wrong and should be punished (generates guilt). The ego-ideal part of the superego has perfectionistic standards for what we should do, feel, and think (generates inferiority feelings or pride when we live up to standards). A well-developed superego is constantly on guard, judging the intentions and plans of the ego for satisfying the impulses and instincts of the id. An overdeveloped superego can make us feel guilty, inferior, and anxious about seeking any pleasures.

Ideal personality development involves a strong ego, able to satisfy the impulses of the id in the real world without irritating the perfectionistic superego whose standards are always in conflict with the pleasure-seeking id.

Freud identified a variety of strategies or **defense mechanisms** that the ego uses to manage the conflict when the ego cannot effectively problem solve.

Ego Defense Mechanisms

Defense mechanisms allow the ego to **repress** or push id impulses and desires that are unacceptable to the superego into the unconscious, thereby reducing the anxiety and tension that accompany them (Freud, 1946). Defense mechanisms do not resolve the underlying conflict and therefore are only temporary solutions requiring a great deal of psychic energy needed to maintain unacceptable impulses and wishes as unconscious processes. This process is called repression. **Repression** is the foundation of all of the defense mechanisms that the ego uses to manage the id versus superego conflict. All defense mechanisms serve to keep impulses repressed into the unconscious. We all use defense mechanisms to protect ourselves from anxiety; they become pathological when used compulsively or repetitively. Freud identified a number of defense mechanisms; however, we are going to focus on those most clearly related to violent and predatory offenders.

Isolation and undoing keep unacceptable impulses and wishes repressed by using distracting obsessive thoughts (isolation) or by engaging in compulsive behavior (undoing) to block out unacceptable thoughts and feelings (Freud, 1959). For example, serial killers often report obsessive fantasies that are frequently precipitated by actual or symbolic events that threaten self-esteem or that trigger feelings of anger and helplessness originating in childhood, possibly at the hands of an abusive parent. Feelings of anger and shame, rooted in childhood molestation, may be isolated/walled off by obsessive fantasies about raping and killing. The actual killing and disposal of victims are often compulsively ritualistic and restore feelings of power and control. In these ways, the killer may be isolating and undoing anxiety generated by unacceptable feelings of helplessness and aggression toward an abusive parent. The *souvenirs* that these killers take from their victims are used later to relive the killing through fantasy, maintaining—at least for a while—the isolation of unacceptable feelings, wishes, and impulses. Later, as these repressed impulses and feelings again threaten to break through into consciousness, causing tension and anxiety, the ego again engages in isolation (fantasies) and undoing (ritualistic murder) to keep them repressed.

Displacement represses sexual and aggressive impulses toward an unacceptable object by redirecting these urges toward more acceptable objects (Freud, 1959). Aggressive impulses towards a parent, on whom a child is dependent and who is both loved and seen as powerful, creates anxiety for the ego. Consequently, the child may redirect these aggressive impulses toward a psychologically safer object such as a sibling, a neighbor child, or an animal. For example, Eric Smith (age 13) lured a 4-year-old neighbor child into the woods, killed him, and sodomized him with a stick. Eric had been the victim of verbal abuse from his older sister and peers at school, rejected by his biological father, and possibly sexually molested by his step-father. A Freudian interpretation would be that Eric displaced his aggression/killing impulses toward his father(s) onto a smaller child in order to maintain the repression of these urges associated with powerful and/or loved others. Many serial killers have a childhood history of abusing, torturing, and/or killing small animals (displacement).

Reaction formation maintains the repression of unacceptable wishes and desires by disguising them as their opposite (Freud, 1959). The disguise is characterized by exaggeration and a compulsive quality. For example, a man who is very dependent and needy (unacceptable) may express exaggerated independence, domination, and machismo toward others. John Wayne Gacy, who sexually assaulted and killed over 30 teenage boys, may have been using reaction formation when he expressed to friends and colleagues strong antihomosexual feelings and attitudes.

Projection maintains repression of instinctual impulses and unacceptable wishes by attributing these impulses to others (Freud, 1959). In other words, instead of accepting our sexual and aggressive impulses, we project these unacceptable feelings and desires onto others. For example, violent hate crimes against homosexuals are, according to Freudian theory, an effort to repress unacceptable homosexual urges by projecting them onto gay men whom the perpetrator then perceives as trying to seduce him. The compulsive use of this defense mechanism leads to general feelings of persecution, and in its most extreme manifestation, paranoid delusions.

Stages of Development

According to Freud (1961), personality development takes place primarily in the first five or six years of life, referred to as the infantile period. This period is crucial in that most of our later actions, feelings, and pathologies are rooted in this early period of development. Freud further divided this important period of development into three stages, each named for the erogenous zones most involved in development during that time (although they do overlap). Intense frustration and ambivalence at any of these stages may result in fixation. That is, we may stay developmentally stuck at a stage of development.

Oral Stage. Babies seek satisfaction through sucking and oral stimulation. Fixation at this stage may result in hostile personality characteristics such as oral sadism, expressed as nail biting, sarcasm, being hypercritical—manifestations of the aggressive instinct. Serial killer Ted Bundy was convicted partially on bite-mark evidence.

Anal Stage. The infant derives pleasure through excretion of feces. Punitive toilet training leads to the development of the anal triad in adulthood, characterized by orderliness, stinginess, and obstinacy (Freud, 1964). During this time, the child also develops an active orientation (dominant, sadistic), a passive orientation (voyeuristic, masochistic), or some combination of the two. The aggressive instinct is further developed during this stage.

Phallic Stage. The focus of pleasure is the genitals with masturbation being a universal activity. It is during this stage that children experience the infamous **Oedipus complex** (Freud, 1961); its resolution provides the foundation for gender identification and the development of the superego.

The simplified version of the development and resolution of the male Oedipus complex begins when the young boy develops sexual desire for his mother and consequent hostility toward his father whom he views as a rival. He discovers that little girls and women do not have penises and concludes that they must have been castrated as punishment for sexual urges. Fear of a similar fate at the hands of the powerful father leads to castration anxiety. To reduce this anxiety, the boy represses his sexual impulses for his mother and identifies with his father; he introjects his father's authority, values, and sense of right and wrong. Thus is born the foundation for the superego and gender identity. Either an absent or a rejecting father or a seductive or an aggressive mother can result in pathological sexual development and negatively affect the development of the superego.

For girls, the realization that they have been castrated (are missing the all-powerful penis) is blamed on their mother. The girl begins her quest for a penis by focusing her libido on her father, who can give her a substitute penis in the form of a baby. This is the female Oedipus complex (Freud, 1964). Resolution comes about when she realizes that she cannot have her father, identifies with her mother, displaces her search for a penis on other males, and strives to have a baby. Problems during the female Oedipus complex result in ongoing penis envy, which can be manifested as the desire to be a man, competition with and hostility toward men, or rejection of sexuality (frigidity). Female serial killers almost always target men.

Other Psychodynamic Theories

Later psychodynamic theorists placed less emphasis than did Freud on biological instincts and emphasized more strongly early relationships with primary caregivers, human contact, and connectedness as the foundation of personality development. Object Relations theorists such as Melanie Klein and Otto Kernberg (Feist and Feist, 2002) point to the infant's introjection of the mother (breast) as both good (nurturing) and bad (withholding). These early object relations create the prototype for later relationships with self and others; love and/or hate for others is born from these early object relations.

Bowlby's **Attachment Theory** (Feist and Feist, 2002) is based on his observations of both human and primate infants. When the primary caregiver is accessible and nurturing, infants develop the ability to establish and reestablish a bond or an attachment with others. However, when primary caregivers are inaccessible and undependable, infants detach permanently. This detachment is maintained in all future human relationships. Although these infants may later develop superficial social skills, they are not able to emotionally bond to others. These are characteristics associated with psychopathy. Sex offenders show high rates of insecure attachment (Ward, Hudson, and Marshall, 1996). Hickey (1997) reported that in his study of 62 serial killers, 48 percentage reported strong feelings of rejection rooted in parental abandonment, neglect, drug abuse, and/or child abuse.

Integration and Application

According to Freud, most mental life is unconscious and driven by sexual and aggressive instincts, and repressed wishes and desires. Early childhood (first 6 years) experiences and relationships with parents are the key to how these unconscious desires are manifested throughout our lives. With regard to violent expression, it is obvious that the development of the superego during the phallic stage plays an important role.

One explanation for psychopathy is that the superego fails to develop, leaving the individual without conscience or the capacity for guilt. Ego function may be intact; but without the "brakes" of the superego, the individual feels free to pursue his or her desires, albeit realistically. According to Attachment Theory, a severely disturbed relationship with the primary caregiver leads to an inability to attach to others later in life. Lack of conscience and attachment commonly describe the primary psychopath.

Freud, however, observed that pathological guilt, an overdeveloped superego, may also lead to antisocial behavior (Freud, 1960). Sexual and aggressive desires and wishes toward a parent may trigger extreme guilt and anxiety that cannot be managed by a weak ego but that can be alleviated only through actual punishment. In other words, the individual acts out his or her impulses in order to be punished.

James Gilligan (Gilligan, 2000), a psychiatrist who worked with male prison inmates for many years, postulates that many of the most heinous and seemingly incomprehensible crimes can be understood as symbolic representations of unconscious intolerable thoughts and desires that cannot be expressed in language but that emerge through actions. Often, he found, these intolerable thoughts had their roots in emotionally abusive early childhood relationships and revolved around feelings of inadequacy as a man—being weak, dependent, a "sissy"—and resultant feelings of shame. Gilligan notes that, when asked what triggered their violent crime, many prisoners report that their victim "dissed" them—disrespected them either overtly, indirectly, or symbolically. "Dissing" that taps into early childhood feelings of inadequacy and shame may evoke the expression of its opposite (reaction formation)—violence, overkill—to keep these intolerable feelings repressed. As we look at the childhoods of most violent and sexual offenders, Gilligan's conclusions appear to have some validity.

To analyze the case of Richard Ramirez, presented at the beginning of this chapter, here are some of the questions you would consider if you were Freud:

- How would you assess Ramirez's development in terms of the relative strength of the three structures of the personality (id, ego, and superego)?
- What ambivalent or unacceptable feelings and wishes might be repressed? Why?
- What defense mechanisms are apparent?
- How was the Oedipus Complex resolved? How might its resolution contribute to his violence?

Case Example: How Would the Psychodynamic Perspective Explain Richard Ramirez?

Baby Richard came into the world with the basic biological instincts of Eros (life and sex) and Thanatos (death and aggression). Freud would find the key to Richard in his first 6 years of life (infantile period). His early childhood reflects a lack of bonding with his mother because of her long work hours. His father was a "rageaholic" who probably elicited intense feelings of both fear and rage in Richard. However, these feelings would conflict with feelings of love for and dependence on a powerful father. Similarly, his mother could not or would not protect him, resulting in conflicted feelings of love and anger toward her also. His child's ego could not resolve these conflicting feelings or find cathartic release for his anger in socially acceptable ways. Consequently, the ego repressed his wishes for vengeance into the unconscious, where they emerged as fantasies of power and control displaced on others. Weak ego development blurred the lines between fantasy and reality; consequently, Richard spent increasing amounts of time in fantasy. During the phallic stage, Richard's desire for his mother conflicted with fear of his violent and erratic father, causing intense castration anxiety. To resolve this, he abandoned his desires and identified with his violent father. The resulting superego punished feelings of anger toward both Dad and Mom, and feelings of being less than a man (which were repressed). The repression was maintained through displacement (substitute for rage toward both Mom and Dad was displaced onto male and female strangers) and reaction formation (need for power and control to disguise feelings of inadequacy). Clearly, his sadism was extreme and perverted by the ascendance of Thanatos (externalized) over Eros.

LEARNING AND COGNITIVE THEORY

If aggression and violence are instinctual human drives, as the psychodynamic perspective postulates, why are there cultures and societies in which violence is virtually nonexistent? The answer, according to learning theory is that violent behavior, whether it is murder or rape, is learned.

Assumptions about Human Nature

Learning theorists assume that we come into this world a blank slate. Whatever we become is the result of learning. Deviant personality development is acquired through the same principles of learning as is healthy personality development.

Learning theorists do acknowledge a role for genetic and biological factors such as IQ and fearlessness, which limit one's ability to learn within genetically determined limits.

In a nutshell, to understand how monsters are created, learning theorists would look at the the monsters' learning history for answers while acknowledging certain biological and genetic limitations on their ability to learn.

Principles of Learning

According to learning theory, our personality is the sum total of our actions and reactions that are acquired through a combination of respondent conditioning, operant conditioning, and modeling/observational learning.

Respondent Conditioning. Through **respondent conditioning,** an association is established between a neutral stimulus and a physiological/emotional response. Responses may be emotionally negative, such as fear, anger, and/or anxiety, or emotionally positive, such as relaxation or sexual arousal (Skinner, 1953).

An unconditioned stimulus (US) naturally elicits an unconditioned response (UR). For example, when a baby is held and cuddled (US) by its mother, the baby naturally feels warm and safe (UR). For a baby, however, perfume is a neutral stimulus that does not naturally elicit good feelings. However, if Mom is always wearing perfume when she holds and cuddles the baby, the scent of her perfume becomes a conditioned stimulus (CS) that elicits good feelings even when Mom is not cuddling the baby. That is, the CS (perfume) alone will now elicit a conditioned response (CR) that closely resembles the original UR. Most of our emotional reactions to stimuli in our environment are learned through this process of respondent conditioning. For example, a sexually abused child becomes fearful and angry (CR) when the offending parent simply comes into the child's bedroom (CS). Further, the ability of the CS to elicit the CR may be generalized to other neutral stimuli that have characteristics similar to the CS. For example, if we have been attacked by a large dog (CS) in our neighborhood, we subsequently experience fear and anxiety (CR) when approached by *any* large dog (generalization).

Let's illustrate the process of **respondent conditioning** with an example that is germane to our study of the development of violent offenders. An adolescent boy experiences sexual arousal when he masturbates. This response is inherent—it does not need to be learned. Therefore, we have an unconditioned stimulus (US) that elicits an unconditioned response (UR):

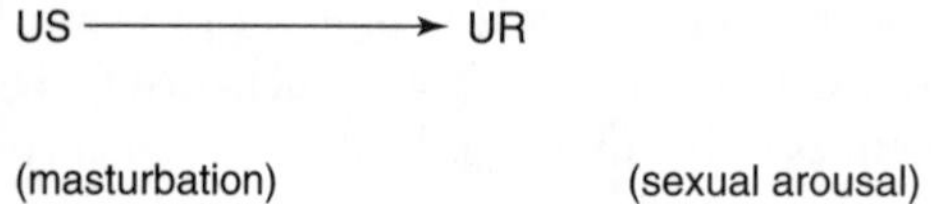

Violent video images do not, by themselves, cause sexual arousal. However, if the violent images are frequently present when the boy experiences arousal through masturbation, an association is made between the violent images (CS) and sexual arousal (US):

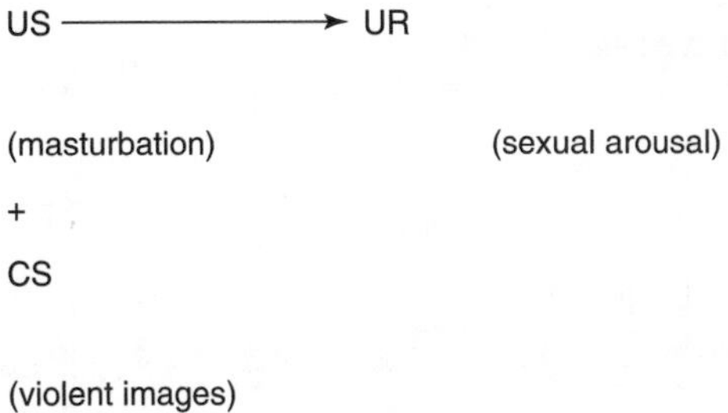

With repeated pairings of masturbation (US) and violent images (CS), the violent images alone will begin to elicit sexual arousal (CR) in the boy even when he does not masturbate (US):

CS - - - - - - - - → CR

(violent images) (sexual arousal)

When the conditioned stimulus and response (CS–CR) association has been established, characteristics of the conditioned stimulus (i.e., the sound of a woman screaming) may be generalized and also elicit the conditioned response of sexual arousal. As a result of respondent conditioning, a budding anger-excitation rapist (sadist) is born. Respondent conditioning is thought to be the principle responsible for the learning of paraphilias such as fetishism, sadism, and exhibitionism.

Operant Conditioning. Through **operant conditioning,** behaviors/actions are learned as a result of either external or internal consequences (Skinner, 1953). Positive consequences such as a compliment, food, money (external), or relief from anxiety, a sense of mastery (internal) increase the likelihood that we will repeat a behavior. Aversive consequences such as a spanking, disapproval (external), anxiety, or embarrassment (internal) decrease the likelihood that we will repeat a behavior. This basic operant conditioning formula is presented in Figure 4–1. To apply operant conditioning to understanding human behavior, we must examine the elements of this paradigm more closely—by itself it is overly simplistic.

Consequences are positively reinforcing when they increase the frequency of a particular behavior (Skinner, 1953). Such reinforcers as food, water, sex, and physical comfort are called primary reinforcers because we do not need to learn that they are reinforcing—they just are. Other reinforcers, such as money, compliments, and the

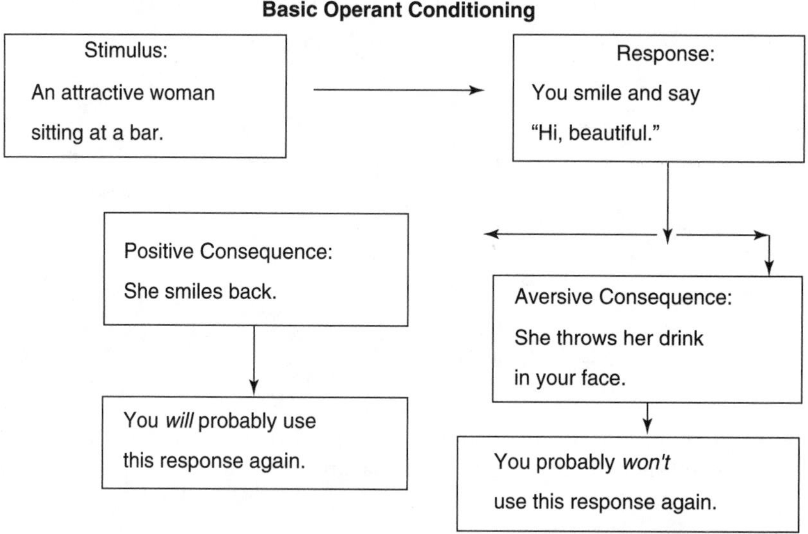

Figure 4–1 Basic Operant Conditioning

like, are called secondary reinforcers because we must learn to value them. Because of our different learning histories, what people find reinforcing is individualistic—"different strokes for different folks." For example, money may be very reinforcing to a stockbroker but may be less reinforcing to a nun. A child who is usually ignored/neglected by parents may find being yelled at reinforcing because he/she enjoys the attention. The only way to tell whether a consequence is a reinforcer is to look at whether the behavior continues as a result of the consequence.

Positive reinforcement is pretty straightforward—we emit a response, and if something good happens, we will do the same thing again. Another way of increasing the likelihood that a behavior will occur is through **negative reinforcement.** Negative reinforcement occurs when we engage in a behavior that removes an aversive or a painful stimulus. Whatever behavior we engage in to remove the aversive stimulus will be reinforced. For example, if a person feels socially anxious at a party (an aversive stimulus), then drinks a couple of beers (behavior) and the social anxiety goes away (negative reinforcement), the drinking behavior has been negatively reinforced and will more likely occur again in a similar situation. Some maladaptive behaviors are learned through direct positive reinforcement. The contract killer is positively reinforced with money (secondary reinforcer) for murder, and a gang member is positively reinforced for killing a rival gang member through the esteem of his friends (secondary reinforcer). However, most maladaptive behavior is learned through negative reinforcement. When a behavior such as taking drugs, killing, rape, or torture removes an aversive internal emotional state like tension, low self-esteem, or helplessness, the behavior is negatively reinforced. For example, the anger-retaliatory rapist finds that his anger toward women (or a particular woman) is temporarily relieved when he successfully attacks a stranger. The act of rape is negatively reinforced. Skinner (1953) acknowledged Freud's defense mechanisms as learned strategies acquired through negative reinforcement.

If we learn to engage in behaviors through positive and negative reinforcement, how are behaviors suppressed or eliminated? The answer is through punishment and extinction.

Punishment is a consequence that temporarily suppresses a behavior. That is, when a behavior is followed by an aversive consequence such as physical or emotional pain or the removal of something pleasurable (i.e., loss of money, withdrawal of affection, etc.) we will probably stop doing it for a while. However, harsh punishment has side effects; the punisher (i.e., parent, teacher), through respondent conditioning, comes to elicit negative emotions such as fear, anxiety, or anger in the recipient. Because of its temporary effect and accompanying side effects, Skinner (1953) viewed punishment as an ineffective and unpredictable learning tool.

Extinction eliminates a behavior by removing the positive consequences. For example, a parent may respond to a tantrum with attention to the child or by giving the child what the child wants (positive reinforcement). If these positive reinforcements are eliminated, the tantrums (behavior) will eventually stop; the behavior has been extinguished.

Respondent and operant conditioning can explain how stimuli elicit physiological and emotional reactions (respondent conditioning) and increase or decrease the likelihood that we will continue to engage in certain behaviors (operant conditioning). However, respondent and operant conditioning alone would limit human learning to chance association and trial and error. How we develop the wide repertoire of human behaviors is not adequately explained. This limitation is overcome with the addition of modeling to our learning repertoire.

Modeling. Bandura (1977) popularized the idea that we acquire most of our behavioral repertoire through observing the behaviors of others. That is, we can learn without actually performing a behavior that is reinforced. Behaviors learned through **modeling** may not always be acted out but may be stored in memory and performed only when an appropriate stimulus situation arises and we anticipate being rewarded for the behavior. We are more likely to act out what we have observed when our model is reinforced for their actions. Further, modeling is not only direct imitation but also an approximation of behaviors we observe in others. All of this requires **cognition:** attention, memory, and anticipation of reward. For example, a child raised by a parent who successfully uses violence to get others to do what he or she want's, is attending to this behavior and is storing it in memory. When the child is later confronted with a peer or sibling who defies him or her, the child is likely to anticipate that violence will solve the problem and therefore to respond violently. If the violent response is successful, it will probably be repeated in similar situations (operant conditioning).

Cognition and Learning

Although Bandura placed cognitive variables into the learning equation, the importance of cognitive processes to what and how we learn has gained full integration into learning theory in recent years. Cognitive processes such as what we attend to and how we interpret environmental and internal stimuli intercede between a stimulus and a response (Beck 1976; Dodge, Bates, and Pettit, 1990). The individual actively interprets stimuli and information; he or she does not just passively receive and encode stimuli and information:

Stimulus ⟶ Cognitive variables ⟶ Response

(attention, interpretation)

For example, a domestic batterer arrives home and dinner is not ready (stimulus). He attends to only the lack of dinner preparations (attentional focus) and not to his spouse's fatigued face. He interprets the lack of dinner preparation as disrespect and lack of concern for him (interpretation). Then he responds with anger and verbal abuse (response). Acquaintance-contact rapists often interpret a woman's "no" (stimulus) as game-playing that really means "yes" (interpretation) and proceed to force sex (response).

A cognitive habit of attentional focus and interpretation related to a particular domain or category such as authority figures, self, other people, women, men, and the like is called a **schema.** Schemas are learned through modeling and previous experiences and are responsible for our reacting consistently, either adaptively or maladaptively, to categories of stimuli. For example, a schema of other people as hostile and aggressive will lead to defensive or aggressive reactions even to neutral or positive overtures. Cognitive distortions and their underlying schemas related to victims and self have been well documented in sex offenders (Ward, 2000). For example, a preferential child molester's schema regarding children may be that children enjoy and want sex with adults. Consequently, any attention from a child is interpreted as an invitation to engage in sexual behavior. Resistance by the child may be interpreted as game playing to make this piece of evidence fit the offender's schema/theory about children's desires. Schemas develop in childhood (during the first 5 years) and are resistant to change—evidence and experiences that do not fit one's schema are often distorted/reinterpreted to be consistent with the schema (Gopnik and Meltzoff, 1997).

The development of schemas begins in early childhood as a child tries to explain and understand his or her interpersonal world through experiences with parents and caregivers. Schemas that are maladaptive in adulthood may have been adaptive in childhood in order to survive in an abusive or a neglectful environment (Ward, 2000). For example, for a child who is repeatedly sexually abused by a parent, attributing sexual and/or aggressive intent to others is realistic and adaptive; in adulthood, the same schema can lead to sexual offending.

Integration and Application

Violent, predatory offenders such as serial killers and rapists often report that fantasy plays a major role in their actions (Ressler, 1988). Learning theory would conceptualize fantasy as an acquired coping strategy/behavior that is learned and maintained through negative reinforcement. Fantasies of control and power decrease aversive internal stimuli such as anxiety, low self-esteem, and so on. The following list illustrates how this perspective might explain the acquisition of fantasy and killing as coping skills:

- Emotional, physical, sexual abuse in childhood results in low self-esteem (negative self-schema), and feelings of helplessness, anger, anxiety (aversive internal stimuli).
  - Parent is also modeling aggression and the domination and humiliation of others.
- Most children daydream and fantasize. In the case of abuse, these fantasies revolve around control and power to compensate for feelings of anxiety and helplessness.
  - The "blueprint" of a real man in Western cultures also emphasizes control and dominance (modeling).
- Fantasies (behavior) of control, power, and aggression provide temporary escape from or avoidance of negative feelings of helplessness and inferiority (negative reinforcement).
- Through repeated negative reinforcement, these fantasies become the child's primary coping skills in response to negative feelings precipitated by events such as rejection, loss, or failure.
- In preadolescence, sexual arousal and masturbation become associated through respondent conditioning with fantasies of control and power.
  - Exposure to violent pornography while masturbating or being sexually aroused may further respondently condition an association between sexual arousal and violence.
- The adolescent acts out fantasies on a nonthreatening victim such as an animal. This act temporarily reduces negative feelings (negative reinforcement) and is repeated.
  - Acting out temporarily enhances the vividness and power of the fantasy since real experiences can now be incorporated into the fantasy.
- The first murder or rape may be opportunistic or spontaneous, but it elicits strong sexual arousal because of the respondently conditioned association between sex and aggression.
  - It also temporarily reduces negative feelings (negative reinforcement).
- The experience is incorporated into and strengthens the fantasy (coping strategy). For a while, the fantasy still works as an escape from negative feelings

(negative reinforcement), but as it weakens, the killer needs to refuel it. Without the fantasy, the killer could not cope with such feelings as low self-esteem, loneliness, anxiety, and the like.

- The next kill becomes necessary to maintain the potency of the fantasy, the killer's primary or only coping skill for reducing negative internal feeling and mood states.

Respondent conditioning, operant conditioning, modeling, and cognition, in combination, are powerful tools for explaining the acquisition of adaptive, maladaptive, and antisocial responses.

Analyze the accompanying case of Richard Ramirez, using the social learning perspective. If you were a learning theorist, you might ask the following questions:

- What behaviors might Richard have learned through modeling?

Case Example: How Would the Learning Perspective Interpret the Career of Richard Ramirez?

This perspective would look at Richard's learning history. Young Richard had many unfortunate models of violent or antisocial behavior: his father Julian (violent), his brother Rubin (burglary), his cousin Mike (sexual sadism), and his sister's husband (voyeur). Rubin directly modeled burglary techniques for Richard, and Richard was positively reinforced (operant conditioning) for engaging in this behavior by what he stole and by the esteem of his brother. In addition, Julian's beatings and violent rages were probably very aversive to young Richard, and he escaped these negative feelings through fantasy and marijuana use (negative reinforcement). Parental neglect and violence, rejection by his peers because of his seizures, and molestation by his teacher may have provided a self-schema of inadequacy and a schema of others as hostile and rejecting. Environmental stimuli situations were interpreted through these schemata to the point that he adopted Satan (evil) as his savior.

In early adolescence, through the pictures and stories of Mike's sadistic adventures, he was respondently conditioned to associate violence and sexual arousal—the recipe for a sadist. This association was also respondently conditioned by masturbating to Mike's sadistic pictures.

Fantasies about sexual and violent scenarios, power, and control continued to be negatively reinforced by providing escape from loneliness, boredom, and negative feelings about himself. Later cocaine and PCP use were positively reinforced because of the feelings of power that they chemically provided.

At 18, Richard completed his first rape, which was positively reinforced by the feelings of power and control it elicited. And the pattern continued, maintained through positive and negative reinforcement.

- What behaviors were strengthened through positive or negative reinforcement (operant conditioning)?
- What emotional associations were learned through respondent conditioning?

Although learning theorists acknowledge a role for genetics in personality development, they do not focus on the particulars of genetic contributions to personality development. The trait/dispositional theorists do.

TRAIT/DISPOSITIONAL THEORY

The belief that genetic factors predispose us to the development of certain personality traits has a long history, especially as it relates to criminality and violence. In 1876, Lombraso put forth the proposition, based on his study of Italian prisoners, that criminals were born, not made (Martin et al., 1990). Dugdale documented the violent and criminal history of the infamous Jukes family to demonstrate the heritability of these traits. These early proponents were looking at genetics and criminality at a macro level—that is, the heritability of criminal personality in general. Contemporary trait theorists, however, postulate that there is no such thing as a genetic destiny for crime or violence—there is no criminal or violent personality gene.

Assumptions

Trait theorists seek to discover what personality traits or dispositions have a strong genetic component. According to trait theory, we do not come into the world as a blank slate but are genetically prewired toward certain dispositions or characteristics. These dispositions or characteristics interact with the environment to produce personality and adaptive or maladaptive behavior. To grasp this concept, think of how different breeds of dogs have different temperaments. For example, I have two dogs—Sami, a West Highland Terrier, who came into the world feisty, territorial, and independent, whereas Scout, a Labrador Retriever, came into the world just lookin' for love and a ball to retrieve. It would be harder, but not impossible, to turn Scout into a guard dog than Sami because of the difference in their genetic temperaments/dispositions.

Temperament refers to a consistent way of responding to the environment, energy level, emotionality, ability to self-regulate, risk taking, and sociability. These temperament characteristics are observed in infancy and early childhood, and they have been found to have strong genetic roots (Kagan et al., 1994; Rothbart and Ahadi, 1994; Thomas and Chess, 1977).

Although temperament may have its roots in genetics, how temperament is expressed behaviorally not only is strongly influenced by environment (particularly parent-child interactions) but also may produce or evoke a certain type of environment. That is, a "difficult" child may evoke different reactions from parents than an "easy" child, creating different parent-child relationships and family environments that, in turn, may result in different behavioral outcomes. There are indications that a child's temperamental style plays a significant role in the development of social consciousness and is affected either positively or negatively by parenting style (Fowles and Kochanska, 2000). Hans Eysenck will be our "poster boy" to illustrate the trait/dispositional perspective.

Highlight 4-2
How Extroverted Are You?

Directions: For each item (do not skip any), circle the alternative that *best* reflects your preferences or feelings.

1. a. I get bored doing the same things every day.
   b. I like the familiarity of routines.
2. a. People who hang glide (bungee jump) must have a death wish.
   b. I would like to try hang gliding or bungee jumping.
3. a. I prefer to live in an area that is safe and secure.
   b. I prefer to live in an area that is exciting, even a little dangerous.
4. a. I enjoy people who are unpredictable, even a little unstable.
   b. I enjoy people who are sensible and mature.
5. a. I like art that is bold and shocking.
   b. I like art that is peaceful and serene.
6. a. I hate to be bored.
   b. I hate to be frightened.
7. a. At the end of a tiring day, I prefer to watch TV or read, and relax.
   b. At the end of a tiring day, I prefer to go out to a club/party with friends.
8. a. I want a job that is exciting and full of variety even if it is insecure.
   b. I want a job that is secure and where I can make steady progress.
9. a. For vacation, I like someplace restful like the mountains or beach.
   b. For vacation, I like big cities where there is lots to do and plenty of excitement.
10. a. I like to hang out with sensible people.
    b. I avoid people who are dull.
11. a. I get bored easily.
    b. I can find something interesting in almost any situation.
12. a. I don't mind sitting in a waiting room for an appointment.
    b. I like walking along crowded, noisy streets.

Scoring: Give yourself 1 point for each answer that matches the following: 1a, 2b, 3b, 4a, 5a, 6a, 7b, 8a, 9b, 10b, 11a, 12b. Add up your points. A score closer to 12 indicates a more extroverted temperament. Scale is for purpose of illustration only.

Eysenck's Trait Theory

According to Eysenck, personality traits are the result of inherited differences in the central and autonomic nervous systems (Eysenck, 1994) that predispose an individual's ability to be socialized by his or her environment. Eysenck identified three high heritibility traits or bipolar dimensions of personality: extroversion/introversion (E), neuroticism/stability (N), and psychoticism/superego function (P), and their biological correlates (see Figure 4-2). Each of these types is an independent bipolar dimension of normal personality. That is, an individual may be high on E (extroverted), low on N (stable), and moderate on P. The distribution of the population on each of these bipolar dimensions follows the normal bell curve; most people fall in the middle ranges, with fewer at the extremes of each dimension.

Extroversion/Introversion (E). The **extroversion-introversion** dimension of personality has been the most extensively researched and has a high heritability factor. The extroversion end of the continuum is characterized by thrill seeking, sociability, and impulsiveness, whereas introverts are unsociable, careful, and controlled. Although these characteristics are the outward manifestation of the two ends of this dimension, the real difference lies in the central nervous system.

At the juncture of the spinal cord and the brain is the reticular activating system (RAS), which regulates the amount of stimuli reaching the cerebral cortex. Extroverts are genetically wired to inhibit stimuli to the cerebral cortex, resulting in low resting levels of **cortical arousal** (Eysenck, 1994). Introverts, on the other hand, are genetically wired to have high resting levels of cortical arousal. In other words, when exposed to an unstimulating environment (i.e., watching grass grow), the extrovert will have very low levels of cortical activity and probably fall asleep. However, the introvert will still have high levels of cortical activity and remain alert.

An optimal level of cortical arousal is moderate—we feel more comfortable when we are not drowsy or bored (low cortical arousal) or not overstimulated (high

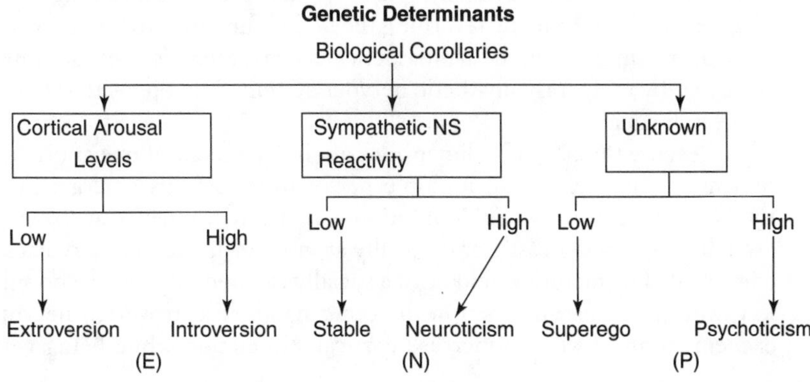

Figure 4–2 Eysenck's Model

cortical arousal). Therefore, extroverts, with their habitual low level of cortical arousal, will seek stimulating environments and experiences that raise cortical arousal to an optimal (moderate) level. They like parties with lots of people and loud music, and they seek out activities that increase arousal such as hang gliding, gambling, or car racing. Introverts, because of their habitual high levels of cortical arousal, would find high stimulation environments and activities aversive. Instead, they seek out soothing environments (such as sitting by a fire reading) that reduce cortical arousal to an optimal (moderate) level. Several studies have found that violent offenders are extroverted, whereas sex offenders, particulary child molesters, are introverts (Eysenck and Gudjonsson, 1989; Gudjonsson and Sigurdsson, 2002).

Twin data, specifically on sensation-seeking (extreme extrovertion), indicates that for the general population, approximately 80 percent of the stable variance related to this trait is genetic (Lykken, 1995). Researchers have found that low physiological arousal at age 3 predicts aggressiveness at age 11 (Raine, Venables, and Mednick, 1997); that adolescents with low arousal are also more aggressive ten years later (Raine, Venables, and Williams, 1990); and that those diagnosed with antisocial personality disorder and incarcerated psychopaths also show lower than average autonomic arousal patterns (Herpertz, Werth, Lukas, Qunaibi, Schuerkens, Kunert, Freese, Flesch, Mueller-Isberner, Osterheider, and Sass, 2001; Raine et al., 2000).

Neuroticism/Stability (N). The **neuroticism/stability** dimension reflects emotional reactivity and has a strong hereditary component. Individuals high on neuroticism are very emotionally reactive and have difficulty returning to a normal or moderate emotional state once they are aroused (Eysenck, 1994). The layman might describe these individuals as emotional, excitable, or high-strung. In contrast, individuals on the stable end of the continuum do not react with emotional excitability to stressful circumstances and may be thought of as individuals who "roll with the punches."

The **neuroticism/stability** dimension is associated with the activation of the **sympathetic nervous system,** which stimulates heart rate, blood flow, and adrenaline in response to stressful events (fight or flight). The parasympathetic nervous system counteracts this activity by returning the bodily functions to homeostasis. For the high N (neurotic) individual, the sympathetic nervous system is easily activated and not well regulated by the parasympathetic nervous system. The opposite is true for the highly stable individual.

Because the E and N dimensions are independent of one another, when the two dimensions are combined, multiple personality portraits emerge. For example, the introverted neurotic would find stimuli-rich environments aversive (cortical overarousal) while being easily emotionally aroused (sympathetic nervous system is easily triggered). The picture would be of a socially isolated individual who suffers from anxiety, worry, and fearfulness. On the other hand, an extroverted neurotic would seek excitement and thrills to increase cortical stimulation while being very emotionally reactive—easily angered, upset, can't calm down. This combination has been associated with criminality and delinquency (Eysenck, 1964). These examples are based on individuals at the extremes of both dimensions; most people fall in the middle range for each.

Psychoticism/superego (P). Eysenck (1976) added the **psychoticism/superego** dimension later in his career, and it has not been as thoroughly researched as the other two. Unlike the outcome for the other two dimensions, Eysenck was unable to discover a biological link to the P dimension. The psychoticism end of this dimension is characterized by an individual who is egocentric, nonconforming, cold, and aggressive. At the other end (superego), individuals are described as empathetic, cooperative, tender-minded, and conforming.

Lykken has identified additional genetic temperament traits that may increase a child's vulnerability to later violent behavior. High psychoticism encompasses the traits of fearlessness (versus harm avoidance) and aggressiveness, identified by Lykken (1995) as having strong genetic roots and being associated with psychopathy, criminality, and violence.

A healthy portion of how parents socialize children depends on children's desires to avoid the emotional or physical pain associated with parental disapproval, restrictions, or spanking. Children who are fearless are not made anxious by the anticipation of punishment and consequently are hard to socialize using traditional punishment-based methods of discipline. They are also more likely to engage in high-risk behavior since they do not fear the consequences. In an analysis of the harm-avoidance (versus fearlessness) scores of MZ twins raised together and apart and tested over time, Lykken (1995) demonstrated that approximately two-thirds of the stable (over time) variance on this trait can be attributed to genetic factors.

Aggressiveness is the tendency to respond to people and situations with physical or verbal attacks. This tendency has been found in a number of studies to be quite stable from childhood to adulthood (Eron and Huesmann, 1990; Farrington, 1991). In his analysis of the Minnesota Twin Study data, Lykken concluded that "about 80% of the stable components of aggressiveness is genetically determined" (1995: 103). Other reviews of twin studies of aggressiveness (Plomin, Nitz, and Rowe, 1989) have concluded that although there is a genetic contribution to aggressiveness, it is much weaker than Lykken's analysis found.

Integration and Application

How these temperament characteristics are expressed in action depends on the environment. An individual with a high P, high N, high E pattern may be channeled by the environment either toward a career as a hockey player or commodities trader or toward a career as a thrill-seeking conartist or thrill killer. Genes load the gun, but the environment points the gun and pulls the trigger.

Extremes on the E, N, or P dimensions would also predict different types of killers or rapists. Let's assume, for purposes of illustration, that all would be relatively high on P (cold, aggressive, fearless, unempathetic) and moderately high on N. However, high P and N in combination with extraversion would yield a possibly charming/manipulative killer who enjoys the thrill of the chase (a Ted Bundy) and taunting the police with clues. A high P and N introvert, on the other hand, would predict a loner who takes few risks.

Trait/dispositional theory provides some intriguing insights into the role of genetic factors in personality development (how the gun is loaded) but depends on learning theory to explain individual differences in how these traits are manifested as behavior. Genetic predispositions affect learning through their impact on conditionability, responsiveness to stimuli, and emotional reactivity.

If you were a trait/dispositional theorist, here are some questions you would address in looking at the case of Richard Ramirez:

- What trait/disposition are evident in Richard's first-degree relatives (parents, siblings)?
- Where would you place Richard on each of Eysenck's dimensions (E, N, or P)?

Case Example: What Contributions Could the Trait-Dispositional Perspective Make to Understanding Richard Ramirez?

According to this perspective, Richard came into this world with genetically based predispositions that might make him more vulnerable (but certainly not destined) to seeking the experiences that he did. Eysenck (1964) found that criminals were more often high on E and N than noncriminals. Entering people's houses (burglary), which Richard and Rubin did regularly, could be seen as thrill seeking (E), and the use of cocaine and PCP (stimulants) would fit with the need to increase arousal. Richard's father, Julian, certainly exhibited high emotional reactivity (N), and he contributed 50 percent of Richard's genes. Finally, Richard (like his brother Rubin) would certainly fall on the high P end of the psychoticism dimension (cold, hostile, psychopathic)—he certainly wouldn't be described as empathetic, altruistic, and conforming (low P). If Richard's parents had excellent parenting skills (which they clearly did not), he could have been socialized onto a more prosocial path. However, his learning history brought out the most antisocial aspects of his genetic vulnerabilities.

So Which Theory Is Right?

The theories presented in this chapter, like the blind men and the elephant, all have different "takes" on how the wide variety of violent and sexual predators became who they are. However, it may be possible to integrate them so that an outline of the elephant emerges.

None of the theoretical perspectives would disagree with the proposition that genetic predispositions for temperament exist and are expressed biologically (dispositional/trait theory). Furthermore, one cannot discount the effects of early childhood experiences with primary caregivers (psychodynamic) as profoundly affecting later behavior, the ability to bond, and attitudes toward others and self. Learning-cognitive theorists would conceptualize these early relationships as learning experiences through which we acquire our first emotional responses (respondent conditioning), behavioral repertoire for coping and interacting with others (operant conditioning and modeling), and patterns of interpreting stimuli (schemas). Through stimulus generalization, environmental stimuli later in life may elicit responses learned in childhood. Both psychodynamic theorists and learning-cognitive theorists agree that we try to reduce subjective aversive feelings such as anxiety and tension and that we strive for pleasure (reinforcement). The two theoretical perspectives differ only in how they describe this process. Freud describes mostly unconscious hypothetical personality structures in conflict (id, ego, superego) and dynamics (defense mechanisms), whereas learning-cognitive theorists describe these as habitual ways of responding acquired through learning principles. Whereas psychodynamic theorists describe the unconscious as a repository of repressed wishes and desires, learning-cognitive theorists describe lack of consciousness as lack of awareness of the contingencies (connections) of reinforcement and learned associations between stimuli, responses, and consequences.

Discussion Questions and Activities

1. Sex and aggression are the basic instincts that motivate all behavior, according to Freud. Identify examples of how these are expressed in socially acceptable (but disguised) ways in everyday life.

2. Identify what personality characteristics might emerge from each of the following combinations: (a) High ego strength and a strong superego, (b) low ego strength and a strong superego, (c) low ego strength and a weak superego, and (d) high ego strength and a weak superego. Pick case examples from Chapters 2 or 3 to illustrate each combination.

3. Think of examples from your own life in which you have used the following defense mechanisms: isolation, reaction formation, projection, and displacement.

4. What is the difference between a positive and a negative reinforcer? What is the difference between negative reinforcement and punishment? Illustrate each with examples of how violent or sexual offending could be learned.
5. Using respondent and operant conditioning principles, and modeling, discuss the pros and cons of the following proposition: We would have fewer violent offenders if parents would spank their children more—"spare the rod and spoil the child."
6. Identify examples from your own life that illustrate the following: respondent conditioning, modeling, positive reinforcement, and negative reinforcement.
7. Identify examples of psychopathic or violent characters from TV, movies, or literature that exemplify each of the following temperaments: extroversion, introversion, neuroticism, stability, and psychoticism.
8. Create a hypothetical example of the development of one of the types of serial rapists (from Chapter 2) or a hedonistic serial killer (from Chapter 3), integrating the trait and learning perspectives.
9. Find a case of a violent offender from the Internet, and analyze how the person developed from either the psychoanalytic or the social learning–cognitive perspective. Use as many concepts from these perspectives as you can.

Key Terms

Attachment Theory
Cortical arousal
Defense mechanisms
Ego
Extroversion/introversion
Id
Modeling
Negative reinforcement
Neuroticism/stability
Oedipus complex
Operant conditioning
Primary process thinking
Psychic determinism
Psychoticism/superego
Repression
Respondent conditioning
Schema
Secondary process thinking
Superego
Sympathetic nervous system
Temperament

References

Bandura, A. 1977. *Social Learning Theory.* Englewood Cliffs, N. J.: Prentice Hall.
Beck, A. 1976. *Cognitive Therapy and the Emotional Disorders.* New York: International Universities Press.
Carlo, P. 1996. *The Night Stalker.* New York: Kensington Publishers.

Dodge, K. A., J. E. Bates, and G. S. Pettit. 1990. "Mechanisms in the Cycle of Violence." *Science 250:* 1678–1683.

Eron, L., and L. Huesmann. 1990. "The stability of aggressive behavior even into the third generation." In M. Lewis and S. Miller (Eds.), *Handbook of Developmental Psychopathology,* pp. 147–156. New York: Plenum.

Eysenck, H. 1964. *Crime and Personality.* Boston, Mass.: Houghton Mifflin.

Eysenck, H. 1994. "Personality: Biological foundations." In P. Version (Ed.), *The Neuropsychology of Individual Differences,* pp. 151–207. San Diego, Calif.: Academic Press.

Eysenck, H. 1997. "Personality and experimental psychology: The unification of psychology and the possibility of a paradigm." *Journal of Personality and Social Psychology 73:* 1224–1237.

Eysenck, H. and S. Eysenck. 1976. *Psychoticism as a Dimension of Personality.* London: Hodder & Stoughton.

Eysenck, H. and G. Gudjonsson. 1989. *The Causes and Cures of Criminality.* New York: Plenum Press.

Farrington, D. P. 1991. "Childhood aggression and adult violence: Early precursors and later-life outcomes." In D. J. Pepler and F. H. Rubin (Eds.), *The Development and Treatment of Childhood Aggression,* pp. 5–29. Hillside, N.J.: Lawrence Erlbaum Associates.

Feist, J. and G. Feist. 2002. *Theories of Personality* (5th ed.). New York: McGraw Hill.

Fowles, D., and G. Kochanska. 2000. "Temperament as a Moderator of pathways to conscience in children: The contribution of electrodermal activity." *Psychophysiology 37:* 788–795.

Freud, S. 1946. *The Ego and the Mechanisms of Defense:* New York: International Universities Press.

Freud, S. 1949. *New Introductory Lectures on Psychoanalysis.* London: Hogarth Press.

Freud, S. 1959. *Beyond the Pleasure Principle.* New York: Bantam Books.

Freud, S. 1960. *The Ego and the Id.* New York: W. W. Norton and Co.

Freud, S. 1961. *The Infantile Genital Organization: An Interpolation into the Theory of Sexuality.* In *Standard Edition,* Vol. 19.

Freud, S. 1964. *New Introductory Lectures on Psychoanalysis.* In *Standard Edition,* Vol. 22.

Gilligan, J. 2000. *Violence: Reflections on Our Deadliest Epidemic.* London: Jessica Kingsley Publishers.

Gopnik, A. and Meltzoff, A. 1997. *Words, Thoughts and Theories,* Cambridge, Mass.: MIT Press.

Gudjonsson, G. and J. Sigurdsson. 2002. "Differences and similarities between Violent Offenders and Sex Offenders." *Child abuse and Neglect 24*(3): 363–372.

Herpertz, S., U. Werth, G. Lukas, M. Qunaibi, A. Schuerkens, H. Kunert, R. Freese, M. Flesch, R. Mueller-Isberner, M. Osterheider, and H. Sass. 2001. "Emotion in criminal offenders with psychopathy and borderline personality disorder." *Archives of General Psychology 58:* 737–745.

Hickey, E. 1997. *Serial Murderers and Their Victims.* Belmont, Calif.: Wadsworth.

Kagan, J., N. Snidman, D. Arcus, and J. Reznick. 1994. *Galen's Prophecy: Temperament in Human Nature.* New York: Basic Books.

Lykken, D. T. 1995. *The Antisocial Personalities.* Hillsdale, N.J.: Lawrence Erlbaum Associates.

Martin, R., R. S. Mutchnick, and W. T. Austin. 1990. *Criminological Thought.* New York: Macmillan.

Plomin, R., K. Nitz, and D. Rowe. 1989. "Behavioral genetics and aggressive behavior in childhood." In M. Lewis and S. Miller (Eds.), *Handbook of Developmental Psychopathology,* pp. 119–133. New York: Plenum.

Raine, A., T. Lencz, S. Bihrle, L. LaCasse, and P. Colletti, 2000. "Reduced prefrontal gray matter volume and reduced autonomic activity in antisocial personality disorder." *Archives of General Psychiatry 57:* 119–127.

Raine, A., P. Venables, and S. A. Mednick. 1997. "Low resting heart rate at age 3 years predisposes to aggression at age 11: Findings from the Mauritus Joint Child Health Project. *Journal of the American Academy of Child and Adolescent Psychiatry 36:* 1457–1464.

Raine, A. P. Venables, and M. Williams, 1990. "Relationships between central and autonomic measures of arousal at age 15 years and criminality at age 24 years. *Archives of General Psychiatry 47:* 1003–1007.

Ressler, 1988. *Sexual homicide: Patterns and motives.* Lexington, Mass.: Lexington Books.

Rothbart, M. K. and S. A. Ahadi. 1994. "Temperament and the development of personality." *Journal of Abnormal Psychology 103*(1): 55–66.

Skinner, B. F. 1953. *Science and Human Behavior.* New York: Macmillian.

Thomas, A. & S. Chess. 1977. *Temperament and Development.* New York: Brunner-Magel.

Ward, T. 2000. "Sexual offender's cognitive disortions as implicit theories." *Aggression and Violent Behavior 5* (5): 491–507.

Ward, T., S. Hudson, & W. Marshall. 1996. "Attachment style in sex offenders: A preliminary study." *Journal of Sex Research 33:* 17–26.

CHAPTER 5

HOW DO SOCIAL SCIENTISTS FIND ANSWERS?

LEARNING OBJECTIVES

After studying this chapter, you will

- Learn to think critically about social science research
- Be able to evaluate the internal and external validity of a research study
- Know the three basic research methods/strategies that social scientists use to answer questions about the causes of maladaptive human behavior
- Understand the strength and limitations of each of the three research methods
- Be able to apply what you have learned about evaluating research studies to those reported in the literature or the popular media

INTRODUCTION

How do you know what you know about what makes people tick—either pathologically or adaptively? Two common, but unreliable, ways of knowing are by relying on authority or relying on casual observations.

We often rely on pronouncements from **authority** figures to answer such questions as Does the death penalty deter murder? or Do broken homes lead to school failure and criminality? These pronouncements usually begin with "experts say" or "researchers have found." However, historically, so-called experts have said that women have smaller brains and consequently less intelligence than men and made other spurious pronouncements that have later been debunked. Another way of knowing is to rely on casual observations—our own or those of others. I call this drawing conclusions by anecdote. You have probably observed or participated in debates that rely on this method: "I have a friend who . . ." to which the reply is "I know of a case where . . ." —the battle of the anecdotes! Casual, unsystematic observations are limited in value by the confines of our own or others' experiences and biases. The methods of social science research provide a more reliable way, based on systematic observations, to answer questions and form conclusions.

Psychologists, sociologists, and criminologists are all interested in understanding what factors lead to and maintain a life of violence and in finding interventions to reduce or eliminate violent behavior. Consequently, they apply the methods of science to try and find answers. An understanding of these methods will prepare you to study the research into factors that contribute to the development of violent, antisocial behavior and to understand the efficacy of potential treatments. As you study these issues, you may go to the research literature to find answers to such questions as these: Does media violence cause violent behavior? Does abuse in childhood contribute to later violence? Is violence the result of damaged brains? Does chemical castration stop sexual predators? Also you may read in newspapers, or hear commentators and politicians on TV often referring to research to support their conclusions about the causes of crime. Therefore, it is important that you develop an understanding of the strengths and limitations of the research methods employed by social scientists.

Although judgments and conclusions based on empirical research are vastly superior to those based on authoritative pronouncements or casual observation, you should not passively accept a researcher's results or conclusions. Empirical studies can be flawed in their methodology, or the research strategy/method employed may be inappropriate for answering a particular question. Students are often tempted (and frequently give in to the temptation) to skip the methods section when reading a research article, and they simply read and accept the researcher's conclusions. However, not all conclusions are valid, and the devil is in the details! In this chapter, we hope to acquaint you with the basic elements of research and the primary methods that social scientists employ to test hypotheses. Further, we want to give you the tools to evaluate and identify potential problems with the methods employed in an empirical study so that you can critically evaluate the validity of any conclusions. Being an active, probing, analytical consumer of research is so much more interesting than being a passive receptacle of others' conclusions!

It is important to remember that no single research design or study can, by itself, provide definitive answers to such complex questions as what causes predatory violence. First, multiple biological and environmental factors are implicated in causing such multifaceted behavior. No single study can account for all possible contributing factors. Second, ethical and practical considerations limit what we can do in the name of scientific study. For example, if we thought that we knew what factors produced a "monster" (i.e., on the basis of theory), ethical and moral considerations would prevent us from taking two identical twins at birth and exposing one to these factors and shielding the other to try and produce one violent predator and one prosocial adult. Consequently, researchers must find ways to study these questions indirectly or through approximations. To do this, they design and conduct empirical studies in both the natural world and the laboratory, using a variety of research strategies or methods.

It is only through the convergence of findings from many studies that our understanding of violence can advance.

BASIC ELEMENTS OF RESEARCH

Social science researchers are people who are curious—they have lots of questions about why people act, think, and feel the way they do. To answer these types of questions, they design and carry out empirical studies that include the following basic elements:

- Observations
- A hypothesis (prediction to be tested)
- Independent variables (predicted causes)
- Dependent variables (predicted effects)
- A sample (representing the group of interest)

Social scientists begin with observations related to a question they want to answer. These may come from observing people in a clinic, prisons, the classroom, institutions, the coffee shop, and so on, and/or from reading about other scientists' observations. From all of these pieces of information, they try to find patterns. Identifying patterns from varied pieces of information is called **inductive reasoning.** Sherlock Holmes was a great inductive thinker, finding patterns in seemingly disparate clues. For example, over the past few years, I have been reading newspaper and magazine articles about children who open fire on their schoolmates. From these observations, through inductive reasoning, I believe that I see a pattern of peer rejection in these children's lives and then develop a hypothesis: peer rejection increases aggressive behaviors in adolescent boys. Hypotheses may also come through deductive reasoning. That is, we may deduce a specific hypothesis from a broader theory. For example, from Freud's theory of repression and displacement, I may hypothesize that hostile impulses toward powerful, rejecting peers will be expressed and displaced as aggression on weaker peers.

A hypothesis is a prediction or an educated guess about what we expect to find about the nature of the relationship between variables. In the preceding example, we are hypothesizing a *causal* relationship—peer rejection *causes* aggression. The variable that we predict will influence the aggression is the **independent variable** (peer

Self-Check 5-1

If we turn our hypothesis around—aggressive behavior increases peer rejection in adolescent boys—the dependent variable is _______, and the independent variable is _______.

Answer: peer rejection; aggressive behavior.

rejection). The variable that we think will be influenced and that we measure is the **dependent variable** (aggressive behaviors). To summarize, in a hypothesis the independent variable is expected to influence or predict the dependent variable.

Our hypothesis also specifies that the causal relationship between peer rejection and aggressive behaviors occurs in adolescent boys. Therefore, the **population** that we are interested in is adolescent boys. Since we cannot test all adolescent boys, we will test a smaller group of adolescent boys. This smaller, representative group is our **sample.**

Hypothesis

Once a social scientist has made observations and identified a question or problem to explore, the next step is to formulate a hypothesis. A hypothesis may be causal, as in the preceding example, or noncausal.

A causal hypothesis predicts a cause (independent variable)–effect (dependent variable) relationship. The independent variable (IV) is manipulated by the experimenter to discover whether or how it affects the dependent variable (DV). Examples of causal hypotheses are the following:

- Chemical castration (IV) of convicted rapists will eliminate sexual assaults.
- Exposure to violent video games (IV) increases physical aggression (DV) in children.

A hypothesis may also be noncausal. That is, rather than predicting a cause-effect relationship, a hypothesis may only predict an association between variables (not inferring that one causes the other) or that a variable is more likely to occur in one group compared with another group—a descriptive-comparative hypothesis (Meltzoff, 1998). Examples of noncausal hypotheses are as follows:

- Lower socioeconomic status is related to higher rates of delinquency (association).
- Preschool boys are more aggressive then preschool girls (descriptive-comparative).

It is important to understand the nature of the hypothesis because the *hypothesis should guide the design of the research study.* If researchers hypothesize a causal relation-

Self-Check 5-2

For each of the following hypotheses, identify whether they are causal (C), predict an association (A), or are descriptive-comparative (D):

- Higher testosterone levels are related to greater aggression.
- Rapists read more violent pornography than do nonrapists.
- Administration of drug X, which increases serotonin, will reduce violent outbursts.

Answers: A, D, C.

ship but use a method that can only demonstrate an association, they are not really testing their causal hypothesis, and their conclusion may be erroneous.

Independent Variables

In research into the etiology of violent offenders, the independent variable (IV) can be biological, psychological, or environmental. For example, we may hypothesize that one of the following independent variables (IV) influences (causal) or predicts (non-causal) aggression (DV):

- High levels of testosterone (biological)
- Low levels of self-esteem (psychological)
- Deviant peer group (environmental)

When researchers test the effectiveness of "cures" for violent behavior, the IV will be a type of treatment or punishment such as a drug, type of therapy, or prison time.

In a true experiment, researchers manipulate the independent variable. That is, they chemically castrate one group of rapists (experimental group) but not another group (control group), or they artificially manipulate participants' levels of self-esteem (i.e., by providing fake test results). When the IV is manipulated by the researcher, it is possible to infer a cause-effect relationship between the IV and the DV. In other types of empirical studies, the IV may be a preexisting or **static variable**—something that participants bring with them such as gender, socioeconomic status, a genetic or biological variable, or personality characteristic. When the IV is a static variable, we cannot infer that the IV causes the changes in the dependent variable, but we can only conclude that they are related.

In an empirical study, the IV must be operationally defined. That is, the researcher must identify what he or she means by levels of self-esteem, a drug, and the like. For example, in our original hypothesis that peer rejection (IV) increases aggressive behavior, how would we operationally define peer rejection? Do we mean that a child is simply ignored by peers or that the peers are actively teased or verbally harassed? It is important to know how a researcher has operationally defined the IV so that we can evaluate how well it represents the phenomenon of interest. For example, if a researcher predicted that strong parental values (IV) reduce delinquency in offspring, would you accept frequency of church attendance by parents as an operational definition of the IV (parental values)? Do you think that church attendance is a good representation of the phenomenon of parental values?

In an empirical study, we want to be sure that any changes in, or differences between, our participants are due only to the effects of the independent variable. This caution means that we want to hold all other possible variables constant so that if we find a change in the DV or a difference between groups on the DV, we can be confident that these changes or differences are due to the influence of the independent variable (IV) alone. Uncontrolled variables that can affect the outcome of a study are called **extraneous variables** or **confounds.** For example, let's say we find that boys who lack a father in the home (IV) are more likely than boys who have a father at home to engage in delinquent behavior (DV). However, in our sample, the boys who lack a father are also poorer than the boys who have a father at home; oops, we have more than one independent variable at work. Consequently, we do not know whether higher rates of delinquency (DV) are related to the lack of a father (IV) or to poverty (a confound). When a study does not control for extraneous variables (confounds), it is said to lack internal validity, which is discussed in more detail in the next section.

Dependent Variables

The dependent variable (DV) is the behavior, attitude, emotion, or other phenomenon that we predict will be affected or predicted by the independent variable. To know whether the IV had an effect, we must *operationally define the dependent variable* and find

Self-Check 5-3

Fill in or circle the correct answer to items 1–4 for this hypothesis: a researcher hypothesized that serial killers would have a higher rate of brain injury than nonviolent offenders.

1. The independent variable is ______.
2. The independent variable is a (static, manipulated) variable.
3. Therefore, we (can, cannot) infer a cause-effect relationship.
4. The researcher did not control for a history of physical abuse that may be related to violence and/or head injury. This is an example of ______.

Key: 1—head injury; 2—static; 3—cannot; 4—an extraneous variable (confound).

a way to *measure it*. If we hypothesize that a treatment (IV) will decrease aggression (DV), we must operationally define what we mean by aggression. Are we including verbal aggression (i.e., threats, shouting, etc.) as well as physical aggression (assault) in our definition? If we define aggression as assault, we must devise a way to validly measure it. Methods that are typically used to measure dependent variables in research studies include self-report, documentary evidence such as arrests or referrals, observer reports, and psychological tests.

To adequately test a hypothesis, the measure of the dependent variable must be **reliable** (consistently accurate) and **valid** (measures what it is supposed to measure). If a psychological test has been assessed for reliability, it will be noted in the research report. When using observer ratings, **interrater reliability** is established by assessing how consistently observers agree on their ratings of the same behavior. Do they independently agree that the observed behavior is aggressive? A measure that has low reliability is as useless as a bathroom scale that tells you at 10:00 A.M. that you weigh 140 pounds, at 10:30 A.M. that you weigh 115 pounds, and so on—it is useless! To be useful, the **validity** of a measure must also have been established—that is, does it measure what it is supposed to measure (aggressiveness) and not actually measure something else (i.e., attitudes)? A measure may be reliable, but not valid, for a particular purpose—a bathroom scale, no matter how reliable, is not a valid measure of aggression!

Sample

Once we have developed a hypothesis, operationally defined our independent and dependent variables, and identified reliable and valid measures for our dependent variable, we need subjects/participants. The characteristics of the population in which we are interested dictate the characteristics of the sample we select. If we are testing a treatment for child molesters, we want a sample selected from a population of child molesters. We also want to be able to generalize the results; we want our results to apply to molesters beyond our sample. Ideally, to accomplish this task, researchers randomly select participants from the population of interest so that there is no systematic bias. Practically, this process is not always possible, and other methods may be used to create a sample. Researchers often use a convenience sample—subjects that are available (i.e., child molesters jailed in a particular facility). Less desirable would be to use a sample of participants who are referred, for example, by prison officials (who may refer on the basis of their own biases), or participants who volunteer. In our example, child molesters who volunteer for treatment are probably different in some systematic way (i.e., more motivated to change) than those who do not volunteer. Using referrals or volunteers to make up a sample may not be a problem as long as the researcher is careful to conclude that the results apply only to a population of referred or volunteer participants. Systematic bias may also occur when there is significant participant attrition (people dropping out) in a sample during a study.

Internal and External Validity

To be a conscientious consumer of research, you need to be alert to threats to the internal validity of a study (see Table 5-1). **Internal validity** refers to the degree to which the results or outcome of a study depend on the independent variable alone and are not due to confounds or uncontrolled extraneous variables (Campbell and Stanley, 1963).

To assess internal validity, you need to *ask whether there are alternative explanations for the outcome* of the study. The following is a clear example of a study with poor internal validity:

> Researchers wanted to assess the effectiveness of cognitive therapy in reducing the violent impulses of incarcerated rapists. They drew a sample of rapists from a prison population and engaged them in tri-weekly therapy sessions for 12 weeks. The results showed that following the completion of therapy, self-reported violent impulses were reduced for this group.

Can you be confident that the reduction was due to the therapy, or are there uncontrolled extraneous variables (confounds) that allow for alternative explanations? Some alternative explanations may be that the results are due to the passage of time (time-tied effects), to receiving attention from the therapist or researchers (Hawthorne effect), or to participants' expectations (placebo effect), rather than to the therapy (the IV). Since there was no control group that was treated identically to the therapy participants in all ways but *one* (did not receive therapy), we do not know whether the therapy was responsible for the reduction in violent impulses. Without proper controls for variables other than the independent variable, the results are uninterpretable, and a study is said to lack internal validity.

Problems with internal validity are a particular risk when researchers use a static variable (preexisting participant or environmental characteristic) as the independent variable. For example,

> A researcher hypothesized that criminal fathers produced criminal sons due to the effects of modeling deviant lifestyles. The researcher found that, indeed, sons of criminal fathers are more likely than sons of noncriminal fathers to be criminals. However fathers' criminality (a static independent variable) is also associated with such variables as lower SES, greater marital conflict and divorce, and probably poorer parenting skills.

Unless the researcher matched the two groups on these variables to control for their effect, it would be erroneous to conclude that fathers' modeling of criminality alone (the IV) was responsible for the differences in the two groups of sons. The study has poor internal validity because the outcome could be due to any or all of these variables. Static variables, especially broad ones like criminality, are usually associated with multiple additional variables that might be responsible for the outcome. Likewise, the

TABLE 5-1

Typical Threats to Internal and External Validity and Control Measures

Threats	Causes	Measures of Control
Faking good/bad	Participants may bias answers to impress experimenters with how good, how bad, or how sick they are	Measures with "lie scales" or questions that hide their intent
Hawthorne effect	Response/performance influenced by being observed or attended to	Comparison group also measured/observed
Placebo effect	Participants change because they expect to change	Control group that receives "fake" treatment or drug
Time-tied effect	Participant's changes due to passage of time rather than due to treatment/intervention (IV)	Comparison group also measured over same time period
Memory bias	Participant's memory for past events may not be accurate or be filtered through present circumstances	Inclusion with additional sources of data
Observer characteristics	Subject alters behavior/ responses because of some characteristic of the observer (i.e., gender, age, SES)	Variation of observers
Observer bias	Experimenters know the hypothesis and see what they expect to see	Observer is blind to the hypothesis and to what group a participant belongs
Invalid operational definition	Definition of IV or DV does not adequately represent the phenomenon of interest or also does not represent uncontrolled variables	Use of validated and reliable measures
Biased sample	Sample differs systematically from population it is supposed to represent	Random sampling or matched

operational definition of a dependent variable may, as for the IV, be confounded because it really measures/includes more than one variable. For example, the use of incarceration rates as a DV may also reflect socioeconomic status, since poor defendants may be more likely to be convicted because they cannot usually afford private attorneys and investigators. When assessing the internal validity of a study, evaluate whether there are uncontrolled extraneous variables that compromise the independent or dependent variable.

Finally, it is important to assess the operational definitions of the independent and dependent variables as they relate to the purpose or hypothesis of the study. This process is sometimes referred to as **study validity** (Meltzoff, 1998). That is, do the operational definitions of the IV and DV accurately or logically reflect the variable of interest, or are either or both poor approximations or abstractions of the variable? An amusing example of this problem is a study in which the researcher hypothesized that women were more likely than men to suffer from penis envy (reject femininity, want to be men). Penis envy (the DV) was operationally defined as whether or not participants kept a loaned #2 pencil when they turned in a scantron test. The operational definition of penis envy was a pencil (long, pointed object—phallic symbol), and more women than men kept the pencil. The researcher concluded that this outcome confirmed the hypothesis that more women than men suffered from penis envy—please! Watch out for erroneous or silly operational definitions that do not logically reflect the variables that they are supposed to represent.

A carefully designed empirical study controls methodologically for confounds and alternative explanations. Sometimes this process is accomplished through statistical controls as well. As you read reports of empirical studies, it is important to carefully examine the methods section so that you can consider threats to internal validity as you make judgments about the conclusions that the author is drawing from the evidence. A summary of typical threats to internal and external validity (Stern and Kalof, 1996) may be found in Table 5-1.

The **external validity** of a study is the degree to which the results and conclusions can be applied or *generalized to the people whom the sample is intended to represent* (Campbell and Stanley, 1963). Results from a study can rarely generalize to broad or universal populations such as all women, all murderers, all adolescent boys, and so on. This limitation is not a problem unless researchers make such a claim when their sample does not support it. Evaluation of the external validity of a study can be made relative only to the intention and claims of the researchers regarding how far the results of the study can be extended beyond the people, time, and place of the study (Meltzoff, 1998).

Integration and Application

To evaluate the results and conclusions of research studies, it is important to evaluate the methods that were used to obtain the results and/or to arrive at the conclusions. As a conscientious consumer of such information, you need to be able to assess the internal and external validity of the study by evaluating each of its elements. The

Self-Check 5-4

Fill in or circle the correct term for items 1–4.

1. A __________ is intended to represent the population of interest in the study.
2. An unbiased, representative sample helps ensure the (internal, external) validity of a study.
3. A measure of a DV is (reliable, valid) if it accurately measures what it is supposed to measure.
4. A researcher would use a matched comparison group to control for confounds to increase the (internal, external) validity of a study.

Key: 1—sample; 2—external; 3—valid; 4—internal.

following summarizes some of the questions to ask about each element of an empirical study.

- Hypothesis:
  - Is the hypothesis causal or noncausal?
  - What is the nature of the relationship between variables that the hypothesis predicts?
- Independent Variable:
  - What is the independent variable? How is the IV operationalized?
  - Is the operational definition of the IV an adequate representation of the variable of interest as stated in the purpose/hypothesis?
  - Are there any uncontrolled for independent variables (extraneous variables) that could also affect the findings/DV (see Table 5-1)?
- Dependent Variable:
  - What is the dependent variable? How is the DV operationalized/measured?
  - Is the operational definition of the DV reliable?
  - Is the operational definition of the DV a meaningful representation of the variable of interest? Is the measure used valid?
- Sample:
  - Does the sample represent the population of interest?
  - Was the sample selected randomly?
  - Are there any potential biases in how the sample was selected?
- Conclusions:
  - Are the conclusions about the relationship between variables consistent with the hypothesis (i.e., causal, noncausal)?
  - Do the conclusions drawn by the experimenter take into account limitations due to methodological problems with the IV, DV, or sample?

Self-Check 5-5

Evaluate the following hypothetical study, using the questions in the preceding list.

Smith and Jones (1996) wanted to discover what factors contribute to the making of a murderer. They hypothesized that the greater the severity of early childhood (first 7 years) experiences of physical and emotional abuse, the greater the level of violence involved in killers' crimes. Level of violence was defined by a formula that included the number of victims, previous violent offenses, degree of emotional and/or physical suffering (sadism) inflicted on victims, and amount of overkill in their crimes.

Their sample consisted of 80 offenders jailed for homicide who were randomly selected from a list of such offenders incarcerated at Kansas State Prison. Researchers developed a series of 10 open-ended interview questions that asked about early family experiences and methods of parental discipline. The interviewers were undergraduate criminology students from a local college who were trained by the researchers to conduct the interviews in male-female pairs. Interviews were recorded and transcripts prepared. Raters, who were trained to use a rubric to assess level of emotional abuse and level of physical abuse, analyzed the transcripts. The interrater reliability following training was .85. The researchers found that 80 percent of the most violent offenders reported moderate to severe emotional abuse and that 71 percent reported moderate to severe physical abuse. Only 51 percent of the least violent offenders reported moderate to severe levels of emotional abuse, and 46 percent reported moderate to severe levels of physical abuse. Researchers concluded that high levels of emotional and physical abuse contribute to the severity and degree of violence exhibited in later offenses.

Key:

Hypotheses: The *purpose* of the experiment sounds causal ("what factors contribute to"), but the *hypothesis* is noncausal and predicts a positive correlation (as levels of abuse increase, so do levels of violence—both are static variables).

Independent Variable: The IV is level/degree of abuse and is operationally defined as self-report (interview) of physical and emotional abuse in childhood. The definition has all of the problems of self-report (faking good/bad, memory bias) as well as the threats to internal validity of observer characteristics (naive college student interviewers) and observer bias.

Dependent Variable: The DV is level of violence of participants' crimes as found in their records—probably reliable and valid.

Sample: Sample was selected randomly from population of prisoners at one prison. Although it represents only prisoners at one facility, the results may have implications beyond this one geographic location.

Conclusions: Hypothesis is noncausal (descriptive—comparative), the variables were static variables (noncausal), but the researcher draws a cause-effect conclusion. Researcher's conclusion does not take methodological limitations into account and goes beyond the data in generalizing about a cause-effect relationship. All the researcher can really conclude is that there is an association between level of self-reported memories of abuse and degree of violence.

RESEARCH METHODS/STRATEGIES

Researchers use a variety of research methods to answer questions about factors that contribute to creating a monster and about treatments or interventions that might change or prevent patterns of violence.

The three methods researchers frequently use to study violence are case study, correlational, and experimental. Each method contributes in different ways to our knowledge and understanding of human thought, emotion, and behavior related to violence. Each method also has its own characteristic vulnerabilities to problems with internal or external validity.

Case Study Method

Although the case study method is not based on the scientific method, it is often used by clinicians or researchers as a way to begin studying a phenomenon. Using the case study method, researchers employ a combination of interviews, psychological tests, histories, reports of family and peers, and naturalistic observation to develop a detailed description of past and present factors in the life of an individual or a select group of individuals. They look for patterns or clues that might explain the individual's current pathology. Because case studies investigate an individual intensively, they are often a good starting point for developing hypotheses that may be tested more broadly by using larger samples. Sometimes the case study method may be the only method available because of the rarity of a phenomenon or pathology of interest. For example, although school shootings have broad impact, there are relatively few school shooters available for study. Therefore, intensive case studies of school shooters are not only a good place to begin our efforts at understanding but also realistically may be the only method available for researching this phenomenon.

Even though case studies may be valuable as sources of ideas for potential independent variables, they are not conclusive by themselves. Although a researcher using this method may be tempted to draw causal conclusions, such conclusions must be viewed as speculations. The case study method is vulnerable to many of the threats to internal and external validity identified in Table 5-1 that make conclusions or generalizations unwarranted.

The most obvious threat to internal validity in case studies is observer bias, since the researchers know what they are looking for and also collect and interpret the information. Researchers, on the basis of a particular theoretical orientation, may see what they expect to see. As we saw in Chapter 4, different theories guide us to look at people through different lenses and to interpret what we see differently. How researchers assess an individual and where they look for relevant information may be influenced by their theoretical orientation. A psychoanalyst is going to look for early childhood conflicts such as mother-child relationships and Oedipal issues, and the psychoanalyst may use dream analysis and/or projective tests to gather information about unconscious wishes/desires. A behaviorist will look for current reinforcers, models, and so on.

The methods frequently used to gather information for a case study, such as histories obtained through interviews and naturalistic observation, are subject to many of the threats to internal validity noted in Table 5-1. Can you identify some of these before continuing? Interviews with the subjects of a case study, with their family and/or friends, with teachers, and so on are particularly vulnerable to faking good or faking bad because of the subjects' desire to impress the interviewer with socially desirable responses or to impress the interviewer with how sick they are (i.e., to invite sympathy or to support an insanity plea). Interview responses may also be influenced by observer characteristics. For example, a prisoner may enjoy exaggerating in order to shock a young female interviewer. Memory bias is also a factor to consider in case history interviews. Our memories of past events are very likely incomplete and filtered through our current attitudes and circumstances. Observations of subjects in a natural setting such as their home and school, and with their peers, are vulnerable to the Hawthorne effect. That is, the subjects' behavior may change because they know they are being observed. Many years ago my family and I were victims of the Hawthorne effect! A college student came to observe my family (my children were 3 and 6) for a class project. Despite our desire to "be natural," we came across like the Brady Bunch—my children and husband were perfectly behaved, and I was acting like the mother of the year (not the usual state of affairs!).

Case studies lack external validity (generalizability) because a single person or even several individuals cannot be representative of a wider population. Observations of a single individual are circumscribed by idiosyncratic histories, circumstances, and experience.

TABLE 5-2

Strengths and Limitations of the Case Study

Strengths	Limitations
It may provide information that can generate ideas for additional research.	It is vulnerable to observer bias and unsystematic observations.
It can be used to study a rare phenomenon.	Findings cannot be generalized beyond the individual studied.
	It cannot draw cause-effect conclusions.

Correlational Method

The correlational method allows researchers to investigate the degree of association between preexisting static variables or subject characteristics, using large samples so that results may be generalized to a wider population of interest. Correlational research is appropriate for testing only a noncausal hypothesis. That is, hypotheses that predict an *association* between static variables or that make *descriptive-comparative* predictions based on static variables, can be tested using this method. Unlike the experimental method, in a correlational study, the researcher does not manipulate an independent variable. Rather, the *variable of interest is static*—the variable already exists within the participants or the environment. For example, a researcher might ask whether parental marital conflict is associated with the children's behavior problems. Are testosterone levels associated with sexual aggressiveness? In each of these examples, the variables already exist; they are static variables. Whenever a hypothesis employs a static variable as the independent variable, it is, by definition, a correlational study. The researcher is simply trying to discover whether the two variables vary in relation to each other in a systematic or predictable way.

Because the correlational method allows us to study preexisting variables, we can study phenomena that we cannot ethically or realistically manipulate, such as brain injury, gender, genetics, and existing personality characteristics such as impulsivity. Using the correlational method, for example, we could test a group of already brain-injured participants to find out if they are more impulsive than non-brain-injured participants.

The strength of the relationship between variables is derived statistically and may be expressed as a correlation coefficient. A positive correlation coefficient can vary from 0 (no relationship) to +1.0 (a perfect relationship) and means that as variable A (i.e., testosterone) increases, variable B (i.e., sexual aggression) also increases. The closer the correlation coefficient is to 0, the less likelihood that the two variables are associated. A negative correlation can vary from 0 (no relationship) to −1.0 (a perfect correlation) and means that as variable A (i.e., self-esteem) increases, variable B (i.e., behavior problems) decreases. A negative correlation of −.80 demonstrates as strong a relationship as a positive correlation of +.80. The negative correlation simply reveals an inverse relationship, whereas the positive correlation demonstrates a positive relationship. In order to test whether a positive or negative correlation is due to a true relationship between variables, researchers apply statistical tests of significance to rule out the possibility that the correlation is due to chance. If the correlation coefficient is found to be significant (not due to chance), we can conclude that there is an association or a bond between the two variables.

A significant positive or negative correlation allows us to make predictions that are likely (depending on the strength of the correlation) to be correct. For example, if we found a significant correlation of +.60 between peer rejection and aggressive behavior, we would have a reasonable chance of predicting that children rejected by their peers will also demonstrate aggressive behavior. When there is a group of aggressive children, we can also predict that they will probably have a higher rate of peer rejection. Because the correlation is not +1.0, we will not be right all of the time.

Although profiling serial killers is both an art and a science, the science part is based on correlational data. Characteristics of known perpetrators were correlated with characteristics of crime scenes. Therefore, identifying certain elements of a crime scene allows a profiler to predict the characteristics of an unknown perpetrator with greater than chance accuracy.

You will notice that in all of these examples of a correlational relationship, we are making no inference that variable A causes variable B. A correlational relationship establishes only an association, not a cause-effect relationship. There are two reasons that concluding a cause-effect relationship between two correlated variables is unwarranted: the *directionality problem* and the *third variable problem.*

Although we may know, on the basis of correlation, that peer rejection and aggressive behavior are associated, we cannot conclude that peer rejection causes aggressive behavior; it may be that aggressive behavior causes peer rejection. This is the **directionality,** or the **"chicken or the egg," problem.** Often the media or the public are tempted to make erroneous cause-effect conclusions on the basis of correlational research. The controversy over the effects of TV violence on children is a good example of this phenomenon. Many of the studies that have been conducted on this issue have been correlational and have found that the more TV with violent content that children watch, the more aggressively they behave (a positive correlation). However, does violent TV cause aggressive behavior in children, or do aggressive children seek out more violent TV shows because they relate to them? Conclusions about the directionality of a relationship are always suspect when based on the correlational method.

A second reason that we cannot conclude a cause-effect relationship on the basis of the correlational method is the **third variable problem.** Because correlational studies examine the degree of relationship between static (existing) variables, it is possible that the relationship is due to a third variable that is common to or underlies both.

For example, if a correlational study found a strong negative correlation between educational level and delinquency (the lower the educational level, the higher the rate of delinquency), it may be that poverty causes both lower educational level (drop outs) and greater delinquency (exposure to gangs and a high crime environment). Consequently, we cannot conclude that low educational levels cause delinquency, because the relationship may be caused by a third variable (poverty). This problem can be partially overcome by using a **matched group design.** For example, a researcher may want to

Highlight 5-1

Because of the third variable problem, correlational studies are vulnerable to producing spurious relationships. An example of a spurious relationship is illustrated in the case of Al Capone and his gang members. During the 1920s, his gang members would rub their bullets with garlic. They believed that the garlic was a poison and would ensure death. After a person was shot 30 or 40 times with the garlic-rubbed bullets, the person would most certainly die. It is obvious that the bullets were the true cause of death, not the garlic. Just as in the case with Al Capone and his gang, the associations between such factors as media violence, gender, or family breakup and violence in children and young adults could be because the relationship has a third variable acting on the situation.

discover whether being raised in federal housing projects is related to higher rates of delinquency. Using matched groups, the researcher would measure the rate of delinquency in children who were raised in the projects and those who were not. The two groups would be matched in terms of any potential third variables that the researcher could think of, such as SES, race, number of children raised by single parents, gender, and so on. Matching controls for the third variable problem only for those factors on which the two groups are matched.

When basing conclusions on correlational studies, it is important to keep in mind the strengths and limitations shown in Table 5-3. In addition, look for specific threats to internal and external validity from Table 5-1 when evaluating the methodology of an individual study.

TABLE 5-3

Strengths and Limitations of the Correlational Method

Strengths	Weaknesses
It is practical; can study a wide variety of existing human phenomena.	It cannot draw cause-effect conclusions.
Results may be generalized beyond the sample.	It is vulnerable to third variable confounds.
It can statistically represent the strength of an association between variables beyond chance.	It cannot infer directionality.
It can be replicated by other researchers.	

Experimental Method

The experimental method is used when we want to draw conclusions about a cause-effect relationship between variables. That is, we want to see whether variable B (the dependent variable) changed or occurred *because of* variable A (the independent variable). In a true experiment, the researcher manipulates the independent variable while controlling for all other possible variables that might affect the outcome. This method is often used to test whether or not a treatment or intervention (IV) has produced a desired effect. When well designed, the experimental method provides the best evidence that the independent variable is responsible for the outcome. The beauty of a true experiment is that it allows the researcher to *control for all variables but one*—the independent variable.

Let's use the following hypothesis to demonstrate the elements of a true experiment: chemical castration (IV) of serial rapists will decrease the incidence of repeat offenses (DV) when they are released from prison. At first glance, you might be tempted simply to take a sample of imprisoned serial rapists who consent to participate, give them the chemical castration injections, and then see what happens when they are released. This, however, is not a true experiment because it does not control for "volunteerism," the passage of time, participants' expectations because they are getting treatment—all confounds. To set this up as a true experiment, a researcher would control for these confounds by using an experimental group and a control group, participants would be randomly assigned to one of these two conditions, and the researcher would employ **double-blind** procedures.

In an experiment, we assess the effect of the treatment by comparing the outcome for participants in the experimental group who receive the treatment to the outcome for participants in the control group who are treated the same as the experimental group in all ways except for one—the IV. In our example, participants in the experimental group would receive "chemical castration" shots on a regular schedule. Participants in the control group would receive shots of an inert substance on the same schedule to control for expectancy (placebo effect), in the same room and by the same nurse as the participants in the experimental group. In addition, the nurse would be "blind" to which participants were receiving the chemical cocktail and which participants were receiving the inert substance. Participants would also be "blind" to whether they were in the experimental or control group. In this way, we have a double-blind experiment that *controls for the experimenters' (nurses') expectations* that could be subtly communicated to the participants and for *participants' expectations.* Finally, to control for any participant characteristics that could bias the outcome, our sample of volunteers would be randomly assigned to either the experimental or the control condition. Random assignment means that each participant has an equal likelihood of being assigned to each group—we could flip coins or draw names out of a hat to place participants in one of the groups.

Although the experimental method allows us to make cause-and-effect conclusions by manipulating the independent variable and instituting methods of control (control group, randomization, double-blind procedures), when it comes to investigating the causes of human behavior, the application of this method may not always be practical, possible, or ethical. Therefore, researchers sometimes employ a subtype of the experimental method called an **analogue experiment.** An analogue experiment tests human or animal subjects in a laboratory setting that is designed to be functionally analogous to a real-life situation.

For example, if we wanted to study the effects of peer rejection on subjects' feelings of hostility toward peers, we could not draw a sample of sixth graders and randomly assign them to an experimental group where school peers are instructed to reject them for the year or a control group where peers are instructed not to reject these subjects. It would certainly not be ethical nor would it be possible to control all the possible extraneous variables (i.e., maybe the peers would not comply with instructions, etc.). However, we could set up an analogue experiment in which subjects are randomly assigned to the experimental or control condition. A laboratory play area would be set up complete with 4 peers who are really confederates of the experimenter.

Before each subject in the experimental group is introduced into the play area, the 4 peer confederates would be instructed to ignore the child and rebuff any attempts that the subject might make to join in the half hour of play. Control subjects would not be ignored or rebuffed by the "peer" confederates. Following this manipulation, all the subjects would be assessed in terms of feelings of hostility. They would then, of course, be debriefed (told how they were "set up"), to prevent any lasting effects.

Analogue experiments require imagination and creativity on the part of the researcher to design an experiment that is as analogous to a real situation as is possible in an artificial environment. However, analogue experiments, by their nature, can only approximate real life—no one would agree that a half hour of play with rejecting peers (our operational definition of the IV) who are strangers is the same as years of rejection by peers whom the subject sees at school every day. With analogue experiments, it is particularly important to note how the IV and DV are operationally defined—do the operational definitions really represent the phenomenon of interest? However, if the effect (peer rejection, hostility) could be demonstrated and replicated in the laboratory, it would be strong evidence of a cause-effect relationship, especially if studies employing correlational methods had also found an association between peer rejection and hostility as it occurs in the real world.

Laboratory animals are sometimes used in analogue experiments to investigate cause-effect questions, by using experimental controls that could not be implemented with human subjects. Questions regarding the effects of maternal abandonment, of damage to certain areas of the brain, and of random punishment are often addressed using animals as "stand-ins" for humans. Of course, when evaluating analogue experiments, we must assess whether the animal analogues are really similar to their human counterparts on the phenomenon being studied.

When evaluating studies that use the experimental method, you should always be alert to any of the threats to internal or external validity noted in Table 5-1.

TABLE 5-4

Strengths and Limitations: Experimental Method

Strengths	Weaknesses
It can control for potential confounds or variables.	Is often limited to phenomena that can be studied in a laboratory.
It can establish cause-effect relationships.	Analogue studies may be artificial and not truly reflect real human experiences.
Findings may be generalized beyond the sample studied.	
Statistical analysis can determine whether chance is the reason for the result.	
It can be replicated by other researchers.	

Integration and Application

Social scientists use different methods to answer different types of questions. The case study method uses the intensive study of an individual not only to answer questions about that individual but also to identify factors that could be studied further using other approaches. The correlational method is used to study large groups of individuals to answer questions about the strength of association between variables that we predict are related, either positively or negatively. The experimental method is the only method that allows us to answer questions of cause and effect.

Each of these methods has limitations on the conclusions that can be drawn from the data obtained. The case study method is particularly vulnerable to the potential subjective bias of the researcher, and findings cannot be generalized to people beyond the individual studied. The correlational method, which allows us to generalize our results to a population of interest, does not allow us to draw conclusions about cause and effect. The experimental method, when well designed, has both internal and external validity, but may be limited by the artificiality of the laboratory. However, research into a phenomenon using each of these methods is like putting pieces of a puzzle together—each piece of the puzzle adds to the clarity of the picture. The following example illustrates how this goal may be accomplished.

To discover what factors produce the lack of empathy or concern for others that is the hallmark of a psychopath, we may begin by intensively studying the life histories of three individuals who have been diagnosed as psychopathic (case study method). If we find that all three suffered maternal deprivation in their first 2 years of life (i.e., because of being in and out of foster care, mother being in and out of jail, etc.) we might want to see whether there is an association between maternal deprivation in early childhood and psychopathic lack of empathy in adulthood in a wider population. To do this, we design a correlational study. We draw a sample of diagnosed psychopaths and nonpsychopaths matched for SES, age, and gender. We would operationalize our definition of maternal deprivation as a child or mother's being removed from the home for (cumulatively) over half of the child's first 2 years, and we would find methods for measuring this (i.e., archival data, interviews, etc.). If we find that significantly more participants in the psychopathic group met the criteria for maternal deprivation, we could conclude that maternal deprivation in early childhood is associated positively with later psychopathy. However, we cannot conclude that maternal deprivation is a cause of later psychopathy.

In order to establish a causal relationship, we would need to use the experimental method, which requires that we manipulate the independent variable (maternal deprivation) and measure its effects. Since we cannot deliberately expose a sample of young children to maternal deprivation, we would have to design an analogue experiment, probably using animals as our subjects. First, we would operationalize our IV (maternal deprivation). For example, we might remove our experimental animal subjects from their mothers (beginning at birth) and place them for defined periods of time with a variety of other female caregivers. Our control subjects would remain with their mothers. We would then need to operationalize our DV (psychopathy) in a way that could be measured on animals. Since we cannot give psychological tests to animals, we would have to define and measure psychopathy as a set of observable animal behaviors that we think are analogous to the human diagnosis of psychopathy (a challenge!). If our results came out as predicted—experimental subjects were more psychopathic than control subjects—we would conclude a cause-effect relationship.

If the results using each of these research methods are consistent (converge) in their findings, we would be on firmer ground in concluding that maternal deprivation is a cause of later psychopathy. The strengths and limitations of each method counterbalance each other and allow us to derive more valid and robust conclusions than could be derived from employing any single method.

Self-Check 5-6

For each of the following, fill in the research method(s) being referred to: CS (case study), C (correlational), and E (experimental).

1. The ______ method manipulates the IV.
2. The ______ method is especially vulnerable to researchers' subjectivity.
3. The ______ method can statistically establish only an association between variables.
4. The ______ method allows us to draw cause-effect conclusions.
5. The ______ method(s) allow(s) us to study a wide variety of human phenomena.
6. The ______ method(s) is/are vulnerable to alternative explanations because of extraneous variables.

Key: 1—E; 2—CS; 3—C; 4—E; 5—CS & C; 6—CS & C.

Discussion Questions and Activities

1. Find a newspaper/magazine article or editorial that presents a point of view about either the causes of criminal behavior or the effectiveness of a type of punishment (i.e., jail term, death penalty) in reducing or deterring crime. Identify examples of the types of evidence (casual observation, appeal to authority, empirical) that are used to support that viewpoint. Using what you have learned from this chapter, critique the "evidence."

2. What is meant by the term "operational definition" as it refers to the independent or dependent variable? Develop two different operational definitions for each of the following variables:
   a. psychotherapy as an IV
   b. aggression as a DV
   c. child abuse as an IV
3. What are the ethical guidelines for research set forth by the American Psychological Association for the following:
   a. Human subjects
   b. Animal subjects

   What is "informed consent"? When is it unnecessary? Go to *www.apa.org/ethics/* to answer these questions.
4. Social scientists debate the usefulness of laboratory research versus research on people in real life. What approach do you favor? Why? What are the advantages and disadvantages of each approach?
5. When studying human thought, motivation, histories, and the like, researchers often depend on self-report. What are the limitations that researchers have to look out for when using self-report by participants?
6. Investigating racial or sex differences as they relate to violence is controversial. Should researchers be restricted on these issues? Why, or why not? What factors should be taken into consideration in interpreting results based on these *static* variables?
7. How might a researcher's own bias or theoretical orientation affect the outcome of a study? What might be done to eliminate this extraneous variable?
8. A researcher hypothesized that prisoners who receive drug treatment while in prison would be less likely to reoffend when released. She searched the records of the California prison system between 1995 and 1998 and identified prisoners who had undergone drug treatment in prison and who had subsequently been released. She found that the recidivism rate for these ex-prisoners was lower than for ex-prisoners who had been incarcerated during the same period but who had not received drug treatment in prison. She concluded that drug treatment during incarceration reduced prisoner recidivism. Were her conclusions valid? Why, or why not? What are some possible alternative explanations for her results? Here are some things to think about in framing your answer:
   a. Is the hypothesis causal or noncausal? What are the conclusions?
   b. What method was used?
   c. Are there any questions you would ask about how prisoners were selected or how they volunteered for drug treatment?

Key Terms

Analogue experiment
Confounds
Deductive reasoning
Dependent variable
Directionality problem
Double-blind
External validity
Independent variable
Inductive reasoning
Internal validity
Population
Reliability
Sample
Static variable
Third variable problem
Validity

References

Campbell, D. T. and J. C. Stanley. 1963. *Experimental and Quasi-experimental Designs for Research*. Chicago: Rand McNally.

Meltzoff, J. 1998. *Critical Thinking about Research*. Washington, D.C.: American Psychological Association.

Stern, P. C. and L. Kalof. 1996. *Evaluating Social Science Research* (2nd ed.). New York: Oxford University Press.

CHAPTER 6

TOXIC FAMILIES AND CULTURE

LEARNING OBJECTIVES

After studying this chapter, you will

- Understand the role of child abuse and neglect on violence
- Understand the role of divorce and family breakup on behavior
- Learn about the role of race and gender on violence
- Gain knowledge about the effects of the media on violence
- Gain knowledge about the social conditions conducive to violent crime
- Learn about the many risk factors associated with later violence

INTRODUCTION

Social scientists have long concluded that crime and violence are the result of a number of interacting factors including, but not limited to, mental aberrations, social deprivation, family dysfunction, media violence, environmental toxins, climate, boredom, and a host of other elements (see generally Adler et al., 2001; Cullen and Agnew, 1999). Some researchers opine that the roots of violence, as with behavior in general, develop in the first two years of life or start at conception (Karr-Morse and Wiley, 1997). However, it is cautioned that with the exception of certain rare head injuries, no one factor or condition by itself predisposes a child to violent behavior. There are multiple factors that combine to cause violence, such as a brain disorder, genetics, and mistakes in parenting, along with the failure of normal protective systems in the environment.

Even though no single factor is considered causal by itself, in certain combinations and with certain dispositions, such combinations can provoke anger, lack of anger management skills, and violence against self or others. Although there are a number of perspectives and criminal typologies, the sociological approaches offer one of the most popular explanations of violent crime.

Social theories of crime generally fall into two broad categories: learning and the environmental conditions. In the former, acceptable or deviant behavior is a learned process resulting from family, peer, or other social influences. Society or environmental conditions, on the other hand, explain criminal behavior through the social economic conditions to which one is exposed, such as poverty, community disorganization, and so forth. In other words, deplorable living conditions are precursors to crime and violence, because there is a lack of legitimate opportunities to succeed or gain acceptance in so-called mainstream society.

Both approaches overlap in explaining one's propensity to crime and violence, because one may be exposed to abuse or neglect (i.e., poor health care, diet, etc.) that is due to poverty, employment, and general deplorable living conditions.

GENDER, RACE, AND VIOLENCE

> "African-American males between the ages of 15 and 24 are almost five times more likely to be injured by firearms than are white males in the same age group. Firearm homicide has been the leading cause of death among young African-American males for nearly 30 years." (Quote from an NAACP press release.)

Before we address learning and environmental conditions, some mention on the dynamics of gender and race are necessary. Males and minorities are often victimized by violent crime and are also the most common perpetrators.

Gender. According to data compiled by the U.S. Bureau of Justice statistics, males are most often the victims and the perpetrators in homicides, and they are 10 times more likely than females to commit murder and sexual offenses.

Despite the emergence of female crime, data continually suggest that males are the more violent gender, and there are a number of reasons why this is so. Gender role stratification is a powerful socializing influence for both males and females.

Researchers argue that there is a so-called "boy code," which insists that boys hide their emotions such as hurt, shame, and weaknesses. The only feelings that society allows a boy to express are those of anger, frustration, and lust. The code is a series of unspoken and unwritten rules of conduct that boys have been raised with for many generations. The code says that boys must be tough and unresponsive to pain (Pollack, 1998). As gender role expectations grow, the boy withdraws, becoming frustrated, angry, and even violent. When men are hurt, physically or emotionally, they learn to suppress fear and sadness and then to express them in gender-appropriate ways such as through aggression and anger. This tendency was demonstrated in a study by Song, Lisak, and Hopper (1996) that found that, when combined with an emotional legacy of abuse, some men's capacity to respond empathetically is inhibited, increasing the likelihood of their committing aggressive acts. In this study, male offenders who were sexually or physically abused manifested significantly more gender-role rigidity and emotional constriction than nonabused perpetrators.

A boy may not feel safe in the psychological world with a culture sending "boy code" messages that cause adolescents to end up "feeling emotional voids filled with media stereotypes, sexists, and chauvinistic attitudes that cloud healthy masculine development" (Gurian, 1998).

In studying men who were domestic batterers, one study suggested that violent men reported significantly higher levels of stress in their lives and were also more likely to report that they repressed emotions. Further, they were more likely to view stressful situations as personally threatening and causing a lack of control in their lives. Men who showed both tendencies—viewing stressful situations as threatening and repressing emotions—were 3.5 times more likely to commit domestic violence than those who didn't share that combination of traits (Williams et al., 2002).

Race. Blacks were over 7 times more likely than whites to commit homicide in 2000. From 1976 to 2000, the Bureau of Justice statistics reported that black victims and perpetrators are greatly overrepresented in homicides involving arguments or drugs and felony murders. However, blacks are less often the victims of perpetration of sex-related homicides, homicide by poison, and workplace killings.

As to early abuse and neglect, white abused and neglected children were no more likely to be arrested for a violent crime than their nonabused and nonneglected counterparts. This finding differs with findings for abused or neglected black children who showed significantly increased rates of violent crime arrests than black children who were not abused or neglected. The differences may be attributed to a number of environmental factors that may be associated with race, including poverty, family characteristics, the type of the abuse or neglect, access to counseling or support services, treatment by juvenile authorities, or exposure to levels of violence in the community (Widom and Maxfield, 2001).

LEARNING VIOLENCE

"Probably the most powerful generator of aggression in living beings is pain. Animals that have been tortured and children who have been severely and repeatedly abused often become extremely aggressive. Animals and humans raised in the company of violent adults is associated with the development of aggressive behavior patterns." (Quote from Dr. Dorothy Lewis, Professor of Psychiatry, NYU.)

Regardless of race and gender, learning is probably the dominant social theory addressing crime and delinquency in the United States (Akers, 1998). As with any other experience, crime and violence are learned through the normal process of interaction with peers, family, and influences. In other words, we learn from teaching, through watching others interact, and through exposure.

A prominent perspective associated with learning theory is known as the **differential association theory.** The theory posits that crime is learned through small, intimate groups and through ongoing encounters (Sutherland and Cressey, 1978). Many violent offenders learn criminal behavior from associates and groups that define criminal behavior as acceptable, thus leading to unacceptable criminal behavior (Leighninger, 1996). In other words, deviant behavior, like normal behavior, is a product of socialization acquired through daily family or peer interaction (Calhoun, 1989).

Parents are probably the most powerful agents in socialization. To exemplify this theory, imagine a child growing up in a home where the parents routinely engage in violent acts. The child would grow up assuming that these acts may not be as wrong as society or the law has defined them. The child may learn to rationalize that such behavior is a natural method for achieving success. Also, if a child is around delinquent peers, one can also learn the activities of these peers and be much more prone to engaging in criminal activity. We will consider the role of the family, peers, and media in addressing learning and violence.

Familial Influences

"Train up a child in the way he should go: and when he is old, he will not depart from it." (Quote from Proverbs 22:6.)

The role of family and parenting has long been a popular research topic in explaining violence. Children raised in families where there is disruption, abrupt change, and the absence of positive role models are more like to have adjustment problems or engage in criminal behavior later in life. Since the family is the primary socialization agent, much of who we are is a reflection of how we are raised. Also, how we treat others and conduct day-to-day activities is often based on the type of guidance received in the home.

For the parents who wish to raise a delinquent child, there are some suggestions in Table 6-1. A child who becomes delinquent and later violent does not necessarily come from a home that is poverty-ridden or dysfunctional. A child may become violent because of enabling or overly protective parents, as well as from abusive and neglectful caretakers.

There are a number of factors explaining the relationship between youth violence and family. Conditions in the home—harsh and ineffective parental discipline, lack of parental involvement, family conflict, parental criminality, child abuse and/or

TABLE 6–1

Ten Steps for Raising a Delinquent Child

1. Begin at infancy to give the child everything he wants. In this way, he will grow up to believe that the world owes him a living.
2. When he picks up bad words, laugh at him. This will make him think he's cute.
3. Never give him any spiritual training. Wait until he is 21, and then let him decide for himself.
4. Pick up everything he leaves lying around—books, shoes, and clothes. Do everything for him so that he will be experienced in throwing all responsibility on others.
5. Quarrel frequently in his presence. In this way, he will not be too shocked when the home is broken later.
6. Give a child all the spending money he wants. Never let him earn his own. Why should he have things as tough as you had them?
7. Satisfy his every craving for food, drink, and comfort. Denial may lead to harmful frustration.
8. Take his part against neighbors, teachers, and the police. They are all prejudiced against your child.
9. When he gets into real trouble, apologize for yourself by saying, "I never could do anything with him."
10. Prepare for a life of grief. You are bound to have it!

neglect, and rejection—also predict early onset and chronic patterns of antisocial behavior (McEvoy and Welker, 2000). When these conditions are present, children may be "literally trained to be aggressive during episodes of conflict with family members" (Forgatch and Patterson, 1998: 86).

Bonding and Early Attachment. A theory posited by Hirschi (1969) argues that everyone has the potential to be law violating and that the primary deterrent against crime is a person's social bonds with others. Violent criminals and other predatory offenders have the greatest likelihood of committing crime, because they have few social bonds at stake. Under this **attachment theory,** there are four aspects of social bonds: attachment, commitment, belief, and involvement. People are less likely to engage in criminal behavior if they are attached to their family, employed, and involved in community activities. In addition, adolescents who are strongly attached to their parents have been found to be less likely to engage in criminal behavior.

Related to social bonds is the importance of early attachment in the development of aggression. The types of attachments an individual has with a caregiver or parent is important in understanding later behavior. A child who is detached emotionally from a parent may feel alienated from others and have difficulty forming interpersonal bonds (Cassidy and Shaver, 1999).

When an attachment figure is not present, fear motivates the individual (such as a small child) to elicit behaviors to reestablish the connection between the attachment figure (parent) and himself or herself (a crying infant elicits parent to hold and comfort him or her). However, when there is a prolonged unavailability of the attachment figure (such as an absentee or a neglectful parent), increased anger and hostility are often observed, particularly if the child is not allowed to openly communicate his or her anger with the missing attachment figure. Many violent offenders lacked attachment to a parent or caregiver, either because the attachment figure wasn't available or because the figure simple didn't care about the child.

Studies have found that sex offenders identify less with their parents than nonoffending comparison groups. One-third to one-half described their relationship with their mother as cold, distant, or hostile (Hudson and Ward, 2000). In addition, as a result of lack of attachment, many sex offenders display intimacy defecits (Hudson and Ward, 2000); they confuse intimacy and sex. This confusion is especially apparent in some child molesters. In the case of serial killers, it has been established from case studies that in approximately half the cases, the biological father left before the child reached 12 years of age. Fathers who remained were more often than not domineering, abusive, insensitive, alcoholic, and expressive of overt anger toward women.

Case Example: Lack of Bonding/Attachment

Richard Allen Davis is a career criminal who kidnapped and murdered 12-year-old Polly Klaas in 1993. Prior to the murder, Davis had a history of violence toward women. Davis was the third of five children. Both of his parents were alcoholics. His mother was strict and is believed to have disciplined Rick for smoking by burning his hand. The couple divorced when Rick was 11. After their divorce, his father won custody of all five kids "because of the mother's immoral conduct in the presence of the children." Young Davis moved around a lot. His father remarried three times, and young Davis would resent all of his stepmothers. Although his father won custody when his marriage dissolved, the elder Davis was sometimes either unable or unwilling to care for the kids, so they were shuttled between paternal and maternal grandparents. Davis's father was mentally unstable and sometimes suffered from hallucinations. He is reported to have taken a gun outside the home and to have shot at mirages. At an early age, young Davis began torturing and killing animals. Davis particularly delighted in dousing cats with gasoline and setting them on fire. He made a point of letting people know he carried a knife, and he used to find stray dogs and cut them.

Source: http://www.crimelibrary.com.

Abuse. Athens (1992) argues that learned violence follows certain steps. From his research on violent offenders in prisons, he determined that people become violent through a process of **"violentization,"** which involves these four stages:

- Brutalization and subjugation
- Belligerency
- Violent coaching
- Criminal activity

In applying this theory, the person (usually a child) is the victim of violence and feels powerless to avoid it (child abuse, neglect, etc.). The child soon becomes belligerent and callous because of his or her violent exposures. As a result, the child learns how and when to become violent and how to profit or manipulate others from the violence. And eventually, it is not long before the child has had sufficient exposure to act on violence by becoming an abuser or violent predator.

The problem of child abuse and neglect cannot be stressed enough. It is a national problem that has increased to epidemic proportions in the United States, and it is a strong predictor of later violence. More than 2.5 million reports of child abuse are made in the United States annually, with hundreds of deaths related to child abuse reported each year. Most runaways, adolescent prostitutes, and teenage delinquents report having been victims of some form of child abuse, and it is also reported that a majority of violent criminals as children suffered abuse, either physical and/or sexual (National Council of Child Abuse and Family Violence, 2002).

Children with a documented history of childhood abuse and neglect, compared with nonabused children from the same neighborhood and born at the same time, are at a two times greater risk for arrest for a violent crime and are also at greater risk for earlier and more chronic involvement in criminal behavior (Widom, 1998).

There is a great deal of literature reflecting an association between childhood victimization experiences and adult risk for mental health disorders and future victimization of others.

High rates of prior sexual victimization have been constantly found in both adult and juvenile sex offenders. The link between sexual victimization and sexual offending was demonstrated by Veneziano, Veneziano, and Legrand's (2000) study of 74 adolescent sex offenders. They found that these offenders would typically reenact their own victimization when abusing their victims. That is, if their own victimization occurred before age 5, they were twice as likely to choose victims under age 5. If they had been subjected to anal intercourse, they were 15 times more likely to abuse their victims in the same way, and so on.

The association between sexual victimization and later offending is not, however, a straight line. Female children outnumber male children as victims of child sexual abuse, yet there are relatively few female sex offenders. Gender-role expectations may impact how the effects are expressed. Female victims are more likely to become depressed and engage in self-destructive activities rather than focusing their feeling outward in the form of aggression toward others (Saunders et al., 1992) as the "boy code" would dictate.

Family Disruption. Divorce, single parent households, illegitimate births, and fatherlessness have been associated with early antisocial behavior in children. Children in homes where both biological parents are present have a much lower incidence of behavior problems and criminal activity. The vast majority of violent juveniles come from broken homes, usually a single-parent household headed by the mother (McLanahan and Sandefur, 1994). Of course, these are static variables that are also associated with poverty, neglect, and dysfunctional communities. It is not just divorce, but also family disruption—either through divorce or illegitimacy—that is associated with greater incidence of crimes such as mugging, violence against strangers, auto theft, and burglary (Elias, 1998). Sociologists from the University of Pennsylvania and Princeton University examined data derived from 6,400 teenage boys over a period of 15 years. Of that group of young men, 13 percent who lived in a home headed solely by their mothers had been incarcerated by the time they were 30, compared with only 5 percent of those whose fathers were present at home. "For each year spent in a non-intact family, the odds of incarceration rise five percent," the sociologists reported (American Family Association, 1999). In general, parents who are available, responsive, and gentle in their interaction with their children are more likely to raise competent and well-adjusted children.

TABLE 6–2

Family Risk Factors for Juvenile Violence

1. Alcohol, tobacco, and other drug dependency of parent(s)
2. Parental abuse and neglect of children
3. Antisocial, sexually deviant, or mentally ill parents
4. High levels of family stress, including financial strain
5. Large, overcrowded family
6. Unemployed or underemployed parents
7. Parents with little education
8. Socially isolated parents
9. Single female parent without family/other support or family instability
10. High level of marital and family conflict and/or family violence
11. Parental absenteeism due to separation, divorce, or death
12. Lack of family rituals
13. Inadequate parenting and low parent/child contact
14. Frequent family moves

Domestic Violence. Children who **witness violence** at home are more likely to become angry, dysfunctional adults later in life. In other words, children who witnessed violence show more anxiety, lower self-esteem, depression, anger, and temperament problems than children who did not witness violence at home. There are estimates that more than 3.3 million children are exposed to physical and verbal spousal abuse each year. This exposure means seeing or hearing the actual abuse, or dealing with the aftermath or trauma of the abuse (Osofsky, 1999).

Children from homes where their mothers were being abused have shown less skill in understanding how others feel and in examining situations from others' perspectives when compared with children from nonviolent households. The lethal combination of being abused and witnessing violence appears to be associated with more

Case Example: A Case of Family Violence

Lisa has just been beaten by her husband. Her attack was like all the others. Her husband arrived home from work to find that dinner wasn't ready. Lisa was running late because she had to stop at the grocery store and the dry cleaners after work and then run to soccer practice to pick up their children. Her husband yelled and threw dishes. Lisa ran toward the back door but could not escape; his fists flew, and she collapsed with bloody abrasions on her face, neck, upper arms, and chest. During the verbal abuse before the attack, her children tried to distract their father with a video baseball game, but the ploy did not work. When he started hitting Lisa, the children jumped on his back but were thrown furiously to the floor. The children are scared. Lisa feels numb and has nowhere to turn. At least this time her injuries won't require stitches. She has been to the emergency room before, for a "slip on the driveway." She does not want to embarrass her children by calling the police and having a patrol car in front of the house. The neighbors don't want to get involved. Her husband controls the money and the car. She doesn't know what to do. Her son yells at her for not having dinner ready. The boy slams his fist into a cupboard, rage pouring out of him. Lisa and her children feel alone, frightened, angry, ashamed, and most of all, hopeless. They fear that they are the only ones who live in a home with this terrible secret. Dad will be home in a few hours, and Lisa is worried about how she will pull things back together over the weekend: the children have homework to do, and she has to drop them off at school early Monday morning. The trap she is in feels overwhelming. The children feel powerless to protect their mother. Lisa is worried about her son—she sees signs that he may be seeking refuge in a gang. He hates school, where he feels like a failure; his teachers and others know that "there is something wrong at home" but feel that it is none of their concern. Lisa's husband grew up in a home with an abusive stepfather who assaulted his mother and frightened the children. He has his own story of rage, powerlessness, and hurt.

serious problems for children than witnessing violence alone. Silvern et al. (1995) found, however, that after accounting for the effects of being abused, adult reports of the witnessing of interparental violence as children still accounted for a significant degree of childhood development problems. We cannot ignore the role of family on the development of future violence.

Peer Influences

Along with the importance of family, sociologists have long acknowledged the importance of the peer group in shaping and supporting the behavior of its members (Rubin, Bukowski, and Parker, 1998). Peer group members are often similar on both demographic and behavioral dimensions. For example, groups or gangs are formed on the basis of similarities in attitudes, race, and other demographic factors (Cairns and Cairns, 1994). Furthermore, group members tend to be similar on behavioral dimensions including smoking (Ennett and Bauman, 1994), aggression (Cairns and Cairns, 1994), and academic achievement (Ryan, 2001).

Negative peer relations such as gang membership is likely to produce such learning as to how to be a better criminal as well as to incorporate rationalizations for crime and violence. Gangs provide youths with both an environment that is conducive to learning criminal values and behaviors and to techniques for engaging in those activities. In other words, Negative peer influence was a distinguishing factor between youths who became delinquent or who maintained their delinquency and those who did not. Those who have means or who are part of the establishment, such as the police, are perceived as enemies.

A longitudinal study, known as The **National Youth Survey,** examined such crimes as assault, fighting, drug use, alcohol use, and weapon carrying. On the basis of this data, Menard (1992) found that adolescents who had a negative peer influence tended to have greater behavior problems. Youths learn that delinquent activities and gun ownership are an acceptable part of gang membership. In other words, gangs may establish their own criteria for attaining status within the group setting, and frequently that status is established by engaging in delinquent activities (Bjerregaard and Lizotte 1995; Sheldon, Tracey, and Brown, 1997). The daily learning activities and habits of gang members are much like most normal adolescent and youth socializing, including talking about local news, sports and recreation activities, music, and so forth. But because their educational and job history is so poor, gang members are often unemployed and have time on their hands, time that is often spent drinking alcohol and taking drugs. During these times, aggressive and violent thoughts often rage to the surface (Vigil, 1997).

Youth participate in gangs during a period of transition from childhood to adulthood. Known as the "**psychological moratorium,**" adolescence is a time of confusion and ambiguity when age and gender identity must be formed. This is particularly so for boys, raised in the female-dominated households that often emerge from the familial stresses of poverty and social marginalization, who must now adjust and conform to the male-dominated streets. The solidarity among gang members helps to reduce the anxiety involved in life on the streets (Vigil, 1997). Gangs and peer groups are important socialization agents for many youth and in many ways replace the family as the major support group.

Media Influences

> "The American Psychological Association has concluded that viewing violence on TV or other mass media does promote aggressive behavior, particularly in children."

The media is a powerful influence in developing value systems and in shaping behavior. Also, there is mounting evidence linking increased aggression to excessive exposure to violent entertainment in the media. It has been found that "the average child watches 1,689 minutes per week" of television (Lockwood-Summers, 1998). Research has associated exposure to media violence with a variety of physical and mental health problems for children and adolescents, including aggressive behavior, desensitization to violence, fear, depression, nightmares, and sleep disturbances.

More than 3,500 research studies have examined the association between media violence and violent behavior; all but 18 have shown a positive relationship (Grossman, 1999). It is not surprising that young kids imitate the actions that they see performed by their favorite actors, actresses, or cartoon characters. These children have grown up watching violence, thinking that acting in such a manner is a social norm. In other words, the media, including videos, music, and the Internet, provides powerful models for many young and immature minds. This is not to say that the media is a direct cause of violence, but it can be a contributing learning influence for some, such as those who are raised in violent or neglectful homes and/or in decaying communities. In 1996, the National Television Violence Study examined the most extensive body of television programming ever collected for the purpose of content analysis. The study found that the majority of all entertainment programming contains violence. Especially disturbing was the fact that the perpetrators of violence went unsanctioned in 73 percent of these violent scenes, since the most effective way of reducing the likelihood of young viewers' imitating violent behavior is to show such behavior being punished (Dubow and Miller, 1996).

According to the National Association for the Education of Young Children (1997), there are three effects of too much media violence on children:

- **Direct action:** When children see characters on TV or in movies triumph by using physical force, they begin to see violence as an acceptable way of resolving conflict. As a result, children use physical or verbal abuse toward others on the playground or at school.
- **Desensitization:** Children may become less sensitive to the pain and suffering of others. Viewing violence encourages children to see other people as "enemies" rather than as individuals with thoughts and feelings like themselves. Children who cannot put themselves in others' shoes may become less desirable playmates.

- **Mean world syndrome:** Children may become more fearful of the world around them. Children's natural anxieties may become magnified by watching TV and movies in which the world is a dangerous place where violence triumphs over peace.

There is research evidence that all three types of effects operate independently. In a study conducted by Aletha Huston-Stein and her colleagues (Stein and Friedrich, 1972), the researchers studied the effects of viewing either violent or nonviolent television programming. In this study, about one hundred preschool-aged children who were enrolled in a special nursery school at Pennsylvania State University were divided into three groups and were assigned to watch a particular diet of programming.

The children watched either a diet of Batman and Superman cartoons, a diet of Mister Rogers' Neighborhood, or a diet of neutral programming (programs that contained neither violence nor prosocial messages). Prior to the children's being exposed to their assigned diet, the researchers observed the youngsters on the playground and in the classroom for two weeks to assess baseline levels of aggressive and helpful behavior displayed by these children. Then the children viewed their assigned program diet one half hour a day, three days a week, for four weeks. The researchers found that the youngsters who watched the Batman and Superman cartoons were more physically active, both in the classroom and on the playground. Also, they were more likely to get into fights and scrapes with each other, play roughly with toys, break toys, snatch toys from others, and get into little altercations.

Additional work on the subject of media violence was conducted by Eron and Slaby (1994). Their longitudinal research began in 1963, focusing on the development of aggression in third-graders and eight-year-olds. In the course of the study, they asked children to report on their television viewing and other things they liked to do, and then to rate the aggression levels of other children. Teachers were also asked to indicate who in the classroom was more aggressive or less aggressive. In addition, the researchers obtained information from parents about children's television viewing and the parent's home discipline practices. Children who reported, or whose parents reported, that the youngsters preferred and often viewed more violent programs were more likely to be the ones nominated by their peers and teachers as more aggressive in school. In a follow-up of these youngsters 10 years later, the most interesting and the strongest relationship was between early television viewing at age 8 and aggressive behavior at age 18.

The researchers again followed up these children as adults at age 30 and found that there was a relationship between early television viewing and arrest and conviction for violent interpersonal crimes, spouse abuse, child abuse, murder, and aggravated assault.

There is research support suggesting that exposure to pornography or graphic violence against women may influence male attitudes toward women and contribute to violence. Studies have indicated that exposure to scenes from R-rated movies that contain sexual content and also present women in an objectified or degrading way have the

Highlight 6-1
Can TV Make You Fearful?

Studies conducted by Gerbner (1993) and his colleagues explored the relationship of the amount of television viewing and mean world syndrome. For example, the researchers would ask questions about viewers' perception of risk in the world, such the following: How likely is it that you are going to be the victim of a violent crime in the next six months? How far from your home would you be willing to walk alone at night? Have you done anything recently to your home to increase its security—added burglar alarms, changed locks? The researchers found that the amount of television viewed predicted fearfulness: heavy television viewers (those who watch four hours or more each day), as opposed to light viewers (those who watched an hour or less per day), were much more fearful of the world around them, were much more likely to overestimate their level of risk, and were much more likely to overestimate the number of persons involved in law enforcement. Although there are different risk levels depending upon residence, those who watched more television were more fearful than those who watched less television. Also, there are special subgroups, such as the elderly, that were more fearful and also tended to watch more television. It appears that the Mean World Syndrome determines one's perceptions of the risks of the world, despite gender, educational level, or income level.

effect of altering the way that men perceive a later account of an acquaintance rape, lessening males' perception of the victim's suffering (Milburn, 2000).

An earlier study by Weaver (1987) showed different groups of participants in a variety of different video scenes, including eroticized violence, male-coerced sex, and female-instigated sex, as well as neutral stimuli. In each of these treatment conditions, participants rated a female target person as significantly more "promiscuous." In other

Case Example: TV Intoxication?

In September 1977, fifteen-year-old Ronnie Zamora was placed on trial for first-degree murder, burglary, robbery, and possession of a firearm in connection with the slaying of his elderly neighbor. At trial, Zamora raised an insanity defense. His trial counsel argued that Zamora's insanity had been caused by "television intoxication." Zamora claimed that his steady diet of watching violent TV programs caused him to kill. Not only did he kill his neighbor, but also the method of killing was similar to that in a plot he had viewed on a popular TV program at the time. This defense was unsuccessful, and Zamora was convicted on all counts. He received concurrent sentences of life imprisonment for murder, twenty-five years each for burglary and robbery, and three years for possession of a firearm.

words, sexually oriented film content as found in X-rated films may have significant negative effects on the ways that males perceive females' resistance to sexual advances. Males tend to perceive female friendliness as sexual interest, in contrast to females' intentions and perceptions (Abbey, 1982). Also, women who accompany men to watch films with scenes that degrade or objectify women may be at a somewhat increased risk of sexual assault (Milburn, 2000).

It is not our position that negative media influences or viewing objectionable material are a direct cause of violent or antisocial behavior. If it were, most children would become violent or criminal. There are a number of learning conditions and experiences that affect legitimate or illegitimate behavior. However, a constant diet of media violence, combined with exposure to family violence, neglect, instability, and so forth may contribute to acts of violence. Contrarily, children in violent environments or adults with violent personalities may be drawn to violet media, raising questions as to whether media violence is a cause or an effect or whether the relationship is due to a third variable that influences both.

ENVIRONMENTAL CONDITIONS AND VIOLENCE

Social structure theories stress that poverty and the deplorable environmental conditions surrounding a community are the root of violent crime. Many violent criminals have grown up in poverty-ridden environments where daily economic survival is a constant struggle. Also, regional survey-based studies have shown that residing in a low-socioeconomic status (SES) neighborhood is associated with more frequent and severe delinquent and criminal behavior among adolescents (Ludwig, Duncan, and Hirschfield, 2001). Offenders commit more crime when there are more opportunities and incentives for committing it. The tendency of certain places or locations to stimulate crime can be gauged from the fact that, in one study of 326,000 calls to the police, 50 percent of the calls were found to come from just 3 percent of the city's addresses (Sherman, 1995).

A host of factors can create opportunities or incentives for crime, such as lax law enforcement (guardians) or a low perceived risk of apprehension (Sherman, 1992). Socially disorganized communities are characterized in part by economic and social flux, high turnover of residents, and a large proportion of disrupted or single-parent families, all of which lessen the likelihood that adults will be involved in informal networks of social control. As a result, there is generally little adult knowledge or supervision of the activities of teenagers and a high rate of crime. In such an environment, it is hard for young people to avoid being drawn into violence. In other words, the combination of poverty with community instability and family disruption is predictive of violence (Elliott et al., 1996).

There are a number of social structure theories associated with the explanation of community or environmental-facilitated violence. One major view is referred to as the **subcultural theory** (Cloward and Ohlin, 1960). The subcultural theory argues that living under conditions of chronic poverty exposes individuals to a different subculture and that adherence to those different subcultural values heightens the risk that an individual will engage in delinquent and/or criminal behavior, such as gang violence. The theory grew out of the so-called **Chicago school,** which focused on human behavior as determined by social and physical environmental factors, rather than genetic, personal characteristics.

According to the Chicago school, the community is a major influence on human behavior. Crime is fostered mainly in the slums, with many unemployed people—male, female, young, and old—becoming transients. A plethora of social problems emerged, ranging from poor sanitation, inadequate housing, juvenile gangs, and so forth. People are no longer closely knit, nor are communities familiar, and many people had no one to turn to during these troubled times. Thus, crime is mainly fostered in the slum areas. Accordingly, people may form their own support groups or gangs, which emphasize deviant values. Individuals at the lower end of the socioeconomic status scale are more likely to participate in crime (Larzelere and Patterson, 1990).

Involvement in crime frequently leads to arrest and imprisonment, and this outcome, in turn, reduces an individual's employment prospects (Fagan and Freeman, 1999). Thus, it is possible to argue that crime leads to poverty and unemployment, rather than vice versa (Fagan and Freeman, 1999). One major longitudinal study found evidence that individuals who are already prone to involvement in crime offend more frequently during periods of unemployment (Farrington et al., 1986). Poverty and unemployment are usually thought to cause crime because they motivate people to offend as a means of overcoming their disadvantage. Likewise, parents in economic stress are more at risk for employing inadequate parenting practices, such as neglect, poor supervision, and inconsistent, erratic discipline. These parental behaviors increase the risk of juvenile involvement in crime (Elder et al., 1985). Thus, it is possible to assume that social and economic stress is an important influence on crime, their effects being mediated by family factors.

Related to this perspective is Merton's (1968) **modes of adaptation theory.** Our culture socializes people to the values and themes of the success goal, which is acquiring material things through hard work. According to the success goal, material things are worth striving for (e.g., automobile, clothes) and are acquired through legitimate means such as legitimate employment. Merton theorized that in reaction to this success goal, people have several modes or typologies of adaptation, which may be either legitimate or unlawful. The legitimate mode is conformity, which refers to the acceptance of society's goals and the means for attaining them. Most people follow this mode of adaptation, by working and attending school to advance their earning power. Others, however, who do not have access to the normative means for attaining material goals because of poverty or other problems, may use illegal methods to achieve those goals. Offenders may innovate, for example, to attain their material goals by robbing a bank in order to obtain their needs.

Social and physical disorder in urban neighborhoods can, if unchecked, lead to serious crime. The reasoning is that even such minor public incivilities as drinking in the street, spray-painting graffiti, and breaking windows can escalate into predatory crime because offenders assume area residents are indifferent to what happens in their neighborhood (Rengert, 1996; Wilson and Kelling, 1982).

There are many disenfranchised people who live in such conditions and who do not commit crimes, and they go on to be productive citizens. Yet, for many, violence is learned, facilitated by community conditions such as urban decay and poverty. In other words, the risks increase for later violence when an individual is surrounded by a number of environmental and family influences that favor or support antisocial behavior. These influences reinforce the beliefs that it is all right to offend in order to achieve success or to get what is deserved.

Many violent offenders often blame their actions on social conditions or early upbringing. In a sense, it may help them to justify or rationalize their violent behavior. Moreover, it is true that social conditions and urban decay are contributors to violence. However, we must recognize that many people exist in such conditions but choose not to participate in violence, suggesting that other variables are operating as a protective force.

Conclusion

Social learning and environmental conditions are the crux of sociological perspectives on behavior. A young person who is exposed to violence at an early age, through abuse or witnessing violence, may express the same violence in later years. In studying violent offenders, a researcher will often discover evidence of negative family or environmental influences, regardless of race or gender. Yet, some are affected by these variables more than others. Many violent offenders have no legitimate bonds to either family members or the community. Although there are exceptions, most violent offenders have been exposed to negative social or family conditions that contributed to their behavior. It is not surprising why many grow to become violent predators. As to communities or environmental conditions, the most common characteristics of crime-prone neighborhoods are poverty, unemployment, and income inequality. In these areas, there is frequently a breakdown in the level of informal social control exercised by local residents against people who threaten to commit crime. Crime also tends to become concentrated at particular locations where there are increased opportunities for committing crime.

Discussion Questions and Activities

1. Explain how violence is learned.
2. Identify the childhood risk factors associated with adult violence.
3. How do social conditions contribute to violence? Illustrate with an example.

4. Select a violent offender, and research the family influences on the development of the offender.
5. Explain Hirsch's theory of attachment and its relationship to criminal behavior.
6. What is the "boy code," and how do you think that it contributes to violence when combined with other influences (i.e., abuse, neglect, racism, family breakup)? Is there also a "girl code"? If so, what does it include, and how might it discourage female violence? Or how might it contribute to the modus operandi of female killers?
7. Referring back to Chapter 5, what type of research is most often conducted on social and family influences on violence? On the basis of this information, what cautions would you recommend in interpreting these studies?
8. Since our media is full of violence (including unpunished violence), explain from an interactionist perspective why most children do not become violent offenders.

Key Terms

Attachment theory
Desensitization
Differential association theory
Mean world syndrome
Modes of adaptation theory
National youth survey
Psychological moratorium
Subcultural theory
Violentization
Witnessing violence

References

Abbey, A. 1982. "Sex differences in attributes for friendly behavior: Do males misperceive females' friendliness?" *Journal of Personality and Social Psychology 42:* 830–838.

Adler, F., G. O. W. Muller, and W. S. Laufer. 2001, *Criminology and the Criminal Justice System.* Boston: McGraw-Hill.

Akers, R. 1998. *Social Learning and Social Structure: A General Theory of Crime and Deviance.* Boston: Northeastern University Press.

American Family Association. 1996. [Online.] *American Family Association Journal.* http://afa.net/. April 09.

Athens, L. 1992. *The Creation of Dangerous Violent Criminals.* Chicago: University of Illinois Press.

Bjerregaard, B. and A. J. Lizotte. 1995. "Gun Ownership and Gang Membership." *Journal of Criminal Law and Criminology 86* (1): 37.

Cairns, R. B. and B. D. Cairns. 1994. *Lifelines and Risks: Pathways of Youth in Our Time.* Cambridge, England: Cambridge University Press.

Calhoun, C., D. Light, and S. Keller, 1989. *Sociology* (5th ed.). New York: Alfred A. Knopf.

Cassidy, J. and Shaver P. R. (Eds.). 1999. *Handbook of Attachment: Theory, Research and Clinical Applications.* New York: The Guilford Press.

Cloward, R. A. and L. E. Ohlin. 1960. *Delinquency and Opportunity: A Theory of Delinquent Gangs.* New York: Free Press.

Cohen, A. K. 1955. *Delinquent Boys: The Culture of the Gangs*, pp. 65–67. Chicago Press.

Cullen, F. T. and R. Agnew. 1999. *Criminological Theory: Past and Present.* (Los Angeles: Roxbury Publishing).

Dubow, E. F. and L. S. Miller. 1996. Television violence viewing and aggressive behavior. In J. M. MacBeth (Ed.), *Tuning in to Young Viewers: Social Science Perspectives on Television*, pp. 117–147. Thousand Oaks, Calif.: Sage Publications.

Elder, G. H., T. Van Nguyen, and A. Caspi, 1985. "Linking family hardship to children's lives." *Child Development 56:* pp. 361–375.

Elias, M. 1998. "Studies Find Dads Make a Difference." USA Today. August 24: p. 1D.

Elliott, D. S. and S. Menard. 1996. "Delinquent friends and delinquent behavior: Temporal and developmental patterns." In J. D. Hawkins (Ed.), *Current theories of crime and deviance*, pp. 28–67. Newbury, Calif.: Sage Publications.

Ennett, S. T. and K. E. Bauman. 1994. "The contribution of influence and selection to adolescent peer group homogeneity: The case of adolescent cigarette smoking. *Journal of Personality and Social Psychology, 67:* 653–663.

Eron, L. D. and R. G. Slaby. 1994. Introduction. In L. D. Eron, J. H. Gentry, and P. Schlegel (Eds.), *Reason to Hope: A Psychosocial Perspective on Violence and Youth.* Washington, D.C.: American Psychological Association.

Fagan, J. and R. B. Freeman. 1999. "Crime and Work". In M. Tonry (Ed.), *Crime and Justice: An Annual Review of Research*, vol. 25, pp. 225–290. Chicago: The University of Chicago Press.

Farrington, D. P., B. Gallagher, L. Morley, R. J. St. Ledger, and D. J. West. 1986. "Unemployment, school leaving, and crime." *British Journal of Criminology 26*(4): 335–356.

Forgatch, M. S., and G. R. Patterson. 1998. "Behavioral family therapy." In F. M. Dattilo (Ed.), *Case Studies in Couple and Family Therapy: Systematic and Cognitive Perspectives*, pp. 85–107. New York: Guilford Press.

Gerbner, G., M. Morgan, and N. Signorielli. 1993. *Television violence profile: The turning point.* Manuscript. University of Pennsylvania, Annenberg School of Communications.

Grossman, D. 1999. *Stop Teaching Our Kids to Kill: A Call to Action Against TV Movie & Video Game Violence.* New York: Crown Publishers.

Gurian, M. 1998. *A Fine Young Man: What Parents, Mentors, and Educators Can Do to Shape Adolescent Boys into Exceptional Men.* New York: Jeremy P. Tarcher/Putnam.

Hirschi, T. 1969. *Causes of Delinquency.* Berkeley and Los Angeles: University of California.

Hudson, S. and T. Ward. 2000. "Interpersonal compentency in sex offenders." *Behavior Modification 24:* 494–527.

Karr-Morse, Robin and M. S. Wiley. 1997. *Ghosts From the Nursery: Tracing the Roots of Violence.* New York: Atlantic Monthly Press.

Kindlon, D. and M. Thompson. 1999. *Raising Cain: Protecting the Emotional Life of Boys.* New York: Ballantine Books.

Larzelere, R. E. and G. R. Patterson. 1990. "Parental management: Mediator of the effect of socioeconomic status on early delinquency." *Criminology 28*(2): 301–323.

Leighninger, L. and P. R. Popple. 1996. *Social Work, Social Welfare, and American Society* (3rd. ed.). Needham Heights, Mass.: Allyn and Bacon.

Lockwood-Summers, S. 1998. "Public TV For The Rockies: Act Against Violence Outreach Campaign. Internet. *http://www.krma.org/six/aav/medialit.html.*

Ludwig, J., G. J. Duncan, and P. Hirschfield. 2001. "Urban poverty and juvenile crime: Evidence from a randomized housing-mobility experiment. *Quarterly Journal of Economics 116:* 655–680.

McEvoy, A. and R. Welker. 2000. Antisocial behavior, academic failure, and school climate: A critical review. *Journal of Emotional and Behavioral Disorders 8:* 130–140.

McLanahan, S. and G. Sandefur. 1994. *Growing Up with a Single Parent: What Hurts, What Helps.* Cambridge, Mass.: Harvard University Press.

Menard, S. 1992. Demographic and theoretical variables in the age-period-cohort analysis of illegal behavior. *Journal of Research in Crime and Delinquency 29:* 178–199.

Merton, Robert K. 1968. *Social Theory and Social Structure.* New York: St. Martin's Press.

Milburn, M. A. 2000. "The Effects of Viewing R-rated Movie Scenes That Objectify Women on Perceptions of Date Rape." Sex Roles 43: 645–664.

National Association for the Education of Young Children. 1997. Washington, D.C.: National Association for the Education of Young Children.

National Council of Child Abuse and Family Violence. 2002. Washington, D.C.

Osofsky, J. 1999. "The Impact of Violence on Children: The Future of Children. *Domestic Violence and Children 9*(3): 33–49.

Pollack, W. 1998. *Real Boys.* New York: Henry Holt and Company.

Rengert, G. 1996. The Geography of Illegal Drugs. Boulder, Col: Westview.

Rubin, K. H., W. Bukowski, and J. G. Parker. 1998. "Peer interactions, relationships, and groups." In W. Damon (Series Ed.) and N. Eisenberg (Vol. Ed.), *Handbook of Child Psychology,* Vol 3: *Social, emotional, and personality development* (5th ed.). New York: Wiley.

Ryan, A. M. 2001. "The peer group as a context for the development of young adolescent motivation and achievement. *Child Development 72:* 1135–1150.

Saunders B. E., L. A. Villeponteaux, J. A. Lipovsky, D. G. Kilpatrick, and L. J. Veronen. 1992. "Child sexual assault as a risk factor for mental disorders among women: A community survey. *Journal of Interpersonal Violence 7:* 189–204.

Sheldon, Randell, S. K. Tracey, and W. B. Brown. 1997. *Youth Gangs in American Society.* Belmont, Calif.: Wadsworth Publishing.

Sherman, L. W. 1992. "Police and crime control." In M. Tonry and N. Morris (Eds.), *Crime and Justice: An Annual Review of Research,* vol. 15, pp. 159–230. Chicago: University of Chicago Press.

Sherman, L. W. 1995. "Hot spots of crime and criminal careers of places." In J. E. Eck and D. Weisburd (Eds.), *Crime and Place,* pp. 35–52. Washington, D.C.: Criminal Justice Press, The Police Executive Research Forum.

Silvern, L., J. Karyl, L. Waelde, W. F. Hodges, J. Starek, E. Heidt, and K. Min. 1995. "Retrospective reports of parental partner abuse: Relationships to depression, trauma symptoms and self-esteem among college students." *Journal of Family Violence 10:* 177–202.

Stein, A. H. and L. K. Friedrich. 1972. "Television content and young children's behaviour." In J. P. Murray, E. A. Rubinstein, and G. A. Comstock (Eds.), *Television and social behaviour,* vol. 2, *Television and social learning,* pp. 202–317. Washington, D.C.: United States Government Printing Office.

Song, P. Lisak, L. & H. Hopper, 1996. Factors in the cycle of violence: Gender rigidity and emotional construction. *Journal of Traumatic Stress,* 9, 721–743.

Sutherland, Edwin H., & Cressey, Donald R. 1978. Principles of Criminology. Philadelphia: Lippincott.

Veneziano, C., Veneziano, L., & Legrand, S. 2000. The relationship between adolescent sex behaviors and victim characteristics with prior victimization. *Journal of Interpersonal Violence*, 15, 363–374.

Vigil, James Diego, 1997. Learning from Gangs: The Mexican American Experience. ERIC Digest. ERIC Clearinghouse on Rural Education and Small Schools: Charleston, WV.

Widom C. S. 1998. Child victims: Searching for opportunities to break the cycle of violence. *Applied Preventive Psychology* 7: 225–34.

Widom, C. and M. G. Maxfield. 2001. "An Update on the Cycle of Violence." Washington, D.C.: National Institute of Justice.

Williams, K., D. Umberson, and K. Anderson. 2002. "Domestic violence often comes from men who repress emotions." *Journal of Health and Social Behavior* No 12: 355–360.

Wilson, J. Q. and G. Kelling. 1982, March. "The police and neighborhood safety: Broken windows." *Atlantic Monthly 249*(3): 29–36, 38.

CHAPTER 7

NEUROLOGICAL CONTRIBUTIONS TO EVIL MINDS

LEARNING OBJECTIVES

After studying this chapter, you will

- Understand the findings regarding the genetics of violent crime and the gene-environment interaction model
- Become familiar with basic neurochemical and neuroanatomical functions related to violence and crime
- Learn about the research into prenatal and postnatal brain impairment and antisocial and violent behavior
- Understand the reciprocal relationship between physiological processes and environment and the way that they interact to produce a vulnerability to violence

INTRODUCTION

Consider the following:

- From gestation to age 7, the neurodevelopmental, cognitive and social foundations for learning, adaptation and behavior are laid (Huttenlocher and Dabholkar, 1997; Loeber and Farrington, 2000).

- Statistics show that some 40 to 95 percent of all violent criminals were severely abused or neglected as children (Meyers, Reccoppa, Burton, and McElroy, 1993, Schumaker and Mckee, 2001), and court records indicate that children under the age of 5 suffer the most severe cases of abuse, including death and disability (Miller, Fox, and Garcia-Beckwith, 1999).
- Genetic research shows that brain function and structure are highly heritable (Thompson et al., 2001).
- Imaging studies suggest structural and functional differences in the brains of violent offenders versus nonviolent controls (Raine, Buchsbaum and LaCasse, 1997).
- Violent criminals display physiological stress response abnormalities that may inhibit normal social learning (Fowles, 2000; Raine, Lencz, Bihrle, LaCasse, and Colletti, 2000).
- Violent criminals exhibit neurochemical imbalances known to cause aggression in laboratory animals (Coccaro, 1989).

The nature versus nurture controversy regarding the causes of violence has been a dead issue in the scientific community for years. It has been replaced by an interactionist explanation: the bio-psychosocial model. In this model, neither biology nor environment are destiny. Rather, both biological and environmental factors may create a vulnerability for violence or pathology that is expressed only when both factors are present. For example, brain impairment may lead to violence only when the psychological effects of an abusive environment are also present. Furthermore, we now know that early brain development is uniquely tied to childhood environment, and the childhood environments of many violent offenders were less than ideal:

> As children, these men were shot, axed, scalded, beaten, strangled, tortured, drugged, starved, suffocated, set on fire, thrown out of windows, raped, or prostituted by mothers who were their "pimps"; their bones have been broken, they have been locked in closets or attics for extended periods . . ." (Gilligan, 1999: 45.)

Although the psychological impact of these environments is easy to accept, it is important to understand that these environments also produce neurological and physiological changes that in turn impact psychological processes and behavior. Even though research into the environmental correlates of violent behavior has proceeded at a steady state for years, the search for neurological correlates to violent behavior has exploded in recent years as a result of advances in technology, especially in brain imaging and computer modeling tools. As a result, researchers are beginning to understand the role of neurology in the development of violence. Current research focuses on several factors associated with violent behavior:

- Genetic influence
- Neurodevelopmental insults experienced either prenatally or postnatally

- Neurological deficits and/or injuries
- Neurochemical and/or hormonal imbalances

As we review the research regarding the neurology of violent behavior, keep in mind that the human brain is an incredibly complex system that interacts not only with other physiological systems but also with the environment as well. This interaction creates several methodological and theoretical limitations for researchers. First, even though we will discuss each neurophysiological system separately, these systems do not in any way function independently of each other. Rather they are intimately dependent upon one another such that pathology in any one system is likely to have repercussions in another. Second, the complexity of the relationship between systems limits and often confounds any data that are collected. Finally, because much of the research in this field uses correlational or animal analogue methodologies, it necessarily suffers from the methodological (discussed in Chapter 5) and theoretical limitations associated with these types of research models. Despite these limitations, the research is exciting and offers new insight into the neurophysiology of violent behavior.

THE SEARCH FOR THE GENETIC ROOTS OF VIOLENCE

For decades, researchers have attempted to link specific chromosomal **genotypes** (genes) to certain **phenotypes** (observable behaviors or traits). Two genotypes in particular have been studied extensively, the XXY *(an extra female chromosome)* and XYY *(an extra male chromosome)* male in relation to criminal behavior.

The XXY genotype, known as Klinefelter's syndrome, appears in about 1 out of every 500 male births. Men with Klinefelter's syndrome show a pattern of endocrine abnormalities, including small stature, little body hair, smaller than normal testes, and some breast enlargement. They also are generally infertile and show some mental retardation (Starr and McMillan, 1997) The behavioral characteristics of males with Klinefelter's include immaturity and a higher than normal degree of mental illness, and they tend to have few or no friends (Nielson and Pelson, 1987). Several studies initially indicated that Klinefelter's males showed a higher than normal propensity to criminal behavior, especially sexual criminality (Neilson, 1970). However, it was later determined that the rate was comparable to that of other men with mental retardation (Neilson, 1970) and thus was considered nonsignificant.

The other genotype studied extensively in relation to criminality was the XYY male (one female and two male chromosomes). This genotype occurs in about one out of every 1,000 male births and is a result of an error in sperm production. XYY males are sometimes referred to as the *super male* or *alpha male* because of the additional male chromosome and the fact that they tend to be taller and larger than other men (Starr and McMillan, 1997). Studies done during the late 1960s and 1970s found that a disproportionate number of XYY males were either in prison or in psychiatric institutions (Gardner and Neu, 1972; Nielson, 1970). It was thus assumed that this genotype was associated with aggressive behavior. However, the methodologies used in many of these studies were inconsistent, and researchers in Denmark later refuted the theory (Mednick and Finello, 1983).

As we are increasingly able to study specific gene variations, research will focus on the effects of these variations on violence and criminality. For example, a recent study in New Zealand looked at the relationship between the gene Monoamine Oxidase A (MAOA) and antisocial behavior, which points to the importance of environment in how a gene is expressed behaviorally (Moffitt, Caspi et al., 2002). Of the 442 men studied, 154 had the gene variation and were also abused (maternal rejection, physical or sexual abuse, frequent changes in caregivers). Of these 154 abused men, 85 percent were involved in antisocial behavior and/or violent crime, whereas none of the nonabused men (who had the same gene variation) were antisocial or violent. The gene variation may create a vulnerability to antisocial behavior that is expressed only when certain environmental conditions occur.

Two popular research models that are used statistically to assess the relationship between genotype and phenotype are twin and adoption studies. Twin studies compare the degree to which identical twins (sharing 100 percent of their genes) also share certain traits/behaviors (i.e., antisocial personality, violent criminality) compared with fraternal twins or siblings (sharing 50 percent of their genes). Adoption studies look at the degree to which parents and their offspring (sharing 50 percent of their genes) also share certain traits/behaviors when the offspring have been adopted into a different family (environment).

Both twin studies and adoption studies suggest a modest genetic contribution to nonviolent antisocial or criminal behavior (property crimes, etc.) and a much weaker genetic contribution to violent or sexual antisocial behavior (Christiansen, 1974; Raine, 1993). However, there is a caveat to this general finding. Although these findings for males point to only a modest relationship between genes and criminality, for females who are antisocial, there is a much stronger genetic relationship (Eley, Lichtenstein, and Stevenson, 1999). Because female socialization traditionally discourages aggression and antisocial behavior, females may require a stronger genetic "push" for both aggressive and nonaggressive antisocial behavior.

In addition to twin and adoption studies, researchers often look to measurements of early temperament and behavior to support the heritability of criminal behavior. Temperament refers to a consistent way of responding to the environment, energy level, emotionality, ability to self-regulate, risk-taking, and sociability. These studies are based on the questionable assumption that if a behavior happens early, it must be genetic (Sapolsky, 1992). These studies are generally longitudinal, spanning from childhood to adulthood, and prospective in that they attempt to predict the probability of future criminality and aggression on the basis of early behavior. Everything from tantruming (Stevenson and Goodman, 2001), fearlessness (Fowles and Kochanska, 2000; Raine, Reynolds, Venables, Mednick, and Farrington, 1998) to skin conductance patterns (Fowles, 2000) have been correlated with adult criminality. But here again we have problems with methodology. Although temperament style is believed to be stable over time and is often present early in life, we know that environmental factors play a huge role in central nervous system development (Jerison, 1997; Teicher et al., 1997) and therefore can significantly influence measurements of early temperament and behavior (Anderson, Damasio, Tranel, Damasio, 2000; Loeber, and Farrington, 2000; Tranel and Eslinger, 2000).

Whether we are looking for the contributions of genetics to violence and crime through gene variations, twin and adoption studies, or studies of early temperament, it is clear that genes alone do not explain this pathology. Instead, the data are more consistent with a **gene-environment interaction.** That is, genetic factors may increase vulnerability to crime or violence, but environmental influences are necessary for the vulnerability to be expressed in behavior.

THE BRAIN-BEHAVIOR CONNECTION

The brain-behavior connection has been studied extensively for over 200 years. It began in earnest in 1848 with the case of Phineas Gage. Gage, a 25-year-old railroad worker, known by bosses and workers alike to be one of the most capable and respected workers on the crew, survived a freak accident that fundamentally altered his personality forever. While laying new railroad tracks in Vermont, an explosion shot a 2-inch-diameter tamping iron through his left cheek at the base of his skull, through the front of his brain. This is an area identified by researchers some years later as the orbital frontal region of the prefrontal cortex. Remarkably, Gage not only survived the accident but also was up and moving within a few minutes. After Gage recovered from the immediate physical trauma of the injury, it became clear that something was not quite right, even though physically and cognitively he appeared to have recovered. The **injury** had radically changed his personality and behavior. Whereas before he was polite, respected, and competent, now he was irreverent, profane, and extremely impulsive. He went from being a respected and capable supervisor at the railroad to being utterly incapable of holding a job (Damasio, 1994; Kalat, 1995). How was it that his cognitive abilities could remain seemingly intact after injury, while his personality and behavior were drastically changed? Or in the case of serial violence, how is it that someone can act so "reasonably" in the commission of such heinous and "unreasonable" acts? The answers, not yet completely understood, lie in the neuroanatomy and neurochemistry of the brain. To understand the brain connection, we need to review some basic tenets of neurochemistry, neuroanatomy, and physiology as a foundation for understanding the research findings on psychopathy and violence.

Neurochemistry

The human brain is a network of billions of neurons (Carlson, 2000) that communicate via the release and synthesis of **neurotransmitters,** or neurochemicals. Researchers have identified many neurotransmitters, but the most widely researched in relation to crime and violence are the following:

- **Dopamine (DA)** regulates perceptions of pleasure, reward, goal-directed behavior, decision-making, and motor control. It is present in less than 2 percent of the brain. Parkinson's patients have too little DA, and persons with schizophrenia have too much (Martin, 1996).
- **Serotonin (5HT)** regulates mood, anxiety, arousal, and appetite. It is present throughout the brain (Martin, 1996). Both depressed and aggressive individuals have been shown to have reduced levels of 5HT (Coccaro, 1989).
- **Norepinephrine (NE)** regulates sleep-wake cycles, alertness, sustained attention, and biological responses to new stimuli such as anxiety, fear, or stress (Martin, 1996). Hyperactivity of NE functioning is correlated with aggressive behavior in lab animals and humans (Kavoussi, Armstead, and Coccaro, 1997).

Communication between nerve cells takes place chemically in what is called the synaptic cleft, or the space between each neuron. The neuron that releases the neurotransmitter is called the **presynaptic neuron,** and the one that receives it is called the **postsynaptic neuron.** Each neuron can have thousands of synaptic connections working together to initiate and regulate all aspects of behavior, cognition, and emotion (Martin, 1996).

Both medical and street drugs affect our behavior and moods by increasing, decreasing, or mimicking the neurotransmitter available in the synaptic cleft or synapse (Leonard, 1992). Drugs that increase neurotransmitter availability are called agonists; drugs that block the effects of neurotransmitters are called antagonists. Cocaine, heroin, and nicotine are dopamine (DA) agonists (increase DA availability), and antipsychotics are DA antagonists (decrease DA availability) (Leonard, 1992). Popular antidepressants such as Prozac are called SSRIs, or selective serotonin reuptake inhibitors. This class of drugs works by inhibiting the reuptake (recycling) of serotonin (5HT) by the presynaptic neuron, which effectively increases the availability of 5HT in the synaptic cleft (Leonard, 1992). Even food mediates the amount of available neurotransmitters. For example, the tendency toward napping (increased relaxation) after Thanksgiving dinner is facilitated by the tryptophan in the turkey. Tryptophan is a precursor to serotonin and therefore initiates an increase in its production, which ultimately puts us to sleep (Kalat, 1995).

Neuroscientists have altered the postsynaptic neurons' ability to "receive" serotonin in mice, creating "outlaw mice." These "outlaw mice" ferociously and indiscriminately attack any mouse that intrudes on their territory (Myslinski, 1997).

Neuroanatomy

Neurochemicals exert their influence across all regions of the cerebral cortex. When we look at a horizontal view (from the top) of the cerebral cortex, we see two distinct regions called hemispheres. For most people the **right hemisphere** is responsible for modulating emotional, creative, and aggressive expression, whereas the **left**

hemisphere controls language comprehension and fine motor movement. Connecting the two hemispheres and integrating the input from both is the job of the **corpus callosum.** Dysfunction in the corpus callosum affects the integration of information between the two hemispheres. (Martin, 1996).

From a sideways section of the cerebral cortex, there are four functionally distinct regions of the brain, called lobes, each responsible for a variety of processes or reactions. Within each lobe are sets of nuclei responsible for more specific behaviors. The two lobes most regularly implicated in aggression and violence are the frontal (inhibitary functioning) and temporal (emotional regulation) lobes (see Figure 7-1).

Within the frontal lobe is an area called the **prefrontal cortex,** which houses two regions that are particularly important to the study of social behavior and aggression; the orbitofrontal cortex (sometimes referred to as the ventromedial cortex); and the dorsal lateral cortex (Gazzaniga, Irvy, and Mangun, 1998). The prefrontal cortex as a whole integrates sensory information from the outside world with internal bodily and emotional states, allowing us to act in a socially appropriate fashion (Bear, 1991). It acts as a **brake on impulses** (Raine, Buchsbaum, and LaCasse, 1997); and when it is damaged, individuals demonstrate risky behavior and a lack of concern for consequences (remember Phineas Gage). The prefrontal cortex is the last area to fully

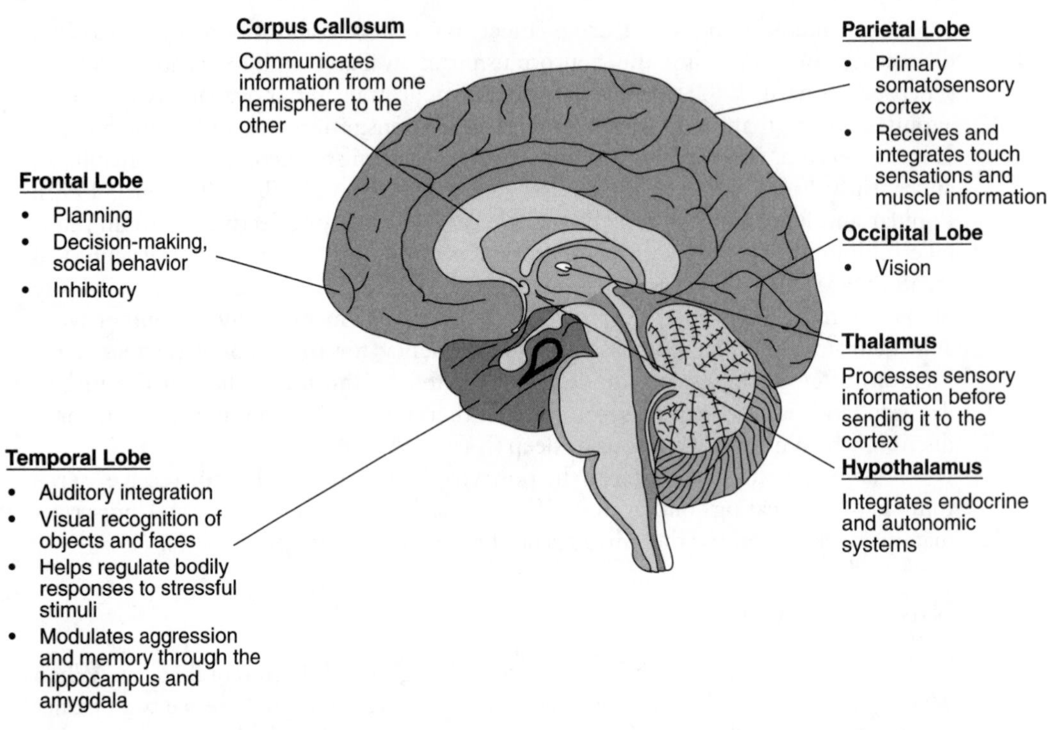

Figure 7-1 The Four Lobes

Orbitofrontal Cortex

- Acts as a braking agent for social interaction
- Individuals with lesions in the OFC show:
  - Impulsivity and disregard for future consequences
  - Little concern for physical safety and often take risks
- Links memories of events to the emotional and physical state correlated with that event

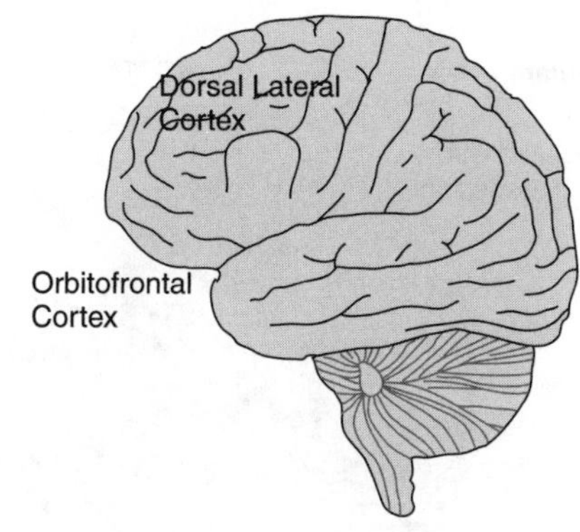

Dorsal Lateral Cortex

- Regulates planning and strategy
- Individuals with DLC lesions
  - Have difficulty planning and organizing information
  - Are unable to complete tasks effectively
  - Exhibit learning and memory deficits
  - Have an especially difficult time with verbal recall

Figure 7–2 The Prefrontal Cortex

mature (make connections), and this process is not complete until about age 20 (Pincus, 2001) (see Figure 7-2).

Implicated in almost every psychiatric disorder is a region of the brain called the **limbic system.** The limbic system is excitatory and part of what some call the **"emotional brain"** because it is the seat of our most fundamental impulses and drives necessary for survival (i.e., aggression, fear, sex). The limbic system comprises two primary structures located in the temporal lobe, the hippocampus and the amygdala, as well as several secondary structures located throughout the brain: the thalamus, the hypothalamus, and the cingulate gyrus. The hippocampus and the amygdala are responsible for several aspects of memory and emotion. (see Figure 7-3).

Hippocampus. The hippocampus codes and organizes emotionally charged cognitive memories and affects several aspects of learning, memory, and attention (Martin, 1996). It also modulates the excitability of hypothalamic neurons (Siegal and Flynn, 1967) that are important for stress regulation. Reduced posterior hippocampal volume has been linked to psychopathy in some samples (Laakso et al., 2001) as well as to problems with memory and attention deficits (Scheibel and Levin, 1997).

Amygdala. The amygdala mediates the expression of aggression (Raine et al., 1997) and influences our abilities to learn and remember. The amygdala controls somatic memory. **Somatic memory** refers to the physiological state associated with a particular event such as increased heart rate experienced during physical or psycholog-

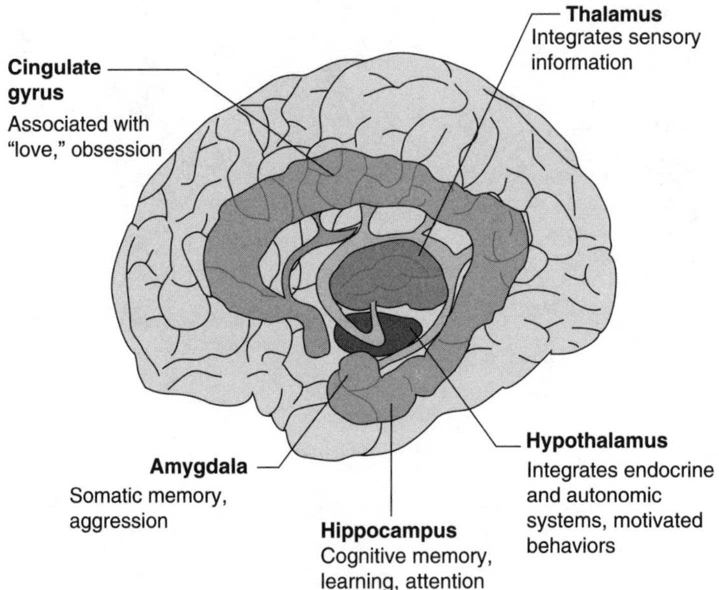

Figure 7–3 The Limbic System

ical trauma (LeDoux, 1996). Damage to certain areas of the amygdala is associated with reduced capacity to make socially appropriate decisions (Raine, Buchsbaum, and LaCasse, 1997) such as when to withdraw from a dangerous situation. Stimulation of the amygdala can produce rage (Tranel, in press), whereas its removal has been found to reduce aggressive and violent behavior in both aggressive/violent animals and humans (Bear, 1991; Tranel, 2000).

The **thalamus** is considered the key integrator of sensory information and receives input from the sense organs throughout the body. It also plays a pivotal role in the regulation of emotion by integrating and relaying input from the limbic system to

Highlight 7-1

Neuroscientists theorize that there are **two memory systems,** the cognitive/explicit memory system and the somatic/implicit system. The **cognitive memory system** regulates explicit thoughts and emotions about an event and is controlled by the hippocampus. The **somatic memory system** regulates the nonverbal, automatic, bodily (fight or flight) responses to an event and is controlled by the amygdala (LeDoux, 1996) Hippocampal memory is slow and thoughtful, and somatic memory is quick and noncognitive.

the frontal cortex. When stimulated, the thalamus along with the hypothalamus (via their connections to the hippocampus and the amygdala) appear to induce rage in cats (Raine, Buchsbaum, and LaCasse, 1997; Watson, Edinger, and Siegal, 1982).

The **hypothalamus** is the primary integrator of the endocrine and autonomic systems. Damage to the hypothalamus results in abnormalities in motivated behaviors such as eating, drinking, temperature regulation, sexual behavior, and aggression or activity levels (Martin, 1996). Lesions to the ventromedial (bottom-middle) region have been shown to induce rage and aggressive behavior in laboratory animals (Siegal and Flynn, 1967; Tranel, in press; Watson, Edinger, and Siegal, 1982). The hypothalamus sends and receives neural projections all over the brain.

Daniel Amenc has compared the **cingulated gyrus** with the transmission in a car. When it is impaired, we have trouble shifting from one thought to another—people get stuck. He found that the cingulate gyrus was hyperactive in the brain scans of murderers, possibly reflecting an inability to shift focus from violent thoughts and impulses (Begley, 1999). However, English researchers studying the neurological correlates of "love," using functional magnetic resonance imaging (fMRI), found that when an individual sees an image of someone with whom he or she is in love, activity significantly increases in the cingulate gyrus, compared with when the person sees an image of a stranger or friend (Bartels and Zeki, 2000). It would be ironic if the cingulate gyrus mediates the obsession with both a love object in normals and a victim in murderers.

To oversimplify, the limbic system excites sexual, aggressive and emotional impulses. The prefrontal cortex acts to inhibit and manage these impulses. Damage in the limbic areas can cause paranoia, whereas frontal lobe dysfunction disinhibits; together these factors are "significant precipitators of violence, especially when combined with a history of childhood abuse" (Pincus, 2001: 209).

General Physiology

The division of the nervous system responsible for regulating internal bodily functions such as heart rate, breathing, and general homeostasis is called the **autonomic nervous system** (ANS). The ANS consists of two main systems that act in concert to maintain homeostasis and respond to threat and stress: the sympathetic nervous system (SNS) and the parasympathetic nervous system (PNS). The **SNS** prepares the body for fight or flight by accelerating the heart rate; increasing lung capacity, sweat, and salivary secretions; and inhibiting gastrointestinal activity. When the threat passes, the PNS kicks in and brings everything back to normal (Starr and McMillan, 1997). Someone with an underactive SNS would not be physiologically alerted to potentially dangerous situations and thus would not be swayed by fear in the same manner that everyone else is. Conversely, someone with an overreactive SNS (panic disorder) would be ultrasensitive to the physiological cues elicited by stress or fear.

THE NEUROLOGICAL CORRELATES OF AGGRESSION

Neurodevelopmental Insults and Violence

Some of the variables repeatedly associated with criminal violence fall under the umbrella of what are called neurodevelopmental insults (NDI). NDI is defined broadly as a factor that disrupts normal central nervous system development and occurs either prenatally (as in the case of genetics, in utero, or during the birth process) or postnatally as the result of injury, disease, or abuse and neglect. Several lines of research link a variety of prenatal and postnatal insults to subsequent criminal behavior in adolescence and/or adulthood. These studies suggest that there are clearly early indicators of criminal behavior, which without intervention appear to traverse a fairly stable course over time.

Prenatal and Birth Complications. The idea that prenatal and/or birth complications might influence a child's cognitive and physical development is not a new one and has received considerable attention in medical journals. However, the idea that a child's social development might also be affected by birth complications is neither as readily accepted nor as clearly illustrated. There have been some interesting studies that correlate higher than expected numbers of personality disorders and criminal behavior with either prenatal or birth complications.

One such study looked at the relationship between severe nutritional deprivation experienced by the mother during her first and second trimesters of pregnancy and the diagnoses of antisocial personality in the adult children of those women. When researchers compared the birth records of children whose mothers had suffered severe nutritional deprivation with later psychiatric records, they found that the incidence of antisocial personality disorder was more than double that of the general population (Neugebauer, Hoek, and Susser, 1999).

Another study looking at the interaction of biological and the social factors that predispose individuals to violence found a significant interaction between birth complications (i.e., breach birth, cord prolapses, etc.) and early maternal rejection (i.e., mother sought abortion, put baby up for adoption, etc.) and later violent behavior. Specifically, 47 percent of those individuals with both factors became violent offenders compared with 20 percent of those who had only one or neither risk factor (Raine,

Highlight 7-2

The critical period for fetal brain development is between 9 and 16 weeks, with the central nervous system development continuing to be sensitive to environmental factors through 38 weeks (Starr and McMillan, 1997).

Brennan, and Mednick, 1994; Raine, Brennan, Mednick, and Mednick, 1996). These findings point to the importance of looking at biological and social factors in combination to understand how violence develops.

Early Onset Brain Injury. From birth to age 7 the foundations for all neurocognitive, neurophysiological, social, and adaptive behaviors are being laid (Huttenlocher and Dabholkar, 1997; Loeber and Farrington, 2000). Until recently it was readily accepted that traumatic brain injuries occurring in childhood showed the highest recovery rates because of **neural plasticity,** or the brain's ability to repair itself (Kolb, Gibb, and Gorny, 2000). This ability is due partly to the rapid synaptic growth (connection between neurons) experienced **during childhood** (Goldman-Rakic and Rakic, 1997; Scheibel and Levin, 1997) and partly due to the intensity of the learning environment experienced during childhood (Goldman-Rakic and Rakic, 1997). Neural plasticity is particularly apparent in most motor and standard cognitive functions such as language, memory, and general intellectual abilities (Eslinger, Biddle, Grattan, 1997; Scheibel and Levin, 1997). However, studies are beginning to document cases where early onset brain injury in the prefrontal cortex leads to a wide array of social and behavioral deficits later in life that closely resemble antisocial personality disorder.

When the records of children with early onset brain injury (EOBI) are reviewed retrospectively, one finds a pattern of severe behavioral deficit and aggression that becomes more prominent as the child advances in age. Indeed, early injury to some regions of the prefrontal cortex are associated with serious and chronic deficits in social behavior and moral reasoning, as well as deficits in impulse control and emotional regulation (Anderson, Damasio, Tranel, and Damasio, 2000; Tranel and Eslinger, 2000). These deficits occur despite the fact that other neurological development appears to proceed as expected and when there is no indication of parental abuse. Furthermore, the **earlier the brain injury, the more severe the behavioral deficits and aggressive tendencies** (Anderson, et al., 2000; Tranel and Eslinger, 2000) This finding indicates that there is a limited window of opportunity for social and behavioral learning. These findings parallel reports of adults whose social functioning is radically compromised after a prefrontal cortex injury (remember Phineas Gage). The behavior change is so extreme that neurologists have coined the term "**acquired sociopathy**" to describe the syndrome (Barrash, Tranel, and Anderson, 2000; Damasio, 1994).

Using positron emission tomography, or PET scans, Raine and associates (1997) found that murderers who pleaded NGRI but who had no self-reported social deprivation/abuse showed reduced brain activity in several areas within the prefrontal cortex. They also found reduced left hemisphere activity, especially in the amygdala, the thalamus, and the hippocampus. What is interesting is that these murderers who had no self-reported history of psychosocial deprivation exhibited less autonomic responsivity and greater prefrontal deficits than their counterparts who had experienced deprivation/abuse. This finding provides further evidence that violent behavior is associated with some form of brain dysfunction. Most researchers suggest that individuals are born with a neurological propensity toward antisocial and/or aggressive behavior and are then either socialized appropriately or not (Fowles, 2000; Lewis, 1990; Lykken, 1995; Raine, Brennan, Mednick, and Mednick, 1996). This study seems to suggest that in some cases, brain dysfunction might lead to violence regardless of the quality of parenting. On the other hand, the simple absence of overt deprivation or abuse (based on self-report) does not necessarily indicate the presence of good parenting.

Early Abuse, Violence and Neuropsychiatric Disorder. Over and over again studies show that child abuse and neglect predict violence irrespective of other factors such as age, gender, or ethnicity (Farrington and Loeber, 2000; Loeber and Farrington, 2000; Wong, Fenton, Lumsden, Maisey, and Stevens, 1997). As mentioned previously, court statistics kept on child abuse and neglect show that the most severe cases of abuse occur in children under the age of 5 years old (Miller, Fox, and Garcia-Beckwith, 1999). This period corresponds exactly to the time when children are experiencing the greatest level of synaptic growth (Huttenlocher and Dabholkar, 1997) and when most prosocial skills are developing (Loeber and Farrington, 2000). It is also during this time that both physical and psychological trauma are likely to have the greatest impact. Preliminary evidence suggests that this is in fact the case. Several brain regions appear to be especially vulnerable to neurodevelopmental insults in early childhood, including the prefrontal cortex (planning, impulse control, social behavior, memory and attention), the hippocampus (learning and memory), the amygdala (somatic memory, regulation of sexual and aggressive impulses) (LeDoux, 1996), and the corpus callosum (hemispheric integration) (Teicher et al., 1997).

Endocrine function is also vulnerable to chronic stress and can initiate a series of physiological events that have recognizable physiological and neurological consequences (Sapolsky, 1992). The social, psychological, and academic indicators of such trauma usually include problems with behavioral inhibition, attention and planning deficits, increased aggressiveness, early onset delinquency, and language and verbal IQ deficits (Scheibel and Levin, 1997).

Considering that most seriously violent offenders were abused (Meyers, Reccoppa, Burton, and McElroy, 1993; Schumaker and Mckee, 2001) and that most violent adults were also violent and aggressive as children (Harris, Rice, and Lalumiere, 2001), it stands to reason that the early indicators of behavioral dysfunction identified in some studies might represent early neurological responses to abuse. Although there is a strong correlation between abuse and violence, not all abused children become violent offenders, and not all violent offenders were abused. However, when we look at the school records of adult or adolescent violent offenders who were abused, we find a pattern of misbehavior, deficit, increased incidence of mood, personality disorders (Silverman, Reinherz, and Giaconia, 1996) and even psychotic disorders from a very early age (Lewis, 1990). For example, in prospective studies of children and adolescents who after psychiatric evaluation went on to commit murder, it was noted that many of these children had displayed several psychotic symptoms. However, because of differences in child and adult symptomology, these children were routinely diagnosed with either conduct or oppositional defiant disorder (Bensley et al., 1999; Lewis, 1990) and consequently not treated for the psychosis. In addition, epidemiological meta-analyses on childhood and adolescent violence show that the road to delinquency and violence begins in childhood around age 7 and gradually progresses in frequency and severity of offense until about age 14 years, a full seven years during which intervention was possible (Loeber and Farrington, 2000).

Early Childhood Aggression and Neurological Deficit

Underlying the behavioral and academic problems that many aggressive children exhibit are a variety of neurological deficits that are linked to dysfunction in several brain regions. Numerous studies show that aggressive and violent children and adults repeatedly perform more poorly than do controls on electroencephalographic (EEG) and some forms of neurocognitive testing (Loeber and Farrington, 2000; Moffit and Lynam, 1994; Raine, Venables, and Williams, 1990). In addition, cognitive testing reveals that violent offenders who were abused as children show marked deficits in the working memory (hippocampus and amygdala), executive functioning (prefrontal cortex), and attention (Raine et al., 2001).

Behavioral Hyperactivity. Prefrontal cortex deficits either can be genetically based or can be the result of physical injury, disease, or chronic psychological trauma. Aggressive children and adults tend to display poor impulse control, increased activity levels, and difficulties in planning and attention that are consistent with prefrontal cortex disfunction and similar to problems in children diagnosed with attention deficit hyperactivity disorder (Lewis, 1990). In fact, several studies have indicated that the two strongest predictors of violence in adolescence are prefrontal cortex deficit per neurological testing at age 7 years (Loeber and Farrington, 2000) and child abuse (Teicher et al., 1997). As one might expect, when both risk factors are present, the probability of violent behavior greatly increases (Harris, Rice, and Lalumeire, 2001; Raine, Brennan, Mednick, and Mednick, 1996). A damaged or poorly functioning frontal cortex may not be able to inhibit the violent impulses engendered by abuse (Pincus, 2001).

Autonomic Hypoactivity. EEG studies on both children and adults with histories of violence repeatedly show autonomic hyporeactivity or an underreactive fear conditioning system (Fowles, 2000; Hare, 1970). Fear conditioning refers to the autonomic responses associated with fight or flight and is controlled by two brain regions, the orbitofrontal cortex (frontal lobe) and the amygdala (temporal lobe) (LeDoux, 1996). Research shows that injury or dysfunction in these regions of the brain impairs social and behavioral decision-making abilities and does so while leaving cognitive ability relatively intact (again, remember Phineas Gage). This finding means that although one might be aware cognitively that a particular behavior is irrational or

Highlight 7-3

The right **frontotemporal regions** are associated with **pain processing** (Flor-Henry, Lang, Koles, and Frenzel, 1991). Many **violent criminals show severely abnormal pain thresholds** and while in prison repeatedly injure themselves and others as a way of "feeling." "At the least violent end of the self-mutilative spectrum, these men cut their wrists or forearms or other areas of their bodies. Then they escalate to swallowing razor blades, screws, or other injurious objects. . . . So common is the practice that surgeons are reluctant to remove these objects surgically unless and until so many have accumulated inside the body that they threaten to cause intestinal obstruction or perforation. When that is not sufficient, many escalate to the point of repeatedly inserting bedsprings or screws or ballpoint pins into their urethras. . . . I have also known prison inmates who have cut off their penis and testicles, others who have taken out their toenails and others who have blinded themselves" (Gilligan, 1999: 40).

dangerous, one is prevented from acting on this knowledge because of the lack of **somatic markers** (the adrenaline rush that causes increased heart rate, breathing, etc.). These somatic markers that our body produces help influence decisions about dangerousness.

Several aspects of this research are particularly relevant to the study of aggression and violence. First, this research implies that physiological and emotional regulatory processes underlie and guide cognitive decision-making (Damasio, 1994). This is contrary to the opinions of generations of philosophers and psychologists who have held that rationality precedes and guides action. Second, although most of this research is done with individuals who sustain injuries to either the orbitofrontal cortex (Damasio, 1994) or the amygdala (LeDoux, 1996), we know from decades of endocrine research that stress chemically alters these and other regions of the brain and produces similar symptoms (Sapolsky, 2000). Considering the number of violent criminals who were abused as children, the environmental requirements of early brain development and the neurological changes that result from chronic or acute stress, it is

Highlight 7-4

When frightened by an event such as walking down a dark alley, the **amygdala,** via its connections to the **hypothalamus,** activates the **sympathetic nervous system** and initiates the array of bodily events that signal dangerousness. The **prefrontal cortex** then links the emotion and its corresponding bodily representation with the event and forwards it to the **hippocampus** for storage. When faced with a similar circumstance in the future, not only will you recall danger cognitively, but your body will also recall the danger physiologically. This type of coding helps you avoid dangerous situations and is called **fear conditioning.**

conceivable that violent and antisocial behavior is tied to the neurophysiological changes resulting from abuse. That is, children who are abused or neglected don't develop the somatic markers necessary for fear conditioning or social decision-making.

In a series of groundbreaking studies, Adrian Raine and his colleagues at the University of Southern California compared the functional magnetic resonance images (fMRI) and volumetric measurements of the brains of violent offenders, abused and nonabused individuals and various control groups. Abuse data were gathered from self-report interviews, and a variety of visual, verbal, memory, and attention tasks were administered while subjects underwent fMRI brain scans. The results indicated that several regions of the brain were affected in those individuals with histories of abuse.

Globally reduced left hemispheric activation in all lobes was correlated with abuse, as was reduced right hemisphere activation in the frontal and temporal lobes. For abused/violent individuals, the right hemisphere, especially the right temporal cortex, showed the lowest level of functioning of all groups. Reduced right hemisphere activation impairs fear conditioning (Hugdahl, 1998). The abused-only (nonviolent) group showed the least amount of activation in the left hemisphere (language, fine motor), which correlated with this group's lower IQ scores. What does this mean? Raine and his colleagues speculate that the reduced right hemisphere functioning in violent individuals who were severely abused as children (AV) might inhibit their ability to recognize emotion in others. This possibility may contribute to their propensity to respond inappropriately to social situations. Since the right hemisphere is also associated with the inability to back off from a socially or physically dangerous situation, it is possible that these individuals don't respond normally to fear-initiating situations and therefore are not swayed by the possibility of danger or punishment. The reduction in right hemispheric activation in the frontal and temporal lobes would then represent a neurological correlate of the deficient fear conditioning and the autonomic underactivity exhibited by many criminals. Without fear, one cannot judge danger or consequences. This fearlessness may also make a child more difficult to socialize through punishment-based discipline.

Stress, Memory, and Behavior

As mentioned before, stress can modify neural pathways and continued and/or high levels of stress can irreversibly alter cellular organization in certain regions of the brain (Sapolsky, 2000). Two regions that are affected by the stress and trauma are the hippocampus and the amygdala. Recall that both the hippocampus and the amygdala play critical roles in the formation, coding, and organization of emotional and associative memory. The hippocampus receives projections from the hypothalamus, which along with the pituitary and adrenal gland modulate the release and synthesis of many hormones. One of the hormones released and modulated through the hypothalamus-pituitary-adrenal axis (HPA) is the stress hormone, cortisol.

Cortisol controls the physiological response to stress known as fight or flight. However, chronic hyperstimulation of cortisol leads to a variety of conditions including cell death within the hippocampus (Nelson, 2000; Niewoehner, 1998). Increased cortisol also alters mood toward manic states and sometimes even psychosis (Niewoehner, 1998).

Recall from our earlier discussion that violent offenders and aggressive and abused children show reduced autonomic reactivity and reduced ability to respond to fear conditioning. An integral part of fear conditioning is associative memory (e.g., the ability to associate the feeling of fear with a particular event), and both the hippocampus and the amygdala are critical to this function (Hugdahl, 1998). We know that excessive stress causes cell death in the hippocampus (Teicher et al., 1997) and that

Case Example: Gene-Environment Interaction, Neurological Damage, and Stressful Childhood

Bobby Jo Long may be the classic case of someone "destined" to become a random killer. He suffered from a genetic disorder characterized by an extra X chromosome, causing his glands to produce abnormal amounts of estrogen in puberty, with the result that his breasts began to enlarge. Surgery removed six pounds of excess tissue from his chest, but the resultant gender confusion remained, exacerbated by his mother, who shared Long's bed until he reached the age of 13 years. Long also alleged that his mother entertained numerous male visitors in their one-bedroom apartment. Aside from genetic and family problems, Long also suffered a series of grievous head injuries beginning at age 5, when he was knocked unconscious in a fall from a swing, with one eyelid being skewered by a stick. The following year, he was thrown from his bicycle, crashing headfirst into a parked car, with injuries including loss of several teeth and a severe concussion. At age 13, Long met the girl who would become his wife and simultaneously gave up sleeping with his mother. Long enlisted in the army prior to marriage, and he crashed a motorcycle six months later, shattering his helmet with the impact of his skull on asphalt. Convalescing in the hospital, he was alternately stricken by blinding headaches and unpredictable violent rages, discovering a new obsession with sex. While still in a cast, Long masturbated five times a day to relieve himself, continuing the practice at home despite twice-daily intercourse with his wife. Still, it was not enough, and soon he began to search for other prey. Between 1980 and 1983, Long terrorized the Florida communities of Miami, Ocala, and Fort Lauderdale as the "Classified Ad Rapist," preying on housewives in midday attacks. Dropping by while their husbands were working, Long typically produced a knife, bound his victims, raped them violently, and robbed their homes before he fled. Unlike the 50 women raped by Long, his murder victims were selected from the ranks of prostitutes or other women whom he viewed as "tramps." Between May and November 1984, he strangled, stabbed, and shot at least 9 victims. Convicted at his trial in early 1985, he was sentenced to die.

those individuals who experience excessive or chronic stress often show memory deficits, and in the more severe cases, they exhibit dissociative states (Teicher et al., 1997). Both aggressive children and adults repeatedly test poorly on tasks related to memory and attention (Lewis, 1990). Furthermore, the few brain-imaging studies done with violent offenders and abused children consistently show a reduction in hippocampal functioning (Laakso et al., 2001; Raine, Buchsbaum, and LaCasse, 1997). This finding means that even if there is no direct physical trauma or injury to a particular brain region, the chronic emotional stress experienced as a result of abuse or neglect many negatively alter brain function.

NEUROCHEMISTRY AND HORMONES

The Serotonin Connection

The connection between serotonin (5HT) and aggression is one of the most researched and highly debated associations in this field. A correlation between the two was first noted in animal research over forty years ago and has been confirmed in clinical studies over the last two decades (Coccaro 1989; Coccaro et al., 1997). However, because of differences in methodology, the research is far from definitive (Berman and Coccaro, 1997).

In animal studies, lower 5HT has been associated with isolation-induced aggression (Coccarro, 1989) and territoriality (Brunner and Hen, 1997). In this paradigm, mice are isolated for up to two weeks before another mouse is introduced into the cage. Researchers find that an isolated mouse will attack an intruder mouse several times faster than its nonisolated counterpart, without provocation and without following the usual social protocols that normally occur in such situations (Brunner and Hen, 1997). When researchers measure the 5HT levels in the isolated mouse, they find that they are in fact several times lower than normal. It is interesting that the more fighting that the mouse engages in, the lower the 5HT levels become, suggesting a reciprocal relationship between the behavior and the neurochemical (Brunner and Hen, 1997) and supporting the old adage that "violence begets violence."

In human clinical studies, diminished 5HT levels have been associated with an entire spectrum of impulsive behaviors including violence, suicide, and drug and alcohol abuse (Coccaro, 1989; Coccarro et al., 1989; Coccarro et al., 1997; Moss, Yao, and Panzak, 1990). Low serotonin is also implicated in depression and antisocial personality disorder (Coccarro et al., 1989; Moss, Yao, and Panzak, 1990). Researchers believe that 5HT modulates inhibition systems and mood states, via input to the hippocampus and amygdala, (Teicher et al., 1997), thereby either raising or lowering one's sensitivity to painful or unpleasant stimuli (Coccarro, 1989). That is, low levels of 5HT heighten one's general irritability and excitability rather than provoking a specific activity or mood state. However, reduced 5HT has not been associated with premeditated violence. Since genetic factors determine the general characteristics of brain function and structure, it is likely that serotonin levels are controlled genetically. Low 5HT levels create a vulnerability to aggression or depression (Lappalainen et al., 1998) that emerge only under certain environmental conditions. Environmental factors that have been associated with lowered serotonin production include neglect, harsh discipline, poverty, and sensory deprivation (Myslinski, 1997).

Hormones and Aggression

Several lines of research have linked testosterone to aggression (Fishbein, Lozovsky, and Jaffe, 1989; Simon, Cologer-Clifford, Lu, McKenna, and Lu, 1998). Testosterone is thought to both organize and initiate brain pathways that elicit aggression (Nelson, 2000). Conversely, the female hormone estrogen is thought to organize the neural networks associated with feminine or nonaggressive behavior (Flor-Henry, Lang, Koles, and Frenzel, 1991). In both cases, the structures associated with these pathways are some of the same ones implicated in 5HT, imaging, and cortical stimulation studies (the amygdala, the hippocampus, the hypothalamus, and the prefrontal cortex) (Nelson, 2000). Testosterone and estrogen are directly involved in the regulation of the 5HT pathways that modulate aggression (Cologer-Clifford, Simon, Richter, Smoluck, and Lu, 1999).

The majority of research into the role of testosterone and aggression is done using animal models with conclusions that are then extrapolated to humans. One such research model is the castration-replacement paradigm (Cologer-Clifford, Simon, Richter, Smoluck, and Lu, 1999). Here, researchers study the effects of castration or ovariectomy (removal of the ovaries) on aggressive behavior. Researchers find that when male mice are castrated before sexual differentiation occurs in the brain (prenatally), they exhibit no aggression. If these mice are then given testosterone in adulthood, they continue to show reduced levels of aggression. If, on the other hand, they are castrated in adulthood and then administered testosterone, only the mice that were previously aggressive become aggressive again, whereas those who were not previously aggressive remain nonaggressive (Nelson, 2000). It is interesting, that when female mice are ovariectomized prenatally and given testosterone in adulthood, they show no signs of aggression, but when they are ovariectomized and given testosterone prenattally, then they too show aggressive tendencies (Nelson, 2000). Findings from these types of studies indicate that there are critical periods of development (at least in mice) when hormones can initiate aggressive behavior.

In human studies, the role of testosterone in aggression is much more difficult to pin down for several reasons. First, testosterone levels fluctuate as social status changes, such that dominance is correlated with increased testosterone, and dependence is associated with decreased testosterone (Mazur, Booth, and Dabbs, 1992). Second, the data gathered from many of the human studies are inherently flawed because of the confounding variables that are necessarily present. For example, studies have noted that from 5 to 10 percent of the most violent and aggressive prisoners show elevated testosterone levels. But since aggression is measured by psychological assessment, questionnaire, and criminal records, and then it is correlated with blood tests, the time between the aggressive or violent act and the blood tests measures may span many years (Nelson, 2000).

Highlight 7-5

It is interesting that low testosterone is correlated with greater marital satisfaction for both women and men (Nelson, 2000).

A counterpoint to the testosterone-aggression hypothesis is the case of sexually sadistic killers who tend to exhibit uniquely feminine hormonal responses during endocrine challenge experiments (Flor-Henry, Lang, Koles, and Frenzel, 1991). This finding is particularly interesting when one considers that serial killers often are sexually sadistic (Meyers, Reccoppa, Burton, and McElroy, 1993). One could speculate that the dominance and the control achieved through sadistic acts are an effort to raise testosterone levels in this type of offender.

Conclusion: Pulling It All Together

As we've seen throughout this chapter, from Phineas Gage to modern neuroscience, personality, behavior, cognition, and emotion are all controlled by brain function, and brain function relies heavily on both genetic and environmental circumstances. Our friend Phineas Gage survived a focal brain injury in the frontal region of the brain that we now know controls many aspects of behavior and personality. The injury was devastating not because of the physical or cognitive impairments that he might have suffered, but because of the behavioral and personality changes that ensued. Had we been able to examine him using modern technology, we might have found that he, like so many of the violent offenders, exhibited autonomic hyporeactivity that precluded him from associating fear or other emotional and physiological responses with particular events. This limitation made it impossible for him to learn from his mistakes and to prejudge the possible consequences of his actions. His behavior after the injury was erratic and unreasonable. He drank. He brawled. He was vulgar and profane, and in some fundamental way his values changed. He had in effect "acquired sociopathy." But he was not violent, just impulsive and reckless.

From the research discussed in this chapter, we know that violent criminals exhibit several behavioral and personality deficits similar to those of Phineas Gage. We also know that violent criminals show deficits in inhibition, attention, and memory consistent with brain injury or dysfunction (in prefrontal, amygdalar, and hippocampal regions). But when we examine the brains of violent men, rarely do we find evidence of specific damage to these areas. Rather, we see evidence of dysfunction and bits and pieces of a picture that is, as of yet, not fully understood. Even with the recent advances in technology, researchers are able only to broadly identify the neural correlates of violence. However, an emerging theory that developed from observations of modern-day Phineas Gages offers insight about the possible neural development of violent behavior.

This theory, which is called the **somatic marker theory** (Damasio, 1994), postulates that certain bioregulatory processes, including autonomic functioning (fear conditioning) exist to help influence our decisions about social interaction, survival, and danger. When the circuits that control autonomic functioning (orbitofrontal cortex, amygdala, hippocampus) are damaged, so too is the ability to "feel." When we can't feel, we can't judge the inhumanity or dangerousness of an act. If this theory is correct, it would mean that the physiological expression of emotion precedes and guides action. Although this might seem obvious, especially to anyone who has ever acted in the "heat of the moment" or under the influence of hormones, it is not obvious. Since antiquity, to act reasonably is to act devoid of emotion. When people are excessively emotional, we call them unreasonable, hysterical, or neurotic. What the somatic marker theory says is that without emotion, reason runs amuck. And this is especially evident in the social arena. When we look at the stories of some of the seriously violent offenders, we see examples of this condition. These people craft and carry out incredibly inhumane and horrific acts of violence that go against all social mores and that are completely unreasonable to those of us who are "in our right minds"; however, these actions have an internal logic that is perfectly reasonable to someone who is devoid of emotion. But what neural mechanisms either elicit or fail to inhibit such horrific behavior? One of the reasons that Phineas functioned as well as he did after his injury (if we can call it functioning well) was that his premorbid (before disease/injury) functioning was quite good. Recall that children with early onset brain injury, who have not yet had the time to develop social functioning skills, actually become quite aggressive and exhibit substantially more behavioral problems than do adults with the same injury. As far as researchers can tell, these children develop behavioral problems as a direct result of the injury and without any indications of parental abuse or neglect. This is one possible scenario.

Now consider the violent offender with a history of severe and usually bizarre early childhood abuse. Recall that during childhood, synaptic growth (connections

Highlight 7-6

It is interesting that many violent serial killers speak of being without emotion and often refer to themselves as the **walking dead.** A good example of this is found in an excerpt from David Berkowitz's prison diary:

> I am a monster. I am the "Son of Sam." I have fear now that I . . . will become a demon or, I may be a demon right now . . . I fear that with the **loss of my humanness** I will become like a zombie . . . Some people thought **I was void of emotions** when they examined me. This is exactly what happens to those possessed. I want my soul back! I want what was taken from me! I have a right to be human . . . **I am willing to die to be at peace** . . . I must be put to death (Gilligan, 1999: 39).

between the neurons) and learning takes place at a rate greater than at any other time during development. When abuse or neglect chronically occur, several processes are likely occurring at the neural level. First, the endocrine stress response is activated chronically and acutely, thus ultimately causing damage to the prefrontal cortex (inhibition, planning), hippocampus (representational and associative memory), and the amygdala (emotional and somatic memory). In addition, the chronic stress may contribute to underactive autonomic responsiveness to make the child unresponsive to potential consequences or punishment (fearless). The hyperstimulation of cortisol (stress hormone) leads to cell death in the hippocampus, causing problems with memory and possibly dissociation. Because of these neurological changes, the child may not be able to inhibit the violent or sexual impulses engendered by emotional, physical, or sexual abuse.

Because the effects of child abuse are both neurological (i.e., disinhibitory) and psychological (aggressive impulses), it stands to reason that serious efforts to prevent abuse would allow more individuals to "enter portals of normal society rather than the gates of prison" (Pincus, 2001: 210).

There are more than two potential scenarios for the development of violence. The research is still in its infancy, and much remains to be discovered. However, it is becoming clear that biological-neurological genetic factors do not operate in isolation from psychological and environmental factors to produce "evil minds." Rather, abuse and/or neglect engenders violent desires while also negatively impacting neurological development. In turn, "neurological dysfunction and psychiatric disorders damage the capacity to check that [violent] urge" (Pincus, 2001: 19).

Discussion Questions and Activities

1. How would the gene-environment interaction model explain the results of genetic studies (i.e., gene variation, twin, adoption) into the causes of violence?
2. For each of the following brain structures, identify the possible effects of damage or lesions. Put your answer on a chart.

   Prefrontal cortex

   Corpus collosum

   Amygdala

   Hypothalamus

   Cingulated gyrus

   Hippocampus
3. What is neural plasticity? What is the evidence that early onset brain injury to the prefrontal cortex is not consistent with the neural plasticity principle?

4. Make a graphic organizer of the neurological consequences of early physical and psychological trauma that create chronic stress and the way that they are associated with the functions of specific brain regions.
5. What are the neurological patterns/correlates of fearlessness? What is the role of somatic markers in the development of fearlessness? What is the role of cortisol?
6. In Raines's study of abused only subjects and abused violent subjects, what differentiated the two groups in terms of neurological functioning, and what were the implications?
7. How are levels of serotonin related to types (impulsive versus planned) of violent acting out? From a neurochemical perspective, how does "violence beget violence"?
8. How does the case study of Bobby Jo Long illustrate the gene-environment interaction model? On the basis of the location and timing of his head injuries and his behavior, what areas of his brain were probably affected?
9. Look back at the case of Henry Lee Lucas (Chapter 3), and note his early childhood environment. Using somatic marker theory, what do you think possibly happened to him *physiologically* that contributed to the kind of man that he became?
10. If you were a juror and clear evidence of neurological dysfunction was found in an offender's brain, how much weight would you give this evidence in deciding the level of his or her responsibility for the crime? Explain the reasons for your decision.
11. If science advances to the point that we can clearly identify early childhood neurological indicators of a propensity for violence, how should we use this information? Should we screen children? Put "damaged" children under surveillance? Intervene environmentally? Explain the reasons for your opinions.

Key Terms

Acquired sociopathy
Autonomic nervous system
Cortisol
Dopamine
Gene-environment interaction
Genotypes
Left hemisphere
Limbic system
Neural plasticity
Neurotransmitters
Norepinephrine
Phenotypes
Prefrontal cortex
Right hemisphere
Serotonin
Somatic memory
Somatic marker theory

References

Anderson, S., H. Damasio, D. Tranel, and A. Damasio. 2000. "Long-term sequelae of prefrontal cortex damage acquired in early childhood." *Developmental Neuropsychology 18:* 281–296.

Barrash, J., D. Tranel, and S. W. Anderson, 2000. "Aquired personality disturbances associated with bilateral damage to the ventromedial prefrontal area." *Developmental Neuropsychology 18:* 355–381.

Bartels, A., S. Zeki, 2000. "The neural basis of romantic love." *Neuroreport 11:* 3829–3834.

Bear, D. 1991. "Neurological perspectives on aggressive behavior." *Journal of Neuropsychiatry 3:* S3–S8.

Begley, S. 1999. "Why the young kill." *Newsweek: Special Report.* May 3.

Bensley, L. S., J. Van Ennwyk, S. J. Spieker, and J. Schoder. 1999. "Self-reported abuse history and adolescent problem behaviors, I. Antisocial and suicidal behaviors." *Journal of Adolescent Health 24:* 163–172.

Bergvall, A., H. Wessely, A. Forsman, and S. Hansen. 2001. "A deficit in attentional set shifting of violent offenders." *Psychological Medicine 31:* 1095–1105.

Berman, M. T., J. Tracy, and E. F. Coccaro. 1997. "The serotonin hypothesis of aggression revisited." *Clinical Psychology Review 17:* 651–656.

Brunner, D. and R. Hen. 1997. "Insights into the neurobiology of impulsive behavior from serotonin receptor knockout mice." *Annals of New York Academy of Sciences 836:* 81–105.

Carlson, N. R. 2000. *Physiology of Behavior.* Needham Heights, Mass.: Allyn and Bacon.

Christiansen, K. O. 1974. "Seriousness of criminality and concordance among Danish twins." In R. Hood (Ed.), *Crime, Criminology and Public Policy,* pp. 63–77. New York: Free Press.

Coccaro, E. 1989. "Central serotonin and impulsive aggression." *British Journal of Psychiatry 155* (suppl. 8): 52–62.

Coccaro, E., L. Siever, H. Klar, G. Maurer, K. Cochrane, T. Cooper, R. Mohs, and K. Davis. 1989. "Serotonergic studies in patients with affective and personality disorders." *Archives of General Psychiatry 46:* 587–599.

Coccaro, E. F., R. J. Karoussi, T. B. Cooper, 1997. "Central seratonin activity and aggression: Inverse relationship with prolactin response to d-fenfluramine, but not CSF 5-HIAA concentration, in human subjects." *American Journal of Psychiatry,* 154, 1430–1435.

Cologer-Clifford, A., N. Simon, S. F. Lu, and S. Smoluck. 1997. "Serotonin agonist-induced decreases in intermale aggression are dependent on brain region and receptor subtype." *Pharmacology, Biochemistry and Behavior 58:* 425–430.

Cologer-Clifford, A., N. G. Simon, M. L. Richter, S. A. Smoluck, and S. Lu. 1999. "Androgens and estrogens modulate 5-HT1A and 5-HT1B agonist effects on aggression." *Physiology and Behavior 65:* 823–828.

Damasio, A., 1994. *Decartes Error.* New York: Quill Publishing.

Dinwiddie, S. H. 1996. "Genetics, antisocial personality and criminal responsibility." *Bulletin of the American Academy of Psychiatry and Law 24:* 95–108.

Eley, T., P. Lichtenstein, and J. Stevenson. 1999. "Sex differences in the etiology of aggressiveness and non-aggressiveness in antisocial behavior: Results from two twin studies." *Child Development 70:* 155–168.

Eslinger, P. J., K. R. Biddle, and L. M. Grattan. 1997. "Cognitive and social development in children with prefrontal cortex lesions." In N. Krasnegor, G. Lyon, P. Goldman-Rakic, (Eds.) *Development of the Prefrontal Cortex, Evolution, Neurobiology, and Behaviors* pp. 295–335. Baltimore, MD: Paul H. Brookes Publishing Co.

Farrington, D. P. and R. Loeber. 2000. "Epidemiology of juvenile violence." *Psychiatric Clinics, of North America 9:* 722–748.

Fishbein, D. H., D. Lozovsky, and J. H. Jaffe. 1989. "Impulsivity, Aggression and Neuroendocrine Responses to Serotonergic Stimulation in Substance Abusers." *Biological Psychiatry 25:* 1049–1066.

Flor-Henry, P., R. A. Lang, Z. J. Koles, and R. R. Frenzel. 1991. "Quantitative EEG studies of pedophilia." *International Journal of Psychophysiology 10:* 253–558.

Fowles, D. 2000. "Electrodermal hyporeactivity and antisocial behavior: Does anxiety mediate the relationship?" *Journal of Affective Disorders 6:* 177–189.

Fowles, D. and G. Kochanska. 2000. "Temperament as a moderator of pathways to conscience in children: The contribution of electrodermal activity." *Psychophysiology 37:* 788–795.

Gardner, L. I. and R. L. Neu. 1972. "Evidence linking an extra Y chromosome to sociopathic behavior." *Archives of General Psychiatry 26:* 220–222.

Gazzaniga, M. S., R. B. Irvy, and G. R. Mangun. 1998. "*Cognitive Neuroscience, The Biology of the Mind.* New York: W. W. Norton and Company.

Gilligan, J. 1999. *Violence.* New York: Vintage Books.

Goldman-Rakic, P. S., J. Bourgeois, P. Rakic. 1997. "Analysis of synaptogenesis in prefrontal cortex of the non-human primate." In N. A. Krasnegor, G. R. Lyon, and P. S. Goldman-Rakic, (Eds.), *Development of the Prefrontal Cortex, Evolution, Neurobiology, and Behavior*, pp. 27–47. Baltimore: Paul H. Brooks Publishing.

Hare, R.D. 1970. *Psychopathy: Theory and Research.* New York: John Wiley & Sons.

Harris, G., M. Rice, and M. Lalumiere. 2001. "Criminal violence: The roles of psychopathy, neurodevelopmental insults and antisocial parenting." *Criminal Justice and Behavior 28:* 402–426.

Hugdahl, K. 1998. "Cortical control of human classical conditioning: Autonomic and positron emission tomography data." *Psychophysiology 35:* 170–178.

Huttenlocher, P. R., and A. S. Dabholkar. 1997. Developmental anatomy of prefrontal cortex. In N. A. Krasnegor, G. R. Lyon, and P. S. Goldman-Rakic (Eds.), *Development of the Prefrontal Cortex, Evolution, Neurobiology, and Behavior*, pp. 6–84. Baltimore: Paul H. Brooks.

Jerison, H. J. 1997. "Evolution of the prefrontal cortex." In N. A. Krasnegor, G. R. Lyon, and P. S. Goldman-Rakic (Eds.), *Development of the Prefrontal Cortex, Evolution, Neurobiology, and Behavior*, pp. 9–26. Baltimore: Paul H. Brooks.

Kalat, J. 1995. *Biological Psychology.* Pacific Grove, Calif.: Brooks Cole Publishing.

Kavoussi, R., P. Armstead, and E. Coccaro. 1997. "The nuerobiology of impulsive behavior." *The Psychiatric Clinics of North America 30:* 395–403.

Kolb, B., R. Gibb, and G. Gorny. 2000. "Cortical plasticity and the development of behavior after early frontal cortical injury." *Developmental Neuropsychology 18:* 423–444.

Laakso, M., O. Vaurio, E. Koivisto, L. Savolainen, M. Eronen, H. Aronen, P. Hakola, E. Repo, H. Soininen, and J. Tiihonen. 2001. "Psychopathy and the posterior hippocampus." *Behavioral Brain Research 118:* 187–193.

Lappalainen, J., J. Long, M. Eggert, N. Ozaki, R. Robin, G. Brown, H. Naukkarinen, M. Virkkunen, M. Linnoila, and D. Goldman. 1998. "Linkage of anitsocial alcoholism to the serotonin 5-HT1B receptor in 2 populations." *Archives of General Psychiatry 55:* 989–994.

LeDoux, J. 1996. *The Emotional Brain.* New York: Simon & Schuster.

Leonard, B. E. 1992. *Fundamentals of Psychopharmacology.* West Susex, England: John Wiley & Sons.

Lewis, D. O. 1990. "Neuropsychiatric and experiential correlates of violent juvenile delinquency." *Neuropsychology Review 1:* 125–136.

Loeber, R. and D. P. Farrington. 2000. "Young children who commit crime: Epidemiology, developmental origins, risk factors, early interventions and policy implications." *Development and Psychopathology 12:* 737–762.

Luria, A. R. 1961. *The Role of Speech in the Regulation of Normal and Abnormal Behavior.* New York: Liveright Publishing Corporation.

Lykken, D. T. 1995. *The Antisocial Personalities.* Hillsdale, N.J.: Lawrence Erlbaum Associates.

Martin, J. H. 1996. *Neuroanatomy, Text and Atlas.* Stamford, Conn.: Appleton and Lange.

Mazur, A., A. Booth, and J. Dabbs. 1992. "Testosterone and chess competition." *Social Psychology Quarterly 55:* 70–77.

Mednick, S. A. and K. M. Finello. 1983. "Biological factors and crime: Implications for forensic psychiatry." *International Journal of Law and Psychiatry 6:* 1–15.

Mednick, S. A. and E. S. Kandel. 1988. "Congenital determinants of violence." *Bulletin of the American Academy of Psychiatry and Law 16:* 101–109.

Meyers, W., L. Reccoppa, K. Burton, and R. McElroy. 1993. "Malignant sex and aggression: An overview of serial sexual homicide." *Bulletin of the American Academy of Psychiatry and Law 21:* 435–451.

Miller, B., B. Fox, and L. Garcia-Beckwith. 1999. "Intervening in severe physical child abuse cases: Mental health, legal and social services." *Child Abuse and Neglect 23:* 905–914.

Moffitt, T., A. Caspi, R. Michael. "Sex differences in antisocial behavior: Conduct disorder, delinquency, and violence in the Dunedin longitudinal study." *Journal of Family Studies 8* (2): 260–261.

Moffit, T. E. and D. Lynam, Jr. 1994. "The neuropsychology of conduct disorder and delinquency: Implications for understanding antisocial behavior." *Progress in Experimental Personality and Psychopathology Research 17:* 233–262.

Moss, H., J. Yao, and G. Panzak. 1990. "Serotonergic reactivity and behavioral dimensions in antisocial personality disorder with substance abuse." *Biological Psychiatry 28:* 325–338.

Myslinski, N. 1997. "Violence and the brain." *The World and I* 2(12): 146–152.

Neilson, J. 1970. "Criminality among patients with Klinefetler's Syndrome and the XYY syndrome." *Journal of Psychiatry 117:* 365–369.

Neilson, J. and B. Pelson. 1987. "Follow-up 20 years after of 34 Klinefelter males with karytype 47, XXY and 16 hypogonadal males with karytype, 46 XY." *Human Genetics 77:* 188–192.

Nelson, R. J. 2000. *An Introduction to Behavioral Endocrinology.* Sunderland, Mass.: Sinaur and Associates.

Neugebauer, R., H. W. Hoek, and E. Susser. 1999. "Prenatal exposure to wartime famine and development of antisocial personality disorder in early adulthood." *Journal of the American Medical Association 282:* 455–462.

Niewoehner, C. B. 1998. *Endocrine Pathophysiology.* Madison, Conn.: Fence Creek Publishing.

Pincus, J. 2001. *Base Instincts: What Makes Killers Kill.* New York: W. W. Norton & Co.

Raine, A. 1993. *The Psychopathology of Crime: Criminal Behavior as a Clinical Disorder.* San Diego: Academic Press.

Raine, A., P. Brennan, and S. A. Mednick. 1994. "Birth complications combined with early maternal rejection at age 1 year predispose to violent crime at age 18 years." *Archives of General Psychology 51:* 984–988.

Raine, A., P. Brennan, B. Mednick, and S. Mednick. 1996. "High rates of violence, crime, academic problems and behavioral problems in males with both early neuromotor deficits and unstable family environments." *Archives of General Psychiatry 53:* 544–549.

Raine, A., M. Buchsbaum, and L. LaCasse. 1997. "Brain abnormalities in murderers indicated by positron emission tomography." *Biological Psychiatry 42:* 495–508.

Raine, A., T. Lencz, S. Bihrle, L. LaCasse, and P. Colletti. 2000. "Reduced prefrontal gray matter volume and reduced autonomic activity in antisocial personality disorder." *Archives of General Psychiatry 57:* 119–127.

Raine, A., S. Park, T. Lencz, S. Bihrle, L. LaCasse, C. Spatz-Widom, L. Al-Dayeh, and M. Singh. 2001. "Reduced right hemisphere activation in severely abused violent offenders during a working memory task." *Aggressive Behavior 27:* 111–129.

Raine, A., G. Reynolds, and C. Shears. 1991. "Neuroanatomical correlates of skin conductance orienting in normal humans: A magnetic resonance imaging study." *Psychophysiology 28:* 548–558.

Raine, A., C. Reynolds, P. H. Venables, S. A. Mednick, and D. A. Farrington. 1998. "Fearlessness, stimulation-seeking and large body-size at age 3 years as early predispositions to childhood aggression at age 11 years." *Archives of General Psychiatry 55:* 745–751.

Raine, A., J. Stoddard, S. Birhle, and M. Buchsbaum. 1998. "Prefrontal glucose deficits in murderers lacking psychosocial deprivation." *Neuropsychiatry, Neuropsychology and Behavioral Neuroscience 11:* 1–7.

Raine, A., P. H. Venables, C. Dalais, K. Mellingen, C. Reynolds, and S. A. Mednick. 2001. "Early educational and health enrichment at age 3–5 years is associated with increased autonomic and central nervous system arousal and orienting at age 11 years: Evidence from the Mauritius Child Health Project." *Psychophysiology 38:* 254–266.

Raine, A., P. Venables, S. A. Mednick, 1997. "Low resting heart rate at age 3 years predisposes to aggression at age 11: Findings from the Mauritus Joint Child Health Project." *Journal of the American Academy of Child and Adolescent Psychiatry*, 36, 1457–1464.

Raine, A., P. Venables, and M. Williams. 1990. "Relationships between n1, p300 and contingent negative variation recorded at age 15 and criminal behavior at age 24." *Psychophysiology 27:* 567–574.

Sapolsky, R. M. 1992. *Stress, the Aging Brain, and the Mechanisms of Neuron Death.* Cambridge, Mass.: MIT Press.

Sapolsky, R. M. (2000). The possibility of neurotoxicity in the hippocampus in major depression: a primer on neuron death. *Biological Psychiatry*, 48, 755–765.

Scheibel, R. S. and H. S. Levin. 1997. Frontal lobe dysfunction following closed head injury in children: Findings from neuropsychology and brain imaging. In N. A. Krasnegor, G. R. Lyon, and P. S. Goldman-Rakic, (Eds.), *Development of the Prefrontal Cortex, Evolution, Neurobiology, and Behavior*, pp. 9–26. Baltimore: Paul H. Brooks.

Schumaker, D. M. and G. R. McKee. 2001. "Characteristics of Homicidal and Violent Juveniles." *Violence and Victims 16:* 401–409.

Siegal, A. and J. P. Flynn, 1967. "Differential effects of electrical stimulation and lesions of the hippocampus and adjacent regions upon the attack behaviors in cats." *Brain Research 7:* 252–257.

Silverman, A. B., H. Z. Reinherz, and R. M. Giaconia. 1996. "The long-term sequelae of child and adolescent abuse: A longitudinal community study." *Child Abuse and Neglect 20:* 709–723.

Simon, N. G., A. Cologer-Clifford, S. F. Lu, S. E. McKenna, and S. H. Lu. 1998. "Testosterone and its metabolites modulate 5-HT1A and 5-HT1B agonist effects on intermale aggression." *Neuroscience and Biobehavioral Review 23:* 325–326.

Starr, G. and B. McMillan. 1997. *Human Biology*. Belmont, Calif.: Wadsworth.

Stevenson, J. and R. Goodman. 2001. "Association between behavior at age 3 years and adult criminality." *British Journal of Psychiatry 179:* 197–202.

Teicher, M. H., Y. Ito, C. A. Glod, S. L. Anderson, N. Dumont, and E. Ackerman. 1997. "Preliminary evidence for abnormal cortical development in physically and sexually abused children using EEG coherence and MRI." *Annals of the New York Academy of Sciences 821:* 160–175.

Thompson, P., T. D. Cannon, K. L. Narr, T. G. M. van Erp, V. P. Poutanen, M. Huttunen, J. Lonnqvist, C. G. Standertskjold-Nordenstam, J. Kaprio, M. Khaledy, R. Dail, C. I. Zoumalan, and A. W. Toga. 2001. "Genetic influences on brain structure." *Nature Neuroscience 4:* 1253–1258.

Tranel, D. In press. "Neural correlates of violent behavior." In J. Bogousslavsky and J. Cummings (Eds.), *Behavior and Mood Disorders in Focal Brain Lesions.* Cambridge, England: Cambridge University Press.

Tranel, D. and P. Eslinger. 2000. "Effects of early onset brain injury on the development of cognition and behavior: Introduction to the Special Issue." *Developmental Neuropsychology 18:* 273–280.

Watson, R. E., H. M. Edinger, and A. Siegal. 1982. "An analysis of the mechanisms underlying hippocampal control of hypothalamically-elicited aggression in the cat." *Brain Research 269:* 327–345.

Wong, M., P. Fenton, J. Lumsden, M. Maisey, and J. Stevens. 1997. "Repetitive and non-repetitive violent offending behavior in male patients in a maximum-security mental hospital, clinical and neuro-imaging findings." *Medical Science and Law 37:* 150–160.

CHAPTER 8

TWISTED MINDS: THE CONTRIBUTION OF MENTAL DISORDERS

LEARNING OBJECTIVES

After studying this chapter, you will

- Be able to identify the symptoms of selected mental disorders that have been associated with violent or sexual offending
- Be able to apply diagnostic criteria for selected mental disorders to case studies
- Be introduced to what is currently known about bio-psychosocial causes of these disorders
- Understand the relationship between selected mental disorders and violent or sexual crime

INTRODUCTION

- Russell Weston, Jr., attacked the U.S. Capitol in 1998, killing two security guards who he believed were cannibals protecting a satellite device that could end cannibalism. He suffered from paranoid schizophrenia.
- Jeffery Dahmer pleaded not guilty by reason of insanity, claiming that he had an uncontrollable urge to have sex with the dead (necrophilia)
- Andrea Yates was diagnosed with postpartum depression before she drowned her five children

- School shooter Jason Hoffman had been diagnosed with depression prior to his shooting spree at Granite Hills High School
- Ed Kemper, Ted Bundy, and other famous serial killers were diagnosed as psychopaths during their incarcerations for their serial homicides

The common reaction to these well-publicized cases is "Aren't they just crazy?" or "They must be insane." The term "crazy" is a lay term that has no useful meaning and simply reflects the public's view that these people's actions are not comprehensible to "normal" people. It is analogous to saying that someone is physically ill—it conveys little information (the person could have a cold or pancreatic cancer!). "Insanity" is a legal term defined by state statutes for use in the criminal court system (this will be discussed in detail in Chapter 10). Except for Weston, none of the people in the preceding examples was found to be legally insane. However, they did meet the criteria for a diagnosable mental disorder, and one could make the case that if the disorder was not present, the violent offense may not have occurred.

Psychologists and psychiatrists use a system of diagnostic categories to identify and differentiate a wide range of mental disorders. Each of the diagnostic categories is based on clusters of signs and symptoms that occur together (a syndrome) and that tend to follow a particular course. Currently, these are described in detail in the latest edition of the *Diagnostic and Statistical Manual of Mental Disorders* (DSM IV-R). In this chapter, we are going to provide an overview of disorders that have been associated in some way with violent crime:

- Personality disorders: Antisocial personality disorder and the psychopath; borderline personality disorder
- Post-traumatic stress disorder
- Disorders of childhood: Attention deficit-hyperactivity disorder; oppositional defiant disorder; conduct disorder
- Substance-related disorders
- Major mental disorders: Schizophrenia; major depression
- Sexual deviations: Paraphilia

Although most people who develop one of these disorders do not commit violent crimes, there is reason to believe that the presence of a mental disorder may interact with other factors (i.e., family and social influences, neurological problems, etc.) to facilitate violent offending. Indeed, from his examinations of numerous serial killers, Pincus (2001) notes that the triad of mental illness, abuse, and neurological deficit have been found in almost all cases. For violent and/or sexual offenders who have a psychological disorder, prevention or early recognition of the disorder accompanied by effective treatment/management of the disorder may have prevented their offense. Therefore, what we know about the signs, symptoms, and causes of these disorders may contribute to our understanding of these offenders and potentially assist in the development of early interventions or effective treatments that would prevent their violent or sexual acting out.

THE PERSONALITY DISORDERS

When you describe someone's personality, what are you referring to? Usually, we mean that an individual has a relatively consistent way of thinking about the world, approaching, and reacting to others, and that their actions are somewhat predictable in various situations. **Personality disorders** refer to lifelong patterns of thinking and behaving that deviate significantly from cultural norms, are maladaptive and, despite this, inflexible. The maladaptive pattern is evident beginning in late childhood or adolescence and is manifested across a wide range of personal and social situations; causes personal distress and/or distress to others; or impairs social or occupational functioning (APA, 2000).

Personality disorders are difficult to treat. There are no quick fixes for lifelong patterns of behaving and responding, and the maladaptive patterns that these people display in their interpersonal relationships are also displayed with therapists and interfere with treatment. For example, someone who has paranoid personality disorder and is chronically distrustful and suspicious of others will also be distrustful and suspicious of a therapist. Furthermore, an individual with a personality disorder usually views his or her problems as due to the actions of others. Because of this lack of insight, they usually do not seek treatment.

Although the DSM IV-R identifies ten personality disorders, we are mainly interested in two personality disorders: antisocial personality disorder and borderline personality disorder.

Antisocial Personality Disorder

The diagnosis of antisocial personality disorder (APD) is the formal diagnostic category in the DSM IV-R that was intended to replace the earlier labels of psychopath and sociopath. Although it is the second most common diagnostic category associated with criminality (can you guess the most common?), only about a third of criminals meet the criteria. APD is three times more common in men than in women (APA, 2000).

The DSM criteria for APD are based on behaviors rather than psychological characteristics. As we shall see, some feel that the restriction of criteria to observable behaviors limits our ability to differentiate the general loser/drifter from the amoral, predatory criminal (Lykken, 1995).

Individuals diagnosed with APD (APA, 2000) must be at least 18 years old and have demonstrated a consistent disregard for and violation of the rights of others, beginning by age 15, that includes three or more of the following:

1. Engaging repeatedly in unlawful behavior
2. Deceitfulness—repeated lying or conning others for personal gain or pleasure
3. Impulsiveness or failure to plan

Case Example: John Wayne Gacy—The Clown Killer

Johnny was a well-behaved child, a Boy Scout with a paper route. Although Johnny loved his father (an alcoholic) and tried hard to win his approval, he was constantly belittled and abused by his father. At age 11, Johnny was hit in the head by a swing and experienced blackouts until a blood clot was removed when he was 16. School records show that he was an unremarkable student who was socially adjusted. He was extremely talkative, and his gregariousness and charm led him into the sales profession.

Johnny married his first wife Marlynn in 1964. He impressed her with made-up stories of his travels and accomplishments. He went to work for her father, who owned a Kentucky Fried Chicken franchise. Later he joined the Junior Chamber of Commerce (Jaycees), where he ingratiated himself by working hard, constantly boasting about his accomplishments, flattering his fellow members, and giving them gifts. He strove for any and all awards, recognition, and positions within the organization. Wanting to be recognized as special, he outfitted his car with a siren and a flashing red dashboard light that he claimed he had been authorized to use, and he sought opportunities to be seen with important people. Often he lied to make himself look important, for example, bragging that the governor had appointed him to committees and boasting about his military exploits (he never served in the military). When caught in a lie, he seemed undisturbed and easily made up another lie to cover the first. So far, his only brushes with the law were speeding and traffic violations. He was impatient with stop signs and drove like a teenager—burning rubber was a favored activity.

Rumors began that Gacy's behavior with his teenage male employees was unusual. Because of his charm and vehement antigay stance, many people did not believe the rumors. Indeed, he was named chaplain of his Jaycee chapter and outstanding vice president for 1967.

However, as a result of complaints by two teenage boys, he was indicted for sodomy in 1968. Both complaints involved coercion and one violence. After his attack on one of the boys (who was able to resist), Gacy acted unperturbed and informed the boy that he was an expert in sex education and indeed had written a book about it. He told friends that the accusations were part of a plot to defeat him for the Jaycees presidency. Months later, he was charged with intimidating one of the complainants and with an unrelated charge for breaking and entering (Brown Lumber Co.). The charges were plea-bargained, and in November 1968, he pleaded guilty to one count of sodomy. The judge noted that Gacy behaved only when people were watching him. Although he was sentenced to 10 years, he served only 18 months before being paroled. He was a model prisoner and indeed became president of the prison chapter of the Jaycees. During this time, his wife divorced him. He made no effort to keep in touch with his children. Upon his release, he returned to Chicago, where he remarried and again sought the limelight in the community. He started his own construction business, thereby allowing him to hire young men. He also began appearing as

(continued)

Pogo the Clown, performing at children's parties and in pediatric hospital wards. Meanwhile, he was luring, torturing, sodomizing, and killing 33 young men and burying most of them under his house. After his arrest and conviction, he blamed the parents of his young victims because many of his victims were male prostitutes. At other times, he claimed that he was framed (other people buried the bodies beneath his house). He also callously joked that all he should have been convicted of was "running a cemetery without a license." He reveled in and boasted of all the women who wrote to him and visited him in prison. Until the end, he claimed that if he could meet with the parents of his victims, he could make them understand. (Linedecker, 1980.)

4. Aggressiveness—repeated physical fights or assaults
5. Demonstrating a disregard for the safety of one's self or others
6. Irresponsibility—failure to sustain work behavior or meet financial obligations
7. Lack of remorse—indifference to mistreating others

Because the preceding criteria can fit a wide variety of criminals and noncriminals (i.e., combine criteria 1, 4, and 7 versus criteria 3, 5, and 6), researchers who are interested in the more conscienceless predatory criminals have developed diagnostic criteria for what they term the **psychopath.** These criteria include not only behaviors but also cognitive and emotional features. Cleckley, in his classic book *The Mask of Sanity* (1982), was among the first to fully describe the characteristics of this group: superficial charm, intelligence, a general poverty of emotion that includes a lack of anxiety and remorse, habitual lying, lack of empathy for others, antisocial actions that appear motiveless (i.e., just for fun), failure to learn from experience and to develop a life plan, egocentricity, and exploitive interpersonal relationships.

Not all psychopaths are criminals, and not all criminals are psychopaths; psychopaths constitute about 20 to 30 percent of the prison population (Barlow and Durand, 2002). Although the individuals described in most of Cleckley's case studies were not criminals (indeed, he identified Scarlett O'Hara as fitting his descriptors), they left a destructive wake behind them. Even when not physically dangerous, they are psychologically dangerous through their treatment and manipulation of others. The man who legally charms and cons widows out of their money leaves his victims

Self-Check 8-1

Which criteria for APD does John Wayne Gacy meet? Which does he not meet?

emotionally damaged. Cleckley's description also better captures the personality characteristics of real-life predators like John Wayne Gacy than does the APD criteria alone. Indeed, sexual and/or violent criminals who are psychopathic are more likely than nonpsychopathic offenders to be repeat offenders (Rice, Harris, and Quinsey, 1991).

Building on the work of Cleckley, Robert Hare developed an assessment tool, the Revised Psychopathy Checklist (PCL-R) (Hare, 1991), which is commonly used to diagnose psychopathy for both clinical and research purposes. The assessment is based on interviews and a review of documents. Unlike the criteria for APD, the PCL-R includes personality characteristics.

Hare's twenty-item checklist (see Table 8-1) has been divided into two factors that are only moderately correlated with each other. That is, a person may be high on **Factor I** (affective-cognitive instability) and low on **Factor II** (behavior-social deviance) or vice versa. As you might notice, Factor II looks a great deal like APD. With regard to the two factors, research (Hare, Hart, and Harpur, 1991; Lykken,

TABLE 8-1

Revised Psychopathy Checklist

Factor I: Affective-Cognitive Instability
Glibness and superficial charm
Grandiose sense of self/narcissism
Pathological lying
Conning/manipulative behaviors
Lack of remorse or guilt
Shallow affect
Callousness/lack of empathy
Failure to accept responsibility for antisocial actions
Factor II: Behavior-Social Deviance
High need for stimulation/easily bored
Parasitic lifestyle
Poor behavioral controls
Early behavior problems
Lack of realistic goals
Impulsivity
Irresponsibility
Adjudicated delinquent
History of violating probation or supervision
Other Factors
Sexual promiscuity, short-term marital relationships, and criminal versatility

1995; Meyer and Brothers, 2001; Slovenko, 1995) has found that compared with high Factor II psychopaths, high **Factor I** psychopaths

- are more likely to be violent;
- are less likely to improve in middle age;
- may actually get worse with traditional forms of treatment such as milieu therapy (they use treatment to sharpen their manipulative skills); and
- are on average more intelligent.

As mentioned before, not all psychopaths are criminals or violent. However, when violent offending and psychopathy are combined, the result is a nightmare. The psychopathic violent/sexual offender may appear normal and even charming, may engage in motiveless-appearing crimes, will not stop on his or her own or as a result of punishment, and the offenses may be particularly sadistic because of his or her inability to empathize with the needs and feelings of others. This offender is a true predator.

The signs and symptoms of psychopathy appear to those who have worked with such people (Hickey, 1997), to demonstrate the psychopath's need to control their social environment through conning, manipulation, and lying. When psychopaths are able to manipulate the reactions, emotions, and behavior of others, they feel a sense of power. Their potential to become physically dangerous may be increased when control is threatened or because physically threatening or harming others increases the heady sense of power and control that they crave. Many serial killers have boasted of the power they feel in controlling their victims and ultimately exercising the power of life and death over them. Similarly, sexual psychopaths use sexual degradation to psychologically break down and control their victims to produce a feeling of power. This treatment may be a way of compensating for childhood humiliations and feelings of helplessness resulting from sexual, physical, or psychological abuse (Stoller, 1975); the abuse also prevents the child from forming early attachments to parents and subsequently to others. This lack of attachment prevents them from empathizing with or caring for others. The case histories of many violent offenders certainly seem consistent with this interpretation. However, most abused children do not grow up to be violent offenders or psychopaths, and many psychopaths seem to come from adequate families.

Lykken (1995) has put forth the proposition that primary psychopaths (high Factor I) are born physiologically fearless and are therefore difficult to socialize. In other

Self-Check 8-2

On which of Hare's criteria would you rate John Wayne Gacy high? Is he more of a Factor I or a Factor II psychopath?

words, they do not form adequate behavioral controls and are able to easily lie and con because they do not experience the physiological arousal necessary to develop a fear of consequences. This physiological fearlessness hypothesis has been supported in a number of studies (Herpertz, Werth, Lukas, Qunaibi, Schuerkens, Kunert, Freese, Flesch, Mueller-Isberner, and Sass, 2001; Lykken, 1995). Consequently, psychopaths live in an emotionally presocialized world in which, like a small child, they are narcissistic, only able to think of their own needs and are unable to relate to the needs or feelings of others (Meloy, 1993). Normal socialization processes do not work with them, and ineffective parenting that includes erratic and harsh discipline, abuse, and lack of supervision can further contribute to poor socialization (Patterson, 1986; Robins, 1978). Furthermore, psychopathy or APD on the part of a parent increases the risk of a child's developing the disorder. The mechanism for this fearless "inheritance" is probably both genetic (low physiological arousal levels, impulsiveness) and environmental (individuals with APD make poor parents).

Neither psychopathy nor APD have yielded well to treatment. As noted before, psychopaths often get worse with traditional talk and insight oriented therapy. If incarcerated, they may superficially engage in therapy and even verbalize insights and remorse if release is contingent on their showing progress. However, this cooperation and progress is only a veneer. The following experience of one of my former students when he started working as a counselor in an institution for offenders illustrates this difficulty. An incident occurred in which an inmate blew up and, seemingly unprovoked, attacked another inmate. An investigation revealed that a third inmate (Mark) had lied to and manipulated the attacker into blowing up. The counselor brought Mark into his office and talked and listened for over an hour. Mark came to express regret, cried tears of remorse, and expressed insight into his actions. He thanked the (naive) counselor for helping him and revealed that he felt that he had really made a breakthrough. Two days later, a similar blow-up occurred with another inmate, and again an investigation revealed that Mark was behind it. When the counselor asked Mark why he had done it again, he said that the inmate had made him mad and that he thought that this time he had covered his tracks better.

Borderline Personality Disorder

Individuals with **borderline personality disorder (BPD)** are characterized by instability and reactivity in mood, as well as unstable interpersonal relationships and behavior beginning in early adulthood. In contrast to APD, it is much more common in women than in men. The fictional character played by Glen Close in the movie *Fatal Attraction* is a dramatic example of someone with this disorder. This character alternated between clinging to and hating Michael Douglas's character, between suicidal gestures and terrorizing him and his family, all based on a brief relationship (a one-night stand). BPD is diagnosed when an individual displays five or more of the following symptoms (APA, 2000):

1. Frantic efforts to avoid real or imagined abandonment
2. Unstable relationships in which the individual alternates between extreme idealization and disparagement of others
3. Unstable sense of self and identity
4. Impulsive behavior that is self-destructive (i.e., reckless sex or driving, substance abuse)
5. Suicidal behavior and/or threats, self mutilation
6. Unstable moods and emotions (intense)
7. Feeling of emptiness (often bored)
8. Intense anger and displays of temper, rage
9. Transient paranoia or dissociation

Although people with BPD are more likely to harm themselves than others, their intense fear of abandonment, reactive moods, anger, and rages can lead to stalking and violence toward others to whom they have become attached but who do not return the attachment. Their attachment to and anger toward someone may be based on a prior relationship, a belief acquaintance, or an imagined relationship (i.e., celebrity stalkers). The intense feelings of those with BPD may be aimed inward, resulting in depression or suicide, or outward, resulting in violence (sometimes both). The stalker is trying to repair a real or an imagined relationship through both clinging to and terrorizing the victim.

The causes of BPD seem to be a combination of genetically based neurobiological reactivity and possibly low serotonin levels combined with parental relationships marked by rejection and neglect, alternating with overcontrol, physical and/or sexual abuse, and/or frequent mother or father substitutes (Comer, 1995).

Highlight 8-1

Dissociative identity disorder (DID)—formerly known as multiple personality disorder—is a rare condition in which aspects of one's personality fracture or split into separate identities complete with their own memories, behavior, attitudes, and even physiological reactions (American Psychiatric Association, 2000). Often one identity (an alter) is unaware of the existence or actions of another. Kenneth Bianchi, the Hillside Strangler, claimed, for example, that an alter personality, Steve, had committed the rapes and murders. He was later found to be faking (although he was convincing for a while). Billy Milligan, who was found not guilty by reason of insanity for a series of rapes and robberies, was found to genuinely suffer from DID. Despite a few high-profile insanity defenses based on claims of DID and soap operas and movies populated with killer "multiples," the disorder is rare, and its association with predatory violence even rarer.

Post-Traumatic Stress Disorder

The histories of serial killers and chronic sex offenders are replete with childhood trauma that is often extreme and/or chronic, usually at the hands of caregivers and experienced at an early age. Although only about 25 percent of people who experience the type of trauma identified in the diagnostic criteria for post-traumatic stress disorder (PTSD) develop the disorder, these factors (early onset at the hands of another and high intensity/multiple traumas) increase the likelihood of developing PTSD (Grant, 2002). Although most individuals with PTSD are not violent, PTSD is also often overlooked as a possibility by a professional when working with violent offenders or in understanding the origins of the behavior. After all, PTSD is the result of being a victim, and violent offenders are victimizers—it is difficult to perceive them as possibly belonging in both categories.

PTSD can occur at any age as a result of exposure to a traumatic event(s) during which the individual experienced or witnessed threats of death or serious injury to himself or herself or to others, and as a result experienced intense feelings of fear or helplessness (APA, 2000). The traumatic event(s) may be unintentional, such as a natural disaster or an accident, or intentionally delivered by human agents, such as in cases of childhood sexual, physical, and emotional abuse; violent crime; or torture. To be diagnosed with PTSD (APA, 2000), the individual must also demonstrate the following symptoms:

- Reexperience the trauma through intrusive recollections, recurrent dreams, flashbacks, or hallucinations; have psychological distress or physiological reactivity when exposed to internal or external cues that resemble the traumatic event.
- Persistently avoid or numb themselves to stimuli associated with the trauma by avoiding thoughts, feelings, activities, places, or people associated with the trauma; experience lack of memory or dissociation; have lessened interest in significant activities; feel detached from others or be unable to feel; and/or have a shortened sense of their own life span.
- Experience symptoms of arousal such as sleep difficulties, irritability or anger, hypervigilance, or an overreactive startle response.

Onset of PTSD may be either immediate (but lasting more than one month) or delayed, in which the symptoms can emerge from 6 months to years later.

When PTSD is chronic and untreated, an individual develops defensive and distortive mechanisms for managing or coping with the symptoms (Grant, 2002). These mechanisms may include, but are not limited to, abusing/using alcohol or drugs to self-medicate against physiological arousal to intrusive thoughts/feelings; escaping into fantasy; engaging in compulsive or ritualistic behavior to avoid internal and external triggers; and becoming emotionally numb and socially isolated (APA, 2002; Horowitz, 1976). Although these are usually expressed nonviolently or self-destructively, violent manifestations of these mechanisms (i.e., fantasies of violence and control, ritualistic rapes and killing) are seen in many predatory offenders. Multiple trauma experiences in early childhood at the hands of caregivers are particularly damaging, since this period is when children develop schemas/beliefs about themselves, others, and the world. For example, personality disorders and the inability to trust or love and care for others can result when early extreme or chronic trauma teaches a child that human relationships result in pain and betrayal (Grant, 2002).

DISORDERS OF CHILDHOOD

Certain mental disorders of childhood have been linked to the later development of violence. They may be early indicators that a child is at increased risk of becoming an aggressive or a violent adult; or the disorder may promote later violence by making a child harder to socialize and by evoking negative responses from family, peers, and teachers.

Attention Deficit Hyperactivity Disorder

We will begin with **attention deficit hyperactivity disorder (ADHD),** since this disorder has been found to frequently co-occur with other childhood disorders and may be a precursor to these disorders (Barkley, 1998). Indeed, some have observed that ADHD along with conduct disorder is probably the "matrix from which later serious violence springs" (Pincus, 2001: 102).

ADHD is much more common in boys than in girls, and it is found across cultures (APA, 2000). Children with ADHD have difficulty maintaining attention, completing tasks, and listening to instructions, and they are easily distracted and forgetful. In addition, they talk excessively, interrupt others, are impulsive, and cannot sit still (APA, 2000). As a result, they often experience school failure, peer rejection, and frustration on the part of parents and teachers. These secondary environmental factors in combination with their impulsiveness, hyperactivity, and inattention often promote later aggressiveness (Frick, 1994).

ADHD children are more likely to engage in early substance use and to drop out of school; both increase the risk for later antisocial behavior. Satterfield, Swanson & Schell & Lee (1994) found that by the time they were 18, ADHD boys were significantly more likely than non-ADHD boys to have committed robbery, theft, assault with a deadly weapon, and other serious crimes.

Although there is evidence that ADHD is more common in first-degree relatives of those diagnosed with ADHD, thus pointing to a genetic vulnerability for the disorder (APA, 2000), the neurological mechanisms that underlie the disorder are not completely understood. However, research using brain scan technology reveals less brain activity in the frontal cortex (which may account for impulsivity) and the basal ganglia (which affects motor behavior) of those with ADHD (Giedd et al., 1994; Pincus, 2001; Zametkin et al., 1990). Evidence of parenting problems, such as depression and alco-

Case Example: Tim

Tim was the second son born to John and Patty Allen. Patty describes Tim as having been a difficult baby and toddler compared with his older brother Mike. As a baby, Tim slept little and was awake demanding attention by 5:00 A.M. As a toddler, he was into everything, often aimlessly unloading drawers and closets, climbing on furniture and kitchen counters, and chattering endlessly, even when nobody was listening. When playing a game or working on a project, he often got distracted and wouldn't finish the project. Patty, a homemaker, found him exhausting. She reported that she frequently found herself at the "end of her rope" and would blow up at Tim, spanking him and yelling that he had ruined her life. Other times she would lock him in his room for many hours. When John came home from work, he would find Patty irritable and angry, leading to arguments and marital discord. John tried to control Tim by holding brother Mike up to him as an example. John and Patty separated for six months when Tim was 6, and his mother began drinking heavily in the evenings. During this time, Tim's constant activity and talkativeness took a more belligerent turn. He had frequent temper tantrums when he didn't get his way and would openly refuse to comply with simple requests from his mother. In school, he would tease and provoke other children (i.e., tearing up their homework, calling them names). The teacher reported that he constantly interrupted when she was giving a lesson and rarely completed assignments in class. He was failing the first grade. Once when another child tattled on him, he flew into a rage and later at lunch he threw milk in her face. Tim, needless to say, was not liked by his classmates. Tim's parents reconciled, and Tim seemed glad to have his father home again. However, when his father told him to do something (e.g., get ready for bed), Tim would argue endlessly with his father, provoking him to lose his temper, to berate Tim, to threaten to leave home again, and often to hit him. His mother continued to drink and seemed to give up on Tim. Tim frequently displayed resentment toward his older brother. When Tim broke something or got in trouble at home, he found ways to blame his brother. This pattern of blaming others for his own misdeeds also carried over into school.

Tim was referred to the school psychologist at the end of second grade because of his failing schoolwork and his attitude toward his teachers. The precipitating event for the referral was an incident in class. His teacher reprimanded him for being out of his seat, and he refused to sit down. When she told him to go to the office, he cursed her out in front of the class.

Does Tim fit the criteria for any of the childhood disorders described in this section?

Self-Check 8-3

Look at the case of Tim described in the Case Example, and decide which of the criteria for ADHD he fits. Give an example from the case for each of the criteria you identify.

hol consumption, have also been found in families of ADHD children (APA, 2000). This behavior on the part of the parents may be the result of, rather than a cause of, the child's problems. Maternal smoking during pregnancy has also been consistently associated with ADHD (Milberger et al., 1996). It appears that neurologically produced factors such as impulsivity, attention deficits, and hyperactivity probably interact with parents', teachers', and peers' reactions either to increase or to ameliorate the behavioral problems.

Oppositional Defiant Disorder

Most children are periodically contrary, temperamental, and uncooperative. However, when the behavior is extreme and pervasive (six months or more) and the pattern is one of negativism, defiance, and hostility, it may be **oppositional defiant disorder (ODD)**. For children with ODD, their behavior interferes with their social and academic functioning (APA, 2000). Their behavior includes at least four of the following characteristics:

1. Having frequent loss of temper
2. Being argumentative with adults
3. Defying rules and requests from adults
4. Deliberately annoying others
5. Blaming others for their own mistakes or misbehaviors
6. Being easily irritated by others
7. Displaying frequent anger and resentment
8. Often being spiteful and vindictive

This pattern appears to be relatively stable through adolescence, and ODD boys are also likely to engage in antisocial behavior and aggression in their teen years (Verhulst, et al., 1993). ODD is often a precursor to the development of conduct disorder (APA, 2000).

The causes of ODD are unclear. It is more common in families in which one parent has a history of mood disorders, ADHD, conduct disorder, APD, substance-related disorder, or ODD (APA, 2000). ODD usually manifests first in the home environment before spreading to school or other settings and is more common in families that have high marital conflict and/or that engage in harsh, inconsistent, or neglectful parenting (APA, 2000). However, it is possible that the difficulty in raising an ODD child could lead to marital strife or inappropriate discipline (APA, 2000). Most likely the child's and the parents' behavior interact with each other. ODD has also been found in children who have experienced a succession of caregivers (e.g., through foster care).

Self-Check 8-4

Looking at the case of Tim, which of the criteria for ODD does he demonstrate? For each criteria you identify, cite an example from the case.

Conduct Disorder

Although **conduct disorder (CD)** shares some features in common with ODD, it also includes more serious behaviors that violate the rights of others as well as laws and rules. The behavior of conduct-disordered individuals must include at least three of the following (APA, 2000):

1. Aggression toward people and/or animals (e.g., bullying, fighting, physical cruelty)
2. Deliberate property destruction (e.g., including arson)
3. Deceitfulness or theft (e.g., lying/conning, breaking and entering)
4. Serious rule violation (e.g., frequent truancy, curfew violations before 13 years, running away from home).

It is much more common in males than in females, and females with CD display less confrontational behaviors than their male counterparts. Conduct disorder may occur as early as 5 years old; the earlier the onset and the more severe the symptoms, the greater the likelihood that the child will develop APD and/or substance-related disorders in adulthood. Serious and early onset conduct disorder seems to be an early warning of high risk for later violence and criminality. In a study of lust killers, Ressler, Burgess, and Douglas (1988) found that over 75 percent had a history of symptoms of conduct disorder in childhood and adolescence. However, children with milder symptoms and later onset often become socially adjusted later in life (APA, 2000).

The etiology of conduct disorder is similar to that of APD and the childhood disorders previously discussed. That is, there is some evidence of genetic vulnerability that, when combined with family discord and hostile or neglectful parenting, produce conduct-disordered children (especially boys).

Self-Check 8-5

Does Tim meet the criteria for CD? Why, or why not?

Self-Check 8-6

Refer to the case study of Tim, and then answer these questions:

1. For which childhood disorders does he fit the criteria?
2. What environmental factors contributed to the disorder(s)?
3. What do you see in Tim's future if something isn't done?

SUBSTANCE-RELATED DISORDERS

Substance abuse and dependence are more strongly associated with crime and violence than any other DSM-IV mental disorder (Rasmussen and Levander, 1996). In fact, Steadman, Mulvey, Monahan, et al., (1998) found that patients diagnosed with a major mental illness (i.e., schizophrenia, bipolar disorder, major depression) were no more likely than non–mentally ill individuals to commit acts of violence unless they also had a co-occurring substance-related disorder. According to these researchers, there was a strong positive relationship between substance abuse and violence for both groups (mentally ill and non–mentally ill).

Although it is common to find that violent offenders either have a history of substance abuse or have used alcohol or drugs before or during their crime, not all violent offenders use, abuse, or are dependent on a psychoactive substance. Chronic use of drugs like phenylcyclidine (PCP) and methamphetamine may induce psychosis and/or high levels of agitation that can directly trigger violence. Alcohol, on the other hand, is a depressant (in the same category as Valium), making its biological relationship to violence more indirect and complex. Despite this indirect relationship, government figures show that the use of alcohol precedes approximately half of all violent crimes (National Institute of Justice, 1999; FBI, 1999).

The common explanation for how alcohol use, abuse, or dependence facilitates violence is that it reduces inhibitions to violent actions. Drinking alcohol depresses the inhibitory centers of the brain; continued drinking depresses more areas of the brain, affecting motor behavior and thinking. Alcohol increases the neurotransmitter GABA (Barlow and Durand, 2002) and thereby reduces anxiety. Reduced anxiety may make people less anxious about consequences, thus reducing inhibition. Alcohol also reduces the neurotransmitter serotonin, which affects moods. As we saw in Chapter 7, lower serotonin levels have been associated with violence.

Some Terms to Know

Substance: Psychoactive substances ingested to alter emotions, thinking, and behaving (depressants, stimulants, opiates, or hallucinogens).

Use: Moderate use of psychoactive substances that does not interfere with an individual's functioning (social, occupational, or educational).

Abuse: Recurrent use of a substance that interferes with an individual's ability to function in one or more areas of his or her life, that exposes him or her to dangerous situations, that causes legal problems, and/or that results in continued use despite these problems.

Dependence: Physiological dependence (i.e., developing tolerance, experiencing withdrawal) and psychological dependence (drug-seeking behavior and preoccupation) (APA, 2000).

Most of us just get silly and stupid when our inhibitions are lowered by alcohol. Why do some people become belligerent, angry, and aggressive? The partial answer is that psychological factors such as expectation influence the behavioral and emotional effects of alcohol (Miller, Smith, and Goldman, 1990). The child of a happy drunk may also be a happy drunk, whereas the child of an aggressive, violent drunk may expect to be more aggressive when he or she drinks and consequently, such is the case. Alcohol consumption may also simply enhance a preexisting mood; a sad or depressed individual becomes more sad and depressed (even suicidal), whereas an angry or aggressive individual becomes more angry and aggressive. Finally, there is evidence that a history of child abuse is what differentiates a violent alcoholic from a nonviolent alcoholic (Asnis, Kaplan, Hundorfean et al, 1997).

MAJOR MENTAL DISORDERS

The common perception is that people with serious mental illness are dangerous and should be feared. Consider the following: people with a major mental disorder such as schizophrenia, depression, or bipolar disorder make up approximately 10 percent of inmates in jails and prisons (Conly, 1999). However, most are incarcerated for petty crimes or crimes of survival such as trespassing, shoplifting, and so on. Indeed, people with serious mental disorders are more likely to be the victims than the perpetrators of crime. For seriously mentally ill persons who do commit violent crimes, the nature of their disorder may contribute to the nature of their crime. Specifically, we are going to look at two serious mental illnesses that, when untreated or inappropriately treated, may contribute to some types of violence: schizophrenia/paranoid type and major depression.

Case Example: Mary

In elementary school and junior high, Mary was an attractive, friendly girl who was active in soccer, enjoyed reading, and participated in 4H. She was a slightly above average student. Throughout her life, her mother had suffered periodic bouts of depression during which she was withdrawn, slept a lot, and left the parenting to her husband. When Mary was 13, her older sister (Ann) was diagnosed with a rare form of bone cancer. She was in and out of hospitals for the next two years. During this time, Mary's parents were naturally preoccupied with Ann's needs, and Mary had a lot of freedom to do what she wanted. Her grades slipped, she dropped out of soccer and 4H, and began spending time at the local mall where she and her friends sometimes shoplifted for entertainment. Ann died when Mary was 15; Mary openly grieved for her sister. A year later, Mary transferred to another high school. At first, she seemed to adapt well, making new friends and doing better in school. After about six months, however, she lost interest in school and became moody and irritable with her friends and family. She also began overeating, putting on considerable weight. Her irritability sometimes escalated to physical threats. She spent a lot of time alone in her room, often sleeping because she always felt tired. She no longer read for pleasure because "nothing held her interest," and she could read whole pages and not remember what she read. She fell in with a new group at school who referred to themselves as "goths." Like them, she began wearing only black, and conversations revolved around death and the meaninglessness of life. She developed an interest in poetry and began writing her own poems, all focused on these same themes. Upon graduation, she remained at home, having no interest in going to college. She continued to sleep excessively and spent most of her time alone; she seemed sad and lonely most of the time. She refused to eat anything at home because she believed that her parents were poisoning her food, just as she had begun to believe that she had poisoned her sister. She began to look for other signs that her parents were trying to kill her. When she heard her mother get up in the night, she believed that she was coming to smother her in her sleep. Finally, one night Mary swallowed a handful of her mother's medication and went into her parents' room and put a pillow over her mother's face to smother her. Her father woke up and stopped her, and she was taken to the emergency room. **Which of the disorders described in the following two sections does Mary exhibit?**

Schizophrenia

Schizophrenia is the most disabling of all the mental disorders (APA, 2000) because it is characterized by impairment across a wide range of functions: attending, perceiving, thinking, behaving, and feeling. The symptoms interfere with or greatly reduce (compared with how the individual functioned prior to the onset of the illness) an individual's ability to work, maintain interpersonal relationships, or care for oneself. (APA, 2000) Schizophrenia affects 1 to 2 percent of the population. A review of the literature on the epidemiology of violence and schizophrenia (Walsh, Buchanan, and Fahy, 2002) found that the proportion of violent crime by young adults associated with mostly *untreated* schizophrenia is less than 10 percent. The diagnostic criteria for schizophrenia must include two or more of the following symptoms:

1. Delusions: Bizarre, unrealistic beliefs that are fervently held despite evidence to the contrary.
2. Hallucinations: Hearing, seeing, or experiencing sensory input that is not tied to the external environment.
3. Disorganized speech: Incoherence, jumping from topic to topic, excess speech with little meaning, and the like.
4. Grossly disorganized or catatonic behavior: Purposeless and repetitive behavior such as pacing or rocking, or an individual's being motionless and unresponsive (catatonic).
5. Negative symptoms: These include flat or blunted emotional expression, lack of motivation or ability to initiate activities, and withdrawal (APA, 2000).

As you can see, most persons with schizophrenia are so severely disabled that they are incapable of planning and carrying out sophisticated crimes. Indeed, if not cared for, many end up homeless and easy targets of crime. However, persons with one subtype of schizophrenia, the paranoid type, are more at risk for violence. A predisposition to perceive threats in the environment accounts for approximately a third of the risk for violence in young adults with schizophrenia-spectrum disorders (Arseneault, Moffitt, Caspi, Taylor, and Silva, 2000).

Schizophrenia/Paranoid Type. Persons with this type of schizophrenia are primarily preoccupied with one or more bizarre **delusions** or experience frequent **hallucinations,** but their cognitive skills remain relatively intact, and they do not display disorganized speech or behavior, or blunted affect. If their delusions are paranoid (i.e., a belief that the CIA or aliens are trying to kidnap them to steal their brains), they may react to these perceived threats by defending themselves. Other types of delusions are delusions of reference (i.e., the person on TV is talking about me); delusions of grandeur (i.e., I am Winston Churchill, or I can control the weather); and delusions of control (i.e., other people or things are controlling my thoughts, feelings, or actions) (APA, 2000). People with paranoid schizophrenia may also suffer from hallucinations. The most common are auditory hallucinations in which they hear a voice or voices talking when nobody is there. These voices may criticize them, warn them of threats, threaten them, or command them to take an action. A study by Hellerstein et al. (1987) found that of those who experienced command hallucinations, 5 percent told them to kill someone (note that 51 percent told them to kill themselves). When a fixed paranoid delusion or delusion that someone is controlling one's thoughts or actions is combined with command or paranoid hallucinations, the possibility of reacting with violence is increased. A serial killer with schizophrenia would most often be described as a visionary killer (Chapter 3).

It is widely accepted that the vulnerability for developing schizophrenia is genetically determined and that environmental stress can trigger the onset of the illness in predisposed individuals. The age of onset is usually early adulthood when people must make the transition to greater independence, a stressful time for most. Prenatal factors have also been associated with the development of schizophrenia. How the vulnerability to schizophrenia is manifested neurologically is the subject of a great deal of research. Although there are no definitive answers, there are some promising leads pointing to abnormalities in the neurotransmitter systems for dopamine and/or serotonin (specifically, excesses of these neurotransmitters) and to abnormalities in brain structure (specifically, enlarged ventricles or spaces in the left side of the brain) (Barlow and Durand, 2002).

Major Depression

Individuals suffering from **major depression** are usually a danger only to themselves. However, in some cases, the hopelessness, feelings of worthlessness, and suicidal impulses associated with depression can contribute to a combined homicide/suicide. That is, the suicidal person may decide to commit suicide and take those persons who they consider either responsible for their misery (e.g., an ex-spouse or schoolmates) or who they feel could not survive without them (e.g., their children) along with them. The "family annihilator" and "disgruntled employee" mass killers demonstrate this pattern. In addition, Pincus (2001) has found evidence of mood disorder in most serial killers he has examined, and he notes that their killings are often committed during periods of depression or mania (feelings of grandiosity, euphoria, irritability). Note that these types of cases do not include suicide bombers, who do not commit homicide/suicide from depression but rather as willing martyrs to a political cause.

A diagnosis of major depression is made when five or more of the following symptoms are present almost every day and impair one's ability to function socially, in work or school (APA, 2000):

1. Depressed mood most of the day, every day (note that in children and adolescents, the mood may be irritability)
2. Loss of interest or pleasure in most activities
3. Unintended weight loss or gain
4. Insomnia or excessive sleeping
5. Either agitated or retarded motor activity
6. Fatigue, loss of energy
7. Feelings of worthlessness or inappropriate guilt

Highlight 8-2
A Therapist Comments on Mentally Disordered Offenders

Following is an interview with Jeffery Teuber, Ph.D., Senior Psychologist, Atascadero State Hospital, a maximum security forensic hospital.

Dr. Kuehnel—What type of patient have you worked most with at Atascadero?

Dr. Teuber—These are people who are in prison and are found to have a mental illness and to be in need of treatment. Some are sent to Atascadero to serve their parole under treatment (they don't usually like that), some of them go back to prison after a period of treatment, while others are with us at the time their sentence expires and are converted to the Mentally Disordered Offender category and consequently, they stay on with us indefinitely. The law says he must have a mental illness that is not in remission and as a function of that mental illness he is likely to be dangerous. It can be extended like that forever, one year at a time.

Dr. Kuehnel—What kinds of mental illness do you see in these offenders?

Dr. Teuber—Mentally Disordered Offenders usually fall into two categories, the schizophrenia spectrum disorders, and affective disorders proper, such as Major Depression or Bipolar Disorder.

Dr. Kuehnel—We know that in general, the public's fear of the seriously mentally ill is unfounded—how does mental illness interact with violence?

Dr. Teuber—Mentally Disordered Offenders tend to come to us when they have been violent, and they are not all violent. We look at violence in three ways. It is affectively driven (under stress their symptoms exacerbate and they become irrationally angry, paranoid and commit a violent act), symptom driven (the symptoms of mental illness were out of control, a paranoid schizophrenic who commits a crime while delusional or hallucinating), and instrumental violence (the person uses sexual or physical assault, in a planned purposeful way to achieve some goal or meet a need—often applied to sexually violent predators).

Dr. Kuehnel—Without breaching confidentiality, could you tell me about . . .

Dr. Teuber—A patient with a schizophrenia spectrum disorder; for example, lived at home, and was not medicated or was insufficiently treated; he became delusional, paranoid, saw himself as Jesus Christ and his mother as the devil and raped and killed the family member while in this state of acute mental illness. Those cases can get pretty bizarre sometimes. We have patients who have killed their mothers for example, sometimes fathers and other family members and will keep the body in the house and have sexual intercourse

(continued)

with the body afterwards. I think anyone can see that these people are extremely mentally ill in a rather complex, serious way and are out of their heads when they do the crimes.

Dr. Kuehnel—In terms of MDOs whose violence is symptom driven, it would seem that the treatment goal would be to control the mental illness; if you control the illness . . .

Dr. Teuber—That is correct. And with that kind of patient, no matter how horrid their crime may have been, we don't target the violent behaviors—we target the mental illness. Appropriately treated, they are not likely to reoffend.

Dr. Kuehnel—How do non-violent MDOs get to Atascadero?

Dr. Teuber—There are many Mentally Disordered Offenders who committed nonviolent crimes. Everyone has seen homeless people in their community, shuffling along and talking to people who aren't there. Those people are unmedicated and untreated mentally ill and they get arrested sometimes for dropping their pants and peeing in public—they will get an indecent exposure charge, especially in a setting like a park where there are children around. We get patients who in their mental illness will sit in a restaurant, this has happened numerous times, and write on a napkin "give me a hamburger or I will blow up this restaurant," or they will write letters to the White House saying "I am going to kill the president." There are many such people in our hospital, which is a prisonlike setting, and I think it is tragic that they are there. They really only need treatment and they haven't harmed anyone, they have just done incredibly stupid and bizarre things that seemed to make sense to them at the time as a result of their untreated mental illness.

Dr. Kuehnel—I would imagine that treating patients that are symptom driven, who have a serious mental illness is easier than treating those that have personality disorders and engage in instrumental aggression.

Dr. Teuber—As you suggest, the people with a true mental illness whose crimes are symptom driven are often very sympathetic characters, regardless of what they have done, because they are prisoners of their mental illness, and they do respond to psycho/social treatments and medications. We see the evidence of successful treatment in people who are in remission, who become good citizens in the hospital, get accepted to outpatient treatment programs and proceed to conditional release programs. That kind of work to me is very meaningful, fulfilling, and I have a sense of serving others and helping people—which seems to be very important to me. The other cases where there is antisocial/psychopathic disorder involved, we have some doubt as to whether we even know how to treat those people or if they can be treated. That is far less rewarding and can be frustrating.

8. Difficulty thinking/communicating
9. Recurrent thoughts of death or suicide

Depression in preadolescents and adolescents looks similar to depression in adults. However, from age 9 to 18 years, motor agitation is more likely to be expressed as aggressive behavior (Barlow and Durand, 2002). Furthermore, conduct disorders and depression frequently cooccur in adolescence, particularly in boys, and researchers found that when the depression either resolved naturally or was treated, the conduct disorder also remitted (Puig-Antich, 1982). School officials, parents, law enforcement, and counselors may be diverted by the aggressive and antisocial behavior of adolescents and may fail to look for and treat an underlying depression. One could speculate that school shootings may be committed by seriously depressed adolescents. Substance-related disorders also frequently cooccur with depression, particularly alcohol use and abuse. The disinhibiting effects of alcohol, combined with depression, increase the probability of both suicidal and violent behavior.

Approximately 5 percent to 15 percent of persons with major depression also have psychotic symptoms (delusions or hallucinations) (APA, 2000) that, in some cases, can contribute to homicide/suicide. The delusions or hallucinations are usually mood congruent. That is, a delusion that one has been possessed by the devil or auditory hallucinations in which voices accuse the individual of worthlessness and evil acts, are congruent with the symptoms of depression. Andrea Yates drowned her five children because she believed that she was the devil (she looked for signs of 666 on her body) and would corrupt their souls if she did not immediately send them to heaven. She probably suffered from major depression with psychotic symptoms. There have been other tragic cases of new mothers, suffering from major depression (postpartum onset) with psychotic features, who kill their newborns in response to delusions or hallucinations. Major depression and psychosis are the psychological disorders most commonly associated with intrafamilial child homicide (Falkov, 1996; Pritchard and Bagley, 2001). In an epidemiological study in Britain, 100 percent of mentally ill male intrafamilial child killers and 25 percent of females also committed suicide (Pritchard and Bagley, 2001).

Family studies suggest that genetic contributions increase vulnerability to depression (APA, 2000). In addition, low serotonin (neurotransmitter) levels, high levels of cortisol (stress hormone), and cortisol-releasing factor (CRF) have all been associated with depressive episodes (Brain Briefings, 2001). Whether these biological changes are the cause or the effect of depression is still a question. Psychological factors that have been associated with depression include stressful life events (environmental) and their meaning (cognitive) for an individual (Monroe, Rhode, Seeley, and Lewinsohn, 1999; Young et al., 2001). In other words what is stressful to you (i.e., your boyfriend/girlfriend dumps you) may not be as stressful to your classmate because of differences between you in how the event is interpreted. Your interpretation may be

Self-Check 8-7

Refer to the case study of Mary, and then answer these questions:

1. With which of the preceding major mental disorders would you diagnose Mary? Why?
2. What biological and environmental factors contributed to her disorder?
3. When did the disorder start, and what were the signs?

catastrophic (I'm a loser and nobody will ever love me), whereas your classmate's may be more moderate (I'll miss him/her, but I'm a good catch and will find love again). Biological vulnerability, environmental factors, and psychological factors interact to produce depression and also affect its severity and duration (Nolen-Hoeksema, 2000).

PARAPHILIAS

People (almost exclusively males) with one or more **paraphilias** experience intense, recurring sexual urges and fantasies that they frequently act on and that involve nonconsenting humans, nonhuman objects, or the suffering or humiliation of themselves or others (APA, 2000). Some of these people always require the paraphiliac stimulus to become sexually aroused, whereas others require it episodically (often during periods of stress). The urges and behaviors cause them emotional distress (i.e., shame) or impairment in important areas of functioning, or cause distress or harm to others. Paraphilias usually begin by early adolescence but become more focused and elaborate in adolescence and early adulthood (APA, 2000). It is common for individuals to have more than one paraphilia.

Paraphilias are usually categorized by the stimulus associated with sexual arousal, and there are many types. Following are descriptions of the paraphilias most commonly associated with sexual and violent offending:

- **Exhibitionism.** The focus of sexual arousal is exposing one's genitals to an unwilling person, often for the "shock" value.
- **Fetishism.** The sexual arousal focuses on nonliving objects. The "souvenirs" taken by serial killers are often used in this way.
- **Pedophilia.** The focus of the paraphilia is on prepubescent children (under 13 years).
- **Voyeurism.** The sexual arousal comes from *secretly* observing others naked or involved in sexual activity.

Case Example: Andrew

Andrew was the youngest child in a family that also had three daughters. His mother was both overprotective of him and rejecting. She constantly reminded him that she had "female complaints" from his birth and that he had been a trial to her. Andrew's father was passive and uncaring, showing no interest in him. When Andrew was six, his grandfather began molesting him. When he told his mother, she punished him for lying and became even more harsh and controlling. Andrew was passive and became a loner with no real friends. He also was the constant butt of his sisters' jokes and teasing, which his mother seemed to encourage and his father ignored. Andrew envied the favored treatment that his sisters received at home. Very early one morning (when he was 11 years old) he got up to go to the bathroom, and one sister's door was partially open. He went in. She had thrown the covers off and was lying on her back in only a tank top and panties. He stood over her and became aroused. Since she was sleeping, she could not berate or reject him; he felt a sense of power that he could do anything to her. Later, in the bathroom he masturbated while thinking about her lying there. He repeated his forays almost every night and even took a pair of her panties to masturbate with while he fantasized in the night. He began renting films like *Chainsaw Massacre,* in which scantily clad females are terrorized, tortured, and killed, masturbating while he watched. He also found Internet sites that specialized in pornography around the themes of torture and death. Throughout adolescence, he had no female friends or romantic relationships. At 16, he began paying hookers for sex, but he insisted that they allow themselves to be tied up and to play dead. He did not harm them, but he fantasized about torturing them and playing with their corpses in order to become aroused.

- **Sexual sadism.** The sexual arousal comes from fantasies or behavior involving the real (not simulated) suffering or humiliation of others.
- **Necrophilia.** The focus of sexual arousal is corpses.

Although when acted on, most paraphilias are crimes, they do not directly lead to violence. Indeed, most paraphiliacs do not escalate to violence. However, sexual predators and serial killers often have a history of multiple paraphilias beginning in childhood or early adolescents (Prentky, Burgess, Rokoust, et al., 1989) that become incorporated into their later violent crimes. For example, Richard Ramirez (the Night Stalker) and Ted Bundy both had a history of voyeurism prior to their first kill. Jeffery Dalmer, Henry Lee Lucas, and Arthur Shawcross were necrophiliacs, and Jerry Brudos had a women's shoe fetish (ultimately keeping the high-heel-clad foot of one of his victims in his freezer). Needless to say, most hedonistic killers and sexual predators are also sadists who are sexually aroused by inflicting pain and humiliation on their victims.

The precise causes of paraphilia are not known. However, Barlow and Durand (2002) created a model of the development of paraphilia based on their clinical experiences that includes the following:

1. Early associations are made (accidentally or vicariously) between sexual arousal and inappropriate stimuli.
2. This association is facilitated by the inadequate development of patterns of consensual adult arousal and/or lack of development of effective social skills needed to relate to adults.
3. The inappropriate association is repeatedly reinforced by fantasies combined with masturbation.
4. Efforts to control or inhibit the fantasy and behavior paradoxically strengthen the paraphilic obsessions (i.e., as dieting increases thoughts of food).
5. The paraphilia is established.

In the case of sadism, the early inappropriate association may come about as the result of physical or sexual abuse in childhood or adolescence. Being the victim of violence causes fear/anxiety, and fear/anxiety can cause arousal (the term "scared stiff" comes from this phenomenon) (Barlow and Sakheim, and Beck 1983), and the inappropriate association between arousal and violence is made before appropriate sexual associations are established. Abel, Barlow, Blanchard, and Guild (1977) found that sadistic rapists displayed strong sexual arousal (measured by erections) to both violent sexual and violent nonsexual stimuli, but little arousal to consensual intercourse stimuli.

Self-Check 8-8

Refer to the case study of Andrew, and then answer the following questions:

1. Which paraphilia(s) does Andrew display?
2. How does the development of Andrew's paraphilia(s) fit Barlow's model of development?
3. Is Andrew potentially dangerous? Why, or why not?

Some Final Thoughts

In any discussion of mental disorders and violence, it is important to remember the principle of multifinality (Barlow and Durand, 2002). That is, any disorder has multiple outcomes—violence being only one of the possibilities. Although the majority of individuals with a mental disorder are not violent, in some cases, a violent outcome could have been averted if the disorder had been recognized and properly treated early on. The triad of abuse/neglect, neurological deficit, and untreated mental disorder creates a "witch's brew" that has frequently been associated with murder and violence. The violence is usually facilitated by substance use or abuse.

The cliché "an ounce of prevention is worth a pound of cure" has relevance to any discussion of the role of mental disorders in violent or sexual crimes. Preventing the traumas caused by abusive or neglectful homes could probably prevent many cases of personality disorders, such as APD or BPD, conduct disorder, and post-traumatic stress disorder. These and other disorders such as schizophrenia, depression, substance abuse, and ADHD can be managed with appropriate bio-psychosocial treatments. However, these treatments are most effective when a disorder is identified and treated early in the course of the disorder. Unfortunately, signs and symptoms are often overlooked or ignored until a crises point is reached or treatment is reduced to what insurance companies are willing to afford (i.e., pop a pill). Furthermore, while comprehensive efficacious treatments have been developed for many of these disorders, access to treatment is sometimes restricted by geography, limited funding, or inadequately trained mental health professionals. A detailed discussion of effective treatments for each of these disorders is beyond the scope of this chapter, but a current abnormal psychology text can provide some answers for those who are interested.

Early intervention and/or treatment can either alleviate or positively impact the course of the disorder, including the possibility of preventing a violent outcome. For each of the four case studies presented in this chapter, can you see where early intervention and/or treatment would have changed the course of the disorder and the outcome?

Discussion Questions and Activities

1. Do you think it is important to understand mental disorders and their relationship to violence? Why, or why not?
2. What differentiates major depression with psychotic features from the schizophrenia/paranoid type?
3. For one of the disorders discussed in this chapter, go to an abnormal psychology text, and find what treatment options are available. Share your findings in a class discussion.
4. Visit the National Alliance for the Mentally Ill (NAMI) website (*www.nami.org*). What is their position on violence and the mentally ill? What is their view on prisons and jails for mentally ill offenders?
5. Using the symptoms of ADHD, develop a scenario of environmental responses that might interact with these symptoms to facilitate later violence.

6. How does depression in adolescents differ from depression in adults? What is the former's role in conduct disorder?
7. Look up some cases of school shooters. Is there evidence of any major mental disorder in these cases?
8. Answer the question posed in the last sentence of the chapter. Explain how and when early intervention might have helped.
9. In your opinion, which disorders (if any) might make an individual not responsible for violent/criminal actions? Explain.
10. Answer each of the questions in the eight Self-Check boxes in the chapter, and discuss your answers with your classmates and instructor.

Key Terms

Attention deficit hyperactivity disorder (ADHD)
Borderline personality disorder (BPD)
Conduct disorder (CD)
Delusions
Factor I
Factor II
Hallucinations
Major depression
Oppositional defiant disorder (ODD)
Paraphilia
Personality disorders
Psychopath
Schizophrenia—paranoid type
Substance abuse

References

Abel., G. G., D. H. Barlow, E. B. Blanchard, and D. Guild. 1977. "The components of rapists' sexual arousal." *Archives of General Psychiatry 34:* 895–903.

APA (American Psychiatric Association). 2000. *Diagnostic and Statistical Manual of Mental Disorders* (4th ed.). Washington, D.C.

Asnis, G. M. Kaplan, and G. Hundorfean. 1997. "Violence and homicidal behavior in psychiatric disorders." *Psychiatric Clinics of North America 20:* 405–425.

Arseneault, L., T. Moffitt, A. Caspi, P. Taylor and P. Silva. 2000. "Mental disorders and violence in a total birth cohort." *Archives of General Psychiatry 57:* 979–986.

Barkley, R. A. 1998. *Attention Deficit Hyperactivity Disorder: A Handbook for Diagnosis and Treatment* (2nd ed.). New York: Guilford Press.

Barlow, D. and V. Durand. 2002. *Abnormal Psychology: An Integrative Approach* (3rd ed.). Wadsworth/Thompson Learning.

Barlow, D. H., D. K. Sakheim, and J. G. Beck. 1983. "Anxiety increases sexual arousal." *Journal of Abnormal Psychology 92:* 49–54.

Brain Briefings, 2001, Oct. Depression and stress hormones. *www.sfn.org/briefings/brain_depression.htm* (retrieved Oct. 16, 2001).

Butterfield, F. 1998, March 5. "By default, Jails Become Mental Institutions. *The New York Times. http://www.nami.org* (Retrieved May 1999).

Cleckley, H. M. 1982. *The mask of Sanity* (6th ed.). St. Louis: Mosby.

Comer, R. 1995. *Abnormal psychology* (2nd ed.). New York: W. H. Freeman & Co.

Conly, C. 1999. *"Coordinating community services for mentally ill offenders: Maryland's community criminal justice treatment program."* Washington, D.C.: U.S. Department of Justice, Office of Justice Programs, National Institute of Justice.

Falkov, A. 1996. "Fatal child abuse and parental psychiatric disorders." ACPC series, Rep. No. 1. London: Department of Health Study Working Together, Part 8.

FBI (Federal Bureau of Investigation). 1999. *Crime in the United States*—1998. Washington, D.C.: U.S. Government Printing Office.

Frick, P. J. 1994. "Family dysfunction and the disruptive behavior disorders: A review of empirical findings. *Advances in Clinical Child Psychology 16:* 203–206.

Giedd, J. N., F. X. Castellanos, B. J. Casey, P. Kozuch, A. C. King, S. D. Hamburger, and J. L. Rapport. 1994. "Quantitative morphology of the corpus callosum in attention deficit hyperactivity disorder. *American Journal of Psychiatry 151:* 665–669.

Grant, R. 2002. "Post traumatic stress disorder: Insight and healing." *Cortex Education Seminars.*

Hare, R. D. 1991. *The Hare Psychopathy Checklist—Revised.* Toronto: Multi-Health Systems.

Hare, R., S. Hart, and T. Harpur. 1991. "Psychopathy and the DSM-IV criteria for antisocial personality disorder. *Journal of Abnormal Psychology 100:* 391–398.

Hellerstein, D., W. Frosch, and D. W. Koenigsberg. 1987. "The clinical significance of command hallucinations." *American Journal of Psychiatry 144:* 219–221.

Herpertz, S., U. Werth, G. Lukas, M. Qunaibi, A. Schuerkens, H. Kunert, R. Freese, M. Flesch, R. Mueller-Isberner, and H. Sass. 2001. "Emotion in criminal offenders with psychopathy and borderline personality disorder." *Archives of General Psychiatry 58:* 737–745.

Hickey, E. 1997. *Serial Murderers and Their Victims* (2nd ed.). Belmont, Calif.: Wadsworth.

Horowitz, M. 1976. *Stress Response Syndromes*. New York: Gason Aronson.

Linedecker, C. L. 1980. *The Man Who Killed Boys*. New York: St. Martin's Press.

Lykken, D. 1995. *The Antisocial Personalities.* Hillsdale, N. J.: Lawrence Erlbaum Associates.

Meloy, R. 1993. *Violent Attachments*. New Jersey: Login Bros.

Meyer, R. and A. Brothers. 2001. "A common path for the development of psychopathy." In J. Aponte and R. Meyer (Eds.), *The psychopath and the mental Health Professional*. Mathwah, N.J.: Erlbaum.

Milberger, S., J. Biederman, S. V. Faraone, L. Chen, and J. Jones. 1996. "Is maternal smoking during pregnancy a risk factor for attention deficit hyperactivity disorder?" *American Journal of Psychiatry 153:* 1138–1142.

Miller, P. M., G. T. Smith, and M. S. Goldman, 1990. "Emergence of alcohol expectancies in childhood: A possible critical period." *Journal of Studies on Alcohol 51*: 343–349.

Monroe, S. M., P. Rhode, J. R. Seeley, and P. M. Lewinsohn. 1999. "Life events and depression in adolescence: For first onset of major depressive disorder." *Journal of Abnormal Psychology 108* 4: 606–614.

National Institute of Justice. 1999. *1998 Annual Report on Drug Use Among Adult and Juvenile Arrestees (ADAM)*. Washington, D.C.: U.S. Department of Justice, Office of Justice Programs.

Nolen-Hoeksema, S. 2000. "Further evidence for the role of psychosocial factors in depression chronicity." *Clinical Psychology: Science and Practice* 7(2): 224–227.

Patterson, G. R. 1986. "Performance models for antisocial boys." *American Psychologist 41:* 432–444.

Pincus, J. H. 2001. *Base Instincts: What Makes Killers Kill.* New York: W. W. Norton & Co.

Prentky, R., A. Burgess, F. Rokous, A. Lee, C. Hartman, R. Ressler, and J. Douglas. 1989. "Presumptive role of fantasy in serial sexual homicide." *American Journal of Psychiatry 146:* 887–891.

Pritchard, C. and C. Bagley. 2001. "Suicide and murder in child murderers and child sexual abusers." *The Journal of Forensic Psychiatry 12*(2): 269–286.

Puig-Antich, J. 1982. "Major depression and conduct disorder in prepuberty." *Journal of the American Academy of Child Psychiatry 21:* 118–128.

Rasmussen, K. and S. Levander. 1996. "Crime and violence among psychiatric patients in a maximum-security psychiatric hospital." *Criminal Justice & Behavior 23*(3): 455–471.

Ressler, R., A. Burgess, and J. Douglas. 1988. *Sexual Homicide*. Lexington, Mass.: Lexington Books.

Rice, M., G. Harris, and V. Quinsey. 1991. "Sexual recidivism among child molesters released from a maximum security psychiatric institution." *Journal of Consulting and Clinical Psychology 59:* 382–386.

Robins, L. N. 1978. "Sturdy childhood predictors of adult antisocial behavior: Replications from longitudinal studies." *Psychological Medicine 8:* 611–622.

Satterfield, J., J. Swanson, A. Schell, and F. Lee. 1994. "Prediction of antisocial behavior in attention-deficit hyperactivity disorder boys from aggression/defiance scores." *Journal of the American Academy of Child and Adolescent Psychiatry 33:* 185–190.

Slovenko, R. 1995. *Psychiatry and Criminal Culpability*. New York: Wiley.

Steadman, H. J., E. P. Mulvey, J. Monahan, P. C. Robbins, P. S. Applebam, T. Grisso, L. H. Roth, and E. Silver. 1998. "Violence by people discharged from acute psychiatric inpatient facilities and by others in the same neighborhoods." *Archives of General Psychiatry 55:* 393–401.

Stoller, R. F. 1975. *Perversion*. New York: Pantheon Books.

Teuber, J. 2002. Personal interview conducted in November.

Verhulst, F. C., M. L. Eussen, G. F. Berden, J. Sanders-Woudstra, and J. Van Der Ende. 1993. "Pathways of problem behaviors from childhood to adolescence." *Journal of the American Academy of Child Adolescent Psychiatry 32:* 388–396.

Walsh, E., A. Buchanan, and T. Fahy. 2002. "Violence and schizophrenia: Examining the evidence." *British Journal of Psychiatry 180:* 490–495.

Young, J. E., A. D. Weinberger, and A. T. Beck. 2001. "Cognitive therapy for depression." In D. H. Barlow (Ed.), *Clinical Handbook of Psychological Disorders* 3rd ed., pp. 264–308. New York: Guilford Publications.

Zametkin, J. A., T. Nordahl, M. Gross, A. C. King. W. E. Semple, J. Rumsey, S. Hamburger, and R. M. Cohen. 1990. "Cerebral glucose metabolism in adults with hyperactivity of childhood onset." *New England Journal of Medicine 323:* 1261–1366.

Part Three

Investigating and Prosecuting Evil

Whereas Section II of this book focused on theories and research into what is currently known about factors that contribute to creating a "monster," the final three chapters address how the justice system responds to sexual and violent crimes.

Once a sexual or violent offense occurs, the legal system mobilizes to find and prosecute the offender. Chapter Nine explores the contributions of forensic experts from the behavioral (i.e., profiling), biological (i.e., DNA, entomology) and physical sciences (i.e., trace and fingerprint evidence) to the investigation of the crime and the identification and prosecution of a suspect. Sometimes these forensic experts also contribute to the exoneration of a suspect prior to trial or, in some cases, after conviction. Chapter Ten provides an overview of the justice process, from the origins of laws through trial and disposition. At trial, the accused may respond with a variety of defenses—some that include the admission that he or she "did the deed" but was acting in self-defense, acted with diminished capacity, or was legally insane when the crime was committed.

Once a serial killer or mass murderer has been convicted he or she is either put to death or isolated in prison for the rest of his or her life. However, sex offenders such as child molesters or rapists usually return to society at some point. In Chapter Eleven, we explore the types and effectiveness of treatment for these offenders. When a sex offender is released following prison without treatment, should we feel safer than if he or she received treatment? As you will see, this is not a simple question to answer given the current state of the art for treatment or for current prison conditions.

CHAPTER 9

FORENSIC INVESTIGATION: THE HUNT

LEARNING OBJECTIVES

After studying this chapter, you will

- Understand the value of forensic science in the criminal investigation process
- Be able to identify the various types of forensic science specialists used in the criminal investigation process
- Understand the limitations of forensic sciences
- Through case study, learn how forensic sciences are used in actual criminal investigations
- Understand basic criminal investigative procedures

INTRODUCTION

"Most crime scenes tell a story. And like most stories, crime scenes have characters, a plot, a beginning, a middle, and hopefully, a conclusion. The final disposition of a crime scene depends on the investigators assigned to the case. The investigators' abilities to analyze the crime scene and to determine the who, what, how, and why govern how the crime scene story unfolds." (Quote from the article *"Violent Crime Scene Analysis: Modus Operandi, Signature, and Staging," in FBI Law Enforcement Bulletin,* February 1992, written by John E. Douglas, Ed.D., and Corinne Munn.)

During the course of the justice process, a number of medical, physical, and social scientists trained in various forensic fields are available to offer technical support to law enforcement and the justice system. Forensic experts are used to assist the police, prosecutors, or defense teams in establishing physical or behavioral aspects of a crime or a crime scene. A forensic scientist or expert is one who analyzes evidence pertinent to his or her field of expertise and offers testimony as to criminal behavior or causes contributing to death, disease, or injury. A forensic expert may be a physician, an engineer, a physicist, a chemist, a social scientist, a university professor, or other person who has a particular knowledge or training.

To assist experts, crime laboratories are used to examine and analyze evidence found at a crime scene. Crime labs are found at the state, county, or local level. However, the Federal Bureau of Investigation operates the largest most efficient crime lab in the world. A number of local law-enforcement agencies utilize the services of the FBI lab because their labs may not have the necessary forensic resources available.

THE CRIMINAL INVESTIGATION

> "A good criminal investigator needs common sense and tenacity . . . these are a couple of attributes . . . he doesn't have to be a brain surgeon or nuclear scientist . . . he has to be intelligent and use whatever resources he's allowed to use or limited by." (Quote by Frank Salerno, retired investigator with the Los Angeles Sheriff's office.)

After a major crime, a police investigator is summoned to the scene. The investigator is responsible for gathering facts and evaluating information obtained from the crime scene for subsequent prosecution. The essential duties of an investigator (Swanson, Chamelin, and Territo, 2000) are as follows:

1. To determine whether a crime was committed.
2. To identify and apprehend a suspect.
3. To recover stolen property.
4. To assist the prosecutor in the prosecution process.

In the course of the investigation, the investigator may work closely with a forensic expert, or the investigator may be trained in a particular forensic field such as ballistics.

The more complicated or high-profile the case (serial killings, etc.), the more likely a police investigator will enlist the aid of a forensic expert to assist in determining key issues such as cause of death, criminal motives, or methods. Generally, the criminal investigation includes an evidence search and analysis, which may continue for months. There are a number of types of evidence that may be found at a crime scene (Swanson, Chamelin, and Territo, 2000): direct, real, demonstrative, opinion, or circumstantial (indirect). All or part may be used either to convict an offender or to indicate that someone else may have committed the crime.

Direct evidence refers to first-hand knowledge of a crime as provided by a reliable eyewitness who can testify that the defendant was observed at the crime scene. Real evidence refers to physical evidence, such as fingerprints, tools, weapons, and so forth. Demonstrative evidence refers to items such as maps, tape recordings, photographs, and sketches. Demonstrative evidence, prepared by forensic experts or police, is often used in courtrooms to provide juries with a realistic understanding of the crime. Demonstrative evidence may be recovered at the crime scene, such as in cases in which a killer tape-recorded or photographed his or her victims before their murder. It is not unusual for serial killers and sadistic sex offenders to tape-record or videotape their victims' pleas for mercy while torturing them.

Opinion evidence is testimonial evidence offered by a qualified forensic expert during trial, such as a medical doctor or psychologist. Also, before offering opinion evidence, the person must be recognized by the court as an expert. In other words, experts possess special expertise acquired through specialized training or employment. Experts are used quite often in cases in which establishing the cause of death or injury is important. Experts range from medical doctors to fiber experts.

Circumstantial or indirect evidence is any evidence other than direct evidence, which implies that a certain person committed the crime (or was at the crime scene). At a crime scene, circumstantial evidence may be real evidence, such as bloody shoe prints, tool marks, notes, and other evidence left by the perpetuator. Such evidence may suggest that a certain person was responsible for the crime.

It is possible that an offender may be convicted of a crime such as murder without finding the body of the victim and with only circumstantial evidence. The following case example is based on an actual case.

The effectiveness of the police in identifying suspects depends to a large extent on how well the crime scene is protected and whether the evidence is properly secured and analyzed. In the case of eyewitness testimony, care must be taken to assure that the testimony is reliable and not the result of mistake or error. Psychologists have conducted hundreds of studies on errors in eyewitness identification. Also, in some cases, witnesses simply lie or mistakenly identify the wrong person. A report published in 1996 by the U.S. Department of Justice, for example, indicated that of the first 28 known cases of DNA exoneration, eyewitness testimony had played a part in about 90 percent of the convictions (Miller, 2000). Eyewitness identification error, usually unintentional, is the factor that is most often associated with wrongful convictions. Scheck et al. (2000) report that 84 percent of the DNA exonerations examined rested in part on mistaken eyewitness identification. Wells (Wells et al., 1998) and other scholars have written extensively about eyewitness perception, how it can be significantly affected by psychological, societal, cultural, and systemic factors, and how police lineups should be conducted in fairness to suspects.

Case Example: Conviction of Murder without a Body

Ann and her husband have had marital problems for years. And Ann, who is much younger than her husband, has been having an affair with a much younger man for several months. Ann suspects that her wealthy husband knows about the affair. Ann knows that if the affair is discovered and he divorces her, she will not benefit from his estate.

One evening her husband went jogging, which was his daily practice. Several hours later, when he failed to return home, Ann reports him missing. His body is never found, nor any trace of his existence. The police investigation revealed that an insurance policy of $300,000 was taken out by Ann two weeks prior to his disappearance. Shortly after his disappearance, Ann takes a cruise and is seen spending compulsively on expensive clothes. Neighbors, relatives, and coworkers indicated that Ann and her husband had a strained relationship, and several people knew of the affair. Her husband had told a personal friend that on several occasions, he feared that he was being followed. A search of Ann's boyfriend's apartment revealed a calendar of Ann's husband's daily activities for the past 30 days, including the time when and the route where he went jogging. There was also evidence that Ann and another man had purchased several large plastic bags, duct tape, and gasoline cans from a local hardware store. The jury found Ann and her lover guilty of first-degree murder.

A case in point is the story of Kevin Green, a California man convicted and imprisoned for beating his wife nearly to death and killing their nine-month-old fetus. His wife, who suffered memory loss and permanent brain damage in the beating, falsely identified Green. More than sixteen years later, DNA taken from the crime scene was matched through the state's DNA database with that of a convicted rapist named Gerald Parker (U.S. Department of Justice, 1998).

Although the police are responsible for collecting physical evidence, research shows that such evidence is collected in fewer than 10 percent of the cases, most often in only the most serious crimes such as homicide and sexual assaults (Horvath and Meesig, 1996; Horvath, Orns, and Siegel, 1998). Accordingly, only a small portion of the collected evidence actually undergoes forensic analysis. However, in cases in which forensic analysis is needed, any number of forensic experts may be employed.

FORENSIC SPECIALTIES

The practice of forensic science is growing, and there is a need for a variety of talents. Along with their use in criminal cases, forensic experts are used in civil cases such as product liability, and accident reconstruction and analysis (aircraft, auto, etc.) and medical malpractice.

TABLE 9-1

Major Areas of Forensic Sciences

A. Forensics in the Behavioral Sciences
• Psychology and psychiatry • Truth deception examinations • Criminal profiling
B. Forensics in the Biological Sciences
• Toxicology • DNA fingerprinting • Entomology • Odontology • Pathology and autopsies • Anthropology examinations
C. Forensics in the Physical Sciences
• Trace evidence • Fingerprint • Ballistics

In order to have a better understanding of the role of forensics and the relationship to the justice process, we will briefly examine the contribution of each forensic science to an investigation. Table 9-1 lists the major specialty areas in forensic science (see FBI, 1999; Wrightsman, Neitzel, and Fortune, 1998; Swanson, Chamelin, and Territo, 2000).

Behavioral Science and Forensics

The use of behavioral science in forensic investigations is widespread. The science relies on human factors in investigating a crime, which include a suspect's lifestyle, associations, behaviors, and so forth. The most common types of behavior forensics address human factors through psychology/psychiatric examinations and evaluations, truth and deception detection (i.e., polygraph examinations), and criminal profiling measures.

Forensic psychology and psychiatry is the interface between psychology and the law. Although psychiatry and psychology are distinguishable, both address human factors or the relationship between behavior and crime. The study of forensic psychology dates to 1908 when Hugo Munsterberg published a book on eyewitness testimony and juries.

Forensic psychologists and psychiatrists provide services that are both clinical and forensic in nature. For example, when psychologists and psychiatrists treat a defendant for a mental disorder prior to trial (so that the defendant is competent to stand trial) or following conviction, they are providing clinical services. Most forensic psychologists work either in a correctional institution (i.e., a prison, jail, or juvenile hall) or in a psychiatric hospital. The forensic psychologist in these institutions will often provide a range of therapies in order to control or eliminate the psychiatric disorder that has led to the offender's criminal acts. Whether these interventions will be successful is highly dependant on the nature of the disorder. Certain disorders (e.g., obsessions, schizophrenia, depression, and addictions) that can be correlated to criminal behavior can often be treated satisfactorily, whereas others (e.g., sociopathy, psychopathy) are far less successfully controlled.

On the other hand; if the expert is asked to provide a report for the court regarding the defendant's state of mind at the time of the crime (as in a "not guilty by reason of insanity" assessment), then he or she is providing forensic services. In such cases, these experts will offer testimony as to the accused's mental state and the way that it contributed to the offense charged. In other words, years of training and experience make psychiatrists and psychologists experts at diagnosing and treating mental illnesses. They can offer testimony on the probable nature and severity of the defendant's illness at the time of the crime. Also, the forensic psychologist may perform diagnosis and psychometric testing (the evaluation of behavior/personality via tests/surveys) in order to evaluate and report to the court the accured's risk of violence and/or recidivism (Decaire, 1999).

A controversial behavioral approach is the use of **truth and deception detection methods.** These methods have been around a long time, either criticized as junk science or revered as highly scientific. The origin of such measures is traced to ancient China, where a suspect was required to place dry rice powder in his mouth during an interrogation. If the powder remained dry, the suspect was deemed guilty, because the Chinese knew that fear of detection would cause the salivary glands to dry up. In ancient India, suspects were told that a magic donkey would cry out when a guilty person grabbed its tail. The donkey, whose tail had previously been dusted with lampblack, was in a darkened room. The guilty suspect entered the room, refused to pull the donkey's tail, leaving with clean hands. The truthful suspect, with nothing to fear, pulled its tail and emerged with lampblack on his or her hands. The Indian interrogators understood that the psychological fear of detection would prevent the guilty suspect from touching the donkey's tail.

Today we no longer use rice or donkeys to determine deception. Investigations into human factor analysis utilize a number of devices. Most common in forensics is the polygraph examination. A polygraph is an instrument that simultaneously records changes in physiological processes such as heartbeat, blood pressure, and respiration. Police departments, the FBI, federal and state governments, and numerous private agencies use the polygraph. It is reported that between 1981 and 1997, the U.S. Department of Defense conducted over 400,000 polygraph examinations to resolve issues arising from counterintelligence, security, and criminal investigations (Cohen, 1998).

The underlying theory of the polygraph is that when people lie, their heartbeat increases, blood pressure goes up, breathing rhythms change, perspiration increases, and so forth. Before administering the polygraph, the investigator may ask some pre-questions to eliminate surprise. A baseline for these physiological characteristics is established by asking the subject questions whose answers the investigator knows, such as, Are you a student? Do you live at such and such address. Deviation from the baseline obtained for these questions is taken as a sign of lying.

Generally, the results of polygraph tests are inadmissible as evidence in a court of law, because polygraph tests are known to be unreliable or because what little benefit may be derived from using the polygraph is far outweighed by the potential for significant abuse by the police (Cohen, 1998).

On the other hand, the "fearless" psychopath (with a hypoactive autonomic Nervous system, as discussed in Chapter 7) may be able to beat the machine. The United States Supreme Court ruled in 1998 (**United States v. Scheffer**) that the results of a polygraph exam could be banned in a criminal trial by either side because there is simply no consensus that polygraph evidence is totally reliable. The National Academy of Sciences has criticized the polygraph as a credible employment-screening device as well (Piller, 2002).

Although the polygraph is an incomplete deception device, there are other technologies used in the science of deception detection. These developments include **voice stress analyzers** that look for the audible tremors that occur whenever a person lies. Developed by army intelligence officers in 1970, the purpose of the psychological stress evaluator (PSE) was to detect levels of significant emotional stress from human-voiced utterances. Like the polygraph, it measures physiological manifestations of psychological stress. Both devices need safeguards to differentiate between stress caused by lying and stress caused for any other reason. Unlike the polygraph, the PSE signal-processes the raw input of a voice. Vocalization can be voiced in person, recorded, and played back, or can be taken from radio or television. In other words, a person can be tested without the subject's being present or even knowing about it. Although many police agencies use the technology, its results have been criticized as just another form of unreliable detection, and its validity has yet to be fully accepted (Wylie, 2001).

Another technology gaining increased attention is **brain-wave monitoring.** The brain MERMER (memory and encoding related multifaceted electroencephalographic responses) is also commonly known as brain fingerprinting or mapping and has been used in criminal cases (Farwell, 2000). This new technology is often used in conjunction with DNA testing. Proponents claim that the MERMER technique can determine what has been stored in the brain and that when used on alleged criminals, it can judge with high accuracy whether that person committed a specific crime. This technique measures brain-wave responses to words, phrases, or pictures presented on a computer screen, and details about a crime are mixed in a sequence with other, irrelevant items. Since only the perpetrator would know the details about the crime, the brain-wave response indicates whether a person recognizes the stimulus or not. Also, if the suspect recognizes the details of the crime, this outcome indicates that he or she has a record of the crime stored in his or her brain. The technique reportedly has been accurate in over 120 tests conducted by the FBI (Farwell, 2000).

Another related behavioral science tool is **psycholinguistics,** or the study of the relationship between linguistic behavior and characteristics or psychological processes of the speaker or writer (Crystal, 1998). Both written and spoken language have features that may reveal an individual's geographical origins, ethnicity or race, age, sex, occupation, education level, and religious orientation or background. Each of us, depending upon where we live, has different speech patterns. Those from the southern portion of the United States, for example, say things differently from those from New England, and there are variations within each location.

Forensic psycholinguistics applies the field of psycholinguistics to criminal and civil cases. Psycholinguists, for example, have identified language features associated with personality traits, such as impulsivity, anxiety, depression, paranoia, and the need for power and control; and, for a number of years, they have used these analysis systems for predicting the behavior of national leaders (Shuy, 1998). Investigators are using forensic psycholinguistic analysis to assist in cases that include threat assessment, authorship identification, false allegations, workplace violence, and statement analysis (Smith and Shuy, 2002).

Another sometimes controversial behavioral technique is **criminal profiling.** Offender profiling is a method of identifying the characteristics of a perpetrator of a crime on the basis of an analysis of the nature of the offense and the manner in which it was committed. Various aspects of the criminal's personality makeup are determined from his or her choice of actions before, during, and after the crime (Douglas, 1997; Teten, 1995).

Before the advent of the FBI Behavioral Science Unit (now the Profiling and Behavioral Assessment Unit, which is under the National Center for the Analysis of Violent Crime) in 1974, criminal investigators used "profiling" that was informally based on their observations of multiple crime scenes and the types of perpetrators who were eventually captured. For example, if a child is murdered in his or her home and there is evidence of a history of sexual abuse, investigators know from experience that the most likely perpetrator is a father or stepfather, and they will look at him as a prime suspect. Similarly, since most murders are intraracial, a black victim will lead police to look for a black perpetrator because the probabilities suggest a black offender.

Profiling took a more scientific turn in the early 1970s when John Douglas and Robert Ressler of the FBI interviewed and collected data on most well-known killers: their motives, methods, choice of victim, personality and background characteristics, and the like. Certain personality and behavioral characteristics corresponded with certain characteristics of the methods of selecting, capturing, killing, and disposing of vic-

Highlight 9-1

Before the popularity of profiling serial killers, social scientists were involved in court cases dealing with the profiling of potential hijackers, illegal aliens, and drug couriers, and the courts have varied widely in their receptiveness.

This type of profiling involves identifying a potential offender (before a crime has been discovered) who fits or matches the characteristics of a known group of criminal offenders. A priori profiling has been used to specially train airport employees to screen passengers for potential hijackers and has also been used in many cases involving drug courier profiling.

In almost all these cases, social scientists were involved in the training of employees to detect such persons and/or involved in defending the practice in court. This type of a priori profiling can also lead to abuse, as in the case of detaining someone simply because of his or her race or ethnic background. Since the terrorist attacks of September 11, 2001, a number of Arab travelers have complained of harassment because they fit the profile of a terrorist. For years, minority motorists and passengers have complained of being stopped on the highway and charged with possession of contraband, a situation that gives rise to a racial profiling defense. They maintain that the evidence against them is inadmissible because the practice of singling out minorities for stops is unconstitutional.

In civil cases, some of which are being supported by the American Civil Liberties Union, motorists who were stopped and not charged have accused police of illegally singling them out because of their race or ethnicity (Peterson, 2000).

tims. These patterns were particularly useful in linking a series of victims to a single serial killer or rapist and for narrowing the pool of potential suspects (Douglas, 1997). Out of this research, modern profiling was born.

The purpose of modern profiling is to provide investigators with the following:

- A behavioral composite of the most probable offender in order to narrow the number of possible suspects
- Techniques for luring or tripping up the offender
- Techniques for interrogating a suspect
- Prosecutorial strategies

Before an offender profile can be constructed, the profiler must examine the specifics of the crime scene and evaluate the offender's modus operandi (what the offender does to effect the crime) and his or her signature (why the offender does it, the thing that fulfills him or her emotionally). They then make a comprehensive analysis of the victim or victims (victimology) and evaluate the preliminary police reports and the medical examiner's autopsy protocol.

The broadest typology used in profiling serial killers by crime investigation is the organized-disorganized dimension introduced in Chapter 3 (see Table 3-1). The crime scene characteristics of an organized killer are (FBI, 1997) as follows:

- The offender will kill in one location and move the body for disposal.
- The body will be either carefully concealed or blatantly displayed to degrade the victim.
- The offender will bring a weapon and take it with him or her.
- The offender will take a souvenir and sometimes give it to a significant person.
- The offender will remove and take the victim's clothing.
- The torture of victims occurs prior to death.
- The offender may amputate a body part.
- The offender will clean up the crime scene to leave little physical evidence.

On the basis of these crime scene characteristics, you would increase your likelihood of being right if you profiled the unknown subject (UNSUB) as someone who is intelligent and educated, is socially competent with a skilled job, drives a flashy car, and lives with a partner (wife or girlfriend) or dates regularly, and who may try to insinuate himself into the investigation or contact police to play games.

In general the crime scene characteristics of a disorganized killer, by contrast, will have the following characteristics (FBI, 1997):

- The victim will be killed and left in the same location as the murder.
- No effort will be made to conceal the body, and it may be displayed for symbolic purposes.
- The offender uses a weapon of opportunity found at and often left at or near the scene (often strangles or beats the victim to death).
- The souvenir is usually a piece of clothing.
- There is uncontrolled stabbing or slashing, cannibalism, or bite marks.
- The mutilation of the victim is postmortem.
- The offender leaves a sloppy crime scene.

Self-Check 9-1

If you came across a crime scene with the preceding disorganized charactertistics, what characteristic would you look for in an UNSUB (use Table 3-1 to create your profile)?

Professional profiling is both an art and a science, and profilers bring insight and intuition based on years of experience to their job. The FBI's Profiling and Behavioral Assessment Unit both assists and trains local, state, and federal law enforcement in these and other techniques.

As to the effectiveness of and the problems with behavioral profiling, studies have found that FBI profiling techniques are of some assistance in 77 percent of cases, assist in solving cases 45 percent of the time, and actually help identify the perpetrator in 17 percent of cases (Teten, 1995). Ressler and Burgess (1985) further reported an interrater reliability that averages 76 to 93 percent.

An example of a profile used for serial rapists is depicted in Table 9-2. The profile is based on the accumulation of demographic information about such offenders.

> "Offenders also usually maintain a buffer zone—a minimal amount of distance around their base, usually their home . . . . Killers want to operate in a comfort zone—their own neighborhoods—but they also want to operate in a place where they have some anonymity." (Quote from Kim Rossmo, Director of Research at the Police Foundation.)

The second type of profiling relies more on geographic relationships rather than offender behavior. This method is referred to as **geographical profiling.** Geographic profiling is an investigative methodology that uses the locations of a connected series of crimes to determine the most probable area of offender residence. It is generally applied in cases of serial murder, rape, arson, and robbery, though it can be used in single crimes (auto theft, burglary bombing, etc.) that involve multiple scenes or other significant geographic characteristics. The basis of geographic profiling is the link between geographic crime site information and the known propensities of serial criminals in their selection of a target victim and location. A key concept of geographic profiling is the "nearness principle." Forensic research has shown that most offenders tend to commit crimes fairly close to home. Also, the extent of an offender's range depends on his or her preferred mode of transportation.

A sniper operating from a vehicle would have more range than one who travels on foot. The geographic profile system incorporates all methods of transportation available to an offender, including buses, subways, and cars when calculating a likely base. The geographic profiling system produces a map of the most probable location of the criminal's center of activity, which in most cases is the offender's residence. When linked with additional information and data sources, such as motor vehicle databases and suspect databases, geographic profiling has proven to be very useful to police investigations.

Serial rapists or killers often operate in a geographical comfort zone, selecting victims close to home or from the same community (Goodwin, 1999). A rapist may prefer victims residing in housing complexes or business areas known to the offender. A serial killer may prefer prostitutes who frequent certain areas of a city. Because these offenders operate in a comfort zone, they have knowledge of escape routes or locations

TABLE 9-2

Profile of a Serial Rapist

Age: 75% are under age 25, 80% under age 30; over 30 if sadistic type.
Sex: Is male normally 100% of the time.
Race: Vast majority are black (75–90% of rapists in prison are black); crime tends to be intraracial; rapists are usually unarmed; 1 in 4 times (25%) uses a knife or an instrument.
Class: Majority are from poverty and of lower-class backgrounds.
IQ: Majority are in normal range 90–110.
Family: Sibling history is more important than family history; may have been sibling bed sharing; overt sexual behavior in family with siblings and/or (sadistic) mother; lack of support from (absent) father; temper tantrums as child.
School: Usually had no learning problems and typically is a high school graduate; some college possible; discipline problems likely, most likely involving pornography interest.
Peers: Has mild to moderate social maladjustments, but normally one of the "boys"; tries to cultivate a reputation as a tough fighter, but known as a punk and low life to many; usually married, divorced, or lives with a woman, in that order, but has demonstrated poor relations with women.
Work: Majority work reliably around women; lack self-confidence to improve self; if sadistic, takes better job.
Criminal History: Majority are successful at avoiding this; average of 2.5 priors, only 2 years served on each.
Drug/Alcohol: These are noted problems in this area.
Mental: Has antisocial personality; defines self as normal in every way except sexually, where suffers a known philia or mania; ritualism may border on psychotic with sadistic type.
Arrest: Frequently leaves clues with victim; plays games with police; is difficult to get confession.

Source: Inside the Mind of Sexual Offenders: Predatory Rapists, Pedophiles, and Criminal Profiles. D. Stevens, and F. Schmalleger, 2001.

where they can take their victims. The more a killer or rapist operates in a particular community, the more valuable the geographical profiling.

The use of geographic profiling has proven successful in locating serial killers. Famed Canadian serial killer Clifford Olsen who raped and murdered eleven young boys and girls was apprehended in part through the use of geographic profiling. By analyzing the crime scenes, interviewing witnesses, and studying area maps, profilers were able to locate the killer's residence within a four-block radius (Hickey, 2002: 316).

Although behavioral or geographic profiling does not solve all cases, it provides a method for managing the large volume of information typically generated in major crime investigations. It is one more investigative tool used to assist in the identification of serial offenders.

Forensics in the Biological Sciences

Forensic investigations relying on biological or life sciences to solve crimes include the examination of toxic substances, DNA, insects, anthropological analysis, conducting autopsies, and the use of odontology (dentistry). While they are distinct fields, they often collaborate in the investigation process.

Forensic toxicology is the study of toxic substances harmful to human beings (FBI, 1999). The work of a forensic toxicologist generally falls into three main categories: (1) routine testing for alcohol in blood or urine samples; (2) identification of drugs such as heroin, cocaine, or cannabis; and (3) the detection and identification of drugs and poisons in body fluids, tissues, and organs. Toxicology examinations determine the circumstances surrounding drug- or poison-related homicides, suicides, and accidents. Because of the large number of potentially toxic substances, it may be necessary to screen for classes of poisons such as volatile compounds (ethanol, methanol), heavy metals (arsenic), nonvolatile organic compounds (drugs of abuse, pharmaceuticals), and miscellaneous compounds (strychnine, cyanide). Toxicology experts may offer expert testimony on the effects of certain drugs or poisons on the human body. Toxicologists are often called upon to testify as to the effects of certain mind-altering drugs such as the so-called date rape drugs.

Forensic entomology is the application of the study of insects and other arthropods to legal investigation. Since the majority of living things upon the earth are arthropods, we tend to come into contact with them regularly. Arthropods are of interest to forensic entomologists because they are important carrion feeders—they eat dead vertebrates, including humans. After death, a succession of fungi, bacteria, and animals will colonize the dead body. The substrate on which the body is lying will also change over time. Leakage of fluids from the dead body will lead to the disappearance of certain insects, and other insects will increase as time goes by.

A forensic entomologist can estimate how long a body has been in a location by looking at the fauna on the body and by sampling soil insects underneath the body.

Sometimes the movement of suspects, goods, victims, and vehicles can be traced also by the type of insects found. The information that a trained and knowledgeable forensic entomologist can provide will include time of death, season of death, geographic location of death, storage or movement of the remains after death, evidence of trauma, presence of drugs or chemicals, detection of human body parts, and neglect or abuse of children or the elderly (Haskell and Haskell, 2002).

An example of applying forensic entomology occurred in 1982, when deputies of the Ventura County, California, sheriff's office noticed that a murder suspect had chigger bites similar to the ones that crime scene investigators had on their ankles and behind their knees. An entomologist was contacted, and by analyzing the bites, connected the suspect to the crime scene where the naked body of a 24-year-old woman was found strangled with her own blouse. Criminologists conducted several tests at different places, but the only place in which they found chiggers was a narrow strip near a eucalyptus tree under which the woman had been found. This discovery meant that the suspect had to be at the crime scene at some point, which was not consistent with his testimony (he claimed to have seen the woman for the last time at a bar). The suspect was convicted of first-degree murder and sentenced to life without parole.

Forensic anthropologists assist medical and legal specialists to identify known or suspected human remains. Forensic anthropologists are "bone detectives" who help police solve cases involving unidentified human remains. The techniques that physical anthropologists use to discover information about humans from their skeletons are also used to discover the identity of the victims of accidents, fires, plane crashes, war, or crimes such as murder (Burns, 1999). The science of forensic anthropology includes archaeological excavation; examination of hair, plant materials, and footprints; determination of elapsed time since death; facial reproduction; photographic superimposition; detection of anatomical variants; and analysis of past injury and medical treatment.

When a skeleton is found, the first step is to determine whether the remains are human or animal. If human, an anthropologist then attempts to estimate age at death, racial affiliation, sex, and stature of the decedent. Although the primary task of anthropologists is to establish the identity of a decedent, increasingly they provide expert opinion on the type and size of weapon(s) used and the number of blows sustained by victims of violent crime. It should be noted, however, that forensic pathologists or related experts in forensic medicine determine the cause or manner of death, not the forensic anthropologist.

Closely allied with forensic anthropology is the science of **criminal odontology.** This field is concerned with offender identification through bite marks on both the living and the dead. The theory of forensic dentistry is that no two mouths are alike and that teeth leave recognizable marks (FBI, 1999). Once a suspect is apprehended, the forensic dentist makes one or more impressions of the suspect's teeth, comparing them with the recorded bite marks; and if called to testify, the dentist renders an opinion of the probability of a match.

Serial killer Ted Bundy often left bite marks on his victims, which were later used as evidence against him. In a Florida case in which he was convicted of murder, investigators immediately ordered impressions of his teeth, to compare with the bite marks left on one of his victims. The match was indisputable, thereby assisting in convicting him of murder.

The science of odontology has been around since at least 66 A.D., the time of Nero. Nero's mother had her soldiers kill an enemy of hers, with instructions to bring back the deceased's head as proof of death. Unable to positively identify the head, she examined the teeth and recognized the discolored front tooth of the victim, confirming the identity. During the U.S. Revolutionary War, Paul Revere, who practiced dentistry, helped identify war casualties by their bridgework. The use of dental charts today, usually recorded and updated on visits to a dentist, means that most people have a dental record filed somewhere.

> "A victim who scratches her attacker's skin will get enough material under her nails for a positive ID. The same applies to any of his hairs she pulls out. Or if the rapist smoked a cigarette, drank from a glass, or chewed gum, he left traces of saliva rife with DNA. It is nearly impossible for someone to commit a violent crime like rape and not leave DNA evidence behind." (Quote by Paul Ferrara, Ph.D., Director of the Virginia Division of Forensic Science.)

We have all heard of **DNA** (deoxyribonucleic acid) and its use in criminal investigation. Not only is DNA testing used to identify offenders, but also its use has extended to freeing offenders wrongfully accused of crimes such as murder and rape. In other words, DNA evidence collected from a crime scene can be linked to a suspect or can eliminate a suspect from suspicion. DNA is the building block for the human body; virtually every cell contains DNA. DNA evidence can be found in saliva, on the skin, in bone, in hair, in semen, and in blood. Also, DNA evidence can be taken from a number of sources such as cigarette butts and pipes. DNA does not change throughout a person's life, and with the exception of identical twins, no two people have the same DNA. During a sexual assault, for example, biological evidence such as hair, skin cells, semen, or blood can be left on the victim's body or other parts of the crime scene. Properly collected DNA evidence can be compared with known samples to place a suspect at the scene of the crime.

The 1980s saw the first use of DNA in crime investigation (Lohr, 1987). This occurred in 1983 when Lynda Mann, aged 15, was found murdered only a few miles from her home. The police were unable to come up with any leads, but the killer left a sample of his semen. Four years later another 15-year-old girl was raped and strangled to death. The police believed that the same offender had committed both crimes. A suspect was arrested and questioned. However, the investigator wanted assurance, and after reading a magazine article about a new forensic technique called DNA fingerprinting, he pressed further. Since DNA had not yet been used to solve a case, it seemed like a good chance to prove its usefulness. The investigators compared the suspect's DNA with the DNA from the semen found at the crime scene. The police were surprised to find that the DNA testing proved that the suspect was innocent. Thus, if DNA evidence proved innocence, then it could prove guilt. Later, another suspect was arrested, and the resulting DNA tests revealed that this suspect was guilty.

The technology of DNA testing is growing, and it has been reported that a portable DNA testing kit is under development in Britain. The device will be smaller than a suitcase and will be linked to the National DNA Database. Details of any match will be sent via the Internet directly to the detective in charge. The results would return in under an hour to the detective's palm-held computer (Innocence Project, 2003).

A precursor to DNA analysis is **forensic serology,** which involves the identification and characterization of blood, semen, and other body fluids usually found in dried stain form on items of physical evidence, such as clothing and furniture. If human blood is identified, attempts are made to determine whether the blood type is A, B, AB, or O. Then, depending upon the size of the dried stain, it may be analyzed further using electrophoresis to determine as many genetic marker protein types as possible (Grispino, 1990).

Case Example: A Case of Innocence Through DNA Testing

On February 20, 1990, a patient at the psychiatric hospital where Mark Diaz Bravo worked claimed that she had been raped in an alcove earlier that afternoon. During the course of police interviews, she named several different people as her assailant. One of those she named was Bravo. She later stated that she was sure Bravo was the attacker. A Los Angeles County jury found Mark Diaz Bravo guilty of rape in 1990. The court sentenced him to a prison term of 8 years.

The prosecution based its case on several points:

- The victim named Bravo as the assailant and made an in-court identification.
- Bravo had misrepresented himself in the past on applications and on his business card.
- Blood tests done on a blanket near the crime scene showed a blood type consistent with Bravo's blood type, which is found in only 3 percent of the population.

Bravo filed a postconviction motion, and in 1993, a superior court judge granted Bravo's motion to release a blanket, sheet, and pair of panties to the defense for DNA testing. Prosecutors received a report from Cellmark Diagnostics on December 24, 1993, stating that none of the tested semen had DNA that matched Bravo's. On January 4, 1994, Bravo's lawyer filed a writ of habeas corpus, and a Superior Court judge ordered Bravo released on January 6, 1994. The judge stated that Bravo had not received a fair trial, that the victim had recanted her testimony, that Bravo's alibi was unimpeachable, and that the DNA tests were irrefutable. Bravo was released from prison after serving 3 years of his sentence (Maloney, 2002).

TABLE 9–3

DNA and Its Sources

Possible Location of DNA Evidence	Source of DNA
Bite mark or area licked	Saliva
Fingernail scrapings	Blood or skin cells
Inside or outside surface of used condom	Semen or skin cells
Blankets, sheets, pillowcases, other bed linens, or pillows	Semen, sweat, hair, or saliva
Clothing, including undergarments worn during *and* after the assault	Hair, semen, blood, or sweat
Hat, bandanna, or mask	Sweat, skin cells, hair, or saliva
Tissue, washcloth, or similar item	Saliva, semen, hair, skin cells, or blood
Cigarette butt; toothpick; or rim of bottle, can, or glass	Saliva
Dental floss	Semen, skin cells, or saliva
Tape or ligature	Skin cells, saliva, or hair

Source: Understanding DNA Evidence: A Guide for Victim Service Providers. May 2001. National Institute of Justice and Office for Victims of Crime: National Institute of Justice.

PATHOLOGY AND THE AUTOPSY

When a body is found and there is some suspicion as to the cause of death, a **medical examiner** is called to establish whether it was a murder, a suicide, or an accidental death. If the death was murder-related or undeterminable, the body is taken to a **pathologist** either to conduct an autopsy or to establish the cause of death and gather other bodily information.

An autopsy lasts approximately 3 to 6 hours, because it usually involves an examination of every organ of the body. During the autopsy, the body is photographed, both clothed (if it was clothed when found) and unclothed. Then it is x-rayed, weighed, and measured, and any identifying marks are recorded. Old and new injuries are noted, along with tattoos and scars. Trace evidence, such as hair and fibers, is collected off the body and from under the fingernails. Fingerprints are taken, and if rape is suspected, a rape kit is used for evidence collection.

In cases of suspected suicide by gunshot, hands are swabbed for gunpowder residue. Blood, urine, bile, and other bodily fluids samples are taken and analyzed. The examination of organ parts from the body is useful in poison cases as well any time that alcohol or drugs are suspected. The inspection of stomach contents is part of every postmortem exam, since it may provide information as to cause of death as well as time of death. Clinical examination also answers questions about age, race, sex, height, weight, and general health condition of unidentified persons.

Case Example: Autopsy of JonBenet Ramsey

The brutal murder of 6-year-old JonBenet Ramsey on Christmas night in 1996 shocked America. Although theories abound, the case remains unsolved with no arrests. The autopsy of JonBenet Ramsey indicated that she was strangled. She was found lying in the middle of the basement floor, wrapped in a blanket. She had duct tape across her mouth. JonBenet lay with her arms above her head, and a white cord was wrapped tightly around her neck. The same cord was tied loosely to her wrists. The broken handle of a paintbrush, measuring approximately 4.5 inches in length, had been looped into the cord to form a garrote. At the time of her death, JonBenet was wearing a sweatshirt over a long-sleeve shirt. The lower half of her body was clad in white pajama bottoms over white panties. The evidence suggests that someone either took the girl from her bedroom by force or lured her to the kitchen with the promise of food, which would explain the undigested remnants of pineapple found in her stomach at the time of her death. She was sexually assaulted, after which she was strangled with the garrote and bashed about the head. There were also abrasions on her back and legs consistent with her having been dragged. There was chronic inflammation of the vaginal tract and a small opening in her hymen. In addition, there were traces of blood in the vaginal area and in the crotch of her panties. (Mahoney and O'Connor, 2002)

THE PHYSICAL SCIENCES

The application of the physical sciences in criminal investigations is crucial, including the examination of nonliving evidence such as trace evidence (hairs, fibers, palynology), fingerprints, and ballistics. This is often the most common type of evidence found at a crime scene. **Trace evidence** can corroborate other evidence or even prompt a confession. Because trace evidence can be any number of things, from a paint chip to a piece of glass to plant debris, there are numerous methods used for analysis. Hair and fiber are the most frequently analyzed trace evidence.

Hair examinations can determine whether the hairs are animal or human. The race of the offender, body area, method of removal, damage, and alteration (that is, bleaching or dyeing) can also be determined from human hair analysis. For example, persons of African descent have kinky hairs, with dense pigments, whereas Caucasian hairs are generally straight or wavy, with finer pigmentation. The hair of an infant or young child tends to be finer than adult hair, but it is difficult to establish gender from hair samples. The animal species and family can be determined from hair analysis (Saferstein, 1995).

Fiber examinations can identify a type of fiber such as animal (wool), vegetable (cotton), mineral (glass), and synthetic (manufactured). Questioned fibers can be compared with fibers from a victim's and a suspect's clothing, carpeting, and other textiles. A questioned piece of fabric can be physically matched to known fabric through composition, construction, and color, and impressions on fabric can be examined. Clothing manufacturers' information can be determined by label searches.

Fiber evidence was used to convict serial killer Wayne Williams, who was responsible for killing 25 black males in the Atlanta areas from 1979 through 1981. The police search of Williams's home and car revealed valuable trace evidence. The floors of Williams's home were covered with yellow-green carpeting, and comparisons with samples removed from victims showed good consistency with this carpeting. The fiber evidence, along with other evidence, was used to convict Williams of the murders.

Another less common type of the use of trace evidence that is gaining recognition is known as forensic palynology. New Zealand leads the world in the use of forensic palynology, including its acceptance in courts of law. It refers to the use of pollen and spore evidence found on persons victimized or considered suspects in a crime. Such evidence may be found on debris, clothing, or shoes. Pollen and spore production and dispersion patterns are important considerations in the study of forensic

Case Example: The Danielle Van Dam Case

On February 1, 2002, 7-year-old Danielle Van Dam was discovered missing from her California home. Her decomposed body was found several weeks later, a victim of murder. A neighbor, David Westerfield, was convicted of the kidnapping and brutal murder of the girl, and he was sentenced to death. The strongest evidence against Westerfield was forensic evidence. Although the police did not find any evidence of Westerfield's being in the Van Dam home, fingerprint, DNA, and trace evidence experts testified that there were many indications of Danielle's presence in the defendant's home and RV. A police fingerprint examiner said that a handprint found above the bed in Westerfield's motor home matched Danielle's. A DNA analyst testified that blood fitting Danielle's DNA profile was found on a jacket that Westerfield had taken to the drycleaners and on the carpet of his RV. Other lab analysts testified that hairs found in the RV and on Westerfield's laundry likely came from Danielle or her maternal relatives, and another expert said that one hair found in the RV's bathroom drain fit her DNA profile exactly. A fiber analyst said that a single strand of orange fiber found in the necklace Danielle was wearing at the time of her death matched 20 to 30 fibers found in Westerfield's washer, 50 to 100 found on top of the washer, another 50 to 100 in his laundry, and 10 to 20 found in the bedding in his master bedroom. Other lab analysts said that animal hair in Westerfield's home and vehicle was consistent with that of the Van Dam's dog and that carpet fibers on his property were similar to those from Danielle's bedroom. Westerfield was convicted and sentenced to death.

palynology. In other words, if the expected production and dispersal patterns of spores and pollen are known from plants in a given region, then it is possible to know the type of "pollen fingerprint" that come from that area (Bryant, 1989). The first task of the forensic palynologist is to try to find a match between the pollen in a known geographical region with the pollen in a forensic sample.

Two of the earliest reported cases using forensic palynology occurred in 1959—one in Sweden and the other in Austria (Erdtman, 1969). The case in Sweden revolved around a woman who was killed in May 1959, during a trip in central Sweden. During the court hearing, a number of experts, including a palynologist, were asked to examine dirt attached to the woman's clothing. The objective of those studies was to determine whether the woman was killed where she was found or whether she had been killed elsewhere and then dumped at the site where her body was discovered. Preliminary studies of the pollen in the dirt samples suggested that she had been killed elsewhere, because the dirt lacked pollen from plants common in the area where the body was found.

In 1892, Englishman Francis Galton developed the scientific classification of fingerprints. Then, in 1896, Edward Henry of England developed a system of matching fingerprints to identify people. By 1900, Scotland Yard adopted the Galton-Henry system of fingerprinting. Fingerprinting in crime investigation was first used in 1911 to identify a robbery suspect. Unfortunately, there were no eyewitnesses to the crime, and several people claimed that the suspect could not have committed the crime because they were with him the night of the robbery. Unless the prosecutor could

Case Example: The Shroud of Turin

The Shroud of Turin, the cloth that some claim was used to wrap the body of Christ before burial, represents a high-profile example in which pollen data were used as a key piece of evidence in the attempt to confirm the origin of the item. During an extensive study of the shroud, it was found that 49 different pollen grains were trapped in the fibers of the cloth. Comparisons of the shroud's pollen spectrum with pollen from regions of Israel and the western Mediterranean revealed similar types. Pollen types reported from the shroud included desert-type plants that still grow in Israel. Other pollen types were similar to pollen found in nearby Turkey, and a few additional types represented plants common to the western Mediterranean region. In addition, some of the pollen (such as beech) on the shroud were of types found mostly in central Europe. The conclusion was that the majority of the pollen recovered from the shroud represented plants from regions in Israel, the nearby western Mediterranean, and Turkey (Wilson, 1978). The European pollen represented materials deposited on the shroud during its display in Europe. More recent scientific studies cast serious doubts on the authenticity of the shroud and on the pollen that was purportedly recovered from the shroud.

present solid evidence, the man would go free. The prosecutor summoned a detective who had found several marks of dirty fingers on the window frame, which matched the finger markings of the suspect. The suspect was convicted.

Fingerprints can be exposed from evidence at the scene of a crime in a number of ways. The most common method is dusting smooth, firm, or light-colored surfaces with a fine powder. The powder sticks to the skin oils left on the surface by the fingers, making the prints visible. Forensic scientists can also use laser light to flood a room, causing chemicals in any fingerprints to fluoresce. Also, the vapor from "superglue" reacts with chemicals in human sweat to produce a white image of fingerprints.

Ballistics is the study of firearms, including the firing, the flight of the bullet, and the effects of different types of ammunition. Ballistics in crime investigation was first formally established in 1923. When a criminal fires a gun, a bullet from a spent cartridge can be traced to a particular weapon. When a gun is made, a hole is drilled in the barrel for the bullet to travel through. The barrel of the gun has ridges, or rifling, to make the bullet spin. When a bullet is fired and travels down the gun's barrel, the spiral rifling cuts markings into the bullet. These grooved markings, which are called striations, from one gun will differ from those caused by any other gun.

At the scene of a shooting, the police look for bullets and spent cartridge cases. If a weapon is found, lab technicians will take the gun and fire test bullets from the gun into a cotton wall or a water tank. Under a microscope, the technician can compare the striations on the test bullets with the marks on the bullet from the crime scene. Ballistic science can also be used to determine whether a person was in close proximity when a shooting occurred. When a gun is fired, tiny specks of primer residue and gunpowder remain on the hand of the person who fired it, and tests can reveal their presence.

In many cases, a ballistic expert can assist in determining whether a death was a homicide or suicide. Kohlmeier et al. (2001) analyzed 1,704 suicidal firearms deaths and determined characteristics of those injuries. In his study, he found that a revolver was used in approximately 50 percent of the cases. In those cases, most injuries occurred in the right temple, suggesting that the victim was probably right-handed. If the victim was left-handed and injury was to the right temple or if no gunshot residue is found on the victim's hand, questions may be raised about the cause of death.

Conclusion

The forensic process is not perfect, and there are definitely a number of examples in which the police and the prosecution have made mistakes, resulting in wrongful convictions. Many of these errors have led to protective legislation. The **Innocence Protection Act** (IPA), which was passed in 2003, is a law designed to address wrongful convictions. This groundbreaking act would grant any inmate convicted of a federal crime the right to petition a federal court for DNA testing if testing would support a claim of innocence. The act would also withhold federal funds to states that do not adopt adequate measures to preserve evidence and make postconviction DNA testing available. In addition, the IPA also sets guidelines for courts to follow when DNA testing has been ordered, and it establishes posttesting procedures. It is important to note that the IPA provides for payment for testing, and for punishment for the unlawful alteration or destruction of evidence. Other important provisions include implementation of new and better standards for legal representation in capital cases; increased funding for federal capital defense and prosecutorial DNA testing programs; and compensation guidelines for state capital cases (including the withholding of federal funds to states that do not comply with the standards set forth).

The use of forensic experts in criminal cases is widely accepted; however, it is important to recognize that acceptance of expert opinions in court is not automatic. The United States Supreme Court has ruled that expert testimony must meet certain tests to be admissible. This ruling is known as the **Daubert Standard.** The case of *Daubert vs. Merrell Dow Pharmaceuticals* (1993) arose from a claim that Bendectin, a drug used to treat nausea, caused serious birth defects when taken during pregnancy. In this case, experts testified about the effects of the drug. The case set forth a two-pronged standard: expert testimony must be both reliable and relevant. To be reliable, the evidence must meet the following guidelines: the scientific theory or technique can be and has been tested; it has been the subject of publication or peer review; the known or potential rate of error has been established; standards controlling the technique's operation must exist or be maintained; there must be general acceptance in the scientific community; and the testimony must be relevant to the case in issue. Fingerprinting, for example, has been subjected to experimentation, study, and observation by fingerprint departments all over the world. It has also been subjected to peer review, testing, and a tremendous amount of empirical review by thousands, if not tens of thousands, of scientists. Therefore, it would qualify as a reliable and recognized science. And, of course, fingerprints found at the scene of a crime would be relevant. Forensic science, used in conjunction with good investigation techniques by seasoned investigators, is what solves the most difficult cases.

Discussion Questions and Activities

1. What are some of the problems associated with the use of forensic evidence? Since it is usually circumstantial (indirect), construct a scenario under which someone could be falsely convicted on forensic evidence alone.
2. Compare the types of forensic methods, and then identify the ones you feel are the most valuable.
3. Using the Van Dam case example, identify the types of forensic experts that you would employ, and indicate what pieces of evidence they would analyze, and why. Put this information into a chart.
4. What is the purpose of an autopsy?

5. Complete Self-Check 9-1, and then compare your profile with those of your classmates.
6. Compare behavioral profiling with geographical profiling. How can both be useful in an investigation of a serial rape offender?
7. What do you think of a priori profiling (Highlight 9-1)? What do you see as the pros and cons of using this to fight crime? If you can interview someone who has been "profiled" in this way (e.g., at the airport), what is his or her reaction?
8. Research a famous murder investigation, and then determine how forensic experts were used in the case.
9. Explain the Daubert rule and its application to forensic science.
10. Go to *www.truthorlie.com* to find out the following: Can you (and if so, how) beat a polygraph? How is a lie detected? Will the test give a false positive? Evaluate the site—is it objective or biased?
11. What do you think might be some reasons for mistaken eyewitness identification? Do some additional research into some common reasons that this occurs.

Key Terms

Ballistics
Brain-wave monitoring
Criminal odontology
Criminal profiling
Daubert Standard
DNA
Forensic Anthropologists
Forensic entomology
Forensic psychology
Forensic serology
Forensic toxicology
Geographical profiling
Innocence Protection Act
Pathologist
Psycholinguistics
Trace evidence
Voice stress analyzers
United States versus Scheffer

References

Bryant, V. M., Jr. 1989. Pollen: "Nature's fingerprints of plants." *1990 Yearbook of Science and the Future*, pp. 92–111. Chicago: Encyclopedia Britannica.

Burns, K. 1999. *Forensic Anthropology Training Manual.* Upper Saddle River, N.J.: Prentice Hall.

Cohen, Sheldon, 1998. "USE OF THE POLYGRAPH IN SECURITY CLEARANCE DETERMINATIONS *Security Management Magazine.*

Crystal, D. 1998. The Cambridge Encyclopedia of Language (2nd ed.). Cambridge, England: Cambridge University Press.

Daubert vs. Merrell Dow Pharmaceuticals 113 S.Ct. 2728, 125 L.Ed.2d 469, 482 (1993).

Decaire, M. 1999. "Forensic psychology: The misunderstood beast. (*http://flash.lakeheadu.ca/~pals/forensics/forensic.htm.*

DNA Testing the Future of Forensic DNA Testing: Predictions of the Research and Development Working Group. (NCJ 183697) *http://www.ojp.usdoj.gov/nij/pubs-sum/183697.htm.*

Douglas, J. and M. Olshaker. 1997. *Journey Into Darkness.* New York: Pocket Books.

Erdtman, G. *Handbook of Palynology.* 1969. New York: Hafner Publishing.

Farwell, L. A. 2000. Forensic Science Report: Brain Fingerprinting Test on Terry Harrington Re: *State of Iowa vs. Terry Harrington* Brain Wave Science *www.BrainWaveScience.com* Human Brain Research Laboratory, Inc. P. O. Box 176, Fairfield, IA 52556)

FBI (Federal Bureau of Investigation). 1999. *Handbook of Forensic Sciences.* Washington, D.C.: United States Department of Justice.

FBI (Federal Bureau of Investigation). 1998. "The national DNA index system." U.S. Department of Justice press release (Oct. 13) available at *http://www.fbi.gov/pressrm/pressrel/pressrel98/dna.htm.*

Goodwin, J. 1999. *Hunting Serial Predators.* CRC Press.

Grispino, R. 1990. *Serological Evidence in Sexual Assault Investigations.* In *FBI Law Enforcement Bulletin.* Washington, D.C.

Haskell, N. and C. Haskell. 2002, May. *Forensic entomology Law & Order;* Wilmette;

Hickey, E. W. 2002. *Serial killers and Their Victims.* Belmont, Calif.: Wadsworth.

Horvath, F. and R. Meesig. 1995. "The criminal investigation process and the role of forensic evidence: A review of empirical findings." Paper presented at the 47th annual meeting of the American Academy of Forensic Sciences. February 1995, Seattle, Wash.

Horvath, F. and R. Meesig. 1996. "The criminal investigation process and the role of forensic evidence: A review of empirical findings." *Journal of Forensic Science 41* (6): 963–969.

Horvath, F. and R. Meesig 1998. "A content analysis textbooks on criminal investigation: An evaluative comparison to empirical research findings on the investigative process and the role of forensic evidence." *Journal of Forensic Science 43*(1): 125–132.

Horvath, F., E. Orns, and J. Siegel. 1998. "Prosecutorial use of physical and non-physical evidence in felonies." Paper presented at the meeting of the American Academy of Forensic Sciences, Cincinnati, Ohio.

Innocence Project. 2003. Benjamin N. Cardozo School of Law. New York. *www.Innocence project .org/*

Kohlmeier, R. E., C. A. McMahan, and V. J. M. DiMaio. 2001. "Suicide by firearms." *Am J Forensic Med Pathology 22:* 337–340.

Lohr, S. 1987. "Genetic fingerprinting." *New York Times,* November 30, p. 5.

Mahoney, J. J. 2002. "Will DNA evidence revolutionize criminal law? *www.crimemagazine.com.*

Maloney, J. J. and J. P. O'Connor. 2002. "The murder of JonBenét Ramsey." *www.crimemagazine.com.*

Mann, Robert, M. A. and D. H. Ubelaker. 1990, July. *FBI Law Enforcement Bulletin.* Washington, D. C.: Physical Anthropologists Department of Anthropology, Smithsonian Institution.

Miller, D. W. 2000. "Looking askance at eyewitness testimony." *The Chronicle of Higher Education.*

Peterson, I. 2000. "Profiling May Mean Dismissals." *New York Times,* November 29.

Piller, C. 2000. "Scientists give the lie to polygraph testing." *Los Angeles Times,* October 13. p. A1.

Ressler, R. and A. Burgess. 1985. "The men who murder." *FBI Law Enforcement Bulletin 54* (8): 2–6.

Saferstein, R. 1995. *Criminalistics: An Introduction to Forensic Science* (5th ed). Englewood Cliffs, N.J.: Prentice Hall,

Scheck, B., P. Neufeld, and J. Dwyer. 2000. *Actual Innocence*. New York: Doubleday.

Shuy, R. W. 1993. *Language Crimes: The Use and Abuse of Language Evidence in the Courtroom.* Oxford, England: Blackwell Publishers.

Shuy, R. W. 1998. *The Language of Confession, Interrogation, and Deception.* Thousand Oaks, Calif.: Sage Publications.

Smith, S. and R. W. Shuy. 2002. "*Forensic psycholinguistics: Using language analysis for identifying and assessing offenders.*" FBI Law Enforcement Bulletin.

Teten, H. 1995. "Offender profiling." In W. Bailey (Ed.), *The Encyclopedia of Police Science*, pp. 475–477. New York: Garland.

Stevens, D. and F. Schmalleger. 2001. *Inside the Mind of Sexual Offenders: Predatory Rapists, Pedophiles, and Criminal Profiles.* Campbell, Calif: Authors Choice Press.

Swanson, C. N. Chamelin, and L. Territo. 2000. *Criminal Investigation.* Boston: McGraw-Hill.

Wells, G. L., M. Small, S. Penrod, R. S. Malpass, S. Fulero, and C. E. Brimacombe. 1998. "Eyewitness identification procedures: Recommendations for lineups and photospreads." *Law and Human Behavior 22:* 603–647.

Wilson, I. 1978. *The Turin Shroud.* London: Penguin Books.

Wylie, Margie. 2001. "Police use of voice stress analysis generates controversy." Newhouse News Service: *margie.wylie(at)newhouse.com*.

CHAPTER 10

THE PURSUIT OF JUSTICE

LEARNING OBJECTIVES

After studying this chapter, you will

- Understand the operation of the justice system
- Differentiate between state and federal law
- Understand what constitutes a crime
- Be able to identify the elements of major violent crimes
- Learn about the major insanity defenses
- Understand the purposes of punishment and prison

INTRODUCTION

The criminal justice system traditionally includes the police, prosecutors, courts, and corrections components. When a crime occurs, the police investigate and collect information useful to the prosecution. Then, if an arrest is warranted, the police will present their evidence to the prosecution for subsequent case filing, thus beginning the arduous justice process. The prosecutor will determine what charges will be filed against the offender. Along with the pursuit of due process, a successful prosecution requires a complete investigation and analysis of evidence crucial to determining guilt or innocence. Defendants may also plea bargain a case at any time after a case is filed for prosecution

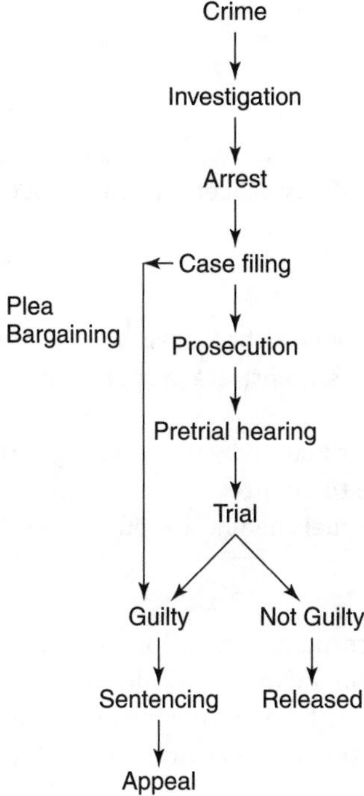

Figure 10–1 Paradigm of the Justice Process

(see Figure 10–1). In a **plea bargain,** a defendant pleads guilty to a lesser charge rather than face trial for the original charge. However, the prosecution, defense, and judge must agree upon a plea agreement. Cases in which there is overwhelming evidence of guilt may not result in a plea bargain to a lesser crime but may entail lesser punishment or sentence bargaining, such as life in prison instead of the death penalty.

THE LAW

American criminal law is based on several sources. The main sources are the Constitution (i.e., **Bill of Rights**), state or federal legislation, and court decisions such as rendered by the United States Supreme Court or other federal appellate courts.

Sources of Law

The constitution, particularly the bill of rights, provides protection for those accused of a crime under the various amendments. The primary amendments pertaining to criminal justice are the first, fourth, fifth, sixth, and the eighth (see Table 10-1). Each of these

TABLE 10-1

Major Criminal Justice Amendments

Amendment	Rights and Protections
First	Freedom of religion; speech; press; peaceful assembly; petition for redress of grievances.
Fourth	Protection against unreasonable searches and seizures; warrants issued on probable cause.
Fifth	Right of indictment by grand jury; right against double jeopardy, self-incrimination, due process, no private property taken without compensation.
Sixth	Speedy and public trial; confrontation by witnesses against accused; notice of charges; assistance to counsel.
Eighth	Excessive bail and fines; no cruel and unusual punishment.

amendments provides protections against governmental intrusions and excesses. For example, an accused person, regardless of how convincing the evidence may be against him or her, has a right to an attorney under the sixth amendment. The accused is also protected from unreasonable searches and seizures as provided for by the fourth amendment.[1]

Another source of law is the legislature. Congress passes laws for the federal jurisdiction, and each state passes laws through its legislatures or assembly. As explained later, Congress, over the years, has passed various crime laws. Both the federal system and each state has its own criminal codes and courts. States crimes, without a federal connection, are tried in state court. State or federal jurisdiction is decided upon by where the crime occurs or the type of offense.

A crime committed on federal property or in violation of a federal statute is adjudicated in federal court. The following are examples of federal law that are applicable to all states.

Unlawful Flight to Avoid Prosecution. Under title 18, chapter 49, section 1073 of the federal code, for example, states the following: "Whoever moves or travels in interstate or foreign commerce with intent either to avoid prosecution or custody or confinement after conviction, under the laws of the place from which he flees, for a crime, or an attempt to commit a crime, punishable by death or which is a felony under the laws of the place from which the fugitive flees is guilty of a federal crime."

It is not uncommon for violent offenders to flee the state or country to avoid prosecution. A visit to the Federal Bureau of Investigation's ten most wanted list confirms the avoidance practices of many violent offenders. The following is an example of a fugitive bulletin sought by the Federal Bureau of Investigation. The offender is charged with multiple crimes, including the federal crime of unlawful flight to avoid prosecution (see *www.fbi.gov/*).

Fugitive Bulletin: Alfredo Reyes

Alfredo Reyes is wanted in connection with the murder of two young Hispanic females, aged 12 and 13. The bodies of the girls were found in an irrigation ditch just outside of Stockton, California, on January 24, 1982. Both girls had been beaten and sexually assaulted. One had been suffocated to death while the other had her throat slit. Reyes and an accomplice, who has since been arrested, were allegedly seen attempting to pick the two girls up at a local hangout and take them to a party on January 23, 1982. When the two girls refused to go with the men, the men allegedly became angry and were seen following the girls around the hangout. After a local arrest warrant was issued charging Reyes with murder, a federal arrest warrant was issued in the United States District Court, Eastern District of California, Sacramento, California, on August 6, 1987, charging Reyes with unlawful flight to avoid prosecution. (Source: *www.fbi.gov/mostwant/fugitive/mar2003/*)

Sex Offender Registration. As part of the federal crime bill approved by Congress in August 1994, the Sexually Violent Offender Registration Act encourages states to create registries of offenders convicted of crimes against children or other sexually violent offenses. Sex offender registration legislation has been adopted in all 50 states (Matson and Lieb, 1996). The law was prompted by the 1994 slaying of 7-year-old Megan Kanka by a convicted sex offender. The law, known as **Megan's Law** in 1995, makes it a standard procedure to inform the community when a sex offender moves into the area. It is clear that Megan's Law is a definite necessity, since it warns people of potentially dangerous individuals (Hudson, 1998).

Hate Crimes Law. In 1968, Congress enacted a **hate crimes** prevention law (Title 18 U.S.C. §245) that covers violent crimes resulting in death or serious bodily injury. The law applies to all states. Crimes that are motivated by a person's race, color, national origin, or religion and that occur while the victim is engaged in a specified, federally protected activity such as walking down the street or simply going about personal business are punishable in every state. Most states have hate crime legislation that follow federal standards.

A final source of law is the **courts.** The courts make laws through the appellate decision-making process. Often appellate courts, such as the Unites States Supreme Court, are called upon to rule on the constitutionality of a law or process. Upon making a decision, the Court is setting a case precedent that binds all other states and federal courts. This process is referred to as setting a precedent or making case law.

Referring to the hate crime laws mentioned before, the United States Supreme Court has ruled on the laws' constitutionality. In the case, a group of young black men and boys gathered at an apartment and discussed a scene from the motion picture

Mississippi Burning in which a white man beat a young black boy who was praying. The group moved outside and observed a young white boy on the opposite side of the street. As the boy walked by, the group ran toward the boy, beat him severely, and stole his tennis shoes. The boy was rendered unconscious and remained in a coma for four days. The assailants were convicted under the state's hate crime statute. The defendants appealed, arguing due process violations, and so forth, but the court disagreed, upholding their convictions (*Wisconsin vs. Mitchell*, 508 U.S. 476 1993).

In discussing the actions of violent predators, we discover that many of them violate both federal and state law. Upon conviction, they may appeal their conviction for years.

Laws often change or are modified either through legislation or judicial decision making. As our technology increases or as criminal sophistication and methods advance, new laws will be written and others modified.

Crime: What Constitutes a Crime?

The justice process is launched upon violation of a law. After a crime is reported, an investigation is initiated to establish whether a criminal case is to be pursued. The most serious crimes are personal crimes such as assault, rape, and murder.

Most crimes consist of two primary elements: a voluntary act, or **actus reus,** which means that the perpetrator acted voluntarily in committing the crime. Also required is a specific mental state or guilty mind known as **mens rea.** Prosecutors must prove that a defendant voluntarily committed the act and possessed the required criminal intent.

Self-Check 10-1

1. Which of the following cases demonstrate *actus reus* for murder?
2. Which of the cases demonstrate *mens rea* for murder?

Case A: A vandal throws a rock through a window with the intent to shatter it, and the rock hits someone inside, causing that person's death.

Case B: In 2002, sniper killer John Allen Muhammad and his teenage companion John Lee Malvo drove around the Washington, D.C. area, shooting innocent people at random. Their vehicle had been modified, allowing them to fire a high-powered rifle undetected through an opening in a rear trunk.

Key: Case A demonstrates *actus reus,* but not *mens rea,* for murder (although the vandal may be convicted for manslaughter). Case B demonstrates premediation through planning.

Case Example: Multiple Crimes

A young women driving home late one evening after attending a party is forced off the road at a deserted intersection. The female victim is pulled from her car, beaten, and driven to an isolated area where she is raped and fatally stabbed several times. At the scene, bloodstains and bullet holes are found inside the vehicle. Several weeks later, a suspect is arrested. Evidence is found in his possession (jewelry, clothing, etc.) belonging to the victim. The suspect is charged with several offenses and is convicted of murder with special circumstance of rape, robbery, and kidnapping. He is sentenced to death.

To prove criminal intent (*mens rea*), evidence of planning and premeditation, such as buying weapons and lying in wait for a victim, is needed. The failure to prove specific intent could result in an acquittal or a conviction of a lesser crime.

Along with intent, there is a need to establish a voluntary act (*actus reus*). The act is required to complete the actual commission of the crime and must not be the result of unconsciousness (e.g., hypnosis) or the result of an uncontrolled reflex, a convulsion, or an accident. Thus, if a person slips on a wet floor and unintentionally falls into another person, causing injury, the person who tripped is not committing a voluntary act.

Descriptions of the major violent crimes are described in Boxes A, B, C, and D, which follow. These are the crimes considered the most threatening to society, and it is common for several of these offenses to be contained in a single crime event. A rape victim, for example, may be robbed, assaulted, or killed. Also, since each is a separate crime, an offender may be tried for each offense.

Following are general descriptions of major crimes. There may some variability among states as to particular elements or degrees. Punishment may increase according to aggravating factors such as the use of a weapon, torture, and so forth.

Box A

Intentional Murder

Intentional murder is the unlawful killing of another through planning and premeditation. The planning may include lying in wait for a victim, stalking, preparing the crime scene, or buying weapons. Intentional murder is conducted with malice (hate) or the desire to achieve some gratification or advantage such as sexual pleasure or financial gain. Many monsters kill their victims to prevent later identification by the victim. Murder can result also from acrimonious, intimate relationships or the need to conceal another crime such as rape.

Box B

Forcible Rape

Rape is the unlawful (nonconsensual) sexual intercourse committed upon another. Rape may or may not involve the use of physical force. Rape charges may be pursued against an offender if the victim was unconscious of the act (e.g., drug induced).

Box C

Aggravated Assault

An aggravated assault occurs when a victim is beaten or assaulted with a weapon (e.g., knife, club). In some cases, an offender may be charged with aggravated assault if the victim is beaten severely through kicking or repeated hitting. When a victim of rape is beaten or injured with a weapon, the offender will usually also be charged with aggravated assault.

Box D

Robbery

Robbery is generally defined as the unlawful taking of personal property through force or fear. To threaten another with bodily harm (with or without a weapon) is robbery if the offender demands property (e.g., vehicle, wristwatch, cash) and the victim is in fear of harm. Robbery often occurs in conjunction with other violent crimes such as aggravated assault and rape.

TRIAL

A person accused of a crime is guaranteed a trial by jury. Usually juries are requested in cases in which the charges are particularly serious, such as murder. However, the accused may ask for a bench trial in which the judge, rather than a jury, serves as the finder of fact.

In both instances, the prosecution and the defense present evidence while the judge decides on issues of law, such as the admissibility of evidence. The trial results in either acquittal or conviction on the original charges or on lesser-included offenses. A judge may order a mistrial, which may occur when a jury cannot reach a unanimous decision. In cases of a mistrial, the prosecution will usually retry the case, requiring a new jury, and the trial process starts over again. The defendant may be released on bail or held in confinement until the conclusion of the new trial.

Prosecution

As addressed in other chapters, serial killers, rapists, and other predators often plan their crimes, including the disposal and concealment of the victim. Their criminal methods may be deliberately organized or spontaneous. But regardless of the strength of evidence against an offender, the case must still be proved beyond a reasonable doubt before a judge or jury.

The prosecutor must convince the jury or judge "beyond a reasonable doubt" of every fact necessary to constitute the crime charged. Beyond a reasonable doubt doesn't mean absolute certainty, but it does require the trier of fact to be convinced of one's guilt on the basis of the evidence presented.[2]

As a way of illustration, suppose that a man discovers that his wife is having an affair with a coworker. Rather than confronting the situation legally, he decides to kill both of them. Upon learning of their next meeting at a hotel, he purchases a gun, drives to the location, conceals his identity with a mask, and waits for both to emerge from a hotel. He follows them to a secluded location and kills them. Absent any mental illness, the distraught man has committed murder, punishable by death or long-term imprisonment. The crime indicated planning and premeditation, which were established by his actions and other evidence, such as a gun purchase, identity concealment, an unstable marriage, and so forth. If a jury is convinced that he killed his wife and her lover, a conviction may follow even though there were no actual witnesses to the shootings.

This presumption of innocence means not only that the prosecutor must convince the jury of the defendant's guilt but also that the defendant need not say or do anything in his own defense. The Fifth Amendment to the Constitution guarantees the right against self-incrimination. If the prosecutor can't convince the jury that the defendant is guilty, the defendant goes free. The presumption of innocence, coupled with the fact that the prosecutor must prove the defendant's guilt beyond a reasonable doubt, makes it difficult for the government to wrongly convict people, although there have been a number of cases in which innocent persons have been convicted of crimes.

Defenses to Crime

When a prosecution is initiated, a defendant may plea bargain to a lesser crime, plead not guilty and request a trial on the original charge, or plead guilty to the original charge to avoid trial. A defendant may offer a straightforward defense to the crime, for example, "I didn't do it, you have the wrong person." Under both federal law and the laws in every state, a number of additional criminal defenses are available to the accused. These fell into two main categories: (1) justifications and (2) excuses.

Highlight 10-1

According to veteran prosecutor Pete Kossoris, in his experience, the more heinous the crime, the less evidence that is needed to convict. Why? The more horrible the crime (e.g., serial killing, sadistic serial rapists) the more threatened the public feels. Jurors are members of the public, and they are more concerned about mistakenly releasing a monster into society than they are when the accused is less threatening (e.g., shoplifter).

Justifications refer to situations in which the defendant doesn't deny that he or she committed the criminal act but does claim that he or she did it for all the right reasons, such as in the case of self-defense.

A self-defense killing is justified when attempting to save one's life (or that of a family member, etc.) from imminent bodily harm, as in the case of an armed intruder's entering the home of another person. Generally, any force used to repel a violent attack is justified.

Another example of a justification is the principle of necessity. Necessity is best explained by the famous 1800s case of ***The Queen vs. Dudley and Stephans,*** in which two men killed and ate a 17-year-old feeble youth (Kaplan, 1978: 1). After a shipwreck, two men and a boy were drifting several days in a lifeboat without food or water. It was decided that the weakest survivor, who was nearly unconscious, should be sacrificed so that the others could live. This is also an example of the choosing of the lesser of two evils or avoiding a greater evil (in the case of cannibalism, choosing to eat the feeble young man instead of letting the whole group starve).

Excuses refer to situations in which the defendant doesn't deny that he or she did it but claims to be not fully responsible for the act because of a lack of volition or free will. Such excuses may include intoxication, duress, postpartum depression (as in the case of Andrea Yates), or a host of so-called abuse excuses such as battered spouse syndrome, post-traumatic stress disorder, and so forth.

Many of these excuses do not relieve anyone of criminal responsibility but are offered either to mitigate their actions or to show that the offender didn't have full cognitive ability in committing the crime. The defense of insanity and diminished capacity are examples of a person's arguing that he or she had less than full cognitive or reasoning ability.

The Insanity Defense

One of the most controversial defenses is the **insanity defense.** This defense is rarely successful and usually seen only when the crimes are very serious and the punishment quite severe. In fact, two-thirds of the states that recognize the insanity defense place upon the defendant the burden of persuading the jury that he or she was insane at the time of the offense, usually requiring proof by a preponderance (more likely than not) of the evidence. A federal statute holds the defendant to an even higher standard, requiring proof of insanity by clear and convincing evidence.

The defense of insanity does not mean that the person did not commit the criminal act for which he or she is charged. It means that when the person committed the crime, he or she could not tell right from wrong or could not control his or her behavior because of mental defect or illness. Such a person, the law holds, should not be held criminally responsible for his or her behavior.

A successful insanity defense is *not* about going free. A person who successfully argues insanity may be indefinitely confined in a forensic hospital, possibly longer than if he or she were actually sentenced for a crime.

Over the years, standard or various tests have been established to determine insanity, including the M'Naghten rule, the irresistible impulse test, and the American Law Institute test (see Table 10–2). All these tests require that at the time of the crime, the defendant's actions were influenced by a mental disease or defect. The tests differ on whether it must be established that the mental disease or defect prevented the person from knowing right from wrong (cognitive prong) or whether the accused could control his or her actions (volitional prong).

The M'Naghten test is the right-wrong test and emerged from the early English case of Daniel M'Naghten. M'Naghten believed that he was the target of a conspiracy involving the pope and British Prime Minister Robert Peel. In 1843, M'Naghten, targeting the prime minister, mistakenly shot and killed Peel's secretary. During the ensuing trial, several psychiatrists testified that M'Naghten was delusional and of unsound mind. A jury agreed, declaring him not guilty. Because of resulting public outrage, British judges set forth the legal standard that has been used for 150 years: under the M'Naghten rule, defendants may be acquitted only if they "labored under such defect of reason from disease of the mind" as to not realize what they were doing or why the act was a crime (Martin, 1998). This legal yardstick established a cognitive standard—did the defendant know that what he or she was doing was wrong?

The irresistible impulse test is a revised version of the M'Naghten rule. The focus is on volition, or whether the defendant had free will or the ability to inhibit his or her criminal behavior. Did the defendant suffer from a "disease of the mind" so strong that the the person lost the power to control his or her behavior and to avoid doing the act? Jeffrey Dahmer (who killed and cannibalized young boys) unsuccessfully claimed NGRI (Not Guilty by Reason of Insanity) due to irresistible impulse. He claimed that he was a necrophiliac (had a paraphilia) and could not control his impulses to have sex with the dead. In other words, he knew that it was wrong but couldn't control himself because of mental disease (the jury didn't buy it).

According to the *American Psychiatric Association Statement on the Insanity Defense*, over half the states have adopted a **test for legal insanity** written by the American Law Institute (ALI) during the 1950s. The test holds that a person would "not [be] responsible for criminal conduct if at the time of such conduct as a result of mental disease or defect he lacks the capacity either to appreciate the wrongfulness of his conduct or to conform his conduct to the requirements of law." This test is basically a

TABLE 10-2

Major Tests of Insanity

Test	Description
M'Naghten test	The defendant is unable to know right from wrong.
Irresistible impulse test	The defendant had an uncontrollable fit of passion.
American Law Institute test	The most popular test. The defendant is not criminally responsible if he or she had a mental disorder or defect at the time of the crime that prevented him or her from knowing right from wrong or from being able to control himself or herself and to follow the law.

combination of the M'Naghten test (cognitive prong) and the irresistible impulse test (volitional prong), and it is widely used. The test, which is sometimes referred to as the substantial capacity test, was successfully applied in the **John Hinckley** case.

Dissatisfied with the aforementioned ALI test, Congress decided to eliminate the volitional prong in the federal test of insanity and to follow the M'Naughten rule. Under federal law, "The defendant has the burden of proving the defense of insanity by clear and convincing evidence" (Federal code 18 U.S.C.A. 17(b).

The legal test for insanity varies from state to state, but in every state, insanity is a legal term decided upon by a judge or jury, not psychologists or psychiatrists. The insanity defense is used in the nation's courts only on very rare occasions. In New Jersey, a review of 32,000 criminal cases in 1982 discovered that the defense was raised in only 52 cases, less than .2 percent of the total (American Psychological Association Report January 9, 1996). In New York City, the insanity defense has been used historically in less than 1 in 700 cases (American Psychological Association Report, January 9, 1996). If a person is found by a jury to be NGRI, he or she will be confined in a forensic hospital setting for an indefinite term.

Although rare, there have been successful cases of insanity pleas. Serial killer Ed Gein (who was the inspiration for the films *Psycho* and *Silence of the Lambs*), was found NGRI for the mutilation, skinning, and murder of several women in the 1950s. Gein was committed to a state psychiatric hospital, where he died in 1984.

In the aftermath of the Hinckley trial, a number of states established a separate verdict of **"guilty but mentally ill" (GBMI).** The consequences of rendering a GBMI verdict are conviction and a criminal sentence. This defense allows the jury to find the accused guilty but requires the defendant to be treated while in prison. Four of the twelve states that adopted the GBMI verdict did so because of the uproar over the Hinckley verdict. Mental health authorities determine whether psychiatric treatment is warranted under the circumstances, and if such treatment is deemed necessary, the offender is hospitalized. If discharged, the offender is sent back to prison to serve the remainder of the sentence (Collins et al., 2003).

Case Example: An Unsuccessful NGRI Defense

Prior to killing her children, **Andrea Yates,** a 37-year-old mother of five children, was diagnosed with psychosis and a severe case of postpartum depression, that is, feelings of overwhelming anxiety, nervousness, and depression affecting many mothers to varying degrees. Despite her periods of depression and emotional problems, antidepressants antipsychotic medications were prescribed, and Yates was allowed to care for her five young children. Yet, on June 20, 2001, Andrea Yates lost the long battle with the visions that she had been having (she had stopped her medication) and that had been tormenting her. She systemically drowned her five children, one by one, in a bathtub. After the killings, Andrea Yates then made at least two phone calls: one was made to her husband, asking him to come home. During the trial, Yates's lawyers argued that in her delusion, Yates believed that she was saving the children from Satan. Prosecutors acknowledge that Yates was mentally ill but successfully argued that she knew right from wrong (cognitive test) and was thus not legally insane at the time of the killings. Yates was convicted of the murderers and is serving a life term. (Bean, 2003)

It is worth noting that because of the subjective nature of the insanity test, several states have abolished the use of the insanity defense altogether. The American Medical Association has voiced its support for the abolition of the insanity defense (Collins et al., 2003). States abolishing the defense continue to admit evidence of mental disorder for the restricted purpose of disproving *mens rea* for the specific crime charged or of proving that a defendant did not possess the special knowledge or intent required for conviction under the charged offense.

Diminished Capacity. Some states allow the **diminished capacity,** or so-called temporary insanity defense. Although limited in use, diminished capacity exists when a defendant has a mental disease or disorder that affects his or her state of mind, as it relates to the commission of a crime (Wrightsman et al., 1998). As discussed, many crimes require that the person "knowingly or purposely" performs some act with specific intent. If a psychological disorder interferes with knowing or purposeful behavior, then this evidence can be presented to the jury for consideration in determining guilt or innocence. Diminished capacity is not the same as an insanity defense, as the person can still be found guilty of a lesser charge that does not require a specific mental state. In other words, the diminished capacity defense may be argued to reduce a charge of murder to a lesser offense of manslaughter. California allowed a plea of diminished capacity beginning in the 1950s. However, the plea came under intense scrutiny during the so-called "Twinkie defense" of 1979 (Dan White case) and is no longer used.

Case Example: A Successful NGRI Defense

On March 30, 1981, John W. Hinckley, Jr., shot President Ronald Reagan, attempting to assassinate him. His defense attorneys did not dispute that he had planned and committed the attack. The attorneys instead argued that he was acting according to the impulses of a diseased or an impaired mind. They further argued that Hinckley had not acted of his own volition but that his life was controlled by his pathological obsession with the movie *Taxi Driver,* starring Jodie Foster. In that movie, the title character stalks the president and fights in a shootout. Hinckley's attorneys said that he saw the movie 15 times, that he identified with the hero, and that he was seeking to reenact the events of the movie in his own life. They argued, moreover, that Hinckley was schizophrenic and that the movie was the actual planning force behind the defendant's assassination attempt against the president. The judge allowed the defense to introduce evidence, in the form of a CAT scan, that Hinckley's brain showed signs of shrunken brain tissue, one of the common symptoms of schizophrenia. The prosecution opposed this evidence on the grounds that the technical nature of the evidence would cause the jury to place too heavy an emphasis on it. The judge rejected this argument on the grounds that the evidence was relevant. Hinckley was found NGRI and remains in hospital confinement.

PUNISHMENT

After a conviction, a criminal sentence is imposed, which may be probation, prison, or death. The punishment may be severe, such as isolated confinement for life, or there may be attempts at treatment or rehabilitation. Unless an offender is sentenced to life without the possibility of parole or is given the death penalty, most violent offenders will eventually be released. Whether these released offenders become recidivists depends upon a number of factors such as age, family supports, offender attitude, employment, psychological conditions, treatment programs, and possibly prison condition.

Prison

The purposes or **goals of imprisonment,** are defined by our society as the following:

- Retribution (an eye for an eye)
- Isolation from society to protect citizens (containment)
- Deterrence (punishment or the threat of punishment to prevent future acts)
- Rehabilitation, so that an individual can be safely reintegrated into society

The high visibility of victims' rights advocates, the public impression that violent offenders cannot be rehabilitated, and saturated media focus on violent offenses have increased the importance of the first three goals and almost eliminated public support for rehabilitation over the last two decades (Chaiken, 2000). Mandatory sentencing laws and three-strikes laws were enacted to keep offenders isolated from society for longer periods of time. Advocating for prison reform and for more humane treatment of prisoners is guaranteed to end a politician's career. Instead, the public wants prison to be as aversive as possible as retribution, as well as to deter repeat offenses upon release or to deter potential offenders by means of having visions of going to "hell"/prison. Supermaximum prisons exist in most states to house serious offenders. This supermaximum model isolates violent inmates in solitary confinement 23 hours per day. This extreme isolation has been associated with the development of serious mental illness and increases the likelihood that inmates will be abused by prison guards (Human Rights Watch, 1997).

Highlight 10-2
Prison Dynamics: Does Power Corrupt?

To examine the effect of power in a prison situation, we will turn to the results of the classic **Stanford Prison Experiment** (SPE) (Haney, Banks, and Zimbardo, 1973). Social psychologists used a variety of psychological tests to screen college males for participation in a simulated experiment in prison dynamics. The subjects were mentally healthy, prosocial young adults who were randomly assigned to be mock-prisoners or mock-guards for two weeks in a mock-prison setup in a basement at Stanford University. The mock-guards soon internalized their role, and many of them began harassing, degrading, and psychologically abusing their peers (mock-prisoners). Even those guards who did not actually participate in the psychological abuse became indifferent to the suffering of the prisoners and turned blind eyes to the abuse. Although in real-life prisons, the majority of violence is perpetrated by prison gangs or fellow prisoners, direct violence by guards or violence tolerated/abetted or instigated by guards is also prevalent (Johnson, 1996; Russell, 1999). The psychologically normal mock-prisoners in the SPE became (in less than a week) more conforming to the whims of the mock-guards and more negative toward each other, and they frequently expressed an intent to harm others (Haney et al., 1973). The experiment, which had to be aborted after six days because of these unanticipated effects, demonstrated the power of situations and roles in transforming the behavior of individuals. The results of the SPE point to the potent effects of psychological abuse on mentally healthy young men who were only pretending to be prisoners for a short time. For real offenders who more often than not experienced psychological neglect or abuse as children, would we expect the effects to be less potent?

Case Example: Diminished Capacity

Dan White, a former city supervisor, shot and killed the mayor of San Francisco, George Moscone, and a city supervisor, Harvey Milk. The crime displayed a high degree of premeditation. Packing extra bullets, White climbed through a City Hall window to avoid metal detectors and shot the two men nine times. White's attorneys argued diminished capacity, claiming that a diet of only junk food had created a chemical imbalance in White's brain (the "Twinkie defense") and that he was depressed over his loss of his city supervisor position. Therefore, he was unable to premeditate murder, one of the requirements for first-degree murder. The jury convicted White of voluntary manslaughter—the least serious charge for homicide. White was sentenced only to a five-year prison term. This light sentence caused an uproar against the diminished capacity plea in California; and in 1982, voters overwhelmingly approved a proposition to eliminate the defense.

Imprisonment of Mentally Ill Offenders

Most offenders with a mental illness are treated in prison rather than being sent to a treatment facility. There are more mentally ill individuals in prisons and jails than in mental health facilities (Winerip, 1999). To illustrate the effects of prison on the seriously mentally ill, consider the case of an individual with paranoid schizophrenia (see Chapter 8) who is in remission upon entering prison. We know that certain conditions predict relapse into an acute psychotic episode: stressful life events, an overstimulating or understimulating environment, high levels of criticism and hostility, and lack of adequate medication (Kuehnel, 2003). In the normal prison environment, stress, sleep deprivation, constant noise, overcrowding, and verbal hostility go with the territory and greatly increase the likelihood of relapse (even with appropriate medication). In a **supermaximum prison,** with 23 hours per day of total isolation, relapse due to lack of stimulation is also predictable. Indeed, in a ruling on California's supermaximum prisons, the judge wrote that these conditions may "press the outer bounds of what most humans can psychologically tolerate" (*Madrid vs. Gomez,* 1995, p. 1267). Imagine the effects on someone who is already mentally ill.

Further, often their mental illness makes it difficult or impossible for the seriously mentally ill to comply with prison rules and guards' demands, resulting in punishment and further restrictions or isolation (Human Rights Watch, 1997). Prisoners with a serious mental illness are also at greater risk for assault by other prisoners (Human Rights Watch, 1999).

The federal courts have mandated treatment in jail and prisons for serious mental, illness which is narrowly defined as acute major depression, paranoid schizophrenia, suicide attempts, and nervous collapse (*Youngberg vs. Romeo*, 1982). The level of treatment provided is usually minimal, and who receives treatment is often at the discretion of wardens. Because of the low level of care and the harshness of prison conditions (most states do not have separate facilities for the mentally ill), most mentally ill prisoners leave prison more ill and disordered, and possibly more dangerous, than when they entered prison (Ditton, 1999).

The Death Penalty

Those convicted of aggravated first-degree murder are normally sentenced to life imprisonment or to death! The decision is made by a judge; or in some states such as California, a jury decides whether the convicted murderer should get life imprisonment or a sentence of death.

States vary on the laws and usage of the death penalty. In 2002, the death penalty was authorized by 38 states and by the federal government. In California, for example, a conviction of first-degree murder may result either in life imprisonment without parole or in the imposition of the death penalty, a fate decided by a jury. In 2001, fifteen states and the federal government executed 66 prisoners for murder. Most were executed by lethal injection, which is considered the most humane method (U.S. Bureau of Justice Statistics, 2002). Although most executions involve men, 9 women have been executed nationwide since 1976. Most women are executed for family killings of their children or spouse. However, all states employing the death penalty provide for automatic appeal in cases involving a death sentence. Among the prisoners executed from 1977 to 2001, the average time spent between the imposition of the most recent sentence received and execution was more than 10 years (U.S. Bureau of Justice Statistics, 2002). As discussed earlier, a conviction for a sex crime may require not only prison time but also life registration as a sex offender. The severity of sentence or punishment is controlled by the seriousness of the offense and associated aggravating factors.

Appeals are subject to the discretion of the appellate court. Prisoners may also appeal their sentences through civil rights petitions and writs of habeas corpus when they claim unlawful detention due to alleged trial error and so forth. There are cases of trial error or other egregious justice mistakes resulting in wrongful convictions in death penalty cases.[3]

It should be noted that appeals are available only to those convicted of a crime. An acquitted defendant cannot be tried again for the same offense even if there is later evidence (after the verdict) that he or she in fact was guilty of the crime for which he or she was originally tried. Such an attempt is termed double jeopardy, the freedom from which is a protection guaranteed under the Fifth Amendment.

Conclusion

The importance of justice and due process cannot be overstated. Although there may be some variability among the states in the law, there is a general consensus on what constitutes a major violent crime. Regardless of the seriousness of the crime, there are constitutional guarantees beginning with the arrest and continuing through conviction. The police must especially be cognizant of the rights of the accused, such as search and seizure and interrogation. If a defendant pleads insanity, a hearing is held to determine whether the accused is in fact insane or is able to stand trial. Despite the amount of evidence against the accused, guilt must still be established beyond a reasonable doubt, that is, the prosecution must convince a jury that the criminal elements were met. Reasonable doubt does not require absolute (100 percent) certainty. In most criminal cases, defendants plead guilty to avoid trial. If there is a trial and conviction, a violent offender is sentenced to prison or death. The offender retains the right to appeal. Also, for those sentenced to death, the appellate process may continue for years, depending upon the constitutional issues involved. The delivery of justice is not without imperfection, and there have been instances of error, such as wrongful convictions. But for the most part, the system generally functions constructively, without numerous constitutional violations.

Discussion Questions and Activities

1. Explain how the laws differ between the federal jurisdiction and the states? How are they similar?
2. What are the major sources of law?
3. What constitutes a criminal offense? Give an example of a murder offense in which the criminal elements have been met.
4. Select one of the defenses of insanity, and then describe how a person could be found not guilty by reason of insanity.
5. Differentiate between diminished capacity and insanity.
6. How do justifications and excuses differ? Find an example of a current case in which each defense was used.
7. The American criminal justice process has often been referred to as one with too may protections. Do you agree with that statement? What should be done to change the process?
8. Do you feel that violent offenders should be allowed to plea bargain? In what types of cases would this be justified?

9. In your opinion, which goal of prison confinement should be primary? Justify your opinion (you may want to use material from previous chapters or to do some additional research).
10. The Stanford Prison Experiment demonstrated the power of situations and roles on behavior and attitudes. Give an example from your own experience (or from something that you have observed) that illustrates this dynamic.

Key Terms

Actus reus
Andrea Yates
Bill of rights
Diminished capacity
Goals of imprisonment
Hate crimes
John Hinckley
Megan's Law
Mens rea
Plea bargain
Queen vs. Dudley and Stephans
Stanford Prison Experiment
Supermaximum prisons
Test for legal insanity
The insanity defense
Unlawful flight to avoid prosecution
Wisconsin vs. Mitchell

References

American Psychological Association. 1996. *Myths and Realities: A Report of the National Commission on the Insanity Defense.* Washington, D.C.

Bean, M. 2003. "Time to think about it: Texas mother gets life in prison." Retrieved from *www.courttv.com.*

Chabria, A. 2002. "The bureaucrat and the boogeyman." *L.A. Times Magazine,* April 14.

Chaiken, J. M. 2000. "Crunching numbers: Crime and incarceration at the end of the millennium." *National Institute of Justice Journal.* Retrieved March 2, 2000, from the World Wide Web: *http://www.ncjrs.org.*

Collins, K., G. Hinkebein, and S. Schorgl. 2003. "The John Hinckley Trial and Its Effect on the Insanity Defense." Retrieved from *www.law.umkc.edu/faculty/projects/ftrials/hinckley/hinckleyinsanity.htm#EVOLUTION.*

Currie, E. 1998. *Crime and punishment in America.* New York: Metropolitan Books.

Ditton, P. M. 1999. *Mental Health and Treatment of Inmates and Probationers* (Special Report NCJ 174363). Washington, D.C.: U.S. Department of Justice, Office of Justice Program, Bureau of Justice Statistics.

Farmer vs. Brennan. 1994. 114 U.S. 1970.

FBI (Federal Bureau of Investigation). 1999. *Crime in the United States—1998.* Washington, D.C.: U.S. Government Printing Office.

Haney, C., Q. Banks, and P. Zimbardo. 1973. "Interpersonal dynamics in a simulated prison." *Journal of Criminology and Penology 1:* 69–97.

Hudson, M. 1998. "Megan's Law Deceptive Experts Say." *The Roanoke Times,* Jan. 25: p. A1.

Human Rights Watch 1997. *Cold storage: Super-maximum Security Confinement in Indiana.* New York: Author.

Johnson, R. 1996. *Hard Time: Understanding and Reforming the Prison* (2nd ed.). Belmont, Calif.: Wadsworth.

Kaplan, J. 1978. *Criminal Justice: Cases and Materials.* New York: Foundation Press.

Kuehnel, T. 2003. Clinical Director Las Posadas Psychiatric Rehibilitation Facility. Personal Communication, 2000.

Madrid vs. Gomez. 1995. 889 F. Supp. 1146. N.D. Cal.

Marshall, W., D. Laws, and H. Barbaree (Eds.). 1990. *Handbook of Sexual Assault: Issues, Theories, and Treatment of the Offender.* New York: Plenum Press.

Martin, J. P. 1998. "The Insanity Defense: A Closer Look." *Washington Post,* Feb. 27.

Matson, S. and R. Lieb. 1996. "Sex Offender Registration: A Review of State Laws." Olympic, Wash: Washington State Institute for Public Policy.

Nicholatichuk, T. 1996. "Sex offender treatment priority: An illustration of the risk/need principle." *Forum on Correction Research 8:* 30–32.

Pincus, J. H. 2001. *Base Instincts: What Makes Killers Kill.* New York: W.W. Norton and Company.

Russell, K. 1999. "Guards accused of setting up rape." *The Washington Post.* Retrieved Oct. 5, 1999, from the World Wide Web: *http://www.washingtonpost.com.*

Silberman, M. 1995. *A World of Violence: Corrections in America.* Belmont, Calif.: Wadsworth.

United States Department of Justice. 2002. *Capital Punishment 2001.* Washington, D.C.: U.S. Bureau of Justice Statistics.

Wilson vs. Seiter. 1991. 501, US 294.

Winerip, M. 1999. Bedlam on the streets. *The New York Times Sunday Magazine,* May 23: pp. 42–49, 56, 65–66, 70.

Youngberg vs. Romeo. 1982. 457 U.S. 307.

Wrightsman, L., M. T. Nietzel, and W. H. Fortune. 1998. *Psychology and the Legal System.* Boston: Brooks and Cole.

Notes

1. For a thorough discussion of law and procedure, see Scheib and Scheib, 1999, *Criminal Law and Procedure* (Boston: West Publishing).
2. A good film to view is *12 Angry Men.* The film portrays the dilemma of a jury's trying to establish guilt beyond a reasonable doubt of a boy on trial for killing his father with a knife. Juror attitudes, evidence analysis, and the like are explored.
3. For a thorough treatment of potential mistakes in the justice process, please consult "The Wrong Man," written by Alan Berlow (*Atlantic Monthly,* November 1999). The author provides examples of the suppression of evidence by police officers and prosecutors.

CHAPTER 11

TO TREAT OR NOT TO TREAT, THAT IS THE QUESTION

LEARNING OBJECTIVES

After studying this chapter, you will

- Understand the issues related to measuring and evaluating treatment effectiveness for sex offenders
- Learn about the elements of cognitive-behavioral/relapse-prevention treatment programs for sex offenders
- Understand how the elements of these treatment programs are applied to sex offender treatment
- Learn about medical/hormonal treatments for sex offenders

INTRODUCTION

- Jeffery Gambord, deemed a sexually violent predator (SVP) by the state of California, wants the state to "just cut of [his] nuts" to free him of his sexually violent compulsions. The state has declined to do so (Blackburn, 2002).
- Having completed a twelve-year sentence and an additional four years of intensive treatment at Atascadero State Hospital under California's 1996 Sexually Violent Predators Law, Patrick Ghilotti petitioned for release. Although

doctors agreed that he was ready, the state of California is blocking his release (Chabria, 2002).

- Approximately 24 percent of rapists and 41 percent of child molesters are convicted of a new sexual offense following release from incarceration (Prentky, Lee, Knight, and Cerce, 1997).

Are there treatments that significantly reduce recidivism for sex offenders? Do laws imposing longer sentences reduce recidivism rates for sex offenders? Current common wisdom is that the answer to the first question is no and that the answer to the second question is yes. However, the answers to both questions are debatable and more nuanced than a simple yes or no. In this chapter, we will provide you with a brief overview of what research has found about treatment effectiveness and the elements of current "state of the art treatments." We focus on sex offenders because unlike mass murderers or serial killers, they are usually released from prison at some point. If not rehabilitated, they pose a continuing threat to the community. This situation has generated efforts to find and evaluate treatment interventions that can reduce the risk of reoffending. Another spur to finding effective treatment has been the passage of sexually violent predator laws, like the one passed in California in 1996. Under this law, those labeled as sexually violent predators can be institutionalized beyond their sentence for treatment. There are legal and moral dilemmas associated with holding sex offenders beyond their sentence for treatment if no treatment (or no effective treatment) is available.

TREATMENT EFFECTIVENESS

The question Is treatment of sex offenders more effective than no treatment? sounds as though it should be simple to answer using an experimental design comparing the recidivism rates of a treated/experimental group to the recidivism rates for an untreated/control group (see Chapter 5). Because of problems inherent in conducting research in real-life settings (i.e., ethical/legal issues, institutional restrictions, problems with follow-up, etc.), the number of participants is usually small in any one study.

To address this problem, researchers investigating the effectiveness of treatment have employed a statistical technique called **meta-analysis.** Meta-analysis combines the results from more than one study for statistical analysis, thereby increasing the overall number of participants. The downside of drawing conclusions based on meta-analysis studies is that the studies that are included in the analysis may vary widely in their methodology, making interpretation difficult. For example, studies included in a meta-analysis may differ in the following:

- Length, type, and intensity of treatment
- Presence or absence of a comparison group

- Manner in which offenders in the treatment group were selected (i.e., random assignment, volunteers, selected by prison officials, etc.) versus that by which the comparison group was selected (i.e., treatment refusers, dropouts, etc.)
- How recidivism is defined (i.e., rearrest, conviction, charged only; does the definition include only sexual offenses or also nonsexual offenses and parole violations?)
- Length of follow-up (i.e., recidivism at 1 year, 3 years, etc.)

Each of these elements of research methodology can affect and potentially bias results. The results of meta-analysis studies must be evaluated in terms of the criteria used for the inclusion of studies in the analysis—remember, "garbage in—garbage out."

Two recent meta-analysis studies (Alexander, 1999; Gallagher, Wilson, Hirschfield, Coggeshall, and MacKenzie, 1999) found lower recidivism rates for treated than for untreated offenders. Gallagher et al. (1999) included only better-designed studies and found positive results for cognitive-behavioral treatments, but not for hormonal and medical treatments.

A major meta-analysis study was conducted by the Collaborative Outcome Data Project (Hanson, Gordon, Harris, Marques, Murphy, Quinsey, and Seto, 2002). They categorized studies on the basis of how offenders were assigned to the treatment and comparison groups, and they included only studies of treatments in current use and cognitive-behavioral treatments delivered after 1980. Almost half of the included studies defined recidivism broadly (parole violations, unofficial community reports), and follow-up periods in these studies ranged from 1 year to 16 years. Sexual offense recidivism (however defined in the original studies) was lower for treated offenders (9.9 percent) than for untreated offenders (17.4 percent) when only studies that used random or nonbiased assignment to treatment and comparison groups were included in the meta-analysis. These results are both statistically and practically significant. Treatment dropouts, as expected, had higher recidivism rates than those who completed treatment. This outcome is probably due to such offender characteristics as hostility toward authority, youth, and impulsivity, which increase both the likelihood that offenders will reoffend and that they will drop out of treatment. Unexpectedly, there was no difference in sexual recidivism between offenders who received treatment and offenders who refused treatment.

Although the findings from the Hanson et al. (2002) meta-analysis of treatment effectiveness are moderately promising, the primary benefits of their analysis are to point out the need for better designed studies (i.e., the consistent inclusion of untreated comparison/control groups) and the importance of developing a consistent and practically useful definition of **recidivism** (outcome). Until there are better-designed studies of treatment effectiveness, the general question Does treatment work to reduce sexual reoffending? cannot be answered with confidence. On the other hand, the alternative is prison with no treatment.

Estimates of **recidivism** following incarceration also vary greatly because of variations in how recidivism is defined (charged versus convicted, sexual versus any reoffense). However, using a sophisticated procedure termed "failure rate" (FR) that includes lifetime risk and new *charges*, Prentky, Lee, Knight, and Cerce (1997) found that following incarceration, 39 percent of rapists were *charged* with a new sexual offense (versus 14 percent convicted) and that 52 percent of child molesters were *charged* with a new sexual offense (versus 41 percent convicted). On the basis of this sample, prison alone is not an effective intervention. Because most sex offenders are returned to the community, finding effective treatments is in everyone's best interest.

CURRENT TREATMENTS

In the past, psychological treatments for sex offenders consisted primarily either of traditional insight-oriented talk therapy designed to help offenders to access feelings and take responsibility for their actions, or of behavior therapies that used respondent conditioning techniques to change sexual arousal patterns (i.e., decrease arousal to images of children and increase arousal to images of adults). The outcomes for both approaches were disappointing over time. Indeed, for psychopathic sex offenders, insight-oriented talk therapy often made them worse. Treatment programs aimed at improving general psychological health (i.e., self-esteem) have not successfully reduced sex offender recidivism (Hanson, 2000; Nicholatichuk, 1996). The current consensus is that comprehensive cognitive-behavior therapy combined with relapse-prevention training is an effective psychological treatment for some offenders. Data from ongoing major studies are still being analyzed, but early reports are promising for some types of offenders. The use of medical/hormonal interventions has a long history accompanied by controversy over mixed results and serious side effects.

Cognitive-Behavior Therapy and Relapse Prevention

Although there is no single cognitive-behavioral protocol outlining the specific therapeutic components that are effective in treating sex offenders, most comprehensive treatment programs use a combination of components that include cognitive restructuring, building coping skills, behavioral reconditioning, and relapse prevention training—this is the "kitchen sink" approach to treatment. Prior to beginning treatment (or as a first step), programs involve offenders in a treatment readiness phase to educate them about their disorder, increase motivation to change, and generate commitment to the program. Psychosocial treatment is a "participatory sport" that requires the cooperation and genuine engagement of the offender.

Cognitive Restructuring

Cognitive restructuring is based on the idea that thoughts (verbal or as images) precede, and therefore influence, emotions and behavior (Laws, Hudson, and Ward, 2000). Thoughts take the form of an inner dialogue that is habitual and automatic in

Highlight 11-1
Confessions of a Forensic Psychologist

This is an interview with Jeffery Teuber, Ph.D., Senior Psychologist at Atascadero State Hospital, a maximum security forensic hospital. Dr. Teuber does not have a specific assigned unit; rather, he is available to all the programs and units that have patients with problematic behaviors. He has worked at Atascadero for six years.

Dr. Kuehnel—Atascadero State Hospital is called a forensic hospital, so have all of the patients been convicted of a crime or found not to be competent to stand trial?

Dr. Teuber—That is correct, all of our patients have gone through the criminal justice system first. We have several different categories, incompetent to stand trial, not guilty by reason of insanity, mentally disordered defender, prisoner in need of treatment, sexually violent predators, and a couple of sub-categories. By the way, we consider our consumers to be twofold. One consumer is the patient himself, being exposed to rehabilitation efforts in hopes of making his life better. The other consumer is the public at-large and we are charged with treating patients so that they don't victimize society.

Dr. Kuehnel—As a therapist, how do you handle realizing some of the things that your patients have done, which have been pretty horrible? Does it ever bother you emotionally? How do you deal with it?

Dr. Teuber—In most cases, I am not consciously aware that it bothers me, I don't know why. Maybe some of us have a built-in protection mechanism where we can detach from the emotional power of the crimes. We have had a number of patients who have raped and/or killed and maybe had sexual relations with the dead body for some period of time or buried family members in the back yard. It is rather bizarre, it is not something that most of us, I think, relate to personally. I can't speak for others but it just doesn't bother me. What I have before me is a person who needs help and they are there for treatment; my job is to treat them so I do it.

Dr. Kuehnel—Are you ever afraid when working with any of these patients?

Dr. Teuber—Often I am working alone, late at night, in back hallways without immediate assistance. If I have a guy who is unstable, a very large man who remains precarious in terms of symptom control while in the hospital, who has tended to be violent numerous times and is behaving in a overtly threatening way, that is kind of frightening. Just once or twice I have had to bluff my way out of the situation—that happens to me infrequently.

Dr. Kuehnel—Is your emotional distance ever challenged?

Dr. Teuber—Yes, I have overheard conversations where two sexual predators are discussing their legal cases and one man will say something like—this is a conversation that I actually overheard, in the patient's library—"Well my attorney says that if I penetrated her

(continued)

with an object but not with my penis yada, yada, yada." The thrust of the conversation is that he can get a lesser charge or plea bargain because he didn't actually have intercourse with this 5-year-old. What he did do was a horrible crime against a child, which she will probably never forget, but these two fellows are talking about their legal situation as if the victim was an inanimate object—a piece of meat or a chair in a room. It is disgusting. Even as a professional it is hard to take.

Dr. Kuehnel—Few anti-social personalities and psychopaths seem to respond to treatment—as a therapist that must be frustrating.

Dr. Teuber—Well, if we use our best efforts to help people that are sent to us learn to overcome violent behaviors and they don't care to respond to treatment, then one feels rather ineffectual, useless in this situation. I'll go on record saying that I am what some people call a "patient hugger"; I love helping people and I have spent my whole life trying to help people. I consider myself very liberal and compassionate in my viewpoint and I am not one of those people who is out to indite all patients as worthless scum. You hear some of this talk in the hospital—they are just worthless scum, they should be caged up and thrown away. I don't have that orientation and yet with the antisocial and psychopathic patients—one can have a sense of getting used up and burned out. They seem tireless in their machinations, utterly at home in their lifestyle and way of thinking no matter how socially undesirable it is to the rest of us. They will ask for and use up therapy time endlessly, never seeming to change at all and often seeming to want to manipulate some therapist into believing that their change is genuine so that they can get a break in court. So that is alienating and frustrating.

Dr. Kuehnel—Many years ago I did some consulting work at Atascadero and it was after a very high profile case here. A 2½ year-old girl, Amy Sue Sikes, was abducted, raped, and killed by a man who had recently been released from Atascadero as rehabilitated. Of course, there was a lot of community outrage. In cases like this where someone is released and they go out and do some horrible thing, as professionals, how do you deal with that type of thing?

Dr. Teuber—It is not easy. There is not only disappointment and frustration but one tends to become fearful on the job that one might make a mistake. One feels that ethically you can't keep a person in the hospital forever, saying that they look ill when they don't. On the other hand, any professional who has worked in forensic mental health long enough has seen himself or his organization burned, so to speak, by people who go back out and harm the community. The community is justifiably outraged, asking why we released this person who raped their daughter. We do the best job we can of predicting who will and who won't reoffend. In defense of mental health professionals, we don't have much control over people once they are discharged. If a person, after he is discharged, decides not to implement the after care program that he committed to and goes without treatment for a certain length of time, I would say that the odds are pretty good that that person will re-offend.

Dr. Kuehnel—As you said, if the patient is, by all objective indicators (no symptoms anymore, they are complying with treatment, a model citizen etc.) "cured," ultimately doesn't the court decide on their release? With psychopaths in particular a psychologist or psychiatrist may have no objective way of documenting that this person is still a danger even if their clinical intuition tells them otherwise. In court, your "intuition" would be made into chopped liver by their attorneys. This is what I have been told by other psychologists/psychiatrists. Is this true?

Dr. Teuber—That is correct. While it is true that the court decides, and I suppose we professionals could hide behind that, the fact of the matter is that the court decides the case on all the available information. If we testified to release such a person and they do go free, then we have to feel some responsibility for that.

Dr. Kuehnel—In your work have you formed any impression about the backgrounds of these psychopathic offenders, do you see any patterns? It seems like many of these offenders had pretty horrible childhoods.

Dr. Teuber—That's true and I don't think that the public has any sympathy for this for obvious reasons—the public suffers from their behaviors and is hurt by them. My experience, since I am able to review the records on every patient I ever treat, is that invariably, I would say that for 80 percent or 90 percent of those with the most antisocial behaviors, I can predict before I look into their record that they come from broken homes, parental alcoholism, experienced rage from their own parents, had fathers that beat their mothers, and drugs were freely available in the house when they were children. Horrific backgrounds. Does that excuse their behavior, no; does it explain their behaviors, quite possibly.

Dr. Kuehnel—I think sometimes the public gets confused between excusing and explaining. But explanation can be useful in developing interventions . . . in terms of prevention, for example . . .

Dr. Teuber—Sure. In terms of prevention I think that if we had the resources and the will in our society to intervene early at 2, 3, 4, 5 years of age, many of these offenders would be saved and many of their victims would also be saved. But we as a society have not chosen to put substantial resources in that direction, nor have we put substantial resources into community based aftercare, which I believe is far more important than anything that can be done in the hospital. What the person receives in terms of guidance and treatment through aftercare, when they are living in real life settings, has a greater impact on protecting the patients and the community than what we provide in the hospital.

certain situations and therefore often below the level of awareness. For sex offenders, these automatic thoughts often have their roots in distorted beliefs or schemas about sex, children, women, and/or violence as a tool. These beliefs/schemas are based on early learning experiences, and the inner dialogue is idiosyncratic to the individual. Figure 11-1 presents the story of Joe, who had a history of raping women. The figure illustrates the role of cognitions (thoughts and beliefs) in facilitating his offending.

The first step in cognitive restructuring is to teach Joe to *identify* the thoughts and inner dialogue that he engages in when confronted by rejection. The second step is for Joe to learn how to *change/restructure* those thoughts that fuel both the feelings of

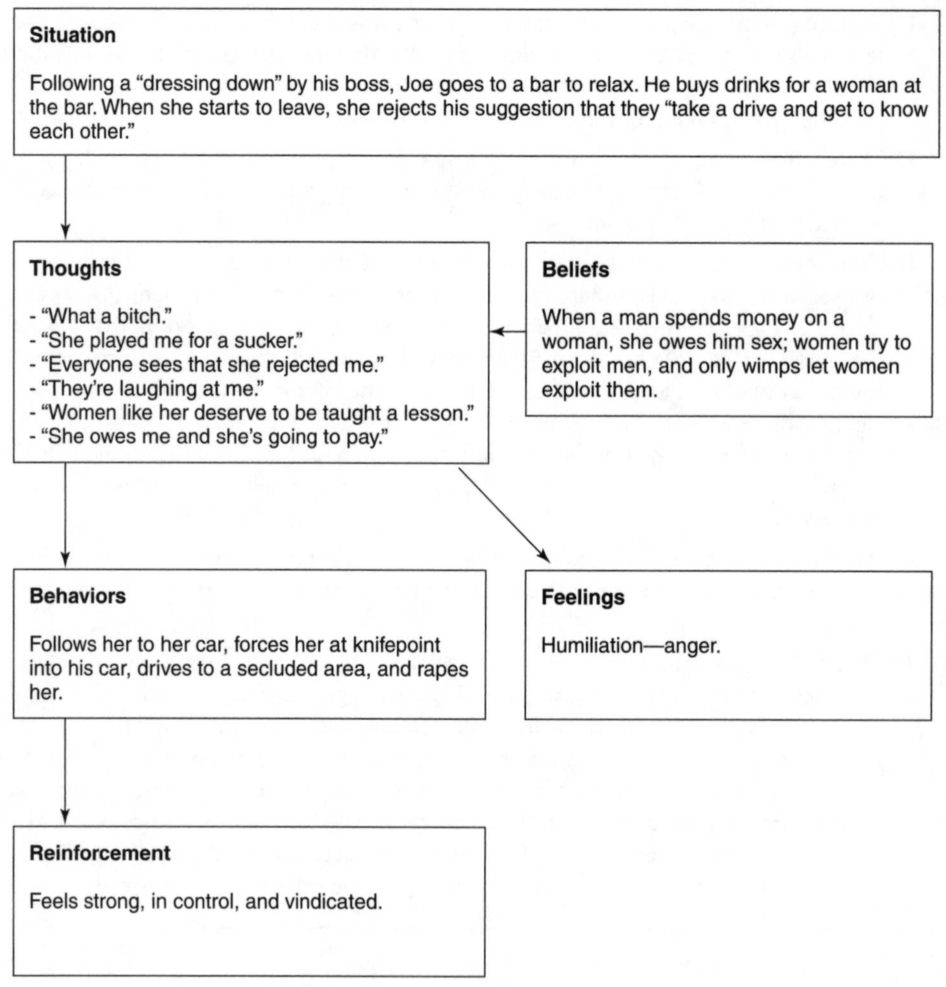

Situation
Following a "dressing down" by his boss, Joe goes to a bar to relax. He buys drinks for a woman at the bar. When she starts to leave, she rejects his suggestion that they "take a drive and get to know each other."
Thoughts
- "What a bitch."
- "She played me for a sucker."
- "Everyone sees that she rejected me."
- "They're laughing at me."
- "Women like her deserve to be taught a lesson."
- "She owes me and she's going to pay."
Beliefs
When a man spends money on a woman, she owes him sex; women try to exploit men, and only wimps let women exploit them.
Behaviors
Follows her to her car, forces her at knifepoint into his car, drives to a secluded area, and rapes her.
Feelings
Humiliation—anger.
Reinforcement
Feels strong, in control, and vindicated.

Figure 11-1 The Role of Cognitions in Facilitating Offending

Self-Check 11-1

Look at Joe's thoughts/inner dialogue. What alternative thoughts/inner dialogue could you propose? Notice that his current inner dialogue revolves around seeing himself as a victim, assuming that others see him as a wimp.

humiliation and anger, and the behavior of rape. The counselor also works with Joe to modify his beliefs about the quid pro quo of buying a drink and expecting sexual favors. **Cognitive restructuring** is based on the assumption that to change behavior, you have to change the inner dialogue that precipitates the behavior. Unlearning a habitual inner dialogue is the same as unlearning any habit: having awareness of when one is engaging in the habitual behavior (thoughts/inner dialogue), replacing the habitual behavior with alternative behavior (new thoughts/inner dialogue), and practicing through visualization and in vivo experiences.

The therapist's task is to help sex offenders reinterpret information. This requires the therapist to elicit and challenge the offender's schemas (theories) that give rise to the maladaptive and antisocial inner dialogues associated with offending. A preferential child molester's schemas may attribute sexual desire to children, whereas a rapist may have well-entrenched schemas about women (controlling and hostile) and himself (sexual dominance = manhood). Both types of schemas control how information is interpreted when the offender is faced with a potential victim and how it guides the inner dialogue of the offender (Ward, 2000). Because schemas develop in childhood and are reinforced through experiences, it is a long and difficult task to change them. It is probably easier to modify the schemas/theories of offenders earlier rather than later in their sex-offending careers.

Building Coping Skills

Sexual offenders usually have developed poor or inappropriate stress management and communication skills (Hanson, 2000). Usually, negative emotions are managed with alcohol or drugs that decrease inhibitions, or through escape into sexual fantasy (Hanson, 2000). Feelings of anxiety or weakness are experienced as inconsistent with self-identity (being a "real man") and therefore are converted into anger, which is more consistent with identity. Often, social skills and the ability to communicate needs and feelings appropriately are also lacking.

Building coping skills includes teaching *stress management skills* such as relaxation techniques, breathing exercises, the use of exercise and physical activity, and so on. Offenders are also taught to identify situations that trigger stress and the early warning signs of stress so that they can intervene early in the chain (e.g., avoid or leave the situation, use a coping inner dialogue, engage in relaxation techniques).

Counselors also teach offenders *social and communication skills* to facilitate appropriate ways of interacting with others and communicating anger and other feelings through words rather than offending behavior. Pedophiles often have serious deficits when it comes to interacting with potential adult partners. Modeling and role-playing with coaching are used to build a repertoire of appropriate social behavior. Assertiveness training teaches offenders to express verbally their feelings, such as anger, disappointment, affection, and concerns, rather than letting these feeling build, feeling helpless, and reoffending. In contrast, for rapists who lure adult victims, social skills training is probably not necessary or even desirable (e.g., Ted Bundy was quite skilled socially).

Self-Check 11-2

In the preceding case of Joe, he was already feeling stressed/anxious before arriving at the bar because of the altercation with his boss. To cope, he chose to go to a bar, drink, and try to pick up a woman. What alternative coping skills could he have been taught to use instead?

Behavioral Reconditioning

In Chapter 4, we discussed respondent conditioning principles in terms of the acquisition of paraphilias and violent fantasies. Cognitive-behavioral treatment programs often employ **behavioral reconditioning** procedures based on respondent conditioning to *modify deviant sexual arousal patterns* such as those associated with pedophilia and sexually predatory/violent behavior.

These procedures are based on learning principles. Reconditioning therapies were developed and used with sex offenders and paraphiliacs in the 1960s and 1970s. Used alone, the results were mixed (O'Donohue and Plaud, 1994); currently these procedures are incorporated as one element of a comprehensive treatment program. To illustrate a sampling of these procedures, we will use the case of Jim, a predatory serial child molester:

> Jim is a 35-year-old man who is described as a loner with a history of poor social relationships with women and exhibitionism. He enjoys child pornography and has molested young girls who were acquaintances and strangers that he would lure into his car as they walked to or from school.

Cautela (1967) first described *covert sensitization* as a method to associate deviant sexual images with negative consequences. The idea is that for molesters like Jim, potential long-term consequences (getting caught) are weak inhibitors of deviant behavior compared with the immediate positive consequence (pleasure/arousal) associated with molesting. For Jim, being discovered by his mother (her shock and disappointment) was the most negative consequence he could imagine. Through visualization/imagination, the therapist trains Jim to immediately associate this consequence with his pedophiliac arousal and behaviors through respondent conditioning.

In multiple sessions, Jim vividly visualizes/imagines his most recent molestation scene along with his most feared consequence:

> He is sitting in his car with a 10-year-old girl; with his right arm holding her around the shoulders, and he runs his left hand up her leg under her skirt. As his arousal increases, the therapist instructs him to imagine his mother opening the car door, her face turning to horror as she screams in shock; her shock turns to contempt, and so on.

With repeated sessions, Jim comes to associate touching little girls with negative emotions of embarrassment, anxiety, and humiliation rather than pleasure. To be effective, these scenes must be designed to be personally meaningful to the offender.

Olfactory aversion therapy is also based on respondent conditioning principles (Marshall, Laws, and Barbaree, 1990). A deviant stimulus is presented to Jim, usually through audiotape or videotape. When Jim begins to feel aroused (often monitored using a plethysmograph, which measures penile erection), Jim self-administers, or the therapist administers a noxious odor, usually ammonia or valeric acid. Through repeated administrations, Jim comes to associate the deviant stimulus with a negative/unarousing stimulus (the noxious odor).

Therapists may also use **masturbatory reconditioning procedures** to decrease arousal to deviant fantasies and/or to increase arousal to appropriate fantasies. We know that sex offenders frequently masturbate to deviant fantasies and/or pornography, thereby strengthening an association between sexual arousal and deviant images. Masturbatory reconditioning procedures use this pattern to weaken/eliminate the arousal patterns by associating deviant fantasies with lack of arousal or boredom (Alford, Morin, Atkins, and Shoen, 1987; Johnson, Hudson, and Marshall, 1992; Marshall, 1979). Using **masturbatory satiation,** Jim would masturbate to his pedophiliac fantasies for long periods of time—usually one to two hours. Although Jim may ejaculate early in the time period, he spends most of the time masturbating and fantasizing to no arousal, boredom, and discomfort. Thus, the fantasy becomes (through respondent conditioning) associated with boredom and discomfort. *Masturbatory*

Highlight 11-2

In the past, covert sensitization procedures were sometimes used "overtly" in forensic hospitals. That is, rather than the offender's experiencing immediate consequences through imagery, the consequences are delivered in real life. On one of my consulting trips to Atascadero, a therapist recounted how he had treated an exhibitionist (flasher) by using this method. The patient was instructed to expose himself several times per day to female nursing staff (they agreed to participate); the nurses were instructed to respond with laughter. After just a few days, the patient begged the therapist to let him stop the treatment because it had become so aversive!

extinction is a variation of this procedure in which Jim would first masturbate to appropriate nondeviant stimuli/fantasies until he ejaculates (maybe more than once). He then continues to masturbate to deviant stimuli/fantasies for an extended period of time during which physiological arousal and ejaculation are very unlikely. In this way, Jim associates pleasure with appropriate images (i.e., adult women), whereas boredom and lack of physiological arousal becomes associated with deviant stimuli (female children). *Orgasmic reconditioning* is a procedure designed to increase arousal to appropriate stimuli (Maletzky, 1991). Jim would be instructed to masturbate to his usual pedophiliac fantasies but to substitute a fantasy of an adult woman just before ejaculation. During later sessions, he would be instructed to substitute the adult female fantasy earlier and earlier in the masturbatory sequence. In this way, Jim would learn to become aroused to images of age-appropriate females.

Behavioral reconditioning procedures require genuine cooperation by the offender in order to be effective. Although these procedures involve a therapist's instructing the offender to engage in different types of fantasies or attend to external images, the therapist cannot control or know what the offender is really fantasizing about. Furthermore, these procedures must be periodically repeated (think "booster shots") to maintain the reconditioning over time.

It is worth noting that the Sex Offender Treatment and Evlauation Project (SOTEP) in California discontinued the aversive conditioning componant of treatment. Even though they found that this treatment reduced the level of arousal to deviant stimuli, this reduction was not related to eventual recidivism (Wiederanders, 2002).

Relapse Prevention

Because most sex offenders return to the community, no comprehensive cognitive-behavior program is complete without a strong **relapse prevention** component to provide the offender with coping skills and to assist the offender in planning to prevent relapse. Relapse prevention (RP) is based on an addiction model and was first developed for use with substance-use disorders and subsequently adapted for use with sex offenders (Laws, Hudson, and Ward, 2000). Offenders are taught to identify early warning signs and high risk situations that may precipitate deviant sexual behavior and to use a variety of strategies to intervene early in the chain to prevent reoffending. RP is a highly individualized approach that is developed by the offender with the guidance and assistance of a therapist. The typical components of RP are to

- Identify the chain of events (E) that led up to the most recent offense.
- Identify thoughts/cognitions (T) and feelings that accompanied the events and that facilitated offending.
- Add coping thoughts/actions (CT and CA) that would have broken the chain leading to reoffense.
- Identify other potential high-risk factors/situations and make plans to intervene and break into the chain early.

To illustrate the use of RP, let's take the case of Lou, who has been treated at a forensic facility following his conviction for a sexual assault on a young adolescent boy. First, Lou identifies the most relevant chain of events (something he or someone else did or said) that led up to the sexual assault: what happened right before the assault, what happened before that, and so on. In this way, Lou created a roadmap of the events that led to his most recent assault; these events are labeled **E** in Figure 11-2.

Next, Lou is asked to write/describe thoughts (T) that accompanied each event (E) in the chain. The counselor then works with him to develop coping responses (coping thoughts and coping actions) that would have reduced the likelihood of his offending. Lou's complete RP assignment is illustrated in Figure 11-2. As you can see, the earlier in the chain that Lou employs coping thoughts (CT) and coping actions (CA), the less likely he is to offend.

The counselor would continue to work with Lou to develop a plan either to avoid or to cope with potential high-risk situations and feelings. The counselor would also use books and videotapes to develop Lou's empathy and awareness of the consequences of molestation and sexual assault on victims.

Relapse prevention assumes that sexual offenses are not impulsive but follow a predictable pattern involving high-risk situations and negative emotions, as well as a series of decisions and actions on the part of the offender (Hanson, 2000). This pattern may not fit all offenders. For example, some child molesters begin with positive emotions (positive anticipation) and then seek out a high-risk situation. Other offenders claim to have acted on impulse, not as a result of a series of events and emotions. Despite the reports of some sex offenders, according to RP, there is no such thing as a truly impulsive offense (Hanson, 2000). These examples point to the need for continued research on multiple types of offense cycles to better match offenders to appropriate treatment—one size probably does not fit all feet.

The success of comprehensive cognitive-behavioral with relapse prevention programs is not perfect, but it is promising. Maletzky (1991) studied over 5,000 sex offenders treated as outpatients in a community-based program, using a combination of the types of treatments previously described. His criteria for success (for from one year to a seventeen-year follow-up period) were the following: no self-reported arousal or behavior, no record of legal charges (even if unsubstantiated), and no deviant sexual arousal as measured physiologically using plethymograph testing. Furthermore, treatment failures included not only those that did not meet any one of the success criteria but also those who dropped out of treatment (even after only one session) for any reason. Although there was no untreated comparison group, the large number of participants and strict criteria for treatment success make these results worth considering. On the basis of these very strict criteria for success, he found the following success rates:

- Heterosexual pedophilia (n = 2,865)—94.7 percent
- Homosexual pedophilia (n = 855)—86.4 percent
- Combined heterosexual and homosexual pedophilia (n = 112)—75.7 percent

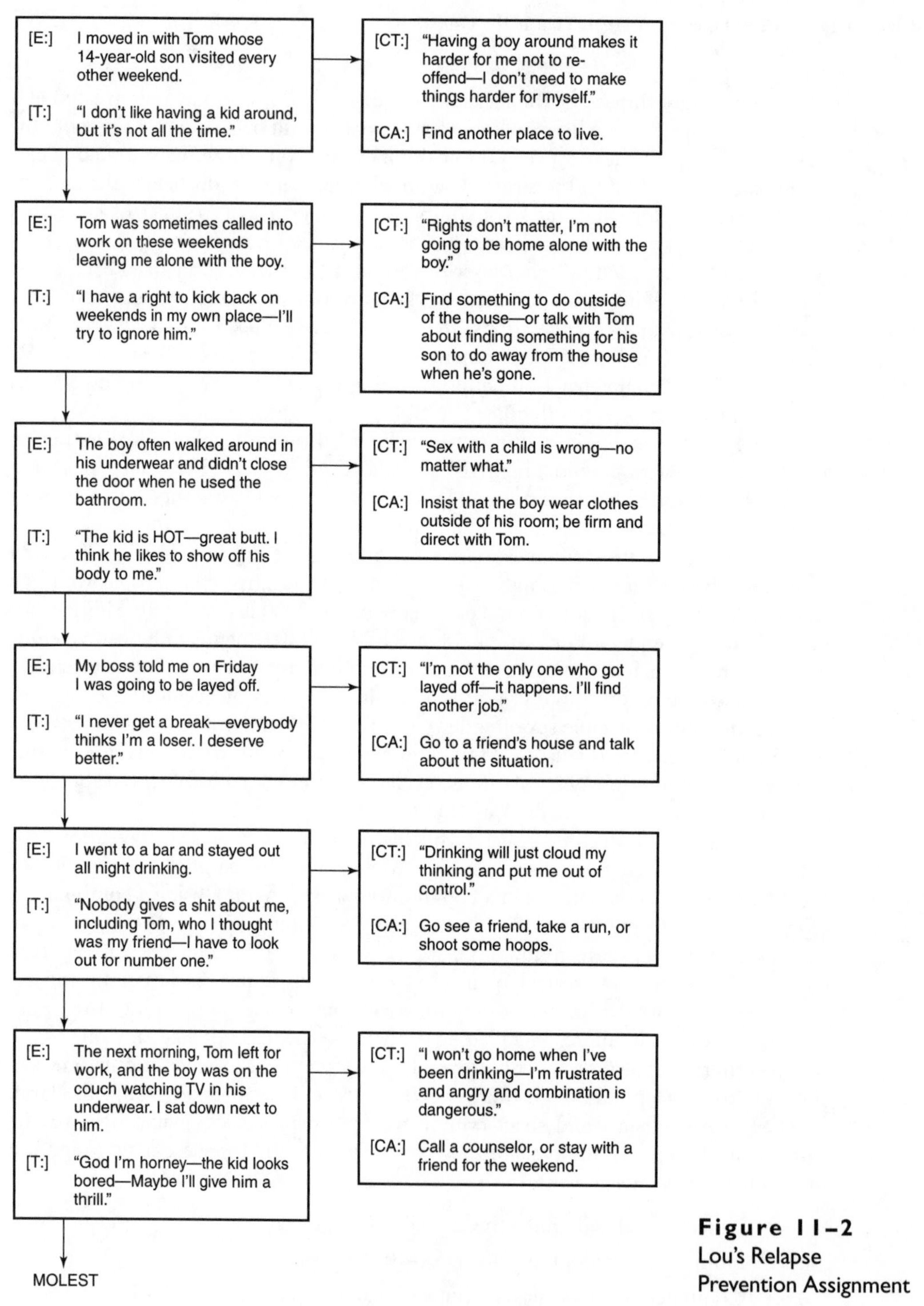

[E:] I moved in with Tom whose 14-year-old son visited every other weekend.
[T:] "I don't like having a kid around, but it's not all the time."
[CT:] "Having a boy around makes it harder for me not to re-offend—I don't need to make things harder for myself."
[CA:] Find another place to live.
[E:] Tom was sometimes called into work on these weekends leaving me alone with the boy.
[T:] "I have a right to kick back on weekends in my own place—I'll try to ignore him."
[CT:] "Rights don't matter, I'm not going to be home alone with the boy."
[CA:] Find something to do outside of the house—or talk with Tom about finding something for his son to do away from the house when he's gone.
[E:] The boy often walked around in his underwear and didn't close the door when he used the bathroom.
[T:] "The kid is HOT—great butt. I think he likes to show off his body to me."
[CT:] "Sex with a child is wrong—no matter what."
[CA:] Insist that the boy wear clothes outside of his room; be firm and direct with Tom.
[E:] My boss told me on Friday I was going to be layed off.
[T:] "I never get a break—everybody thinks I'm a loser. I deserve better."
[CT:] "I'm not the only one who got layed off—it happens. I'll find another job."
[CA:] Go to a friend's house and talk about the situation.
[E:] I went to a bar and stayed out all night drinking.
[T:] "Nobody gives a shit about me, including Tom, who I thought was my friend—I have to look out for number one."
[CT:] "Drinking will just cloud my thinking and put me out of control."
[CA:] Go see a friend, take a run, or shoot some hoops.
[E:] The next morning, Tom left for work, and the boy was on the couch watching TV in his underwear. I sat down next to him.
[T:] "God I'm horney—the kid looks bored—Maybe I'll give him a thrill."
[CT:] "I won't go home when I've been drinking—I'm frustrated and angry and combination is dangerous."
[CA:] Call a counselor, or stay with a friend for the weekend.
MOLEST

Figure 11–2
Lou's Relapse Prevention Assignment

Food for Thought

Can Treatment Be Counterproductive?

There is evidence that comprehensive treatment for **low-risk** sex offenders (i.e., incest offenders) may actually increase recidivism (11 percent) (Nicholatichuk, 1996) compared with no treatment (3 percent), whereas the same program decreased recidivism for **high-risk** offenders (6 percent) compared with their untreated counterparts (15 percent). Why? Perhaps treatment for low-risk offenders inadvertently communicates to them that they are dangerous and likely to relapse—and they believe it!

- Rape (n = 145)—73.5 percent
- Sadomasochism (n = 25)—80 percent

Maletzky also found that the following offense and offender characteristics significantly increased the likelihood that offenders would be treatment failures:

- Having more than one victim
- Victims being strangers
- Total denial of allegations
- Use of physical force in sexual offense(s)
- Being unemployed or having had 3 or more job changes in 3 years prior to offense
- Being divorced or separated, or living alone

The results with incarcerated offenders have been more mixed. The results of the Sex Offenders Treatment and Evaluation Project in California are currently being analyzed—see Highlight 11-3, which contains an interview with Dr. Mark Wiederanders, who is currently analyzing the data.

HORMONAL/MEDICAL TREATMENT

Because the large majority of sex offenders are male, it has long been assumed that the male hormone testosterone contributes to these offenses. Therefore, it seems reasonable to assume that treatments that reduce testosterone levels should reduce sexual arousal, thereby reducing sexual fantasy, preoccupation, and behavior. There are two methods for accomplishing this goal: surgical/physical castration and chemical castration.

Surgical/physical castration, the removal of the testes, to inhibit sexual desire goes back to ancient cultures in which eunuchs (castrated guards) were entrusted to watch over the women's quarters. Surgical castration is an irreversible and a highly

Highlight 11-3

This is an interview with Dr. Mark Wiederanders, Research Program Specialist. Dr. Wiederanders is currently analyzing the clinical and follow-up data for California's Sex Offenders Treatment and Evaluation Project (SOTEP) at Atascadero State Hospital. The project is run by Dr. Janice Marques.

Interviewer: Tell us about the SOTEP program. Why was it started, and what types of offenders were included in the program?

Dr. W.: The participants were molesters and rapists who had prior sexual offenses and were incarcerated following a serious felony conviction. The State Legislature authorized the program in the early 80s to test out state of the art clinical treatment on incarcerated sex offenders, so the program recruited volunteers to this special unit at Atascadero State Hospital.

Interviewer: Did they use an experimental design?

Dr. W.: Yes, the volunteers were randomly assigned to treatment versus no treatment. The no treatment group got the usual prison stuff—maybe a little counseling—not much—it wasn't a true placebo condition. The design was messy—we weren't able to obtain data on many of the measures for the control group (i.e., some wouldn't agree to take them, etc.). But the design was better than most of the studies out there—real-life research is often not pure and clean unfortunately.

Interviewer: So what kind of treatment did the treatment group receive?

Dr. W.: The treatment was Relapse Prevention, based on the AA model with cognitive behavioral therapy. They would get these offenders to see offending as a kind of addiction that was messing up their lives—so what do they have to learn in order to stop? They used the RP model, cognitive restructuring, social skills rehabilitation . . . some of these offenders were very inadequate socially—didn't know how to ask for what they wanted, especially in relationships.

Interviewer: What did they learn?

Dr. W.: The treatment group definitely mastered the RP and cognitive skills—they were using the terms and identifying the high-risk situations and chains that led to offending. There were also gains (more accurately losses!) compared to baseline in the physiological measures of arousal to deviant stimuli—they improved.

Interviewer: Can't the physiological measures be faked—they could use distraction, think of a nonarousing image to control arousal?

Dr. W: That was probably going on to some extent because the recidivism rates didn't match the data on these measures. Actually, the results for the skills and attitude change measures (i.e., not taking responsibility, seeing themselves a victims, etc.) was mostly successful—not completely. But—and it's a big "but"—there was no significant (or even approaching significant) difference in recidivism between the treatment and no treatment groups, and recidivism, of course, is what everyone cares about.

Interviewer: Really? Nothing in terms of reoffending? They learned the concepts, but "no cigar" in terms of recidivism?

Dr. W.: Well, when I say nothing, there is some evidence that those that were treated and are reoffending are doing so less violently. There is a scale of sex offending, from touching over the clothes to penetration, etc., and sexual assault alone versus with battery. There is evidence that the treatment group reoffends lower on the scale—less violent, less likely to penetrate the victim.

Interviewer: Any other small rays of hope?

Dr. W.: I have been working on the data from what we call the "Got It" scale—ratings of 1–7 in terms of the degree to which participants mastered the program, how well they did on all the test, etc. Those that rated high on the "Got It" scale—did significantly better in terms of recidivism than those that didn't "get it."

Interviewer: That makes sense—you wouldn't expect that those who didn't learn the program well would be influenced in their later behavior. Any other subgroups that did better?

Dr. W.: It is probably naive to assume that all sex offenders are the same and will respond the same to treatment. Some are more motivated to change—some pathetically so—and they did significantly better than those who were less motivated. We used a "Motivational Questionnaire" to measure this at the beginning—those that were highly motivated and expected that treatment would help, did in fact do better—it stands to reason.

Interviewer: Motivation and expectation of success are key factors in predicting the success of therapy for any type of client. What about sex offenders who are considered high versus low risk based on static actuarial data (i.e., age of first offense, stranger versus known victim, molests girls versus boy victims, etc.)—were there any differences in treatment outcome?

Dr. W.: That type of data is pretty strong for predicting recidivism—stronger than treatment versus no treatment. Static risk variables also seem to interact with treatment effect. Those in the SOTEP treatment group who were identified on these static variables such as age and offense history as high risk but who mastered the treatment material (as measured by the "Got It" scale on posttreatment test scores) had recidivism rates that were more like those of lower-actuarial-risk subjects. In other words, treatment that "took" seemed to partly ameliorate high-risk factors like history of sex offending. For low-risk offenders there were no treatment versus no treatment differences. It's kind of counterintuitive. Of course, the high-risk group has more room to change.

(continued)

Interviewer: I guess it's like weight loss—the more weight you have to lose, the easier it is to lose the first 10 lbs. So to sum up, while overall, there was not evidence that treatment was better than no treatment in reducing recidivism . . .

Dr. W.: True, but for those that were highly motivated, who learned the program components well, and who were high risk to begin with, there was some definite improvement. I think future efforts will focus more on finding ways to identify those that will most likely benefit from treatment rather than looking for overall treatment effects for sex offenders.

invasive procedure and, therefore, controversial. In a review of studies on the effects of surgical castration, Prentky (1997) found that the recidivism rate for castrated sex offenders ranged from 1.1 percent to 7.4 percent, clearly lower than outcomes for other forms of treatment or for untreated offenders. However, because physical castration is voluntary (and probably requires strong motivation), there may be consistent differences between offenders who volunteer and those who opt for less extreme types of treatment. The Association for the Treatment of Sexual Abusers (ATSA) opposes the use of surgical castration (1997) because there are alternative treatments (i.e., chemical castration) available, and replacement male hormones can be obtained and taken to nullify the effects of surgical castration.

Chemical castration is most commonly accomplished through the administration of medroxyprogesterone (MA), a derivative of progesterone, or cyproterone acetate (CA). Both significantly reduce testosterone levels, sexual fantasies, and arousal, and recidivism rates in sex offenders, but these effects disappear when the drug is removed (Bradford, 1997; Meyer and Cole, 1997). Both drugs have been associated with serious side effects including weight gain, depression, high blood pressure, and in the long term, diabetes, cancer, and thrombosis. Several studies have successfully used long-term low doses of MA to inhibit deviant sexual function while maintaining normal sexual function (Kravitz, Haywood, Kelly, Liles, and Cavanaugh, 1996). Triptorelin is a monthly injected drug that inhibits gonadotropin secretion, decreasing sensitivity to androgens in men. In addition to the practical advantages of monthly injections, there are also fewer reported side effects with this drug. Rösler and Witztum (1998) found that treatment with triptorelin reduced sexual fantasies, deviant desires, and deviant behavior in a sample of 25 pedophiles. However, outcome measures were self-report, and there was no comparison group. Further and better designed studies are needed to evaluate the effectiveness of this drug treatment.

Given the serious side effects and the temporary effects of these drugs, chemical castration has usually been considered a last resort treatment and recommended only when administered along with psychosocial treatments (ATSA, 1997).

IS PRISON THE BEST TREATMENT?

As we have seen in previous chapters, violent and sexual offenders very often have a childhood history of sexual, physical, and psychological abuse. Although these environments alone cannot be blamed for an offender's later crimes, it is evident that they contribute to the bio-psychosocial causes of later offending. Is prison a rerun of the conditions that helped produce a child molester or sex offender in the first place? In many ways, it may be; there are some parallels. In childhood, the authority figures are parents; in prison, the authority figures are guards and/or gang leaders to whom guards have ceded power in exchange for help in maintaining order and discipline (Johnson, 1996). These authority figures control every aspect of a prisoner's life, often with impunity.

Beginning in 1981, the Eighth Amendment, which bars cruel and unusual punishment, has almost evaporated along with the 1975 Federal Inmate Bill of Rights. Harsh treatment or gross negligence by prison authorities (e.g., failure to stop a prison rape) are not considered violations by the Supreme Court (***Farmer vs. Brennan***, 1994) unless the demonstrable intent of prison authorities was to inflict harm on a prisoner—an almost impossible standard (*Wilson vs. Seiter, 1991*).

Physical and sexual assault are also part of the fabric of prison life. Prison gangs use violence to enforce discipline and to protect turf (Johnson, 1996). In a harsh and violent environment, prisoners are socialized to ignore the suffering of others, to employ violence as both a means to an end and preemptively to protect themselves from attack. This violence and the threat of violence are an ongoing part of life in prison, as is homosexual rape. All are intended to assert dominance and debase the victim. Child molesters, homosexuals, and small/slightly built prisoners are particularly vulnerable to gang rape (Silberman, 1995). Only successfully fighting off an attack or retaliating against the perpetrator can protect the victim from further attacks (Silberman, 1995). As discussed in previous chapters, sex offenders are much more likely than nonoffenders to have been sexually molested in childhood or adolescence. Sexual assault in childhood and/or in prison increases the likelihood that the victims themselves will later sexually offend. So, do sex offenders get their "just desserts" (retribution)? Probably. Do they "learn a lesson," (deterrence)? Maybe—but what lesson do they learn?

CONCLUSIONS

As we have seen in this chapter, there is no firm answer to questions of treatment effectiveness for sex offenders. First, to answer this question, researchers must address both the lack of consistency and the adequacy of how recidivism/reoffending is defined and measured. Without solving these problems, comparing the efficacy of different treatment interventions or the relative impact of treatment versus punishment is almost impossible. Second, when it comes to treatment, there is no "one size fits all" intervention. It is becoming clear that the search for treatments will require the development of specialized interventions for subgroups of offenders. The offender with a serious mental illness requires a different approach from that for a primary pedophile or a sadistic high-risk rapist.

Although the development of treatments for sex offenders is still in its infancy, it is also clear that imprisonment to isolate/contain offenders is only a temporary solution—eventually, most sex offenders will be released into society. Prison conceptualized and implemented as retribution or deterrence through punishment may work for some offenders but may actually make others more violent and more dangerous. Perhaps, as Dr. Teuber suggests, society should be putting more focus and resources into prevention and early intervention strategies.

As we have seen in the chapters in Part Two, in most cases, sexually predatory behavior has biological, psychological, and social roots that begin in childhood or even prenatally. Prenatal care, support, and training for high-risk parents; prevention of sexual, physical, and psychological abuse when possible; and aggressive treatment and intervention when abuse occurs may do more to protect society from sexual predators than any intervention can accomplish after they begin to offend. Although comprehensive and sustained early childhood programs have been found to be effective for preventing child abuse and neglect (Currie, 1998), many studies have not included a matched control group or have not had the resources to assess longitudinally whether the reduction in child abuse and neglect translates into lower rates of later violence in the community (Pincus, 2001). Instead of prioritizing prevention/early intervention programs or the treatment of childhood/adolescent mental disorders, our society, unlike Scandinavia, Europe, and much of Asia, pours resources into what to do with the "monster" after he or she has been created.

Discussion Questions and Activities

1. If you were going to look at the research literature to pick an effective treatment program for sex offenders, what issues/problems with the research would you need to be aware of?
2. It appears that no current treatment is universally effective with all sex offenders. Should more tax money be spent to identify subgroups of offenders that may respond to treatment? Why, or why not? Similarly, should tax-supported research into developing new treatments be continued? Why, or why not?
3. Given what you learned about psychopathy in Chapter 8, what would your reaction be if you were told that rapist Jim X (diagnosed as a psychopath) was being released because he had successfully completed a cognitive-behavioral with relapse prevention program. That is, he had completed all assignments and passed tests measuring attitudes towards women, rape, victims, and so on? Explain, specifically, the reason for your answer.

4. Either support or dispute the proposition that for sexual predators, chemical castration should be a condition for parole. Do some additional research to support your view.
5. Some states, like California and Washington, have implemented sexually violent predator laws that extend incarceration for SVPs beyond their sentence for purposes of treatment. What do you feel that the psychological effects would be on their motivation for and engagement in treatment? What issues/barriers would counselors/therapists need to address with these offenders?
6. Construct an RP assignment for yourself (like the one in Figure 11-2) for some action that you recently engaged in that you wish you had not (hopefully not a violent action!). Some possibilities might be overeating, skipping class, verbally attacking a friend, blowing off an assignment, or telling a lie. Do you think that completing this assignment would help you to not repeat the action? Why, or why not?
7. As a therapist, what would you recommend in the way of treatment for each of the following types of sex offenders? Justify your answers.
   a. An intrafamilial child molester
   b. An adolescent pedophile (first offense)
   c. A date rapist
   d. A high-risk offender (multiple stranger victims, etc.)
   e. A person with paranoid schizophrenia who raped and killed a family member
8. Review what you have learned about the etiology of violent/sexual predators (Part Two). If you were "King of the World," what *prevention* strategies might you implement on the basis of a bio-psychosocial model?

Key Words

Behavioral reconditioning
Chemical castration
Cognitive restructuring
Farmer vs. Brennan, 1944
Masturbatory reconditioning
Masturbatory satiation
Meta-analysis
Olfactory aversion therapy
Recidivism
Relapse prevention
Surgical/physical castration

References

Alexander, M. 1999. "Sexual offenders efficacy revisited." *Sexual Abuse: A Journal of Research and Treatment*" *11:* 101–116.

Alford, G., C. Morin, M. Atkins and L. Shoen. 1987. "Masturbatory extinction of deviant sexual arousal." *Journal of Behavior Therapy and Experimental Psychiatry 1:* 59–66.

(ATSA) Association for the Treatment of Sexual Abusers. 1997. "Anti-androgen therapy and surgical castration." Position Paper, Feb. 7.

Blackburn, D. 2002. "Take Them Off, Please." *New Times*, April 25–May 2, pp. 10–11.

Bradford, J. 1997. "Medical interventions in sexual deviance." In D. Laws and W. O'Donohue (Eds.), *Sexual Deviance: Theory, Assessment and Treatment.* New York: Guilford Press.

Cautela, J. 1967. "Covert sensitization." *Psychological Reports 20:* 459–468.

Chabria, A. 2002. "The bureaucrat and the boogeyman." *L.A. Times Magazine*, April 14.

Chaiken, J. M. 2000. "Crunching numbers: Crime and incarceration at the end of the millennium." *National Institute of Justice Journal.* Retrieved March 2, 2000, from the World Wide Web: *http://www.ncjrs.org*.

Currie, E. 1998. *Crime and Punishment in America.* New York: Metropolitan Books.

Ditton, P. M. 1999. "*Mental health and treatment of inmates and probationers.*" (Special Report NCJ 174363). Washington, D.C.: U.S. Department of Justice, Office of Justice Program, Bureau of Justice Statistics.

Farmer vs. Brennan. 1994. 114 U.S. 1970.

FBI (Federal Bureau of Investigation). 1999. *Crime in the United States—1998.* Washington, D.C.: U.S. Government Printing Office.

Gallagher, C., D. Wilson, P. Hirschfield, M. Coggeshall, and D. MacKenzie. 1999. "A quantitative review of the effects of sex offender treatment on sexual reoffending." *Corrections Management Quarterly 3:* 19–29.

Haney, C., Q. Banks, and P. Zimbardo. 1973. "Interpersonal dynamics in a simulated prison." *Journal of Ciminology and Penology 1:* 69–97.

Hanson, R. 2000. "What is so special about relapse prevention?" In R. Laws, S. Hanson, and T. Ward (Eds.), *Remaking Relapse Prevention with Sex Offenders.* Thousand Oaks, Calif.: Sage Publications.

Hanson, R., A. Gordon, A. Harris, J. Marques, W. Murphy, V. Quinsey, and M. Seto. 2002. "First report of Collaborative Outcome Data Project on the effectiveness of psychological treatment for sex offenders." *Sexual Abuse: A Journal of Research and Treatment 14*(2): 169–197.

Human Rights Watch. 1997. *Cold Storage: Super-maximum Security Confinement in Indiana.* New York: Author.

Johnson, P., S. Hudson, and W. Marshall. 1992. "The effects of masturbatory reconditioning with non-familial child molesters." *Behavior Research and Therapy 30:* 559–561.

Johnson, R. 1996. *Hard Time: Understanding and Reforming the Prison* (2nd ed.). Belmont, Calif.: Wadsworth.

Kravitz, H., T. Haywood, J. Kelly, S. Liles, and J. Cavanaugh. 1996. "Medroxyprogesterone and paraphiles: Do testosterone levels matter?" *Bulletin of the American Academy of Psychiatry and Law 24:* 73–83.

Kuehnel, T. 2003. (Clinical Director, Las Posadas Psychiatric Rehibilitation Facility.) Personal communication.

Laws, R., S. Hudson, and T. Ward (Eds.). 2000. *Remaking Relapse Prevention with Sex Offenders.* Thousand Oaks, Calif.: Sage Publications.

Madrid v. Gomez. 1995. 889 F. Supp. 1146 (N.D. Cal. 1995).

Maletzky, B. 1991. *Treating Sexual Offenders.* Thousand Oaks, Calif.: Sage Publications.

Maletzky, B. 1998. "The paraphilias: Research and treatment." In P. Nathan & J. Gorman (Eds.), *A Guide to Treatments that Work.* New York: Oxford University Press.

Marshall, W. 1979. "The modification of sexual fantasies: A combined treatment approach to the reduction of deviant sexual behavior." *Behavior Research and Therapy 11:* 557–564.

Marshall, W., D. Laws, and Barbaree H. (Eds.) 1990. *Handbook of Sexual Assault: Issues, Theories, and Treatment of the Offender.* New York: Plenum Press.

Meyer, W. and C. Cole. 1997. "Physical and chemical castration of sex offenders: A review." *Journal of Offender Rehibilitation 25:* 1–18.

Nicholatichuk, T. 1996. "Sex offender treatment priority: An illustration of the risk/need principle." *Forum on Correction Research 8:* 30–32.

O'Donohue, W. and J. Plaud. 1994. "The conditioning of human sexual arousal." *Archives of Sexual Behavior 23:* 321–344.

Pincus, J. H., 2001. *Base Instincts: What Makes Killers Kill.* New York: W. W. Norton & Co.

Prentky, R. 1997. "Arousal reduction in sexual offenders: A review of antiandrogen interventions." *Sexual Abuse: A Journal of Research and Treatment 9:* 335–348.

Prentky, R., A. Lee, R. Knight, and D. Cerce. 1997. "Recidivism rates among child molesters and rapists: A methodological analysis." *Law and Human Behavior 21*(6): 635–659.

Rösler, A. and E. Witztum. 1998. "Treatment of men with paraphilia with a long-acting analogue of gonadotropin-releasing hormone." *New England Journal of Medicine 338:* 416–422.

Russell, K. 1999. "Guards accused of setting up rape." *The Washington Post,* Oct. 5. Retrieved Oct. 5, 1999, from the World Wide Web: *http://www.washingtonpost.com.*

Silberman, M. 1995. *A World of Violence: Corrections in America.* Belmont, Calif.: Wadsworth.

Teuber, J. 2002. Interview conducted Nov.

Ward, T. 2000. "Sexual offenders' cognitive distortions as implicit theories." *Aggression and Violent Behavior 5*(5): 491–507.

Wiederanders, M. 2002. Interview conducted July 7. *Wilson vs. Seiter.* 1991. 501, US 294.

Wilson vs. Seiter. 1991. 501, US 294.

Winerip, M. 1999. "Bedlam on the streets." *The New York Times Sunday Magazine,* May 23, pp. 42–49, 56, 65–66, 70.

Youngberg vs. Romeo. 1982. 457 U.S. 307.

GLOSSARY

Acquaintance contact rapist—Rape in which the offender and victim are acquainted with one another. This is the most common type of rape, however their crimes are rarely reported because the victims know their offenders from casual dating or through a social or business relationship.

Acquired sociopathy—An extreme change that includes behavioral deficits and aggressive tendencies due to a childhood brain injury.

Active victim precipitation—Refers to situations in which victims provoke violent encounters or use words to cause a physical confrontation with another.

Actus reus (bad act)—The action or inaction in the case of criminal negligence which, in combination with the mens rea ("bad mind"), produces criminal liability in common-law based criminal law. According to criminal jurisprudence, there must be a concurrence of both *actus reus* and *mens rea* for a crime to have been committed.

Aileen Wuornos—Female serial killer who killed seven men in Florida whom she had solicited for sex. She tried to defend herself saying she killed the men in self-defense because they tried to rape her; the court found her to be lying and convicted her.

Analogue experiment—To test human or animal subjects in a laboratory setting that is designed to be functionally analogous to a real-life situation.

Andrea Yates—Defendant who used the excuse of postpartum depression in an attempt to avoid responsibility of killing her five children. Prosecutors acknowledged Yates was mentally ill but argued that she knew right from wrong and was not legally insane at the time of the killings. Yates was convicted and is serving a life term.

Anger-excitation rapist—Often referred to as sadistic, this rapist takes pleasure and sexual arousal from inflicting pain and punishment on the victim.

Anger-retaliatory rapist—One who has a deep anger toward women and use sex as a means to punish or get even.

Attachment theory—A social-psychological perspective on delinquent and criminal behavior which holds that the successful development of secure attachment between an child and his or her primary caregiver provides the basic foundation for all future psychological development.

Attachment theory (Bowlby)—A theory that states when the primary caregiver is accessible and nurturing, infants develop the ability to establish and reestablish a bond or attachment with others. However, when primary caregivers are inaccessible and undependable, infants detach permanently.

Attention Deficit Hyperactivity Disorder—Characterized by either inability to focus attention by overactive and impulsive behavior, or both.

Autonomic nervous system (ANS)—The network of nerve fibers that connects the central nervous system to all the other organs of the body.

Ballistics—The science that deals with the motion, behavior, and effects of projectiles, especially bullets, aerial bombs, rockets, or the like; the science or art of designing and hurling projectiles so as to achieve a desired performance.

Behavioral profiling—A technique to solving a crime where there is an attempt to determine the type of person who may have committed the crime. This technique was started by the FBI.

Behavioral reconditioning—Based on respondent conditioning principles, to modify deviant patterns of arousal.

Bill of Rights—The first ten amendments to the U.S. Constitution, which protect people's basic human rights

Borderline Personality Disorder—Characterized by instability and reactivity in mood, unstable interpersonal relationships, and behavior beginning in early adulthood.

Brain-wave monitoring—New form of science technology able to determine what has been stored in the brain and when used on alleged criminals, can judge if that person committed a specific crime or not.

Chemical castration—Most commonly accomplished through the administration of Medroxyprogesterone, a derivative of progesterone that significantly reduces testosterone levels, sexual fantasies and arousal, and recidivism rates in sex offenders.

Civil Commitment Laws—Laws designed to commit convicted sex offenders if there is any indication of possible recidivism even though they may not have committed a crime.

Cognitive restructuring—Based on the idea that thoughts (verbal or images) proceed, and therefore influence, emotions and behavior.

Conduct disorder—Characterized by children who repeatedly violate the basic rights of others by displaying aggression and sometimes destroying others property, lying, cheating, or running away from home.

Confounds—Uncontrolled variables that can affect the outcome of a study.

Correlation coefficient—A mathematical index used to measure the magnitude and direction of the relationship between two variables.

Correlational method—A research procedure used to determine how much events or characteristics vary with each other.

Cortical arousal—A level of arousal within the cerebral cortex that can be from low to moderate to high depending on an exposure to a stimulating or unstimulating environment. Extraverts have low resting levels of cortical arousal.

Cortisol—A hormone that is secreted by the adrenal glands in response to physical or emotional stress.

Deductive reasoning—To deduce a specific hypothesis from a broader theory.

Defense mechanisms (Freud)—Techniques, such as repression, reaction formation, sublimation, and the like, whereby the ego defends itself against the pain of anxiety.

Delusions—Bizarre, unrealistic beliefs that are fervently held despite evidence to the contrary.

Deoxyribonucleic acid (DNA)—A nucleic acid that carries the genetic information in the cell and is capable of self-replication and synthesis of RNA. DNA consists of two long chains of nucleotides twisted into a double helix and joined by hydrogen bonds between the complementary bases adenine and thymine or cytosine and guanine. The sequence of nucleotides determines individual hereditary characteristics.

Dependent variable—The variable in an experiment that is expected to change as the independent variable is manipulated.

Desensitization—A behavior modification technique, used especially in treating phobias, in which panic or other undesirable emotional response to a given stimulus is reduced or extinguished, especially by repeated exposure to that stimulus.

Deviant lifestyle—Lifestyle that departs from the social norm.

Differential Association—The sociological thesis that criminality, like any other form of behavior, is learned through a process of association with others who communicate criminal values.

Diminished capacity—Refers to a defense by excuse; via which a defendant argues that that although they broke the law, they should not be held criminally liable for doing so, as their mental functions were "diminished" or impaired.

Directionality problem: chicken or the egg—A common error made by the media or the public of cause-effect conclusions based on correlational research.

Disorganized killers—Killers who are careless and leave clues at the crime scene.

Dopamine—The neurotransmitter that regulates perceptions of pleasure, reward, goal-directed behavior, decision-making, and motor control.

Double-blind design—Experimental procedure in which neither the subject nor the experimenter knows whether the subject has received the experimental treatment or placebo.

Ego (Freud)—The province of the mind that refers to the "I" or those experiences that are owned by the person. The only region of the mind in contact with the real world, it is said to serve the reality principle.

Entomology—*Forensic* Entomology is the use of the insects and their arthropod relatives that inhabit decomposing remains to aid legal investigations.

Erotomania—A disorder in which a person holds a delusional belief that another person, usually of a higher social status, is in love with them.

External validity—The degree to which the results and conclusions can be applied or generalized to the people the sample is intended to represent.

Extraversion/Introversion—A dimension of personality that characterizes one end of the continuum of extraversion as thrill seeking, sociability and impulsiveness, while introverts are unsociable, careful, and controlled.

Family risk factors—Family risk factors relate to those variables associated with delinquency such as divorce, low income, alcoholism, etc.

Fantasy cycle of serial killers—Cycle consisting of four phases—fantasy, hunt, kill, and post-kill—in which serial killers generally go through each time before they kill their next victim(s).

Fixated molesters—Child molesters who prefer certain traits of victims.

Forensic anthropologist—Scientists who help police solve crimes involving human remains. They are considered "bone detectives" who to help identify victims of accidents, fires, plane crashes, war, crime, etc.

Gene-environment interaction—Genetic factors and environmental influences interact to produce behavior, disorders, etc.

Genotype—Internally coded, inheritable information carried by all living organisms.

Geographic profiling—Profiling the location or physical area to determine crime patterns.

Hallucinations—Hearing, seeing, or experiencing sensory input that is not tied to the external environment.

Hate crimes—A crime in which the defendant's conduct was motivated by hatred, bias, or prejudice, based on the actual or perceived race, color, religion, national origin, ethnicity, gender, sexual orientation, or disabilities of another individual or group of individuals.

Hebephilia—The condition in which an adult is responsive to and dependent on the actuality or imagery of erotic/sexual activity with an adolescent boy or girl in order to obtain erotic arousal and facilitate or achieve orgasm.

Id (Freud)—The id is the home base for all the instincts, and its sole function is to seek pleasure regardless of consequences.

Independent variable—The variable in an experiment that is manipulated to determine whether it has an effect on another variable.

Inductive reasoning—Identifying patterns from varied pieces of information.

Innocence Protection Act—A law passed in 2003 designed to address wrongful convictions by granting any inmate convicted of a federal crime the right to petition federal court for DNA testing if testing supports claim of innocence.

The insanity defense—A defendant may argue that they should not be held criminally liable for breaking the law, as they were mentally ill or mentally incompetent at the time of their allegedly "criminal" actions. This defense is based on a principle that punishment is only reasonable if the defendant is capable of both controlling their behavior and understanding that they have committed a wrongful act. It is argued that some people suffering from mental disorders are not capable of knowing or choosing right from wrong, and should not be punished. A defendant making this argument might be said to be pleading not guilty by reason of insanity.

Internal validity—The degree to which the results or outcome of a study depend on the independent variable alone and are not due to confounds or uncontrolled extraneous variables.

John Hinckley—John Hinckley was adjudicated insane for his attempt to kill former President Ronald Reagan.

Kansas v. Hendricks—A 1997 Supreme Court case challenging the constitutionality of sexual predator statutes that require sexual offenders judged likely to reoffend to be civilly committed until they are judged to be no longer a risk; the Court confirmed the constitutionality.

Killer cults—Made up primarily of disciple murderers who follow the commands of a cult leader. The leaders are usually charismatic megalomaniacs who pit themselves and their beliefs against society, follow apocalyptic visions, and are absorbed with lust and power and need for control over their followers.

Left hemisphere—Part of the brain that controls language comprehension and fine motor movement.

Limbic system—Responsible for normal human functioning, especially emotional arousal, and include the olfactory cortex, the amygdale, and the hippocampus.

Major depression—Characterized by symptoms of depression that are disabling and are not caused by such factors as drugs or a general medical condition.

Masturbatory reconditioning—A procedure to decrease arousal to deviant fantasies and/or increase arousal to appropriate fantasies.

Masturbatory satiation—Based on respondent conditioning principles, to associate fantasy with boredom and discomfort.

McDonald triad—Early signs of violence found in serial killers such as fire setting, cruelty to animals, and bed-wetting.

Mean world syndrome—The feeling that the world is evil.

Megan's law—Neighborhood notification law: an amendment to the Violent Crime Control and Law Enforcement Act of 1994, requiring community notification when a paroled or released sex offender moves into a neighborhood.

Mens rea (bad mind)—Prior intention to commit a criminal act without necessarily knowing that the act is a crime. For all but some minor statutory offenses, mens rea is basic to establishing the actual guilt of somebody alleged to have committed a crime.

Meta-analysis—A statistical technique that integrates the data from many studies into one comprehensive statistical analysis.

Modeling—How we acquire most of our behavioral repertoire through observing the behaviors of others. Increases the probability that a response will be repeated.

Modes of adaptation—Criminals adapt to their environment by committing crime rather than working.

NAMBLA—The North American Man-Boy Love Association is a U.S.-based organization of pedophiles which claims that sexual intercourse between grown men and boys should be legal.

National Crime Victim Survey (NCVS)—The ongoing victimization study conducted jointly by the Justice Department and the U.S. Census Bureau. The NCVS surveys victims about their experiences with law violation.

National youth survey—A longitudinal panel study of a national sample of 1,725 individuals that measured self-reports of delinquency and other types of behavior.

Negative reinforcement—Occurs when we engage in a behavior that removes an aversive or painful stimulus.

Neural plasticity—The brain's natural ability to repair itself in childhood.

Neuroticism/Stability—A dimension of personality that characterizes one end of the continuum as very emotionally reactive and have difficulty returning to a normal or moderate emotional state once aroused, while the stable end of the continuum do not react with emotional excitability to stressful circumstance.

Neurotransmitters—Chemicals that, released by one neuron, crosses the synaptic space to be received at receptors on the dendrites of neighboring neurons.

Norepinephrine—A neurotransmitter that regulates sleep-wake cycles, alertness, sustained attention, and biological responses to new stimuli such as anxiety, fear, or stress.

Occupational related victimization—Workplace violence or assault on the job.

Odontology—The branch of science that studies the teeth and their anatomy, development, and diseases.

Oedipus complex (Freud)—A term used to indicate the situation in which the child of either sex develops sexual feelings for the parent.

Olfactory aversion therapy—Based on respondent conditioning principles to associate a deviant stimulus with a negative (smell) stimulus.

Operant conditioning (Skinner)—A type of learning in which consequences, which are contingent on the occurrence of a particular response, increase or decrease the probability that the same response will occur again.

Oppositional Defiant Disorder—Characterized by children that argue repeatedly with adults, lose their temper, swear, and feel intense anger and resentment.

Organized killers—Killers who plan their crime with little or no evidence of the scene.

Paraphilia—A disorder characterized by bizarre or abnormal sexual practices that may involve recurrent and intense sexual urges, fantasies, or behaviors focused on nonhuman objects, children, nonconsenting adults, or experiences of suffering or humiliation.

Passive victim precipitation—Occurs when a victim unknowingly provokes a confrontation with another.

Pathology—The scientific study of the nature of a disease and its causes.

Pedophilia—Sexual offenses targeted at children.

Personality disorder—Refers to lifelong patterns of thinking and behaving that deviate significantly from cultural norms, is maladaptive, and despite this, inflexible.

Phenotype—Anything that is part of the observable structure, function, or behavior of a living organism.

Plea bargaining—A negotiation in which the defendant agrees to enter a plea of guilty to a lesser charge and the prosecutor agrees to drop a more serious charge.

Population—The entire group of people of interest in a study.

Power anger rapist—Most feared rapist; divided into four types: power-assertive, power-reassurance, anger-retaliatory, and anger-excitation.

Power-assertive rapist—Where forceful aggression and intimidation of the victim are used to meet the predator's need to control and dominate the victim.

Power-reassurance rapist—Rapist who uses a planned attack, often stalking the victim, with the thought that the victim will enjoy the sexual encounter and subsequently fall in love.

Preferential child molesters—Often referred to as classic pedophiles because they are attracted to children and frequently fantasize about having sex with children.

Prefrontal cortex—A region in the brain responsible for planning, structuring, and evaluating voluntary, goal-directed behavior.

Primary process thinking (Freud)—A reference to the id operations, in which it processes thought through images rather than symbolic thought such as language.

Psychic-determinism—Freud's idea that all behavior has a cause, and often the cause is unconscious.

Psycholinguistics—A discipline concerned with relations between messages and the characteristics of individuals who select and interpret them; it deals directly with the processes of encoding (phonetics) and decoding (psychoacoustics) as they relate states of messages to states of communicators.

Psychopath Factor 1—Affective-Cognitive Instability

Psychopath Factor 2—Behavioral-Social Deviance

Psychoticism/superego—A dimension of personality that characterizes one end of the continuum as egocentric, non-conforming, cold, and aggressive, while the other end as empathetic, cooperative, tender-minded, and conforming.

Rape kit—Weapons, bindings, and any sexual apparatus in which the anger-excitation rapist brings to the scene.

Recidivism—The rate of re-offense

Regressed molesters—Their acts of child molesting emerge when they are adults and are usually precipitated by external stressors such as alcohol or drug use problems.

Relapse prevention—A program to provide an offender with coping skills and assist them in planning to prevent a relapse from occurring.

Reliability—The extent to which a test is consistently accurate.

Repression (Freud)—The forcing of unwanted, anxiety-laden wishes into the unconscious as a defense against the pain of that anxiety.

Respondent conditioning—An association that is established between a neutral stimulus and a physiological or emotional response.

Right hemisphere—Part of the brain that is responsible for modulating emotional, creative, and aggressive expression.

Routine Activities Theory—This theory addresses how particular situations influence interactions between victims and offenders. The routine activity approach assumes that most criminal acts require the conditions of motivated offenders, suitable targets, the absence of capable guardians, and inability to control the actions of the offender.

Sample—The people included in a given study who are intended to represent the population of interest.

Schema—A cognitive habit of attentional focus and interpretation related to a particular domain or category such as authority figures, self, other people, women, men, etc.

Schizophrenia/Paranoid type—Characterized by becoming primarily preoccupied with one or more bizarre delusions, or experience frequent hallucinations, but the cognitive skills remain relatively intact and there are few signs of disorganized speech or behavior.

Secondary process thinking (Freud)—A reference to the ego, in which the process is symbolic thinking such as language.

Self Report Studies—A research approach that requires subjects to reveal their own participation in criminal acts.

Serology—A blood test that detects the presence of antibodies to a particular antigen (i.e., rheumatoid factor, HIV test).

Serotonin—A neurotransmitter that regulates mood, anxiety, arousal, and appetite.

Situational child molesters—Have many different motivations for their crimes that are often not of sexual origin and usually act on opportunity and seek vulnerable victims, not necessarily children.

Situational victimization—In most cases it is a stranger who commits violent crimes under these situations. The key to understanding situational victimization is the relative unpredictability of the circumstances.

Somatic marker theory (Damasio)—Certain bioregulatory processes, including autonomic functioning, help influence our decisions about social interaction, survival, and danger.

Somatic memory—Refers to the physiological state associated with a particular event such as increased heart rate experienced during physical or psychological trauma.

Spree killers—Someone who embarks on a murder rampage. This is an ambiguous term, related to mass murderers and serial killers. The Bureau of Justice Statistics defines a spree killing as: "[involving] killings at two or more locations with almost no time break between murders." The definition is especially close to that of a serial killer; perhaps, the primary difference between the two is that a serial killer tends to "lure" victims to their death; whereas, a spree killer tends to go "hunting."

Stanford Prison experiment—An experiment done to address the question, "does power corrupt?" using mentally healthy young men pretending to be prisoners. The experiment demonstrated the power of situations and roles in transforming behavior of individuals and the potent effects of psychological abuse on mentally healthy young men.

Static variable—A pre-existing variable that participants bring with them such as gender, socioeconomic status, a genetic or biological variable, or a personality characteristic.

Subcultural theory—A sociological perspective that emphasizes the contribution made by variously socialized cultural groups to the phenomenon of crime.

Substance abuse—A pattern of behavior in which people rely on a drug excessively and regularly, bringing damage to their relationships, functioning poorly at work, or putting themselves or others in danger.

Suicide by cop—A form of suicide where people intentionally provoke police officers into shooting them.

Superego (Freud)—The moral or ethical processes of personality. It operates on the morality principle and is developed mostly through parental influences as they socialize us to the values and morals of society.

Surgical castration—The removal of the testes, to inhibit sexual desire.

Sympathetic nervous system—Stimulates heart rate, blood flow and adrenaline in response to stressful events.

Temperament—Refers to a consistent way of responding to the environment, energy level, emotionality, the ability to self-regulate, risk taking, and sociability.

Tests of insanity—standard or various tests established to determine insanity. Examples include M'Naghten test, irresistible impulse test, and substantial capacity of American Law Institute test.

Third variable problem—Another variable that might be responsible for the degree of relationship between correlated variables.

Toxicology—The scientific study of the chemistry, effects, and treatment of poisonous substances.

Trace evidence—A type of non-living evidence such as hairs, fiberspalynology, paint chips, etc., used to corroborate other evidence or prompt a confession.

Types of mass killers—Five types: disciple murderer, family annihilator, disgruntled employee, pseudo commando, and set-and-run killer.

Types of serial killers—Four subtypes: visionary, mission, hedonistic, and power-oriented.

Uniform Crime Report (UCR)—Large database, compiled by the Federal Bureau of Investigation, of crimes reported and arrests made each year throughout the United States.

United States v. Scheffer—A Supreme Court case in 1997 stating that the results of a polygraph exam could be banned from use in a criminal trial by either side because there has been no consensus that polygraph evidence is completely reliable.

Unlawful flight to avoid prosecution—When offenders move or travel in interstate or foreign commerce with the intent to avoid prosecution.

Validity—The extent to which a test measures what it is supposed to measure.

Victimology—Explores the dynamics of victim offender relationships, and studies how and why some people are victimized by crime. While criminology and criminal psychology focus on criminal behavior and motives, a victimologist seeks understanding as to the relationship between the victim and offender.

Violentization—Process involving four stages—brutalization and subjugation, belligerency, violent coaching, and criminal activity—by which a person, usually a child, passes through turning them into a violent individual.

Voice stress analyzers—New technology in the science of deception detection which looks for audible tremors that occur whenever a person lies.

Wisconsin v. Mitchell—Upheld convictions of a group of young black men who beat a young white boy into a state of unconsciousness and put him into a coma for four days. The young black men were convicted under the state's hate crime statute.

INDEX

F

G

Q

R